King Fisher

The Story of Rally Legend Bertie Fisher

by Fergus McAnallen

project coordination by Kieran McAnallen

Cottage
Publications

Published by Cottage Publications,
an imprint of Laurel Cottage Ltd.
Donaghadee, Northern Ireland.
Copyrights reserved.
© Fergus McAnallen 2016.
Photographs are reproduced by permission.
All rights reserved.
No part of this book may be reproduced or stored on any media
without the express written permission of the publishers.
Printed in Slovenia
ISBN 978-1-910657-06-5

Publication of this book has been promoted by the
Armagh Tigers Charitable Trust

A tribute by Gladys & Roy Fisher

Bertie and I met in 1968 when I was working in the parts department in County Cars, now Donnelly Brothers, on the Irvinestown Road in Enniskillen.

We were married in 1972 and settled in Ballinamallard, where Bertie had been raised. I quickly became part of village life and realised that business and rallying were going to be a large part of my life.

Our children, Mark, Emma and Roy, were born at two year intervals from 1973 until 1977. During these years the business was known as Thomas Fisher and was based at Drumkeen in the village. My parents-in law worked tirelessly to build a future for their family. Bertie and his brothers were drawn into the business from an early age and by the time Tommy expanded to the premises at the Mill Bertie and Ernie had taken on more responsibility.

While the business was growing so was Bertie's rallying career. His parents had always been supportive but couldn't help but worry about their eldest son's safety. Indeed, on his first overnight event his mother Elsie busied herself baking cakes all night. This was the first of many anxious days and nights, but they also enjoyed seeing their son partake and succeed in the sport he loved.

Bertie's driving progressed from club events to Irish Championship events. In those days Bertie's co-driver was Austin Frazer. His wife Doreen and I found ourselves feeding the crew out of the boot of Doreen's Nova. In later years we acquired a motor home, which was mostly driven by a group of strong women including the late Carol Meeke, George Campion, my daughter Emma and occasionally myself. I have fond memories of the days in the motor home and all those who enjoyed the hospitality in the service area.

Fisher Engineering continued to grow with iconic buildings such as The Waterfront Hall and the Odyssey Arena placing huge demands on Bertie. The success of the business was paramount to him and left less time for motor sport, or any other hobby.

Mark was interested in cars since before he could reach the pedals. He was keen to emulate Bertie's success in business and rallying. Mark was also a driven character and achieved a first class honours degree in Engineering at the University of Ulster as well as a place on the World Rally Championship.

Emma also had an interest in motorsport, joining the Queens motor club in her first year of university. She also achieved a first class honours degree, attaining a Bachelor of Medical Science in Podiatry.

Our youngest child Roy had little interest in rallying or engineering, however if we were staying in a hotel with a swimming pool he was happy to attend. Roy went on to achieve a second class upper division honours degree in Communications, Advertising and Marketing at Jordanstown.

For some time Bertie had shown interest in flying. He became a helicopter pilot, but unfortunately Bertie, Mark and Emma didn't survive the helicopter accident of January 2001 which changed the lives of Roy and I forever.

A Word from the Author

From a young age I have always been into cars, attending my first rally as a child in the mid-80s to watch Audi Quattros tramp along the local boreens on the Ulster Rally and soon, like many of my friends, I was a rally nut.

In my early days of spectating nothing excited me more than getting up close to drivers and cars at service areas and stage starts but, being a shy introverted fan, despite cousin Kieran McAnallen's involvement with Bertie, I was so star struck that I rarely got chatting to drivers. It is to my eternal regret that I only muttered a few awkward words to Bertie once or twice and never even got a photo with him although I did send him a letter congratulating him on one of his wins and he replied with a big signed poster and stickers, which I cherish greatly… I still have them in the original envelope, stamped 'Ballinamallard P.O.'.

Coming from a family of historians, I took a keen interest in rally nostalgia and wanted to know more about Irish rallying folklore and its legendary personalities, the very mention of whose names would make my eyes light up. Watching rally videos over and over, as well as collecting rally magazines and programmes became a nerdy obsession for me and, while other teenagers had pictures of rock stars or football icons in their bedrooms, my walls were plastered with pictures of rally cars!

As I started university at Jordanstown my interest in rally nostalgia never waned and, having set up one of the first Irish Rallying fan websites, I started to make profiles of Irish rally stars past and present although for me one always stood out and that was Bertie Fisher.

I made many trips to Esler Crawford's office in Belfast to look through his photo archives, purchasing those that caught my eye, and soon I had amassed quite a collection. But like any devoted collector I could never have enough and, having seen old photos in magazines and programmes credited to Colin Taylor's Photographic agency, I visited him several times in Kent before eventually buying his complete collection of British and Irish rally negatives. Around half a dozen more collections followed in the next ten years to the point that I now have in excess of 400,000 images in the 'Rallyretro' archive.

Having followed Bertie's career closely and witnessed the esteem he was held in by many I knew I would not be alone in my devastation in January 2001 when the news of the tragedy in Fermanagh filtered through. However it was only when I attended the funerals a few days later did the true extent of this grief become clear as thousands gathered on that dark, wet January day in Ballinamallard to pay their respects and grieve as the three hearses passed by in a row.

I had always wanted to do something with all the photos and material I had collected about Bertie so that others could share in the nostalgia and fond memories that Bertie's name conjured up for rally fans in Ireland and further afield.

This desire was brought into sharper focus with the loss to natural causes of my own brother Cormac in 2004 and when empathising with the Fishers on our respective family losses, the idea of publishing a book was mooted – but the time was not right as the tragedy was still too raw.

However the idea, once out there, never really went away and in late 2013 Kieran, along with the Armagh Tigers Charitable Trust, gave the project the kick start it required, and I jumped at the chance to be involved.

It has been over two years since the beginning of this project formally, and they have been two very long years, with many late nights, a few sleepless nights, and moments I wondered if I'd ever get to the finish line, but as I write this now I can say that, for my part, to be involved in publishing this book has been a huge personal privilege and honour, a labour of love and passion, for Bertie is my hero – always was, and always will be.

Fergus McAnallen

Acknowledgements

This book would not have been possible without the help of many people and I owe a debt of thanks to: the Armagh Tigers Charitable Trust including Kieran McAnallen, Colm Quinn, Kevin Toner, Emma Gribben and others on the committee for their help and research and time spent with me pulling everything together; to Sinead Slane and Laura O Neill who assisted in the transcription of some of the interviews carried out; to the following people who I interviewed: Canon Paul Hoey, Father Brian D'Arcy, Austin Frazer, Derek Smyth, Rory Kennedy, Brian Quinn, David & Georgina Campion, Paul Howarth, John Lunny, Sean Quinn, Roy Cathcart, Michael Kirby, Dr Frank O'Donoghue, Austin McHale, Hugh O'Brien, Stephen Finlay, Freddie Patterson, Sydney Meeke and all of the former Sydney Meeke Motorsport mechanics we met including: Ian Cuddy, Jimmy Graham, Wesley Emerson, Norman Burns, Gary Wilson, Bob McKeown, Adrian Kirkland.

I am also indebted to the following people whose help and ideas, research and assistance in collating and chasing up photos, facts, contacts, stories, etc were crucial for the book: Andrew Bushe who was responsible for the researching and writing the Mark Fisher chapter, Joe Duggan for research, Kevin O'Driscoll for photo scans and research, Eddie Fitzgerald for advice and research, David Johnston for information and help, Helen Stuart for information on Tommy Fisher, Gerry Cavanagh for contacts and nostalgia, Alan Elliott for research and following up leads, Ivan Fuery for help in tracing photographs, Gary Milligan and the Omagh Motor Club for research assistance, John McIlroy for his assistance in looking through the LAT archives, and Belfast Central Newspaper Library.

With thanks to the following people who submitted photos or who took photos which are included in this book including: Rallyretro Archive, Seamus Counihan, Esler Crawford, Trevor Foster, Martin McCorriston, Dermot Kelleher, Ger Leahy, Colin Courtney, Jonathan MacDonald, David Maes, Fergal O'Keefe, Roy Dempster, Adrian Crawley, Derek Smyth, Raymond Humphreys, Ian Lynas, Paul McIlroy, Harold Moffett, Derek Graham, Podge Newe, Conor Edwards, FD Kullas, Val Fegan, Brian McDaid, Steve Breen, Malcolm Moorehead, Stuart Billington, Ian Richardson, Patrick Browne, Billy White, Pat McKenna, Michelle Cooper Galvin, the archive of Jim Bamber, Paul Howarth, Brian McLean, Brian Regan, Sydney Meeke, Austin & Doreen Frazer, Robin Parkes, Victor Patterson, The archive of Joe Lane c/o Graham Lane, Jeremy Clifford, Mark Griffin, John Crone, LAT Photographic, Harrison Photography Belfast, Sutton Images, Ernie Fisher, Derek Graham, Pat Burns and all associated unknown photographers care of Carsport, the Photographers of the Belfast Telegraph, the staff of the Fermanagh Herald, Ulster Herald, Impartial Reporter, and the various unknown sources of photos who had submitted photos for use in the Bertie Fisher special 50th 'King Fisher' book. All attempts were made to try and obtain contact information for all of the sources of images used in this book and we are sorry if not everyone could be contacted.

Excerpts from the following publications and corporations have been used in this book: Carsport, Motoring News, Autosport, Belfast Telegraph, Sunday Life, Ireland's Saturday Night, Impartial Reporter, Ulster Herald, Tyrone Herald, Fermanagh Herald, Irish Independent, RPM Motorsport, RTÉ News, BBC News, UTV and other unknown sources.

Thank you to everyone who submitted stories or tributes by email or via the website.

Other acknowledgements include Cormac Knott of Netstretch who built and supplied the bertiefisher.com website for free. The domain bertiefisher.com was also kindly donated by Colm Cassidy from the Irish Subaru Drivers Club. To the Armagh City Hotel for assisting in meeting facilities.

A special thanks to the Fisher family including Gladys, Roy, Ivan, Ernie, and Kenny for allowing the book to go ahead and who have been helpful in researching and fact finding.

Finally thanks to my family, to my friends, and to my employees in Benburb, all of whom have put up with me whilst I have missed out on many family, social and work functions I found difficult to attend due to the amount of time I have put into the book over the past two years.

Contents

Introduction

As the news of the tragic helicopter accident in Fermanagh filtered out during that grey January in 2001, a wave of grief and sympathy for the Fisher family swept across Fermanagh, Ireland and beyond, for the loss of Bertie Fisher, his son Mark (27) and daughter Emma (25), was a tragedy not only for the family but also for the worlds of business and motor sport.

Joining the business established by his father, Bertie was a key driving force in developing it into the internationally recognised leader in the structural steel industry it had become by the end of the millennium. And as if this wasn't enough, at the same time Bertie established himself as one of Ireland's most successful rally drivers, achieving 20 victories in the Irish Tarmac Championship, including three Circuit of Ireland victories in 1995, 1997 and 1999. For over three decades he had dominated the local rally scene and as news of his passing spread tributes began to pour in from all over the world.

Bertie was the eldest of four sons born to Tommy and Elsie Fisher. The eldest of eight children from a Co. Leitrim farming family, Tommy's life story is worth a book in itself. Used as slave labour while a Japanese Prisoner of War for three years during the Second world War, he finally settled in Ballinamallard in Co. Fermanagh and, in 1950, opened a farm machinery repair shop in a small shed. By the time he handed over the reigns to Bertie and his other sons in the 1970s Thomas S Fisher employed a workforce of 14 staff and under Bertie's leadership it expanded to become one of the leading structural steel fabricators in Europe.

Tommy was a great advocate for Co. Fermanagh in general and Ballinamallard in particular. He was a great supporter of his local football club, who named their second pitch Fisher Park in his honour. His work as founder and chairman of the Erne Training Services was formally recognised when he was awarded an MBE in 1994. This ethos of helping others was passed on to the next generation as one friend remembers *'[Bertie] liked to see those around him thriving, that was the way he worked. He was very much a community man.'*

However it was as a rally driver that Bertie captured the minds and hearts of his countrymen. John McIlroy, writing for Autosport.com in January 2001 recounts:

'Irish racing … is much more low-key than anything found at Silverstone or Brands Hatch. But when the roads were closed and Bertie and his rivals hit the rally stages, thousands – tens of thousands – hung off every vantage point to catch a glimpse of the action. And Bertie was at the heart of it all'.

It was typical of Bertie to let his driving do the talking because he was a man of relatively few words. Open, honest and entirely down-to-earth, despite the financial comfort that his hard work at the family company brought, he had little time for pontificating or empty talk.

After three decades in the sport, Bertie was beginning to pick and choose which rallies he entered. But when he did get behind the wheel he was still very much at the top of his game, winning the Circuit of Ireland in 1995 and 1997. His son Mark was also beginning to emerge as a major force on the Irish and British scene and if he wasn't competing himself, Bertie was there as his most loyal supporter and adviser. As the report on BBC NI on the tragedy said: *'Yet class is permanent and he saw off all-comers to win his third Circuit of Ireland in 1999. No-one was more delighted than Fisher when it was announced in November* [2000] *that the 2001 Circuit was going to be based in his beloved county. His beaming smile at the press announcement told of a great pride.'*

This book is intended to be a tribute to the 'King' Fisher: a devoted husband and father, successful businessman, kind friend and awesome driver. As John McIlroy said:

'His name of the entry list meant he was there to win, because he didn't know any other way. This was a man who didn't know the meaning of the word 'second' – in life, in business or in sport.'

1968 - 1972

'The Rally Bug' · The beginnings of a
rally legend

This is the story of Bertie Fisher, a legend, a hero, and Ballinamallard's own. For three decades Bertie was at the top of Irish Rallying and, with an ultra-professional approach to what was essentially an amateur sport, he was highly regarded as an ambassador for Irish Motorsport and Irish Sport in general in the 1980s and 1990s. Many of the successes and records he broke in Irish Tarmac International Rallying still stand today. With Four Irish Tarmac Rally Championships and Twenty Championship round wins to his credit, as well as a multitude of wins at national and local level he was one of Ireland's most successful rally drivers of all time. It is over a decade and a half after his untimely passing but he has never been forgotten by the rally fraternity and his legacy means that his name will be around for many more decades to come.

Bertie had always had an interest in speed and engineering as school friend Neil Paget recalls:

'Fishers were the ultimate attraction in Ballinamallard and as a young boy I was never out of the workshop. Of course Bertie was always about and we played together in and around the workshop and yard. There were lots of interesting bits and pieces to get involved with. Stock cars were in vogue at that time and one or two were about that we could start and shunt around the yard. One of my earliest memories is of Bertie trying to power slide a Ferguson TVO tractor around the petrol pumps on the forecourt and no it didn't have a roll over bar. It did leave tell-tale black tyre mark on the concrete that took some explaining to his Dad!'

Given these early signs it should have been no surprise that as soon as the young Fisher obtained his licence that he would be keen to get involved in motorsport and the earliest records we have indicate that the first event in which he competed was the Erne Safari Rally,

right: Bertie on his first Circuit of Ireland as driver in 1971 with John Magee co-driving, seen here on the Borlin stage

A newcomer to motor sport. 18-year-old Bertie Fisher of Ballinamallard (on left) son of Mr. and Mrs. Thomas Fisher, connecting up his spot lamps for the Erne Safari Rally on Friday night. He is helped by his navigator, Neil Paget of McQuaid Villas, Ballinamallard.

October 1968, driving an 848cc Mini. The Enniskillen Motor Club event which is still held today was a gruelling all-night event featuring a 200-mile route made up of 180 navigation and 12 forestry stage miles covering parts of County Fermanagh and the Clogher Valley region of County Tyrone with a halfway petrol halt in Clogher. Of the 81 listed entries due to start at Toppings Garage in Enniskillen, Bertie started right down at the tail of the field at number 79, but he was among the 54 weary crews that managed to reach the finish at Manor House at around 6 am. Neil Paget who was navigating for him on the occasion and for whom it was also a first time, can't remember the exact finishing result but recalls that there was much nervousness leading up to the event. *'I remember sitting in the car trying desperately to plot the route and the sense of trepidation at the thought of taking part in my first rally.'*

The initial trepidation he felt was soon replaced by an overriding sense of desperation! *'We got utterly and completely lost half way through the first half of the rally. It was a case of find a main road, work out how to get to the petrol halt and try to do better in the second part. This we managed to do and as far as I can remember we dropped very few points between the petrol halt and the finish. My claim to fame is to be the first navigator to get Bertie lost!'*

1969

With his first event over, Bertie had the taste for more rallying and just a few months later, competed in his second event, the Pre-Circuit Rally. This was an Omagh Motor Club event which was run several weeks before the Circuit of Ireland, mainly as a warm up for local drivers for the then marathon 5-day 1000 mile route of the Circuit. Once again Bertie was in the Mini and with John Brown as co-driver this time, they won Class 3 on the circa 100 mile event run over back roads in Tyrone on a Friday evening in March 1969.

Around the time of the Pre-Circuit Rally that year, Ernie Campbell from Tempo in County Fermanagh gave Bertie an opportunity to have his first taste of international rallying in the Gallagher Tobacco Circuit of Ireland International Rally as a co-driver. The Tempo man had been rallying for several years by that time, mostly competing in Minis.

Ernie picks up the story of that year's Circuit of Ireland outing. *'I had entered into the Circuit that year with a chap called Jonathan Isherwood as my co-driver. About 6 weeks or so prior to the event, one evening he was returning from Greenmount Agricultural College when he had a road accident.'*

With his listed co-driver in hospital, and unlikely to make the Circuit, Ernie needed a co-driver to replace the injured Isherwood.

It was then that he remembered hearing about a young man finishing the Erne Safari the previous Autumn and, knowing Bertie's family, he decided to contact him. *'I first met Bertie as a teen working on the anvil at the blacksmiths in their Engineering works. I knew Bertie's parents*

below: An off during the Circuit of Ireland in 1969

above: The route in 1969 when The Circuit of Ireland "did what it says on the tin"

right: Bertie co-driving for Ernie on the 'Circuit in '69.

Easter weekend each year saw large crowds of spectators come out to watch the Circuit of Ireland Rally, a huge event in its day which travelled the length and breadth of the island through many of its scenic rugged and mountain passes like this section. It was Bertie's first taste of International rallying, and what a way to debut!

and had read in the local paper that Bertie had been doing some *Enniskillen Motor Club rallies.'*

After having been asked, the youthful Bertie jumped at the chance to compete in such a prestigious event as the Circuit of Ireland. *'Bertie was young, enthusiastic, and working very hard in the family business at the time and when I asked him about it, he was thrilled.'*

As Ernie also pointed out though, the registration process for Bertie wasn't entirely straight-forward! *'He had to get his father Tommy to sign up the documents to give permission to allow Bertie to compete since he was classed as a minor.'* Tommy agreed to sign the form and many years later at one of Bertie's gatherings, remarked

jokingly that, *'He blames me for all this rallying, for having to sign the form to start this!'*

Ernie and Bertie headed off their little 848 Mini. Ernie remembers that Bertie was getting better by the mile and by the time they got close to home on the Monday night of the event at the halt at Manor House at Killadeas things were looking good. But on that final long night in Donegal, and with the fatigue kicking in and concentration levels perhaps not at 100% after the gruelling four days completed so far, there was an error. *'I think we had lost a timecard or it had got messed up. At that point we were having an in-house conference when we arrived on to this big sweeping corner and I never dropped her*

lying came from the young Ballinamallard driver, Bertie Fisher, and navigator Neil Paget, who finished third in Class II in their Mini, behind a more powerful Mini Cooper 'S' and Twin Cam Escort.'

Bertie finished the year off by competing in the Erne Safari, the event which had started it all off the previous year. For the first time that year the club decided to run it as a daytime event with a finish around 5pm. Although he led his class for a period of the rally, he retired on the 3.8 mile final section in Castle Arch-

down a cog at all. There were stone chips and out she went out in a full slide and we rolled the whole lot into a ditch, the two of us in on top of each other, and that put paid to that event.'

With that first taste of International Rallying, Bertie was hungry for more. Although it would be a full year before he competed in another international rally, he did compete on several smaller events in 1969 as driver with Neil Paget as his co-driver.

At the Omagh Motor club's Scallon Cup Rally, he finished 3rd in Class 2, the Novice Class, and won the Novice Award on the final stage, SS13 Gortin Glen 2. An excerpt from Motor Week in Sept. 1969 stated:

'Perhaps the greatest achievement of the day's ral-

dale grounds. Neil Paget, for whom this would be his last regular appearance as co-driver, recalls one event from this rally in vivid detail, *'On one particularly rough stage the centre speedo cluster came loose and we could warm our hands on the red hot exhaust through the resulting hole.'*

Between '69 and '70, Bertie went through at least three Minis. It wasn't so much that they were destroyed but rather that he was always looking for more powerful and competitive. If you wanted a ready to rally car there were people such as Mervyn Johnston whose main business was purely the selling, preparation and fixing of rally prepared Minis. Some of Bertie's Minis came from Mervyn, but more often than not Bertie carried out much of the work himself.

Very often people in the rally family became specialists in a particular field and Bertie's particular specialisation was sump guards for Minis. *'Many of the Mini rally cars in and around Fermanagh were fitted with Fisher* sump guards. I remember Bertie trying to sell them to motorsport outlets in Belfast and to that end I became part of the distribution chain having several sump guards stored in my spare bedroom in Belfast', Neil Paget explained.

Neil also fondly recalls another late night when engines had to be swapped between a road going Cooper and Bertie's 850cc Rally Car

'I remember spending a Saturday night in the work-shop swopping things over. We had a car each to remove the engines from and it was a race to see who could get theirs out first. I cannot remember who won. Of course nothing goes smoothly with these things and the 850 mini required holes cut in the floor to accommodate the Cooper gear change. We tipped it up on its side on a couple of tyres and Bertie set to work with the acetylene cutter. Several hours later the swop was complete and the re-engined Mini got its first test drive out the Enniskillen

right: Bertie on his second Circuit of Ireland in 1970 as co-driver to Ernie Campbell when they did not last as long as their first outing together the previous year.

left: Bertie and John Magee on the 1971 Circuit

below: Bertie on a rare occasion of competing on an autotest, and winning novice award!

Bertie Fisher, the novice award winner, throws the nose of his 998 cc Cooper.

road at one o'clock on the Sunday morning still minus it's silencer. It's a wonder we didn't get locked up for disturbing the peace. During such workshop sessions we were supplied with lashings of hot tea and very tasty tomato sandwiches by Bertie's cousin who worked as a secretary in the works office. She later agreed to become my wife so rallying has unexpected spin-offs!'

1970

The new year's rallying started for Bertie by competing in his second Gallagher Circuit of Ireland Rally, navigating for Ernie Campbell in a Mini. *'We decided to do the Circuit again the next year, 1970.'* Remembers Ernie, *'That was our last event together for some time, because Bertie wasn't really much of a navigation or map man.'*

Irrespective of that lack of experience handicap, Ernie felt Bertie's skills had improved in the intervening year. *'Bertie was a quick learner, especially considering in those days the timing and documentation was very much part and parcel of it. He was very business-like in the car. He approached it in a structured manner and weighed up the situation before reaching a decision. He was good*

company. He wasn't easy put down; he didn't just drop at the first hurdle, even at that young age you could see that personality coming through.'

Unfortunately time penalties meant that they were disqualified before they reached the border in South Armagh. Up until that point in time they had been doing incredibly well, with a fastest time in their class on all of the previous six stages up to that point.

Although there was one further occasion in 1983 when Ernie sat with Bertie, this was the last event in which they competed together in a Mini.

Looking back on that time together as a team, Ernie remarks *'Bertie was great company to rally with. He enjoyed it, and he liked the driving and I think he was a very applied chap because when I look back on it, Bertie, from the beginning, was watching the way a car was driven and what it was doing, and then he was working it out what he would do himself. The more he navigated, the more he learned, he didn't waste his time and he could see where maybe he could make better time than the man driving the car.'*

For the remainder of the 1970 season, Bertie switched sides once again to the driver's seat. He competed in an Enniskillen Motor Club Autotest, held that year in the grounds of the Manor House Hotel, in his 998 Mini Cooper winning the Novice Award Overall. Later in the year he competed in the Erne Safari Rally again, this time with John Magee in the navigator's seat.

1971

John, who is sadly no longer alive, continued to co-drive for Bertie for several more rallies at the start of 1971, in the Omagh Pre-Circuit Rally and in the Gallaher Circuit of Ireland Rally where they would be up against some 200 other competitors as they tackled the 5-day marathon event.

Bertie, unfortunately, had a non-finish due to John becoming unwell on the final night of the event when they were in County Donegal. And in the Manx Rally in September it was another non-finish when, lying second in their class at the fourteenth stage, they had to retire with a damaged gearbox, not the last time Bertie would retire from the Manx due to mechanical gremlins!

Around this time Bertie had become quite friendly with John Lunny, originally from Maguiresbridge but now residing at Trory near Enniskillen, who worked at the Autopoint garage owned by Tom Graydon in Tamlaght a few miles outside of Enniskillen town. The garage was a popular hub for local rally enthusiasts and Bertie would often use the garage as a workshop to build and prepare some of his earlier rally cars. During 1971 Bertie had helped John build a modified Mk1 Escort for rallying and

when the Erne Safari came round again at the end of the season Bertie was a competitor but this time as a navigator, in John's Escort.

Although they finished well up the leader board the rally wasn't all plain sailing as John explains *'We did do a lot of damage on that one, we went off at least 3 times and one of those times we had come round a corner where the Forestry Division had stacks of timber all built up at the side, We hit the pile and we busted the passenger's door and had to hold it on with the seat belt to get to the finish!'*

Overall though, John was pleased with their successes and he told me that the Erne Safari was probably the most memorable rally they had together as either combination of driver/co-driver.

HEK 158G

left: EMC Chairman at the time, Billy Jackson, clocks out John Lunny & Bertie from a control point on the Erne Safari

John recalls the competitive and sometimes ruthless side of Bertie's nature.

'Bertie took it very seriously in the car, more serious on the navigator side than he was behind the wheel. He was a trier, always keen, and pushing hard, always urging "Don't ease her off."

On the Erne I would have known a right few of the stages that were used, particularly the ones out round Big Dog which I knew like my own lane. At one point we came up behind a boy in a Cooper who wouldn't let us past, and as we were coming down through a big sweeping bit, I tried to take him on the inside and I can still see Bertie, his exact words were "Just push him off!" So I gave him a dunt and away on I went and Bertie says "That's the way to knock them off!"'

1972

For 1972 Bertie decided to build a new car and John well remembers its arrival at Tamlaght

'One Saturday night I was just closing the doors of the garage and Bertie came up with a mini shell on a car transporter behind his orange BMW 2002 road car and I said to him jokingly "Sure the dump's closed!" not a bit fazed he retorted "I'm after buying that shell from Mervyn Johnston. It's all seam welded and you and I are going to build her... Make a bit of room for her in the ga-

rage"'. Fired by his enthusiasm Bertie and his friends at Tamlaght Autopoint, often then working until 3 or 4 in the morning, built AIL 6222 in time for the 1972 Galway International Rally.

With Bertie in the driving seat with John as co-driver they were soon setting some impressive times which were raising a few eyebrows as this extract from the 1980 Circuit of Ireland Programme illustrates: –

'Derek McMahon, the baron of Donegal was studying

right: Bertie and John Lunny walk away from their crippled car at the 1972 Galway International Rally.

Bertie's assertion in the Circuit of Ireland Programme that his car 'broke a tie rod' is a masterful understatement when compared to John Lunny's recollection of the event which gives a better picture of how hard Bertie was pushing:–

'We came down to a T junction on what I think was the second last stage of the rally and I said to Bertie "Ease off, Cool her" but Bertie was having none of it and claiming "I'm not lifting, This things flying" he went down through the junction. I'd just time to close my eyes before, at the very same place where David Agnew had went off, we hit the stone wall on the left hand side, travelled another 110 yards through a left hand corner and that was her parked up, that was the end of our Galway. We took the front wheel clean out, drive shaft and all was sitting down the road'.

the 1972 Galway International results board in the Great Southern Hotel "We are leading the class by a minute and a half" he announced to everyone within 100 yards radius. "No you're not. I am" said a curly haired youngster in a quiet Fermanagh accent. "And who the ...... are you" demanded the burly McMahon. "The name's Fisher and I'm in front of you" came the reply.

Few among competitors or spectators on this year's Circuit of Ireland will have to ask who Bertie Fisher is now, his pristine Bush Performance/Team Castrol Ford Escort among the most striking on all of Ireland's major international rallies.

But back in 1972, Fisher was very much an unknown when he first met up with McMahon. "Big Derek wasn't too pleased and he went out on Saturday determined to

catch me" says Bertie. "But we never got into a battle. My Cooper broke a tie rod and that was me out".

Given that he had just signed up with Castrol and a finish would have brought in some welcome funding, Bertie must have been doubly disappointed at this retirement.

However he couldn't dwell on it too long for by the Summer of '72 the wedding bells were ringing in Ballinamallard as Bertie and Gladys Gawley got married in July that year – although Gladys claims they had to cut short the honeymoon so that Bertie could compete on a local sprint event in the car they went off in on their honeymoon!

The story of Tommy Fisher, MBE

The story of Tommy (Thomas S) Fisher is an amazing one, from being a pillar of the local community for half a century, to serving in WWII and being a POW in Singapore and Japan for years; from starting a business in a quaint blacksmith's hut to

developing it into what has become a major player in construction in Ireland and beyond. Tommy, the eldest son of a family of eight, was a modest, unassuming man who grew up in the 1920s and 1930s in the idyllic rural valley region of Newtowngore, not far from the border of Counties Leitrim and Cavan. With the country in deep financial depression at the time, and farmers struggling to make ends meet, Tommy began work at his father's farm at the age of 13 as soon as he had finished at the then mixed religion primary school. It was a simple way of living, but one with a plentiful amount of food from their own lands and stock, they had humble social lives based around ceilidhing with friends and neighbours.

In his memoirs, Tommy recalls how particular his father was, paying great attention to detail, and this trait is a recurring theme that has been carried down through the generations from Tommy in his work as a farmer and engineer, and on to Bertie and later Mark with

their meticulousness in business dealings, and in preparations for rallying exploits, amongst many other things.

It was also apparent that Tommy, much like Bertie and Mark, had a competitive streak too. His father persuaded him to take up competition ploughing and, after a year of trying, success came for Tommy in 1940 when, still in his late teens, he won the Killeshandra Creamery Prize Cup at the Ardlougher competitions and got the prize for the best finished furrow in the field.

As Tommy grew into a young adult, the world was descending into the horrors of World War II. Though there was no conscription in Ireland at the time, Tommy was keen play his part, the service that caught his attention being the Royal Air Force. Despite being advised not to get involved, Tommy went straight to the local Army office in Enniskillen and signed up.

It was early 1941 when he joined up, initially being stationed in various parts of England as he underwent training before being posted overseas. After travelling for months at sea, visiting Cape Town and Bombay along the way, he arrived in Singapore, still under British control at the time although everything changed soon after as the city came within range of the advancing Japanese forces. Tommy was witness to the brutal and intensive fighting as the Japanese over-ran the island's ill-prepared defences he, along with a band of his comrades attempted to escape after the city surrendered but while travelling through Java by train in an attempt to make it to a boat to escape to Australia, they were ambushed by Japanese troops and the survivors including Tommy were taken as prisoners of war. Brought back to Singapore Tommy along with other POWs were used as forced labour in harrowing conditions loading and unloading railway trucks and on jungle clearance for what is now Changi International airport, before he was moved to Japan to work in copper mines near Nagasaki.

When the war ended in 1945 the POWs were released and brought to an American camp in the Philippines to recuperate after their ordeal to begin their re-assimilation into civilization and to catch up on what had been happening in the wider world during their imprisonment, including news from home that he had a 'new' baby brother who by the time he received the letter was three years old!

Arriving home he was reunited with his parents, who had been totally unaware of his whereabouts or wellbeing during the three years that he was held as a Prisoner of War and only became aware of his release just before

Tommy with Bertie at the Ulster Rally in 1995

he arrived back home. There were of course a lot of home coming parties and it was at this time that Tommy made his first acquaintance with Ballinamallard where his aunt and uncle had bought a farm.

Still in the forces, Tommy was sent to a rehabilitation unit in Lancashire in England for further recuperation and preparation for demobilization. Training in various trades was offered and Tommy took a particular liking to welding, sowing the seeds of his future decision to go into the welding and metalwork business.

Following demobilization he struck up a relationship with Elsie (Kathleen Charlotte) Richardson who, like Tommy, had grown up in the Newtowngore area and whom he had known since childhood. Tommy's brother had taken over the farm while Tommy was away fighting in the war so he initially moved to Bel-

Tommy and Elsie at a family wedding

Bertie (front centre with trombone) in the Ballinamallard silver band which Tommy had also played in and helped with fund raising activities

with ever increasing amount of work to do due to the unrest in the nearby Palestine region, the workload could have become overwhelming. However he was able to enlist the services of German ex-prisoners of War at the same camp who helped clear his backlog of work and soon he had a fully functioning productive workshop running like clockwork.

After a full two years of service at Suez, Tommy was getting homesick and, missing Elsie, lovesick! He applied for compassionate posting home on the basis that seven of his nine years spent to date in the RAF were abroad, and with permission granted he headed home in October 1948 where he began an RAF posting much closer to home at Castle Archdale in Fermanagh, a flying boat base on the shores of Lough Erne.

When he could get release at weekends, Tommy cycled the 72 miles round trip to see Elsie only later graduating to a motorbike he acquired for the journey, although at the time the process for going across the border with motorised vehicles requiring bonds made the trip nearly easier on a bicycle! Irrespective of the difficult in seeing his sweetheart, a short time later the couple got engaged, and in February 1949 they were married and shortly

fast in search of work but, although he tried a number of different jobs, none seemed to appeal until one day he spotted a RAF poster which advertised 'Sign on for a 4 year bounty and learn a trade' and he took the opportunity to embark on a course in blacksmithing and welding.

Tommy became really engrossed in his initial six-month course and he came through with good results. So good in fact were his results that he was immediately posted by the RAF to the Suez Canal, to a station where he was thrown in at the deep end as he was the only welder present with only an Egyptian labourer for help.

Tommy's main work was making windscreen shields and tow bars for army vehicles and,

after that they moved to Ballinamallard village where Bertie, the eldest of their family of four boys was born in 1950.

The Fisher boys 1967 back L-R Ernie and Bertie, front L-R Ivan and Kenny

From the 1950s to the end of the 1980s Tommy threw himself into building up his business, the engineering firm of Thomas S. Fisher, in the village of Ballinamallard, and providing for his young family.

Despite his commitments to work and family, Tommy continued to have a very active life in the local community, as he had from the time he arrived there. A significant member of life in the village, he was a founder member of the Ballinamallard Development Association. In 1994 he was awarded an MBE for his Services to Education and Training in recognition to his community work in the Erne Youth and Community Workshop (later known as Erne Training Services, and a government backed organisation who catered for young people unable to find employment and who came from mostly disadvantaged homes) which he

Tommy Fisher and wife Elsie outside Buckingham Palace on the day he received his MBE award

Fathers supporting their sons, Jim Kennedy (Rory's father) and Tommy in Donegal 1992

was chairman of since its inception 12 years earlier. He was also a member of several lodges including the local Orange lodges where for 32 years he held the active title of the Worshipful Master and District Master for a period. He also played in and helped fund raise for the local Flute Band and later Silver Band.

Having always supported and having had an avid interest in the Ballinamallard United Football Club's exploits, he was their Club President for many years and in 1998 he provided a field to the then committee of the club so they could build a new park, later known as Fisher Park in recognition of this fact.

At the age of 78, Tommy passed away on the 22nd August 2001 after a lengthy illness, just seven months after Bertie's fatal accident. Posthumously though, Tommy's legend lived

on, and in May 2002, a new footbridge which was opened by the Duke of Edinburgh in Ballinamallard across the Ballinamallard River was named after Tommy.

Over ten years after Tommy's passing, his wife Elsie passed away on the 19th April 2012, aged 93. Elsie herself was a very active community person, being involved in Magheracross Parish Church and being a founding member of the Magheracross Mothers' Union. She was also a member of the Irvinestown branch of the Royal British Legion. The legacy Tommy and Elsie left behind was huge – their name being marked in involvement of every aspect of social, community, church, business and sporting life in the Ballinamallard and Fermanagh region entirely throughout the second half of the Twentieth Century.

1965

1975

1985

1995

2005

1973 - 1977

The Mk1 & Group 1 years

1973 marked the end of an era for Bertie. Faster and more powerful Ford Escorts were gradually taking over from Minis as the car of choice in the local rallying fraternity and Bertie's interest had been aroused when he saw a Mexico Escort being competed by Rodney Burrows and Brian Quinn from Castlecaulfield in the Circuit of Ireland.

When he first met Bertie, Brian Quinn had been working as a mechanical engineer at Armstrong's garage in Castlecaulfield and already had many years rally experience on both sides of the car. When, shortly afterwards, he moved to Enniskillen to work as an engineer at the Erne Hospital, he developed a friendship with Bertie and, with his rallying background, he soon started to navigate for Bertie in the Night Navigations.

The Omagh 'Pre-Circuit' Rally in 1973 was the first time that Bertie and Brian competed together in a Ford Escort. They finished second overall, the event being won by Trevor Fleming. It was the start of a long and success-ful pairing of Bertie and Escorts, both in their Mark One and Mark Two guises, at home and abroad.

Runner-up in Omagh Motor Rally

Bertie Fisher of Ballinamallard (right) who was runner-up in the Omagh Motor Club's pre-Circuit rally on Friday night last. With him is navigator Brian Quinn of Castlecaulfield.

For the Circuit itself co-driving duties were taken over by Tony Anderson in an event that netted Bertie his first worthy notable result in an International Rally – 17th overall, with a 2nd place in Class 4 and 3rd in Gp1.

This was quite an achievement considering that this was just his second time out in the new car and also that

right: Bertie with Tony Anderson on the Circuit in 1974

It is interesting to note the names of Bertie's sponsors who were mostly all local business-es at the time including David Kettyles, J.A. Knaggs & Co, F.R. Cathcart, Walter Watson, Tamlaght Autopoint, Auto Sport, and Fisher Engineering'

left: Action from the Circuit of Ireland in 1973 including top left the start ramp ceremonies, unusually that year at Landsdowne Crescent, Portrush

he had lost a big chunk of time when he rolled the car in the third stage of the rally.

Later that year, Bertie tackled the Donegal International for the very first time, and with Bertie's first navigator Neil Paget back for a one off, they set out for the hills, but the outing was cut short as Neil explained. *'We suffered engine failure and rear wheel lockup on the stage after Atlantic Drive. If it had happened on the Atlantic Drive stage we could well have ended up with very wet feet!'*

In July Bertie entered the Erne Trophy Rally Sprint in Donegal. He finished 2nd in Class 3, just 2.7 seconds behind Alan Tyndall, later of RPM Motorsports TV productions fame.

To finish off the year Bertie tackled another of the Omagh Motor Club championship events, the Scallon Cup Rally with Brian Quinn once again in the navigator's chair. Brian remembers this event where they finished 3rd Overall, 3rd in Class fondly although, as he explained, they didn't get off to a good start.

'Coming up to that event we had done a few things to the car to get her going well including taking the air filters off to get more power although the Webers had a bad habit of firing back through and they could go on fire.

So there we were at the start line of the first stage on the Scallon cup, ready to head off when sure enough she fired back and up the Webers went. I still had my old mechanical overalls in the back seats of the car so I grabbed them, lifted the bonnet, stuffed them on top of the carbs, closed the bonnet and got the fire out

Although the fire was out, the timekeeper was still counting us down and as I jumped back in to the car, off we started and I remember saying to Bertie "Give me a minute to get sorted here but I know this road, watch out for the yump about half a mile down".

So there I was getting everything sorted, putting my

belts on, head down finding my maps when the car gave a wee kick up and Bertie said "That wasn't much of a yump" just before she took off like a rocket over the actual yump I'd warned about, before landing nose first, taking the front two spotlights clean off. Bertie got her straightened up and on we went although the lighting was a bit limited which wasn't good on a night time event, but we went well anyway.'

1974

Due to the notable results in the Omagh Motor Club Championship rallies that year, Bertie Fisher and Ronnie McCartney were jointly presented with the Omagh Traders' Trophy at their annual prize-giving dinner dance in the Knocknamoe Castle hotel in January 1974. This was the first time in 35 years that two drivers tied for 1st and the trophy.

To usher in the next season Bertie bought a brand new car, an RS2000 prepared

Mr. Ronnie McCartney (left), formerly of Omagh, and Mr. Bertie Fisher, Ballinamallard, who were jointly presented with the Omagh Motor Traders Trophy at Omagh Motor Club's annual prizegiving dinner in Knock-na-moe Castel Hotel. It was the first time in the 35 years since the institution of the trophy that two drivers have tied for first place — and the trophy.

by Derby Road Garages; TMM 17M, and Brian Quinn recalls Bertie bringing him the car to see *'He pulled in to the Hospital I was working in on his way home from the boat in the car for me to see her. He had driven her from the boat to get a feel of her with all this kit sitting in the back seat and he said to me "We'll go out in this thing next"'*

And go out in that thing they did! Just five days after its

left: Flying on the '74 Circuit of Ireland and the celebrations at the prize-giving

purchase, its debut was the Omagh pre-Circuit rally. *'He wanted to get her out to get her organised to see what worked and what didn't, before the Circuit.'*

For the 5-day 'Benson and Hedges Circuit of Ireland International Rally', which that year started at the Manor House in Killadeas, Co. Fermanagh, at 6pm on Good Friday, Bertie was joined by Bangor man Tony Anderson, known for his driving of a rapid Riley Elf in club events. Starting the event seeded at a lowly 88, by the time they arrived in Killarney there were a few surprised faces around as they had worked their way up to 19th place overall. As the rally progressed a big battle developed between Bertie, Will Sparrow in his Vauxhall and Russell Brookes in a similar Escort to Bertie's. The Sunday run saw a particularly fierce struggle with Russell Brookes where, over some 100 miles of stages in the Kerry area, Bertie came out on top by just 8 seconds and in the process won the Killarney Traders prize for the fastest time in his class on the Sunday stages. He finished the event as Winner in Class 3, 2nd overall in Group 1 and 12th place

overall.

On the 3-day Donegal International Rally in June, when he teamed up again with Brian Quinn. Sponsored by Breton of Fivemiletown who placed a full half page advert in the local newspaper wishing Bertie and Brian the best of luck in the rally, They were the highest seeded Group 1 crew although Russell Brookes was still the man

right: Bertie on the 1974 Donegal International with Brian Quinn who expressed in his own inimitable way some thoughts on Bertie's speed

'He did so well on the braking. When he was coming down to any of the junctions you would have thought he was never going to brake her but that's where he won it. I could tell when he was on song and when he wasn't and when he was his judgement on the brakes was magnificent – as the man says he drove her to the death'

But it wasn't all about Bertie's driving skills as Brian explains, *'A lot of his success was down to attitude and temperament. In the car when he was competing he WAS a serious competitor – no doubt about that, he gave it his all. He always wanted to win, even on night navigation rallies when we were experimenting with the car, he still wanted to win and he had a good competitive edge. Outside of the car he would have spoken to anybody, if there was a bit of knowledge to be gained. In everything he was very competitive, and I liked that in him'*

to beat. Brian remembers that *'We hadn't had time to do the recce for Saturday or Sunday's stages so Terry Harryman donated a set of his notes. Despite that, at the end of the 1st stage we were 3 seconds faster than Russell Brookes and apparently he sent a posse back to see who these bloody 'yokels' were that were beating him – at that stage he knew nothing about Fisher, but it wouldn't be the last time he heard of him.'*

Bertie had started out the rally on high performance road tyres never having tried full race tyres on the car but when, during a discussion reviewing the first day's events, Brian said that he had a set of racing tyres at home a decision was quickly made to give them a go in an effort to put one over on Brookes. Jumping into Brian's road car he headed for Dungannon, hooked up the racers, changed rims and headed back up the road arriving back in Donegal in the early hours of the morning."

Off the pair went to the first stage of the day, Stage 10, Letterleague, revelling in the performance boost from the new tyres as Brian explained *'He couldn't believe the grip they had – he was very comfortable in these racers and he was flying'*

Then disaster struck. Just before a tricky hairpin (which by all accounts appears to have caught out several other drivers), they went off the road, rolled and landed in boggy ground where they were stranded.

Thus it was with very confidence sapping Donegal

Look out for the

FORD ESCORT RS 2000

Driven by

BERTIE FISHER & BRIAN QUINN

and Sponsored by

BRETON (ULSTER) LTD.

Fivemiletown, Co. Tyrone

Telephone Fivemiletown 454; Belfast 44311 (Ext. 326)

A NEW COMPANY NOW MANUFACTURING

S P I R O L L

PRE-CAST PRE-STRESSED
CONCRETE FLOOR & ROOF SLABS

memories in their minds that they turned their attention to the Texaco Rally, a special stage event mainly in Counties Antrim and Down and run by Larne Motor Club the following weekend

It was going to be tight going to get the car ready in time, and before they could even get started they had to hide the car from Mr Fisher Senior !

Brian takes up the story *'We got her home, but we didn't want Tommy to see her, so we headed to Tempo with the car, and put her in Ernie Campbell's garage. We worked at her solidly to get her squared up again as best as we could to make her road worthy. By really burning*

the midnight oil we got panels and stuck them on but we didn't even get time to paint them. On the Texaco we were sitting down outside a forest stage near Newcastle when Terry Harryman came walking up past. With three or four different colours of panels on the car, it must have grabbed his attention for he stopped, looked and just said "My God"'.

Unfortunately their efforts were all for nothing as half way through the rally they had to retire with a mixture of mechanical problems and Bertie succumbing to a dose of the flu, no doubt not helped by too many late nights.

The next event for Bertie was the Erne Trophy Rally sprint, a two-day event held in July at St Angelo's Airfield near Enniskillen and close to home for Bertie. There, after three laps of the twisty airfield course, he won his Class overall for Unmodified Saloon and Sports Cars, Class 4A, and got fastest time of the day. He narrowly beat Ronnie McCartney who was in a Mazda RX3, by less than a second.

Bertie's last rally of the year was the Cookstown Motor Club run 'Wynns' Autumn Rally'

Some of the Fermanagh competitors at the rallysprint, discussing their performances. They are from left—Harry Cathcart, Wesley Abraham, Bertie Fisher, Terry Pearson and Jim Stephenson.

based in the Cookstown, Magherafelt area. Bertie was seeded Number Two for this rally, testament to his previous recent successes. He had Roy Sloan along with him for this event and it started off well with several fastest

The 'Autumn Rally' was the last time Bertie used TMM 17M as he felt that the car was getting quite tired. He sold it to Fermanagh man Roy Cathcart who remembered, *'I bought that car from Bertie and sort of used it as a road car. I would have had a few accounts out over at Belcoo which I would have visited with her and she was great fun on the back roads on the way home although she was a bit twisted of herself'*

right: His replacement car was the ex-Russell Brookes RS2000, GVX 833N which is pictured here on the Welsh in 1975 at Llandow track in an unusual shot with Bertie alone in the car because part of the event there included a driver only race around the track

1975

stage times but a few stages in when the rally moved to Magherafelt territory, a slippery downhill left-hander sent Fisher's car off the road.

Around this time, Bertie started a long-time partnership with Sydney Meeke, a rally preparation specialist from the rural village of Bush in County Tyrone, after he offered some service area assistance to the ailing Fisher team on the Circuit of Ireland in 1973 by patching up the rear quarter panel after his day one roll. Sydney was no stranger to rallying being a former Ulster Rally Cham-

pionship winner and also having regularly competed on events in the sprint and navigation rally scene. The relationship developed and from around 1975 Sydney's preparation team would be involved in one way or another with all of Fisher's rally cars.

In the spring of 1975, Fisher acquired an ex- Russell Brookes Group 1 Mark One Escort RS 2000, GVX 833N which Brookes had been using up to and including the Circuit of Ireland in 1975, which Bertie missed. It was in this GVX car that Bertie had his first proper Group 1 successes when a debut in the Welsh Rally brought him 2nd Overall in Group 1 out of 42 Gp1 competitors followed

left: Bertie with co-driver Derek Smyth at the Donegal Rally

As Derek remembers it, his seat with Bertie happened more by chance than anything: *'For the Donegal Rally that year, Brian Nelson and I had done the recce in anticipation of doing the rally with a car from Germany that never materialized. So shortly before the rally I was left without a drive. At the same time Bertie had done the recce with Peter Scott and they had prepared pace notes but Bertie was to be co-driven by an English journalist named Tony McMahon. Tony had some sort of family emergency at the last minute so he couldn't compete. So Bertie was without a co-driver and I was without a driver. Since Peter had made the recce with him, he asked me did I think I could read his notes, although Brian and I had prepared our own notes, and I didn't feel that was going to be a major issue at all. And so, we were match made by Peter to go on the rally'*

up by an even better result in the Donegal International where he finished 1st in Group 1 and 10th overall, his first Top Ten finish in an international rally.

The Donegal Rally that year was also the first time that County Tyrone man Derek Smyth sat with him. With that last minute pairing, off the new team went to the 'Hills. But even from the very start of the rally, Derek notes that it started with a particularly spectacular close shave with the scenery. Here he recalls an incident on Stage one, Carn Hill, just outside Letterkenny: *'There's a spot on the stage where we went over a wee kink and out on to the road and over the bridge. We went onto two wheels before we even came near the junction, rode up the bank, went out across the road on two wheels and ended up*

right: Action from Donegal in 1975 including top right Atlantic Drive stage near Downings village

off the road on the other side. We managed somehow to drive up and out, avoiding hitting the bridge parapet, but he snicked off the door handle on my side, brushed a back tyre and we drove the rest of the stage with a flat tyre!'.

After that first stage fright, they settled down and for the rest of the weekend it was a matter of catching up with everybody else. Their opposition that year was made up of such people as Derek McMahon, James McDaid, and a tall, blonde haired young Finn by the name of Ari Vatanen. Ari, who was partnered by Dave Richards, and in an Opel Ascona, was rallying on tarmac for the very first time ever was and also competing for the first time on Irish soil.

With the success of a great weekend in Donegal over him, Bertie went with high hopes to The Texaco Rally, on that occasion a small single venue event run by Larne Motor Club in Boyd's Quarry, County Antrim. It would not be just as successful an event for him though as the

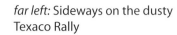

far left: Sideways on the dusty Texaco Rally

left: Bertie and Sydney Meeke share a light hearted moment

surfaces were so rough that he broke a rear suspension spring carrier early on. It could have been fixed but given how rough the event was and the punishment it was inflicting on the car, he decided to pull out.

Shortly after the lack lustre Texaco Bertie took time out of the special stages to do his home Erne Trophy Rallysprint held in mid-July at the St Angelo Airfield venue where he shared the car with Sydney

A class-winner at Friday's races at St. Angelo was well-known Rally man, Bertie Fisher from Ballinamallard.

right: Derek Smyth recalls navigating for Bertie on the Bushwacker rally :
'We had a fabulous run together, and he was so far ahead of the other Group 1 competitors that I had difficulty getting him to go slowly since there was nothing more to be gained other than in his case the enjoyment of driving on the stages !'

The Clanabogan stage on that rally was just an unbelievable experience, – when a driver says he knows a road that's always a very scary time for a navigator! There's a phone box on that stage that sits right out on the edge of the road and I was sure I was going to lose my door handle on it but he knew the lines and it was just an incredible piece of driving. He always drove very, very hard and was very competitive in the car

With Bertie scheduled to do the Manx Rally just two weeks after the Bushwacker, Derek was mindful of unnecessary over exuberance, but it came at a price! : *'Bertie was a very funny guy to be with, what with his dry sense of humour, and he could defuse any kind of a difficult situation very easily. I got the nickname 'Eaasy' because every time he was in attack mode I would be telling him 'Take it easy' in relation to preserving the car.'*

Meeke, Bertie finishing 1st in his Class (Class A, LSD).

Bertie's following rally was the 'Bushwhacker', run by Omagh Motor Club. It was the first time the event was run with that title, and it is still going today. Nowadays it

is a forestry event but then it was mainly on tarmac and based in County Tyrone. Partnered by Derek Smyth once again, they appeared to have a continued recipe for success, finishing first in Group 1 again, winning Class 2 (Gp1 over 1600) and 7th Overall, as well as coming away with the 'C.A.M Perpetual Trophy'.

Next followed the Manx Rally. Bertie had competed on the Manx once before in 1971 in a Mini when he had retired with a broken gearbox. This time the end result, a non-finish, would be the same, only with a different cause.

With Derek as co-driver once again, shortly after the start of the rally they led Group One and were surprising a few of the regular international competitors around at

the time. However this happy state of affairs was not to continue long as Derek takes up the story. *'On a stage in Abbeylands area, as he turned the car into a right-hander it just rolled onto its side. There was no impact or no big sideways moment – as he turned the car it simply rolled over and slid on its side down the road, into a gateway where we hit the end of the bank head on and cart-wheeled up on top of the bank. The back of the car was caught against a tree and so it was sitting with its nose pointing down into the bank. We were both OK – a bit shook up – but we got our seat-belts off and got out of the car and fell down off the back of the bank.'*

Although they were safely out of the car the incident appeared a lot worse than it actually was and the stage was temporarily halted until it was confirmed the pair were OK.

At the time they didn't know what had caused the accident but the next day while the rally continued elsewhere on the island, Bertie wanted to take a closer look at the site of the accident because he couldn't quite understand why the car rolled over on its own. Derek explained, *'He felt if there was an assignable cause, he'd be a lot happier. So, while the rest of us were standing where the accident had taken place, he walked up and down the stage and, away back up the road, he found the little castellated nut with the end of the anti-roll bar still in it. The end of the anti-roll bar, no doubt weakened in a heavy impact we'd had with a kerb on a previous stage, had broken off and the bottom arm which located the wheel had pulled out causing the car to roll'*

This story itself shows even at an early point in his career, how meticulous Bertie was to identify anything which might impact his performance.

The car was so badly damaged after the roll incident on the Manx Rally that it had to be re-shelled and Sydney Meeke remembers the aftermath of the Manx and the rush to get the car ready for the Forward Trust Rally, the car's next event.

'We brought the car home from the Manx and it was in a bad way needing a new shell. On the Monday we went over to Cal Withers in England to get a new body shell, took it home, got it rebuilt and painted in time for Bertie to take to the Forward Trust rally at Aghadowey. I couldn't make it to the rally that day, but as the event was being televised live that day, I turned on the TV – and there he was, going out over a barrel, end over end, another shell needed!'

Although he completed the day, albeit with a very sore car, it was a very dispiriting result and Bertie was reputed to have sold the now wreck of a car at the end of the event for a sum of £2,500.

1976

The disappointment of the Forward Trust and Manx crashes, which occurred at a time when a major expansion to the family business was taking priority, meant that Bertie left rallying for a while. He did no more events for the rest of 1975 and, in fact, didn't drive competitively for around 15 months until his return in early 1977. He did however return to the co-driver's seat again in 1976, one event being the Galway International Rally in February where, alongside James Davison of Ballymena in an Escort, they retired on the third stage with a blown alternator.

While Bertie may not have done much rallying in 1976, he was still very much involved in the sport. He took up

"Permapost" Rally on Saturday

Mr. Bertie Fisher (second right) of Fisher Engineering Ltd., Ballinamallard, handing over a trophy to Mr. Gordon Jackson, secretary of Enniskillen Motor Club, for the highest placed driver of a Group I car in the club's "Permapost Rally". On right, is Mr. Peter Stuart of B.C. Stuart & Son, Enniskillen, who also donated a trophy. Included is Mr. Arthur Finlay, sales manager of Ballycassidy Sawmills, sponsors of the "Permapost Rally".

some organisational posts during this period, including sharing the position of results officer with Austin Frazer on the Enniskillen Motor Club Winter Rally. And the family firm, Fisher Engineering, also first sponsored a trophy for the Permapost that year (the rally's inaugural year) for the highest placed Group 1 driver.

1977

Bertie was back in action for the 1977 season, campaigning a distinctive orange ex-Wesley Abraham RS

Fermanagh's main hope for overall victory in the Group 1 section of the Circuit of Ireland International Rally at Easter, lie with Bertie Fisher and Wesley Abraham from Ballinamallard, in their William Bell Tractors sponsored Escort RS 2000. Included are (from left) Mr. William Bell, Mr. Bertie Fisher, Mr. Wesley Abraham and Mr. William McElroy of William Bell Tractors, Fivemiletown.

2000 Mark Two, KIA 2220, and with backing from Lindsay Cars and William Bell Tractors in Fivemiletown, as well as promoting the Fisher Engineering family firm, he had a good sponsorship package for the year.

From the cars debut on Enniskillen Motor Club's 'Snowspinner' Rally, a small navigation winter event held in January, it was instantly competitive in Bertie's hands. There he finished first place in class 1 and second overall behind John Gilleece. This was followed up by a class win and sixth overall on the Auto Extra Hellfire Rally despite engine problems on the final stage from where he barely limped to the Finish. The Hellfire was

hand at a bit of circuit racing at the Official Opening of the Castlederg Car Club's new Track. It wasn't a discipline Bertie would have been particularly familiar with but ,given he had been invited, it wasn't something he was going to let up the opportunity to try out. In his race, he finished a credible third overall behind the Lotuses of Pomeroy man Mike Nugent and John McCullough, cars which were set up for racing while Bertie's had his normal rally set up.

Just a few days after that Castlederg Race Circuit opening was the Burmah Rally. A predecessor to the Lurgan Park Rally, this one day event was organised by the North Armagh Motorcycle and Car Club, and based around the forests of Rostrevor in County Down. Bertie's one off co-driver for the day was Dessie Wilson who recalls the rally being a bit of a dingdong battle *'... fighting with the*

the first round of the Irish Shell National Rally Championship and an event which had a considerable number of top entries including Roy Cathcart, Sean Campbell, Ger Buckley, etc. so this was a significant result.

The following Benson & Hedges Circuit of Ireland didn't bring just as much success. Bertie and co-driver Wesley Abraham (the cars former owner) were in 9th place overall and leading Group 1 half way through the rally but a broken steering during the Sunday run put them out of the rally completely.

A few weeks after the Circuit of Ireland, Bertie tried his

far left: On the Circuit of Ireland

left Bertie and Dessie Wilson after the Burmah of which Dessie has many fond memories including about the Meeke service team

'In those days the Meeke team had quite a humble set up, and travel arrangements for any of the parts or equipment were quite primitive. Our service barge was my Fiat 127 which I'd bought at a closing down dealers in Lurgan for £300. Sydney drove bringing his wife and Gladys along with a big tool box, the exhaust fell off halfway and Syd got a garage in Warrenpoint to drop everything and lend him the lift and it was sorted – ah there's only one Sydney!'

A Favourite for "Permapost" Rally

Bertie Fisher, Ballinamallard, one of the favourites to win Enniskillen Motor Club's Permapost Rally this weekend driving his Escort RS2000.

great *Ronnie McCartney in an RS2000 as well as Winston Henry etc., all these guys now departed, I feel so privileged having sat with them and I'm the only one left.'*

That Burmah was a tight affair in the end resulting in Bertie recording a narrow eight seconds win from Ronnie McCartney, who was in a similar RS2000. *'Going into the last stage we were 11 seconds up on him and then he had a real go on the last one. Those were the days'* said Dessie.

On the Burmah he gained maximum points with his win to take joint lead in the championship with Robin Lyons but McCartney, who played second fiddle on the Burmah, got his own back on the next round of the championship, Bertie's 'home' rally so to speak, the

Permapost, organised by Enniskillen Motor Club.

All of the Permapost Rally sections were in Fermanagh's forests, which that weekend were blessed with glorious sunshine making conditions ideal for the 75 starting crews. Partnered this time by his younger brother Ivan, by the half way point, the Ballinamallard pair were doing very well trailing McCartney by two seconds. That gap waxed and waned but in the end he finished where he had been all day, second overall behind the Larne garage man putting McCartney into the lead of the championship, where he would stay until the end of the year.

In June, Bertie took his annual trip to Donegal for the International, now a highly acclaimed classic rally with many international visitors and entries from all over Ire-

left: Bertie passes through picturesque Donegal landscape on the International Rally in 1977

land, the UK and Europe. This year would be different for Bertie as he got his first Top 5 placing in an International Rally, finishing 5th overall and winner of Group 1. On the rally itself, up against some well experienced opposition such as Sean Campbell and Henry Inurietta, Bertie drove very well, and charged hard despite some late brake troubles. A set of photos from the stage which travelled through Ramelton shows just how hard Bertie was trying on this rally, as he is well up on two wheels and he manages to get away with it but is quite dramatic compared to the other drivers on the same corner.

A month after the high of the top 5 Donegal finish, Bertie was 3rd fastest on the Erne Rallysprint, and first in Class 4 and things were looking good for the rest of the summer but with the vagaries of rallying nothing is certain.

An eventful Tour of the Sperrins which followed saw Bertie stall on the first and second stages, put the car off the road and get a puncture, losing so much time he decided to retire from the rally. Although retired from the rally proper, that wasn't Bertie finished for the day. Acting as Course Car for the remainder of the rally, he

right: Action from the Donegal in 1977 including top left and bottom right at various locations of the Ramelton town stage

managed fastest time on the last stage despite losing his brakes!

In August Bertie travelled to Scotland in his only overseas event of the year to compete on the 'Burmah International', a 480 mile Glasgow based event in the forests of Scotland. He and Trevor Hughes completed the first few stages but on stage 4 dropped a wheel over the edge of the track and into a 'firebreak' ditch. Extracting the car took some considerable time and they ran out of time forcing their retirement from the rally.

After that run of unfortunate rallies, some better luck was just around the corner as Bertie, with Robert Harkness navigating, took on the second running of the Belfast Telegraph Ulster International Rally. A successful run saw them finish 11th Overall, and 2nd in Group 1 behind SMT Magnum charger Jimmy McRae claiming a number of significant scalps along the way including Graham Elsmore who at the time was a works supported Ford Group 1 driver.

left: Action from the Ulster Rally in 1977 where Bertie was partnered by Robert Harkness, who later became Clerk of the Course of the Ulster Rally

The Fisher Engineering Story

In mid-1950, with a family on the way, newly-weds Tommy and Elsie Fisher moved to Ballinamallard where an in-law had helped find a suitable house. It was there that Tommy and Elsie settled and started their family and, with the experience Tommy gained working for the RAF at home and abroad, the time was right to go out on his own and set up his own business.

Leaving his job at the Castle Archdale RAF base where he was a maintenance blacksmith and welder Tommy started out working from the back of his house doing small welding and repair jobs for people in the locality but with a £50 deal done for a ¾ acre site in Ballinamallard, the remnants and roof off an old Shell Oil Co building that was being demolished soon became the main components of a new 50' x 30' shed, the first home of 'Thomas S Fisher'.

In their first few years the fledgling firm and its handful of staff concentrated on the maintenance of minor farming and household appliances helped by the arrival of reliable electricity supplies in rural areas which permitted the use of electric welders and power tools.

With the mechanisation of farming came a surge in work converting and redesigning old machinery designed for horses to operate with new farm tractors. In time the company began to produce equipment of its own design including a modern tractor pulled potato planter invented by Tommy with a wheel operated bell to ensure evenly spread seed. Before very long farming machinery production became a niche for the firm which set them apart from other engineering firms in the area. As Tommy himself remembered many years later *'At that time the big change over was coming in agriculture - the horses were going out and the tractors were coming in. There was a massive amount of work converting the machinery for the tractors. It kept the business going for a year until I built our first manufactured item - a potato planter, which has been in use every*

Tommy Fisher with the potato planter and timing wheel he developed

year since.'

Buck rakes, link boxes, trailers, digger buckets and the likes were the order of the day, all produced by Thomas S Fisher Engineering who were drawing in custom from further and further afield.

Sean Quinn (of the Quinn Group) recalls on an occasion in the 1960s travelling from where he lived on the border of Fermanagh and Leitrim near Derrylin to Ballinamallard to get an implement fixed at Fisher's. *'Shortly af-*

Tommy Fisher with tractor mounted back-end shovel

ter my father died when I wasn't that great a farmer, I had a buck rake with twisted teeth. I went to Tommy who straightened them out and he was laughing at me, saying "What were you doing with this buck rake, it's in an awful way". He wasn't overly impressed with my buck-rake skills anyway! I suppose it was a fair oul spin down to him to get a buck rake straightened but there weren't that many people who did that kind of thing around this part of the world at that time'.

Progressing through to the 1960s the company started doing agricultural buildings, making trusses for lean-to houses and silo pits, and in time this led to prefabricated industrial buildings, paving their main direction in future years. Although most contracts were for agricultural and industrial buildings they were prepared to adapt their skills to other fields and one of their first major buildings was in the ecclesiastical sector with the erection of

steel roof trusses for Colaghty church. This ability to think outside the box was demonstrated again in the same sector when, in later years, they designed and fitted a steel fabricated spire on St Michael's Church in Enniskillen. The church originally had plans for a stone built spire but the architect felt the foundations would not carry it so, with the help of Bertie, a steel spire was designed, manufactured and installed by Fisher Engineering.

By the late 1960s the company was expanding rapidly as a new factory extension and extensive new concrete yard for stock storage were added. Key in all this business expansion were the important back room staff including a young Jim Henderson who initially 'kept the books right' for Tommy and would later become company secretary to Fisher Engineering.

Of Tommy and Elsie Fisher's four boys, three went on to work for the family firm in one way or another and Bertie, being the eldest, was the first to get involved. He had studied part time at Hereford College England from around 1965 before working full-time in the business in 1969. In the intervening years, he

had continued to work at the business in his spare time gaining practical experience (including 'on the anvil' at the blacksmiths shop), and this experience allied to the knowledge gained on his Hereford course gave him an extra level of knowledge and indeed confidence, which would be crucial in the following few years in the family business.

Of course the late sixties was also the time when Bertie was starting to rally; any spare time from work was largely spent on car preparations, and he soon became known as much for his skills in car part manufacturing as he was for blacksmithing or steel fabricating as Tommy mentions in his memoirs *'Bertie and his friends built and prepared many cars with assortments of parts including homemade roll bars and sump guards'.*

In the early 1970s, when the business expanded into structural steelwork, Tommy formed a partnership with a man in Ballinamore, Co. Leitrim, where they opened an engineering works called North West Engineering Ltd. With plenty on his hands at Ballinamallard, Tommy found it hard to juggle the needs of both premises, and as a result of problems with staff in the first few months, he sent Bertie to look after the new venture. Bertie was thrown in to the deep end, but as Tommy suggested in his memoirs, it was a very important step for him and for Bertie. *'In hindsight, this was probably the best thing ever happened. I was unable to give him much assistance, only managing to get up to Ballinamore occasionally, and my partner was a local contractor who, although he was easy to work with, had no knowledge of the engineering business, and so could offer only limited assistance. Bertie carried the whole load – manage the business, as well as buying and selling, and pricing contracts.'*

Bertie continued to cut his teeth in Ballinamore for a few years before returning to work in Ballinamallard where, the workforce of 14 had outgrown the small workshops, Bertie's help was much needed as Tommy pointed out in his memoirs.

'I was so busy I felt Bertie would be more vital with me at home. Also, he had just got married, and Gladys was not happy about him being away so much. Added to that it was the beginning of the troubles, and crossing the border was risky at times'.

Private Limited Company Status came in 1974 and with it, the new name Fisher Engineering Ltd. In the following two years, there was a massive step up in operations and in size too, expanding their site to 11 acres with a new £250,000 3,000 sq. metre factory, the first sod of the project being turned by Lord Hamilton, Chairman of the Western Panel of LEDU in May 1976. At the time the factory was being built it was regarded as being the only one of its kind in the West of the province. Bertie had a big part to play in the expansion of the business, which meant that he took an almost complete hiatus from rallying in 1976.

Also in 1976 Bertie's brother Ernie had joined the business and was another major catalyst to the step up in operations. Ernie was well qualified by the time he joined the firm, having studied at Portora College and gaining an OND at Lisburn Technical College before completing a HND in Engineering at Jordanstown.

Just as Bertie had done, Ernie initially worked on the factory shop floor but specialising in computing and other new technologies which were playing an increasing role in the business. The two worked very well together – Bertie carried out PR and marketing to win new contracts while Ernie focussed on how the firm would manage them.

Of the two younger brothers Ivan and Kenny, Ivan joined the business in 1978, while Kenny followed a different course taking up employment with the finance department of the Erne Hospital although he shared with all his brothers a love for cars and rallying and for many years has been involved in helping to run rallies in various different capacities including serving as secretary of Enniskillen Motor Club.

Fisher Engineering Ltd. continued down the route of heavy structural steel fabrication, gaining their first major job in the field with the Lakeland Forum in Enniskillen and its 130ft span.

Other similar sized projects followed but the job which really gave them the next big step up in stature was the steel contract for the new DeLorean factory motor plant at Dunmurry on the outskirts of Belfast. They had never tackled anything of that size before, and the job was a major success and as a result of their work on the DeLorean plant the firm received much recognition from architects and engineers all around the city, and from that point forward the business sold itself as Tommy observed *'We did not have to advertise – all we had to do was rely on our name for high-class quality work and delivery on time'.*

The positive chat in the industry about the company was soon followed by more formal recognition as a number of prestigious business awards came their way. One of the first was in recognition for their part in the construction, with improvements, of a Gravel Tunnel Drainer, which won the supreme award in the Machinery Awards at the Balmoral Show in Belfast, winning the Leyland Cup and Silver Medals followed by the Gallagher Business Challenge award in 1979. On the technical side of the business another high accolade

Joe Pat Prunty with the award winning gravel tunnel drainer at Balmoral Show

The next large scale project undertaken was that of the 4000-tonne steelwork for the 120+ shop and services Castlecourt Shopping Centre structure in Belfast city centre. At the time Castlecourt was the largest shopping, office and car park complex in Ireland and, as if that was not enough, at the same time Fisher Engineering Ltd. were engaged for the steelwork on the new Quinn Cement Factory which required around 2000 tonnes of steel. That both contracts were successfully delivered in an 18 month period between March 1987 and November 1988 was a remarkable achievement.

Part of what set Bertie and indeed all of Fisher Engineering apart when it came to the projects they got involved with was in their meticulous and precise approach to planning and pricing allied to their considerate and helpful nature in advising clients. The Quinn Group was a particularly big client for Fishers, with a large number of manufacturing factories in Derrylin, and the UK including glass, cement, radiators, prestressed concrete, roof tiles production, amongst others but also an insurance company. Sean Quinn, who built the companies up from scratch, gives an insight into Bertie Fisher the businessman as well as the client care that made Fishers' Engineering so unique.

'Bertie was a decent fella, and in any of the dealings we had with him, of which there were many, we never once had an argument. Fishers did all of the steelwork for all of the factories, north and south of the border but also some further afield too. The factory in Elton [Runcorn] built in 2004 was probably the biggest

above: Steelwork for the Castlecourt complex

*below:*Construction on one of The Quinn Groups factories near Derrylin on the Fermanagh-Cavan border

ard ISO 9001 for structural steelwork.

Around the same time as this accolade, after having built up the business over four decades to being one of the biggest and best in its field and with three of his sons now fully engaged in its management, Tommy began to gradually wind down his involvement and by 1988 Bertie had become Managing Director, although Tommy continued as Chairman of the Company until his death in 2001.

came in 1989 when they were the first company in Ireland to be awarded quality stand-

project they did for us and that was huge, the biggest glass factory in Europe. But whether it was myself or some of my men dealing with him, the reason we never had an argument was because of the way he would work, clearly stating things out like "OK, the structure is x high, y wide, etc. etc. I'll come back with the plans".

A good example of this, and how the Fishers in general worked, was on the second cement factory. FLSmidth, the Danish Company, had prepared the plans for the steelwork but Bertie, having looked at the plans, came back and said "I can do it according to the plans, Or, I can do it better and cheaper. Which do you want?" Of course I said "Are you sure?" and he said "I'm 100% sure!", outlined to us why and how he could do it better and cheaper – and he did!'.

Expanding on that example, Sean explained the unique nature of how Bertie would boldly and intelligently reconsider the designs of a market leader and in the process significantly improve them.

'It's worth considering here in relation to Fisher Engineering that 99% of the engineering firms throughout the world who would get a design for a plant from a manufacturer of cement producing equipment like FLSmidth (who were the biggest in the world at that time), wouldn't change the designs – nobody except Fisher Engineering. Bertie asked us to send his spec to Denmark to see would they accept it and, because normally you couldn't change it, we expected they would turn round and say this doesn't suit... But FLSmidth were

very impressed by his re-design which made it a better, stronger, simpler and cheaper structure and adopted his amendments for future projects.

Bertie had a very versatile mind when it came to putting his thoughts to designs of completely different types of jobs or applications. He would have an inquisitive mind for how things could be done. A lot of people just follow the leader, but Bertie particularly, and Fisher Engineering generally, was always looking to simplify and improve the quality of work they were doing.'

Sean continued, explaining some of the integrity Bertie and the Fishers had as business people. 'They had a good team, and Bertie was never mean, he paid good staff, and he wouldn't be looking to do it on the cheap or come half fisted saying "I think it will be such and such a price". There would be no thinking, he would have his design there, he would have the weight of steel there, he would have all the measurements there, everything he needed, and he would be down to pounds, shillings and pence. Of course we would then start a bit of horse dealing – that's the way it was done – but at the end of that he would have done it in such detail, there couldn't be a potential argument, and there wasn't. If there was extra work to be done, there was extra work to be

Pictured at the opening of the extensions to the factory. From left to right, Wesley Knox, Bertie Fisher, Bruce Robinson (IDB), Tommy Fisher, Ernie Fisher, Dennis McConnell

done, but if he was happy to sign off on the design, we were happy to accept his sign off. Sometimes you get people in to do work for you and all of a sudden when they are half way through it they would come back and say "There is a problem here" or "there is a problem there". Well Fisher Engineering never operated that way, they were always professional enough that they could foresee any potential problem and they would outline it in advance making them a very easy company to deal with.'

It wasn't just massive jobs entirely that Bertie and indeed Fisher Engineering took on. Friend, former rally team mate, and business client Ernie Campbell had this to say about Bertie Fisher the business man he knew and how he helped him for a small project Ernie was working on. After asking Bertie for advice, Bertie did a lot more than just advise him on

Erecting the main spine of the roof of the Waterfront Hall in Belfast

it. '*Bertie was a great help whenever you ever needed to discuss anything that you were doing for he had a good head on him. On this occasion he said there was a building going out from the factory and that it was the same size that I needed so I wouldn't need any plans drawn up because they would already have the template from the other project. He told me to get a particular person to do the footings and they would take it all from there. He wasn't miserable with money but had a good respect for it, and when he decided he was going to do something he would put his weight to it. That was the type of fella he was.*' As Ernie points out, just like his father had done, Bertie very often worked for and helped many locals do projects with the help of his knowledge and business, even when it wasn't for finan-

cial gains, but would reap good rewards: '*He liked to see those people around him thriving, that was the way he worked. He would have dropped a lucrative job to attend to them; he was very much a community man.*'

Another business that had numerous dealings with Bertie throughout the 1990s, and that can vouch for Bertie's helpfulness is Ardmac Performance Contracting, which was set up by Brendan McAnallen in the 1970s. Brendan remembers how helpful Fishers in general, and Bertie in particular, were to him in business. '*Over the years I would have got to know Bertie and Ernie reasonably well as we worked on numerous projects together. They were very helpful, co-operative, and very efficient in their dealings with us. On one occasion we got a large IDB foreign investment

project in Belfast and we came across a problem where the roof decking had got damaged in a way that made it almost impossible to repair. We were basically being held for a considerable amount of money by the contractor until they would clear the work, so the architect at the time asked Fishers if they could come up with some solution. Bertie went to the bother of putting another single deck on top of the existing deck, a solution which was accepted by IDB and everyone involved so the whole thing was settled very reasonably and efficiently and the factory was handed over on the due date.*' Expanding on the Bertie he knew from the various meeting and projects they were at, Brendan went on to say, '*He took a personal interest in every job he did – he would take a look at the job, he would be the engineer, he would have been there at the site meetings and when the thing was going up he would have been there and very active. He would have been big into attention to detail*'

As the big jobs such as Belfast's Waterfront

Concert Hall and the Odyssey Arena rolled in, more people were required, and by the early 1990s the workforce was up to 80 working in a total production space of 10,000 sq. metres. The well-established Fisher Engineering now stood as a shining light in the construction industry, not only in Northern Ireland but also across the whole island and beyond. The recognition that successful completion of such large-scale jobs brought meant they were now starting to win major contracts in the rest of the UK: in London, Newcastle-Upon-Tyne, Manchester and Scotland.

The larger projects amongst them required massive amounts of steel and men for the job but perhaps more important was the project management and the logistics needed, which were on scales not witnessed before in Northern Ireland, from the roads needing closed off for the extra wide and long loads which had to be moved to the multiple site cranes used to synchronously manoeuvre the steel beams into place, and much more. With the ever rapidly developing computer aided design and computer controlled machining it was essential to keep up to date with the latest advances and throughout the 1990s the company heavily invested in technology and totally computerised its detailing office.

As the Celtic Tiger roared all over Ireland in the mid-1990s, Fisher Engineering too were booming, with massive contracts across the island including Intel at Lexilip, Kildare; the Liffey Valley Shopping Centre in Dublin; the Coca Cola plants in Drogheda and Ballina plus many more.

Brothers Bertie and Ernie Fisher pictured standing on the bridge in Ballinamallard, Fisher Engineering's new office block behind

But with all this work, the Fishers faced a dilemma – they wanted to address some inefficiencies in directional flow of material being processed through the factory, but were limited by the physical constraints of the site which was bounded on three sides by the Ballinamallard River, ultimately restricting further growth. Major thought was given during 1996 as to how they could address this: either to stand still at the size they were, up-root and move to a greenfield site or try to expand the existing site. In the end they opted for the latter and an additional three acres were acquired from neighbouring farmers and the mammoth task of diverting the river and expanding the factory space to some 15,000 sq. metres got underway.

The Intel factory at Leixlip built during the Celtic Tiger years

Fisher Engineering's complex, Boxing Day 2000

By 2000 the company employed 160 staff and Bertie's name was held in such high regard in the industry that he was appointed as Deputy President of the British Constructional Steelwork Association (BCSA), the first person from Northern Ireland to hold such a position. The BCSA are the national organisation representing the (at the time) £2 Billion per annum steel construction industry which provided employment for over 100,000 workers. The role was a most prestigious appointment and involved making representations to the government on behalf of the industry, as well as attending functions and presenting awards.

While Bertie continued to lead from the top, the third generation of Fishers was getting involved in the business. Bertie's son Mark had completed university and got involved in the business from 1997 onward. While he was initially involved in the drawing office side of the business, he was making significant progress within the Company, moving on to be Structural Design Team Leader on some projects, and was showing the promise to be a future Managing Director. Indeed much like his father, Mark had a great personality, high effervescence and dedicated approach to work, and he would often be heard using the phrase "Look boys this job is not rocket science we can make it work" amongst the staff.

Speaking about Mark Fisher the businessman, Sean Quinn, who had regular dealings with the Fishers throughout Mark's time at the firm, had this to say. '*We as a company and the Quinns as a family would have rated Mark equally as high as his father and that was extremely high. He was responsible as a project manager on the new cement factory and he was an extremely respectful young man. He used to call me "Mr Quinn", and I used to tell him on a daily basis "Forget about Mr Quinn, it's Sean" but the next week he would still*

come back and it would be "Mr Quinn" again, and he wasn't putting that on. It was just how the lad was brought up and that's the way he was. I thought he and his father's personalities were very alike.'

Everything changed in early 2001, initially after Bertie, Mark and Emma's untimely passing and later in the same year when the Company's founder and Chairman Tommy also passed away.

The mood at the time was movingly summed up when Ernie addressed the workforce on the 29th January 2001.

'*I would like to thank the reverend gentlemen and David Bolton for their attendance here this morning to help us all come to terms with what has happened as a result of the helicopter accident last Sunday. Even though the Fisher family are still grieving the tragic loss of Bertie, Mark and Emma I felt the need as acting managing director to speak to every member of the Fisher Engineering workforce today before they start back to work to assure them that there is a very positive future for Fisher Engineering despite the loss of Bertie and Mark.*

I have never been a deeply religious person or a keen public speaker but I honestly do believe that God and the prayers of thousands of people have given me the strength to write these words over the weekend and hopefully the strength to deliver them to you this morning.

First of all Ivan and I wish to thank you all on behalf of the Fisher family for your condolences, help and thoughtfulness over the past week, and the pride and absolute respect that you showed along the route of the removal from the Erne Hospital to the church, and again during the funeral service. I can safely say that Bertie, Mark and Emma would have been very proud of you all.

Kenny, Ivan and I owe a great debt of gratitude to Wesley Knox, Jim Henderson, the management and staff of Fisher Engineering, Austin Frazer, Canon Hoey, the Enniskillen Motor Club and a large number of Bertie's personal friends who took over and organised the complete funeral arrangements. Bertie and Mark would have called it a 'slick operation'. Sean Quinn commented to Ian Cochrane afterwards that he would have expected nothing less from Fisher Engineering, and that is high praise from him.

Looking on from the background during the week and throwing my own thoughts in here and there, I could see a great bond developing between the whole workforce. Everybody seemed to want to help in some way, no matter how small. I hope that that bond between the workforce will grow and develop in the times that are ahead. I could see this past week that you all felt that you too had lost loved ones who were a major part of the Fisher Engineering family.

My wife Joan has decided to give up her part time job as a school nurse in order to carry the bulk of my share of the family commitments in caring for the welfare of Gladys and Roy who are still in the Royal Victoria Hospital and my father and mother who still have to come to terms with this tragic loss. Gladys and Roy are

now fully aware of the outcome of this tragic accident. Joan and I went to see them yesterday along with Canon Hoey. Gladys is still in intensive care but is making steady progress, and was able to speak yesterday morning for the first time since her operation. Roy is in Ward 42 with all his close friends from Belfast around him. He is in very high spirits, even though he has just had fourteen pins and two plates fitted in his left arm, and has still to cope with the pain of two fractured vertebrae.

I would like to go on now to convey to you some of my thoughts over the past few days as they may help all of you to come to terms with what has happened.

A friend of mine came to the house on Thursday morning a few hours before the funeral and to be honest I did not want to see anyone. He apologised for calling at such a time but said that he wanted to see me before the funeral to offer me some advice that he had been given in somewhat similar circumstances but had not taken. He said that I should never ask the reason why this tragic accident had happened as I would never find the answer and if I kept on asking I would eventually destroy my faith in God. I thought about this during the funeral service and also noted that Canon Hoey gave the same advise in his address. Before the end of the service I decided to take that advice and I would suggest that all the people here should give it consideration also.

With regard to the future of Fisher Engineering I have decided to look at it like a gearbox in Bertie or Marks rally car that has had two

cogs sheared off its primary gear wheel in the middle of a special stage in a rally. I know that all of you have enough engineering knowledge to understand that as long as those two cogs have not been side by side then the gear wheel will still be able to turn and drive all the other wheels in the gear train.

Both Bertie and Mark would have realised that in this situation they would have had to slow down for a while in order to reach the next service point and have the gearbox replaced in double quick time by an expert service crew.

The longer serving members of staff will remember that when my father Tommy was managing director of Fisher Engineering he was renowned throughout the country as the best man at rebuilding sheared cogs on cast iron gear wheels. Many times he even put together gear wheels that had completely shattered and some of them I am sure are still working today.

I take great pleasure in telling you that my father came home from hospital yesterday and is making a good recovery. I have absolutely no doubt that with his guidance as company chairman and that of many other close business associates as my councillors we can rebuild the primary gear in our gear box in double quick time and go on to overcome this setback and win many more rallies for Fisher Engineering in the future.

Roy Fisher said when he went into the Royal Victoria Hospital that he would be glad to see any of his friends or relatives as long as they came in with a happy face. I ask you all to be

above and below: Construction of Central Park complex, Dublin and the resulting awards

will do your utmost to achieve that objective.

As most of you know Bertie and I worked in the same office for the past twenty years. We were both on the same wavelength and shared the many complexities of running Fisher Engineering. You are also all aware that Bertie had an exceptionally high public profile, however he would have been the first to admit that Fisher Engineering was always a team operation.

My primary objective is to ensure the continued success of this company and to protect the jobs of everyone employed here. The fact that these words were written yesterday in the back of Canon Hoey's car on the way to and from Belfast and typed last night jointly by my son and daughter shows the strength of resolve that I have to see this objective achieved.

Ernie's trust that the momentum Tommy, Bertie and Mark had helped build up in the company would stand Fisher Engineering Ltd in good stead was not misplaced. Despite the turmoil and adversity, 2001 turned out to be the most operationally successful year to that point in their 51 year history and was capped off by picking up a prestigious European Steel Design Award in Venice for Block E of the Central Park project in Leopardstown, Dublin. There to pick up the award was Ernie, who had taken over management of the company, along with his wife Joan, Gladys and Roy. In his acceptance speech Ernie dedicated the award to Mark who had been construction manager on the project.

The following year saw further expansion, with a 6000 sq. metre extension to produc-

as strong and positive thinking as Roy, have happy faces and go to work thinking of the Fisher Engineering slogan "Constructing The Future Today".

It would have been Bertie's determined wish that Fisher Engineering continues its operations and that we pull out all the stops to ensure that the week of slippage that we have had in our programme is made up and that all our contracts be completed on target. I am confident that each and everyone of you here

tion facilities taking total production space to 21,000 sq. metres. In addition a new staff car park was added and linked to the works by a new footbridge over the river.

On May 14th 2002 Fisher Engineering Ltd and Ballinamallard were honoured with a Royal Visit from Her Majesty the Queen and His Royal Highness The Duke of Edinburgh as part of the Royal Jubilee Celebrations.

Ernie recalls *'Preparation for this visit had been ongoing for many months with numerous meetings in the FEL boardroom in order to plan all the necessary details and security arrangements. We were not informed officially until the week before the visit who our Royal Visitors would be and the visit was almost cancelled in the days prior to the event due to last minute security concerns.*

The Queen was entertained to tea along with the local senior citizens of the village in a marquee erected in the Fisher staff car park and the Duke of Edinburgh toured the factory and officially opened the new footbridge which was dedicated to the memory of Thomas S Fisher founder of Fisher Engineering. It was a day that will live long in the memory of Ballinamallard residents and the other guests present. The honour was much appreciated by the Company and the Fisher Family given the terrible events that had happened in 2001'

2002 also saw the Company finally sign the contract for the supply and erection of 26,000 tonnes of structural steelwork for Dundrum Town Centre outside Dublin.

This contract had been under negotiation during Bertie's time as Managing Director but

had been beset with funding problems and the fallout from the September 2001 crisis in America.

With the addition of structural metal decking, staircases and fire protection packages this project remains today as the largest single contract carried out by any Structural Steel Fabricator in the UK and Ireland.

Dundrum Town Centre Development opened in March 2005 and was awarded European Shopping Centre of the Year in 2007.

The Company continued to expand its facilities and employment to meet the ever increasing workload from the 'Celtic Tiger' and by 2007 they employed over 260 people with an annual turnover exceeding £50 million.

With the Irish economy showing signs of unsustainable growth the Company Direc-

Royal Party on Tour,
Hillsborough Castle,
14th May, 2002.

Dear Ernie,

I am sure that The Duke of Edinburgh's team will be writing to thank you for your help in his visit to Fisher Engineering Ltd. But could I pass on The Queen's gratitude for your assistance in arranging such a warm welcome from Ballinamallard in your grounds this morning. It was a pleasure to meet so many people in the local community, as well as be given the chance to meet a number of your own family.

Her Majesty is always conscious that a visit like today's puts great logistical demands on a host, and when that happens in the context of Northern Ireland, with all the other issues facing visits of this sort, The Queen is exceptionally grateful to those who are prepared to offer hospitality in this way. Thank you for your help; and our best wishes for the continued prosperity of the business.

Yours ever,
Tim

TIM HITCHENS
Assistant Private Secretary

Ernie Fisher, Esq.

Her Majesty the Queen and His Royal Highness The Duke of Edinburgh with Ernie Fisher during the Royal Visit

tors and Shareholders wanted to protect the reputation and employment within Fisher Engineering and took the decision to accept an offer to purchase the Company. A deal was concluded with Severfield Rowen PLC in September 2007 which gave Fisher Engineering full access to the much larger UK market for Structural Steelwork.

From 2008 to 2015 Fisher Engineering (Now Severfield (NI) Ltd.) have gone on to carry out many major projects in the UK and London markets.

Some of the steelwork for many of the new iconic landmarks in London such as the Cheesegrater and the Shard was manufactured in Ballinamallard.

Severfield (NI) Ltd. is still managed and operated by 280 local staff and remains the preferred structural steelwork partner for many of the top project management companies in the UK.

above: The Dundrum Town Centre Shopping Centre

far right: A small selection of the many tributes received by the company after the accident

STEYR-PUCH MANX RALLY

J.E. Skinner G.I. Fire E.
6 Berkeley Street, Douglas, Isle of Man, IM2 3QA
Tel: (01624) 626543 · Fax: (01624) 661314
Email – johnskinner@manx.net

The Fisher Family,
Goblusk House,
Ballinamallard,
Co. Fermanagh,
Northern Ireland.

24th January 2001

Dear The Fisher Family

I was numbed on hearing of the tragic accident that claimed the lives of Mark and Emma and more so on hearing that Bertie had lost his fight for life. Words cannot express the sadness felt on hearing of these sad events.

Bertie was a thoroughly perfect gentleman and probably one of, if not the last "great character" in rallying and his passing will leave a huge unfillable void in Motorsport. I would say that the reason many people had so much time for Bertie was because of his integrity and honesty. In all the time I knew him he never went outside the Regulations of any event he entered.

I had long been a fan of Bertie's when I had my first direct contact with him in 1987 when he along with Austin Fraser came to compete on the Manx National Rally and won in an Opel Manta 400. He subsequently competed in and won two further Manx Nationals 1989 and 1992 with Rory.

I was privileged and indeed honoured in 1995 when Bertie agreed to take me on the Test Stage prior to the Manx International Rally. For nearly three minutes I sat beside him both speechless and spellbound just watching a Master at his Craft unable to take it all in. To my delight in 1996 Bertie again offered me a run over the Manx Test Stage, which I immediately accepted and on this second occasion I was able to appreciate what was happening around me.

Mark had inherited many of Bertie's attributes although he brought to rallying his own talent and brand of humour. Like his father he always took time to acknowledge his friends and fans, a rare gift in this day. Always full of fun and devilment no one more than Mark was extremely focused and committed to what he was doing and the world has lost a potential champion.

I never met Emma but having seen tributes to her on Ulster Television it was obvious she was a person who brought so much joy and happiness to those she worked with.

Although having been through my own personal tragedies recently I can not even begin to imagine how Gladys and Roy will be feeling at losing so much.

I consider it a great honour to have had my life touched by that of the Fisher Family and my memories of Bertie and Mark will stay with me forever.

May Bertie, Mark and Emma rest in peace and God although having dealt this cruel blow remain with Gladys and Roy who are in the thoughts of everyone in the Manx National Rally.

John Skinner
Clerk of the Course
Manx National Rally

Ernest McMillen

14 Ballydrain Road
Cattogs,
Comber, Newtownards,
Co. Down, BT23 5SR
Northern Ireland
Tel. 028 9187 2540
Fax 028 9187 1937

20 January 2001

PLEASE FORWARD

Ernest Fisher Esq
c/o Fisher Engineering Limited
Ballinamallard
Enniskillen
Co Fermanagh

Dear Ernest

I was sorry that I did not have the opportunity of speaking to you on Thursday. I tried to explain the occasion to Alma but really it was just so moving and sad that it cannot be expressed in words but only in thoughts and I was so glad to have been part of that enormous crowd

Bertie and I had been good friends throughout his motoring career and we even had a business relationship with your Company until such time as it was necessary to move to Quinns. I always greatly enjoyed my visits to the Works and made a point of coming along for the meetings. I, of course, knew and admired Mark greatly and the extraordinary thing is that, for such a young man, at every rally in which we happened to be competing together, he would always have made a point of coming and talking to me which I found very refreshing and it was especially nice for this young man to seek me out for a chat bearing in mind that I must be the oldest and slowest

From the point of view of the Family business and what it means to the countryside it is good for everybody that there are wise heads around, although it will take a while to cover the loss of your magic leader

I am thinking of you all and will never forget Thursday

Regards
Ernest

Motorsport Ireland

34 Dawson Street
Dublin 2, Ireland

Tel: (01) 677 5628
Fax: (01) 671 0793

20th March 2001

Mr. Ernie Fisher
C/o Fisher Engineering
Ballinamallard
Co. Fermanagh

Dear Mr. Fisher,

I am writing in my personal capacity as Chairman of Motorsport Ireland and on behalf of everybody involved in motorsport here.

Some weeks have now elapsed since the tragic events of January 21 and first and foremost I want to say that Gladys and Roy are still very much in the thoughts of many of us as they endeavour to regain their health.

Secondly, may I express continuing and sincere sympathy to everybody affected by the deaths of Bertie, Emma and Mark. Words cannot adequately describe the shock and sadness felt by so many enthusiasts on hearing of the accident and it's far reaching consequences.

As I am certain you already know Bertie had many supporters in the south and many have expressed their great sense of loss at his untimely death. For this reason we set up a facility to accept messages which people might like to send and these are enclosed. Perhaps they may prove of some consolation to family members.

The whole episode has proved a sad experience for everybody involved in motorsport and indeed beyond and we are all the sadder for having been part of it.

Oh that we might have more competitors like Bertie and Mark, both fine examples of how to go about motorsport. As often happens, however, life doesn't pan out like that.

In closing and now of ultimate importance, the sincere hope is that Gladys and Roy are making progress in what to them must be a tremendous battle in every way to regain some semblance of normality to their lives.

Yours sincerely,

Cecil Sparks
Chairman

RIAC · a member of FIA

H.R. HOLFELD GROUP

H.R. Holfeld Limited

Wesley KNOX
Financial Director
FISHER ENGINEERING LTD
Ballinamallard
Enniskillen
County Fermanagh BT94 2FY
Northern Ireland

2-4 Merville Road, Stillorgan
Dublin, Ireland. Europe

Telephone: 01 288 7361
+353 1 288 7361

Facsimile: +353 1 288 7380

RRH/MM/49
24 January 2001

Dear Wesley

Words fail to express the disbelief and shock we all feel about this family tragedy. Since we spoke on Monday, the magnitude of what has happened is slowly beginning to sink in.

Loosing Bertie, Mark and Emma must be an unimaginable blow to family, friends, the local and international business and motorsport community. We hope that Gladys pulls through and that Roy continues to improve.

The contribution and commitment of Bertie to the Company was unfailing. He was a great example to others and a wonderful man, always upbeat and cheerful. Having known him originally through motorsport and recently through business, I was always struck by his competitive streak and determination to succeed. We recently had the opportunity of spending some personal time together and with Mark on some British events last year. I was very taken by his frank attitude to life, friendliness and openness, always thinking about the next project or deal. Over three decades of rallying, Bertie was the most complete and stylish driver, a joy to watch in action and a great Ambassador for motorsport in Ireland. His zest for life was quite extraordinary. He extended advice and encouragement unfailingly.

On behalf of the extended HOLFELD Family, the Shareholders, Management and Staff of the H.R. HOLFELD GROUP, please accept our sincerest condolences on your tragic loss and we appreciate how difficult a time this is for you, the FISHER family and in particular his brothers Ernie, Ivan and Kenny.

Please accept our deepest sympathies and our thoughts are with you. Would you please convey my sincere respect to the family and your colleagues.

Yours sincerely
H.R. HOLFELD LIMITED

RICHARD HOLFELD

Date: 26 January 2001
Our Ref:
Your Ref:

SPORTS COUNCIL NORTHERN IRELAND
making sport happen for you

Mr E Fisher
Managing Director
Fisher Engineering Ltd
Ballinamallard
Co Fermanagh

Dear Mr Fisher

As with so many people in Northern Ireland and much further afield who knew Bertie Fisher, we were appalled and very saddened by the tragic accident on Sunday last which claimed the lives of Mark and Emma. The wonderful tributes that have poured in to him and to the whole family circle since Sunday have shown us what a fine man he was in all that he did; and what a fine husband, father, sportsman and businessman he was. The three of them had clearly been highly respected and much loved by many outside your family circle.

Our thoughts are with all your family at this time of grieving but in particular with those family in hospital - Bertie's wife Gladys and his son Roy as they recover from their serious injuries, and his father as he recovers from heart surgery. There is little that one can say at a time like this except that our thoughts are with you all in your sadness.

Our Council Member, Mr Ronnie Trouton, who is deeply involved in motor sports, was present at the funeral and represented the Sports Council for Northern Ireland.

Please accept the sincere condolences of members and staff of the Sports Council for Northern Ireland.

Yours sincerely

Professor Eric D Saunders
Chairman

Phone/Fax 0907-30006

**Parochial House,
Ballyhaunis,
Co. Mayo.**

23rd January 2001.

Dear Mr. Fisher,

I would like to extend to you and your family my deepest sympathy on the terrible tragedy which has befallen you, resulting in the tragic and untimely deaths of your brother Bertie, his son and daughter in the helicopter accident last Sunday.

The name Fisher Engineering had become very familiar to us here in Ballyhaunis because the steel frame for our Millennium Spire was erected by your firm on St. Patrick's Church in October 1999. During that time the names Bertie and Ernie Fisher were used so often by our architect, Tom Mullarkey, that I felt I knew you both personally. However, I did come to admire immensely your business-like and efficient work and I can tell you there is a palpable sadness in our town today because of this tragedy.

I assure you of our prayers and we ask God to give you the strength to cope in this time of grief.

Yours sincerely,

Fr. Joseph Cooney, P.P.

1978 · 1982

From Group 1 to Group 4,
CIL 999 successes

In early October of 1977, Bertie sold the RS2000 he had been rallying throughout that year on to County Tyrone businessman Freddie Patterson as he sought to move up the ranks from Group 1 to Group 4 with the purchase of an RS 1800, BIL 5700, from fellow Fermanagh man Roy Cathcart.

Bertie's first event in the new RS1800 Escort was the B&I Line Cork 20 International Rally, which was also the very first rally Austin Frazer would sit with Bertie. What would become a successful professional partnership together spanning some 13 years until the end of 1989 came about after a conversation at the prize giving for the Donegal Rally a few months earlier. Everyone was in good spirits as the drink had been flowing in to the early hours, when Bertie went to congratulate Austin, who had co-driven, Billy Coleman to take the overall honours in the Chequered Flag Lancia Stratos. Austin recalls Bertie's off the cuff comment *"Well Frazer, Wouldn't you and I make a quare team?"* and several months later that casual suggestion became a reality when they came together as a team.

As a result of the newness of their relationship in the car, and of the car itself, Bertie had initially wanted to hold back, be apprehensive and take things as they came, keeping an eye on other competitors times, but by the end of the first day they were revelling in the car and conditions and setting fastest stage times.

So quick was Bertie that on the first two stages on Sunday morning, he cut 40 seconds from the 92 second lead held by Ger Buckley, but after those shock times, and a problem with the rear brakes, Bertie and Austin decided to settle themselves in second place where they finished overall, 56 seconds behind Buckley.

It was an amazing way to start their partnership with Bertie pushing hard to record his best finish to date on an International Rally. Austin remembers the event well.

right: Bertie and Austin Frazer on the Caragh Lake Stage on the '79 Circuit of Ireland in Co. Kerry

56

we spun the car and that had an effect on him so he settled down a bit after that. It was his first proper run in a Group 4 car which was very different from Group 1, and only in competition could you get used to it; it takes time to get the feel of it and find your limits.'

Following the car's maiden outing in Bertie's hands on the Cork '20 Rally, he entered the Enniskillen Motor Club 'Autumn Rally', a short 75 mile route, 30 entrant event, as an opportunity to build experience with the car. He led the event until the fourth time control when the alternator failed forcing retirement and spoiling the opportunity of receiving a trophy from his wife, Gladys, who was presenting the awards for that year's event!

Following on from the Cork 20 Rally, with a little more experience under their belts, Bertie and Austin rolled on to the one day Strand Inn' Donegal Highlands Rally a few weeks later which they won outright with some 26 seconds to spare from one of Bertie's main Northern Ireland Championship rivals from earlier that year, Ronnie McCartney. The rally, based in the Buncrana town area of County Donegal, had an entry of around 100 crews to compete on the 12 special stages over some 85 miles and it certainly wasn't an easy win by any means.

McCartney was fastest on SS1 while Fisher broke an anti-tramp bar. Subsequently, they almost ran into maximum lateness after some frantic welding in service to repair the car but on the following six stages Bertie was flying and established a lead of nearly a minute from Ronnie. In the dying stages he suffered further mechanical problems but this was his day, and well deserved.

'I think one of the things that stand out in my mind was that Bertie was driving very near the limit most of the time. I felt he was pushing it too hard and on one particular stage I told him to cool it but he didn't listen to me! I said it again, "Cool it or you're going to have an accident", again he paid no heed but a few corners later

far left top: Austin co-driving Cahal Curley to one of their many rally wins on the inaugural Ulster Rally in 1976, a rally which Austin would later go on to win twice alongside Bertie in 1982 and 1987

below: Bertie and Austin on the Cork 20

Although Austin had not co-driven for Bertie before, living near to each other in Fermanagh they knew each other well.

By the time Austin joined up with Bertie he was already an internationally renowned co-driver, having had many national and international successes although he reflects on how the sport had changed over the years since he had got involved in the 1950s. With no closed road sections and events mainly made up of mixed navigation and trial sections, Austin remembers his first ever rally, a Dungannon Motor Club run navigation event in 1959 when he was co-driver to school pal Ian Turkington from Cookstown. Competing in a Morris Minor 1000 owned by Ian's father, Ian had brought along two other friends for the spin so there ended up three navigators. *'On a certain cross roads one navigator said go right, one said go left and the other said straight on, so you can imagine what sort of night that was!'* said Austin.

From that odd first outing, Austin went out on a number of other rallies with Ian before doing his first international rally in 1964 on the Circuit of Ireland with Ted Hobson in a Mini.

The following year he began

sitting with Cahal Curley, in a partnership that would last right until 1976, when Cahal decided to 'retire' leaving Austin free to team up with Bertie.

Despite his achievements as a co-driver Austin's contribution to rallying was not limited to this role.

After he had moved to Enniskillen in 1963 to work at a local pharmacy he was approached by a former member of the recently disbanded Enniskillen & District Motor Club to help get another new motor club up and running. The new Enniskillen Motor Club was founded in January 1964 and Austin has been a committee member ever since.

In the wider rally administration field Austin served as Clerk of the Course for the Donegal International for the first five years of the event's existence between 1972 and 1976.

right top: Prizewinners with their trophies at the annual Enniskillen Motor Club Dinner Dance. They are (front, from left) David Hopper, Wilfred Anderson, Bertie Fisher, Trevor Haydock, (back row) Drew Wilson, Drew Baxter, Stuart Thompson, David Johnston, George Ogle, David Henderson and Ken Beatty

He had previously won forestry rallies, his classes and groups in rallies, but this to be the first time he was a fully-fledged winner of a closed road special stage tarmac rally and signalled his arrival onto the Tarmac Rally leader boards. A fantastic result for only his second time out in the car, the RS1800 was making a big impact on the stages.

Towards the end of the year, he was declared 'EMC Club Champion for 1977', a year in which he also continued with his work within the club, including duties as Clerk of the Course for the Erne Safari Rally that year, an event partly sponsored by Fisher Engineering. At the 14th Enniskillen Motor Club Annual General Meeting in December 1977, he was elected as the new Chairman for the club for the incoming year of 1978.

1978

Bertie's first competitive outing of the new year came in February with the Henley Forklifts Galway International which saw the red colour scheme his car had sported at the end of 1977 replaced by a distinctive Blue over Yellow Colour Scheme signifying sponsorship from Castrol. Sponsorship was also provided by Lindsay Cars Ltd whose Managing Director, David Lindsay, was quoted at the time in the Impartial Reporter [09/02/78] as saying,

New Sponsor for Fisher/Frazer Team

Championship round wins and 4 Tarmac Championships, this particular first taste of Tarmac Championship Rallying was not so successful, retiring with mechanical failure after five stages on the Friday.

However it wasn't long before he was back to his winning ways, winning the Hellfire National Rally outright later in February ahead of Donie Keating who finished over a minute behind in second place. Billy Coleman (who had originally planned to do this event in the Lancia Stratos but ended up driving a RS1800 similar to Bertie's, belonging to his cousin Ger Buckley) retired after nine stages with head gasket failure. At the time he was some 46 seconds behind Fisher who appeared to have the upper hand, including a first stage time of 13 seconds faster than Coleman, often dubbed the 'Millstreet Maestro'. Quite a feat considering Billy's status in Irish and International rallying at that time.

With Bertie gaining maximum Shellsport National Championship points on the Hellfire, it was with a great air of confidence that he decided to tackle the second round, the West Cork Rally based in Clonakilty. Despite an off on the first stage he set a string of fastest times in heavy rain before his engine blew, putting him out of the rally.

He faced a similar fate on the Benson & Hedges Circuit of Ireland where, after being as high as fourth and ahead of the likes of Roger Clark at one stage, a water leak, followed by a broken gear lever on the final of the stages on Saturday dropped him back before the car called it a

'We are confident that Bertie with his tremendous ability and press-on style of driving will be competitive in the overall results classification'

The 1978 Galway International was the first ever round of the newly created Irish Tarmac Rally Championship. While Bertie could later look back on a record 20 of these

left top: Bertie on the Galway International driving sideways 'on the rim'

bottom: Battle scarred after a first stage off on the West Cork

right: BIL5700 on the Circuit of Ireland

Before Bertie owned it, BIL5700 had belonged to fellow Fermanagh man, Roy Cathcart who explained how Bertie came to own the car *'The deal with it was I swapped him the car for a warehouse which he built for me in Derrycharra (which is now known as number 10 Derrycharra). I think at that time probably the warehouse was in and around £8500 so we did a swap... I swapped the car and he built the shed although then I bought the car back from Bertie a year later when he built the fuel injection car CIL 999.'*

KING FISHER?

Bertie Fisher – catching Ari or staying ahead of Billy?

Seventy five cars heading off from the Ballyraine Hotel to Rathmelton and special stage number twenty seven Portlien 1. This is all that remains of the 150 cars that started this Donegal International Rally on Friday.

Tacked on behind are the Sunday runners, competitors out of the rally proper, but trying for a special prize. Ten stages remain and only one of the fabulous classics in Knockalla done twice to-day. The top four cars in the battle are locked together with Vatanen edging away from Fisher, Coleman trying very hard , and McCartney poised a few minutes back, waiting to slot into a new berth should it be vacant.

Heading the rally within a rally, the Group one section, John Lyons is looking unbeatable as he two wheels through the fast corners and holding overall in the Red RS 2000. That super rally pairing Mock and Ann O'Connell have brought their super car up to sixth place. They must be worried about Big Derek.

far left: Donegal Rally in 1978 saw the second coming of the tall fair haired Finn Ari Vatanen in the David Sutton 'Black Beauty' Escort RS 1800 X-Pack

left: The 'Ballyraine Bugle' was an on-event newspaper from the Donegal International in the latter half of the Seventies. In 1977 five high quality editions were issued, a major achievement given the technology of the day and only possible through the efforts of numerous people including photographs from Esler Crawford, news items from Sammy Hamill with a bit of humour thrown in by Plum Tyndall among many other contributors

This edition from 1978 seems to have been the origin of Bertie's nickname 'King Fisher'

day at the top of Moll's Gap when the clutch exploded.

The Circuit of Munster saw Bertie pushing for the lead early on but once again mechanical troubles ruled him out of contention and sent him heading home early.

Next up was the 1978 Castrol Donegal International Rally, regarded by many who were there as one of the finest Donegal's to date. That year saw the second coming of the blonde haired Finn Ari Vatanen who since the first time he had been in 1975 had been making a huge name for himself on the British Rally scene with around half a dozen International Rally wins and a string of other top finishes.

Bertie did really well for the first two days being the only driver able to keep in touch with Vatanen's David Sutton prepared Escort 'Black Beauty' as it was affectionately known. In fact on one stage he was fastest overall, two seconds faster than the Finn.

Interestingly John Taylor, head of Ford Racing at the time, was quoted at this rally to say *'A private entrant in*

a privately run Escort shouldn't be able to get anywhere near Vatanen'.

On Sunday however, with bubbling tar on the melting roads due to the ferocious heat, Fisher crashed twice on the Fanad stage, the second time bringing instant retirement.

In an interview with Plum Tyndall for the Donegal Rally programme in 1991 many years later, Bertie said, *'We had a fabulous battle with Ari Vatanen in 1978. I led initially, then dropped to second, and then took the lead again. On boiling tar on Fanad we went off the road and dropped some time. Then in our efforts to make up this time on the next stage, we crashed heavily. We could have won that event'.*

It has to be said that perhaps Bertie was looking at 1978 with slightly rose tinted glasses, and that a rally win may not have been as simple or easy as Bertie claims it could have been .

Possibly partly due to the disappointment of Donegal, Bertie did not compete on any more major rallying for the following six months apart from a few minor outings including a late entry on the Fermanagh based forestry

right: Action from Donegal including its famous stages through the houses of Glen Village (top right) and Ramelton (bottom left)

Rally, the Permapost (now known as the Lakelands Rally) where, with Belfast Telegraph journalist Sammy Hamill alongside him as co-driver, he finished fourth overall, winning the RC Stuart & Son Perpetual Trophy for the highest placed Fermanagh Driver. So late was the entry for this rally that the car was only prepared right through the night before. Initially he led the rally after the opening Castle Archdale grounds stage, but his clutch had been slipping from the start. In the end he finished 1 minute 7 seconds behind the winner Hugh O'Brien with Jimmy Logan taking second Ger Buckley third.

In the middle of the summer he stepped away from the special stages to compete on the Erne Trophy Rallysprint at St Angelo Airfield where he finished 1st in the Saloon Cars 1650 – 2000cc Class and, completely away from the rallying discipline, the following day he tried his hand at a Monaghan Autocross event. He ended up winning that event outright after raising the suspension on his Escort by one and a half inches by the time of the third run to perfect the performance and punch in a fastest time of the day.

1979

That event in July of 1978 was essentially his last motorsport event until early 1979. Over Christmas Bertie took a family holiday in Greece, but rallying was never far from his mind and eager to get back on the stages again, he made a phone call to his friend Sydney Meeke, asking him to build a brand new Group 4 RS1800 Escort, very much the car to be reckoned with on the national and International scene at the time.

The car which resulted from this phone call was a car he would use for several years and would become widely known by its Fermanagh based registration, CIL 999. With an AVJ fuel injected engine and strong sponsorship from Castrol, it was both a distinctive and lively car.

The car's first planned rally was the Henley Forklift Galway International in February but the car wasn't quite ready despite round the clock efforts by the Meeke team so it was on the Leitrim/Cavan based Hellfire Rally later in February that it made its debut. Bertie had won the rally the previous year but possibly as a result of acclimatising to his new mount on this occasion he finished at the tail end of the leader board in tenth overall.

The Hellfire event was followed up by a Fourth Overall on the West Cork Rally and then on the Hills of Donegal in the same month, Fisher was back to his winning ways

left top: Bertie 'relaxing' at a local motor club event

far left: Monaghan Autocross

above: Action on the West Cork passing through Rossmore village

below: Action on the '79 Circuit of Ireland

right: Bertie and Austin drift their way to a 4th place overall on the West Cork Rally

on tar again, first overall. This was Fisher's second Hills of Donegal win, and it was a dominant win, finishing 39 seconds ahead of nearest rival and fellow Fermanagh man Ernest Kidney. Kidney went into the lead after stage 1 and held the lead until the sixth stage when he dropped 19 seconds with a puncture. The second loop was a tight battle between Fisher and Kidney throughout but Kidney never gained back enough seconds to retain the lead and on the last two stages Fisher increased his lead to 39 seconds.

The Benson & Hedges Circuit of Ireland which followed is regarded by some as one of his best ever performances finishing 3rd overall behind winner Finn Pentti Airikkala

in a works Vauxhall Chevette HS and second placed man Billy Coleman in an Escort. He also picked up the HA Bryson Trophy for the highest placed Northern Ireland finisher. Although there was generally no mechanical gremlins on this rally, his crew took out and inspected the gearbox a total of three times to make sure it was in good condition, given the particularly long route of the five day marathon event. In an Impartial Reporter Report about the rally, Bertie praised his team, saying *'They were magnificent, although the car never gave us any trouble. It was preventive servicing and they never missed a thing.'*

That successful Circuit of Ireland was followed up by

left: Action from the 1979 Circuit of Ireland

right top: Circuit winner Pentti Airikkala

The stage times Bertie punched in on this rally did not go unnoticed by Pentti and Bertie's co-driver at the time Austin Frazer talks of an incident that happened late into the rally,

'Going through Donegal on the last night in the pitch dark, we were having close times with Pentti, and whether he wasn't driving as quickly in the dark as Bertie I'm not sure but we were taking time off him. He accused me of giving him duff times. After that we agreed that he wouldn't ask us for our time because I wouldn't be giving it to him'

far right centre: Bertie on the 1979 Donegal

bottom: Former racing driver Brian Nelson from County Down who in 1979 went on to win the Tudor sponsored Tarmac Championship in a David Sutton RS1800 Escort.

a second overall on the Longford Rally, aka the Midland Moto Rally. There he finished 32 seconds behind winner Cork man Ger Buckley. A few weeks later was the Erne Trophy Rallysprint, held that year on the second week of June at St Angelo's Airfield and with 46 cars taking part in six classes, once again he brought home silverware, winning Class 10 outright on this occasion.

Come June and once again it was time for the Castrol Donegal International Rally with, on this occasion, Bertie arriving home second overall behind the Tuca Tiles Escort of Brian Nelson. With eleven stages completed on the first day, Nelson had built up a comfortable lead of three minutes over Bertie which he extended through Saturday and Sunday to take his second Donegal win by some four minutes.

Following a disappointing 'Permapost' (his home rally) where a spin dropped him well down the leader board, in August Bertie took a trip to Great Britain for two events starting with a loose event in Scotland on the Saturday known as the 'Andrews Heat for Hire Rally'. Having finished a credible 5th Overall on the event, the prize giving was barely over before Bertie, Austin and the service crew had to set out on the 180 mile journey south to the Tyneside rally due to start the next day. At Tyneside he finished an impressive second overall, behind Willie Crawford and ahead of Yorkshire man Steve Bannister clearly demonstrating that, while familiarity with the Irish stages was a benefit on his home events, Bertie was equally capable of great results on unfamiliar territory.

Shortly after he got home from his trip across the water, was the Omagh Motor Club run Bushwhacker event

left top: Bertie on the Andrews Heat for Hire Rally

below: Fellow Fermanagh man Ernest Kidney and co-driver Nicky Moffitt who finished just one second ahead of Bertie on the Bushwhacker in 1979. Kidney went on to win the Northern Ireland Stage Rally Championship of which the Bushwhacker was a round. Here he is pictured on the Manx Rally the month after the Bushwhacker.

where a very closely fought contest throughout the ten stages resulted in second overall, just ONE second behind fellow Fermanagh man Ernest Kidney in the similar RS1800 and just three seconds ahead of third placed finished Ronnie McCartney. The margin could not have been much closer!

The last two rounds of the fledgling Irish Tarmac Championship, that year sponsored by 'Tudor', were on the Haltone Cork 20 and the Belfast Telegraph Ulster Rally where he finished 3rd and 5th respectively. The Ulster was not without its moments as he lost first gear, then third and fifth gears due to the gear stick detaching, and on the Cork 20 an incorrect gamble on tyre choice and a spin on the Mullaghanish stage costing more than 30

above: Action from the Cork 20

right: A minor off on the Ulster

When Austin Frazer was asked about Bertie's behaviour in the car, especially when things were going wrong, he said *'He was calm and collected. In his earlier days when he maybe sometimes was getting to know his limit, he would have easily overstepped the mark if the opposition was either chasing him or he chasing them, but that was just inexperience really.*

He had a businessman's mind and thought nothing was impossible. You would have been very much 'on the ball' with him and you had to keep in touch to know what he was doing. Sometimes he would go and do things that you needed to know about single handily and wouldn't say anything to you about it unless you asked him why or how or what – you would've had to try and read his mind sometimes, and he would have been like that at work too.'

seconds all dropped him down the leader board but, despite these disappointing results Bertie finished the Championship in 2nd place behind Brian Nelson – not a bad return from his first year in CIL 999.

RALLYING

Fermanagh Crews Take Top Places in Championships

Fermanagh rally crews who have been successful in recent championships, with their trophies. They are (from left) Bertie Fisher and Austin Frazer; Ron Neely and David Johnston; and Ernest Kidney.

1980

For the opening rally of the year, the Henley Forklifts Galway International, Bertie swapped his usual Dunlops to try out tyres from French company Kléber. He ended the rally impressed with the French company's interest and support, although he did admit to having not found the perfect tyre for the wet and treacherous conditions. An initial puncture on Stage 16 on Saturday cost three minutes and then, trying to make up some lost time on the subsequent stage whilst driving on slicks in ever changing conditions, an overshoot on a corner put him off the road costing a further two minutes. He eventually finished third overall, nearly three minutes behind

right: Similar lines from Billy Coleman (top) and Bertie (below) on the Circuit of Ireland

Billy's car is the Ford of Ireland supported Escort Monte Carlo special which Bertie later bought and used for several events in 1981

Ger Buckley in second and one of only 39 of the original 86 starters making it back to Galway for the finish of the rally after two hard days rallying.

On the Benson & Hedges Circuit of Ireland he held a consistent third place throughout the first few days setting, equal fastest time on SS28, Molls Gap with rally leader Jimmy McRae in the DTV Vauxhall Chevette who was engaged in an epic battle with Ari Vatanen in his Rothmans-Sutton Escort. However a blown head gasket on Stage 34, Been Hill, near Glenbeigh in County Kerry drew a premature curtain on Bertie's rally.

A run of local successes began with an outright win on the very first Lurgan Park Rally (then named the

left: Sligo Rally with co-driver Dr. Frank O'Donoghue

It was Dublin Psychologist Dr. Frank O'Donoghue's first rally with Bertie and he recalls how it came about

'I was spectating at the Midland Rally in Longford in 1980 when Bertie, standing near me, came over and asked me if he could have a word! I was a motorsport journalist at the time with Auto Ireland and used to take the hand out of drivers so I wasn't quite sure what way to take it when I asked him "Is it serious" and he replied "It could be"! I immediately started worrying, trying to think what I'd said about him but fortunately he just wanted to ask me would I navigate for him to which I said "yeah of course"'

Frank has some vivid memories of that Sligo rally especially one particular jump

'I distinctly remember on the Ladies Brae running north to south out the Sligo/Mayo direction and I was calling it "Straight, Straight, Straight" but of course you can't call the jumps well from the map and we took off over one where the road dipped and then came back up. We were going quite hard and the car slapped straight into the rising road on her nose. I think it was the worst impact that I ever had on a jump on a rally – it was savage – broke Bertie's seat, a gearbox mounting, the radiator mounting and the alternator mounting as well. Fortunately we got to the end of the stage where Sydney Meeke was able to patch it all up and we went on to win'

'Burmah Rally') which was followed by a class win on the annual Erne Trophy Rallysprint and a 3rd overall on the Bushwhacker before moving on to the very first running of the Sligo Stages Rally (run by the Ballina Motor Club for the only time as the Sligo Motor Club took over thereafter). On that rally he completely dominated to finish top of the time sheets, three and a half minutes ahead of John Lyons in an Opel Kadett, but it all came at a price. He hit a major jump on SS3 (of 14 stages) at over 90 mph so badly twisting the car that after the rally

right: Action from the 1980 Donegal Rally which ended after an incident with spectators which contributed to a curtailment of Bertie's rallying activity for the year although business pressure might also have been a factor as Fisher Engineering was rapidly expanding at the time. Bertie often had to juggle the demands of his sport and his business as the following story narrated by Austin Frazer illustrates:-

'On one occasion we were doing a recce for a rally and Bertie says "I have to be in Belfast for 5 o clock" so I had to plan the route to make sure we were able to get to Belfast at this time for him. So we did the stage and immediately after headed into Belfast to this particular office. He didn't say what it was about but when we left I said "What was that all about" and he said "I just met the deadline by a few minutes for the tender for the building of the DeLorean factory," You know, you never knew what he was at – we'd be doing a recce for a rally and he'd be making phone calls about the business at the same time. However once the rally began everything was shut out unless it was critically important and had to be dealt with immediately in which case he would have been very quick to get it done and attended to'

below: Bertie did not compete on the Ulster Rally in 1980 but helped to do Course Car duties with organiser Robert Harkness. The rally was won by Dessie McCartney, his first and only International win. Dessie, who started rallying in the early 1960s is still competing in 2015 five decades on

it needed a new shell. Although he was able to continue, he commented after the rally that *'It was like dropping the car off a two-storey building'.*

Next up was the Castrol Donegal International Rally and with a fresh shell and colour scheme along with a new co-driver in Peter Scott, Bertie set off into the hills. Initially it was John Lyons who led the charge, holding a lead from the start until Stage 5 when he dropped time with a high speed spin on Knockalla leaving regular visitor to Irish shores, Jimmy McRae in the DTV Chevette, in a comfortable lead. Bertie was lying second but on a stage near Ardara town on the Saturday he came over a crest upon an approach to a tight junction too fast and, faced with an escape road full of spectators, drove the Escort up onto a grass bank on the approach to the junction to try to avoid them. Unfortunately he was only partially successful and struck several spectators in the process. Fortunately, although four went to hospital, from newspaper reports of the time it would appear none were seriously injured. For his part Bertie retired from the event shortly thereafter and, perhaps somewhat deflated from the incident, competed in no more rallies in Northern Ireland for the rest of the year.

However, unlike other occasions in his career, this time it wasn't a complete break from the sport and, perhaps to gain some confidence back, he did do Sweeper Car on the Ulster Rally alongside Robert Harkness, before later in the summer of 1980, picking up the pieces on the Galway Summer Rally in late August. Co-driven by Dr Frank O'Donoghue, Bertie finished a close second by just 7 seconds from Ger Buckley after the lead had seesawed between them with Buckley just pipping Bertie in the closing stages by that narrow margin.

A few weeks later was the Wexford Rally, in those days a two day rally fought out between some of the top competitors of the day such as Brendan Fagan, Austin

Jimmy McRae in the Vauxhall Chevette HSR and that was the end of Bertie's rallying for 1980.

Bertie's co-driver Dr Frank recalls the Cork '20 accident. *'We were doing well against Jimmy McRae with me reading off the maps since there were no pacenotes. I called an upcoming 60 left and he drove accordingly but the back slid out and on the bend there was one of those big circular stone gate posts. The wheel got caught on it and just peeled that whole section back like it was plastic and that was the end of our rally.'*

left: Action from the Wexford Rally of which Frank O'Donoghue comments *'That was a fairly uneventful except once where we came clattering into a 90 left and we weren't making it because the road was very slippy. However there was a gate straight ahead and boom, we went into a field and out again and were able to carry on.'*

McHale, John Price, Sean Campbell and many more. Bertie won this event with a comfortable but amazing four minutes margin to spare from Dublin's Brendan Fagan in the Chevette.

This was to be Bertie's last success with CIL 999 for on the following event, the Cork '20 in October, he had a heavy crash where he hit a bridge and damaged the car beyond repair whilst in second place overall behind

1981

1981 saw the arrival of a new car, one of only four special edition 'Monte Carlo' wide body Escorts ever built. GVX 489T had originally been Russell Brookes' car which he used to win the Manx Rally in 1979 and was then driven by Billy Coleman to win the West Cork Rally in 1980, so with its history of success was Bertie in for the same fortune?

A third overall on his debut outing with the car on the W.I.P. Plant Galway International Rally, despite having to deal with a multitude of problems (including colliding with a rock and damaging the steering, a small in car fire, and changing a driveshaft) seemed to bode well, given that the rally was a coefficient 2 round of the European Rally Championship as well as being part of the Irish Tarmac series.

This excellent result was followed up by a not so successful non-finish on the Golden Jubilee anniversary running of the Circuit of Ireland where the car now

right top: Bertie and Frank O'Donoghue

far right top: Cork driver, and cousin of Billy Coleman, Ger Buckley had many tussles with Bertie. Here he is pictured in his Chevette HSR in on the 1981 Circuit of Ireland.

below: GVX 489T showing some unusual front suspension geometry in action from Galway

donned a striking two tone blue striped colour scheme with major sponsorship by Fisher Engineering. Although Bertie and co-driver Frank O'Donoghue had been as high as fourth place at one point, the accelerator cable broke shortly after the start of the nine-mile Babylon Hill stage and the only way they could get to the next service opportunity was with Frank lying under the bonnet operating the throttle by hand resulting in considerable time loss. *'I burned the backside off myself sitting on top of the oil cooler, but I didn't feel the pain at the time, we were just trying to get to the end of the stage.'* Frank recalls.

Following this excitement, the car

left: The newly liveried GVX 489T on the Circuit of Ireland. Although eventually forced out by mechanical issues, that wasn't their only problem according to co-driver Frank O'Donoghue

'There was a long road section which went through Banagher and Bertie said he wanted to sleep for a while because of the fatigue due to the long day's rallying so he asked me to drive for a bit. I had never driven anything like that before so he said "there's two things to remember, the first is that it's very hard to start because of the 24 volt starting systems", (which meant nothing to me) "so don't stall it, and the second thing is that there's a very wide back axle in it do don't snag it off anything". So we came into a T Junction Left in Banagher where there was a very high kerb and I done both at the same time, snagged the back wheel and stalled her! All I could see from underneath the rally jacket he had pulled over his head was the eyes coming up and I was quickly vacated from the driver's seat'.

right top: Sydney Meeke with Hugh O'Brien, the Dromore, County Tyrone man affectionately known as 'The Flying Vet' who went out to the Haspengouw Rally in Belgium in 1981 as part of a three-car Irish team from the Sydney Meeke stable of Fisher, O'Brien and Castlederg man Willie John Dolan

below: Bertie takes his second win in a row on the Burmah Lurgan Park

continued to suffer a series of mechanical gremlins which eventually forced the pair's retirement in Killarney.

With fellow Fermanagh man Roy Cathcart in the navigator's seat for a one-off, Fisher followed up on his previous year's win on the Burmah Lurgan Park with a repeat performance which he backed up with a class 4 win on the Erne Trophy Rallysprint.

The next outing on the agenda, The Haspengouw Rally, was altogether new territory for Bertie on several different levels.

Named after the region of Belgium in which it is based, it is a rally which has always attracted a wide range of works entries and privateers alike from all over Europe and 1981 was no different with over 100 of the 160

left: Action at the Haspengouw.

Austin recalls, *'... was a handful, and was not as predictable in handling as previous Escorts would have been.'* In addition, the Escort was having starter motor trouble and, when the spares of those ran out, they had to push start the car on a number of occasions including, at least once, in a control area which did not go down well with officials present – although a quick witted bit of Irish charm got them safely on their way without any penalties.

Most of the other Irish drivers who travelled to the event acquitted themselves well with Derek Boyd in a Lotus Sunbeam 17th and the Castlederg team of Trevor Cathers and Willie John Dolan 9th in Group 1 and 34th overall. Unfortunately Hugh O'Brien, who had started very promisingly, developed clutch and gearbox problems resulting in his retirement from the event which was won by Belgian Patrick Snijers in an Escort, with Jimmy McRae second in an Ascona 400 from third placed local man Guy Colsoul.

It would seem that Bertie was not entirely happy with GVX 489T for a month later on the eve of the Donegal Rally he sold the car to Vincent Bonner. In fact, Vincent took the car to Donegal complete with all of the Fisher Engineering livery still on the car!

At the start of July was Bertie's home rally and the opening round of the Northern Ireland Stage Championship, the Fermanagh Lakelands. For the event, his first since Haspengouw in May, he used RRM 912R for the first time, an RS1800 Escort that had been built by Sydney Meeke from a bare shell purchased from Malcolm Wilson. Co-driven by Meeke team mechanic Trevor Mc-

Austin recalls a conversation between Bertie and 'OB' (as Hugh O'Brien was fondly called) at this rally.

'After our recce, Bertie and 'OB' were comparing notes as to how they handled the unique stages. Bertie said "Well, When I'm coming up to something I'm not sure about I'm tending to come down a gear until I see what's what"… and OB laughed "Oh I just keep her in top gear and sort it out then when I arrive at the hazard."

A few stages later Bertie and me came on a bend that was hidden by barley that was head high. We just caught the side of the road and slid off although not enough that we couldn't retrieve it and keep going without any problems and I remember Bertie saying to me "It will be interesting to see how OB's theory on braking will work out this time" and sure enough OB went straight into the barley in a major off!'

strong entry being from outside Belgium.

An enticing 'all expenses paid' trip offered by the organiser was no doubt instrumental in attracting a strong Irish contingent including, besides Bertie, Derek Boyd, Hugh O'Brien, Robin Lyons, Willie John Dolan and Trevor Cathers.

The event itself, which permitted the use of pace notes, was made up of 300 miles tarmac, concrete and cobbles over 50 stages weaving through vast flat fields of high growing barley, making reading the road almost impossible and placing a big responsibility on the navigator reading the pace notes. As Bertie's co-driver Austin Frazer explained *'It was totally different experience and terrain to what we would have been used. There are no hedges and you could come over a crest and find the road goes immediately 90 left or 90 right.'*

Bertie and Austin finished 7th place Overall which was a good result given the quality of the field and various problems they were still having with the car which as

right top: At speed on the Ulster

bottom: banter with Jimmy McRae

On the Ulster Frank O'Donoghue was reading the maps and he recalls:

'After we lost second gear on the sixth stage the Meeke boys were left with an impossible 12 minute window to change the gearbox but they managed it in a remarkable 14 so, although we picked up road penalties, we were still in the hunt

The next three stages were around Ballinamallard and as I was reading off the map Bertie said to me "Put away the map". Well, he may have known what he was at and where he was going but I must say I was sitting there getting lower and lower in the seat because we were going over blind crests in the dark and a navigator hates that, he likes to know where he is going, and since I had no map, no map light, turned everything off I had no idea where we were.

By the morning halt in Omagh we were right back up with Jimmy and on the way to the next stage Bertie said "I'm going to give this one everything we can, 10 10ths, have it out to the last thread"

Afterwards as far as I recall we were eight seconds behind McRae, when Bertie turned to me and he said "That's it, I can't go any quicker, if I go any quicker we'll go off the road, I'll settle for second".'

Gaughey, Bertie dominated the rally finishing some 45 seconds ahead of the Sunbeam of Robin Lyons, with fellow Sunbeam driver Ernest Kenmore one second further back in third.

Next up in the same car was the Belfast Telegraph Ulster Rally where, despite having some issues including gearbox changes before the start and again during the rally as well as a failing clutch and water pump on his RS1800, he finished a very credible 2nd overall behind Jimmy McRae in the Opel Ascona 400 just ahead of some other strong local opposition in the shape of Brendan Fagan and Ronan Morgan in their Vauxhall Chevette.

Bertie then competed on a handful of small Rally sprints followed by The Manx International where although he was competitive on the first few stages, punching in some top ten times against World Class teams and opposition, he and co-driver Robert Harkness retired on Stage 6 after the head gasket failed on the Escort.

With mass production of the Mark 2 Ford Escort having ended in 1980 shells were becoming scarce and rally car builders started to look else where for their raw materials. Although the new Escort Mark 3 production line was now in full swing, it's front-wheel-drive set up made it a much less attractive proposition for rallying than the well balanced rear-wheel-drive mark 2. Sydney Meeke, ever the entrepreneur, saw a gap in the market and with help from car body builders Gartrac created a hybrid vehicle based the new Mark 3 Escort known as the G3 which, with its modified transmission train and extended wide arches to make it rear wheel drive, could tap into the extensive knowledge base the rallying fraternity had built up on the mark 2.

The G3 was debuted by Billy Coleman, partly as a test session in competitive special stage rallying, on the Cork 20 in October 1981 and a few months later Meeke asked Bertie to try the car on the Gleneagle Hotel Rally of the Lakes in Killarney. Although it was a useful test it wasn't a very successful outing with the car suffering from an initial misfire and electrical problems followed by an accident when Bertie hit a bridge parapet on Stage 6, Caragh Lake,. The bodywork could not be bent off the wheel in order to continue and he retired from the rally.

1982

1982 got underway with Bertie ordering a new car to be prepared in the Meeke workshops. A brand new RS1800 shell with an engine from Mass Racing in England and top of the range specifications, specially built for Irish

left top: Bertie's last run in RRM 912R on the Manx.

left below: The new G3 draws admiring glances at the Gleneagle Hotel Rally of the Lakes in Killarney, a rally which Bertie would not compete on for another six years but would eventually go on to win a record six times between 1990 and 1996

Tarmac Stages, this new car would run with the plate of the car he had driven in 1979 and 1980, CIL 999, and was designed to be ultra competitive on the Irish national scene and indeed the international rallies Bertie would compete in it on.

With work on the new car still underway early in the year Bertie's season did not get underway until March when things kicked off with a weekend trip to the Longleat, estate and Safari Park in Wiltshire, England. Where he competed on two rallies, both in the same G3 which he used in Killarney the previous December. On the Saturday there was a Rothmans National Stages Rally where he finished third overall and on the Sunday a Rothmans Rallysprint, finishing fifth overall.

And, still waiting on the new car, it would be a full two months later on the Lurgan Park Rally, then known as the 'Burmah Rally' that Bertie came out again. It was his first Irish rally since the Rally of the Lakes in December the previous year and he would be competing, not in his own car or a Meeke built G3 Escort, but in a Mk2 Escort loaned to him by John Burns from Castleknock in County Dublin. At the time John was one of many drivers who made use of Sydney Meeke's Bush based team for his car preparation and building. It was through that link with Meeke that, the weekend previous to the Burmah, John had been rallying in his car using an engine borrowed from Bertie. With Bertie's brand new car on the way but not just quite ready by the time the Burmah came round, John returned the favour by lending Bertie his car for the rally.

right top: Competitors from the Rothmans Rallysprint at Longleat including (back row from left): Bob Fowden, Unknown, Rob Arthur, Unknown, winning driver Jimmy McRae, Henry Thynne, 6th Marquess of Bath, Winning co-driver Ian Grindrod, Russell Brookes, Terry Kaby, Phil Collins, John Price. Front row from left: Alexander Thynne, 7th Marquess of Bath, Desi McCartney, Bertie Fisher, Tony Worswick

below: Number plate CIL 999 finds a temporary home on the Meeke built G3 round the lanes of the Longleat estate

On the event itself, Bertie had a great initial battle with early leader Sean Haveron in another Escort before John Lyons, also in an Escort, blasted through the final stages to win with Bertie finishing a close second by just four

left top: Bertie surveys the condition of the tricky tree lined stage of Lurgan Park with friend and future sponsor Kieran McAnallen, after Sean Campbell's Opel Ascona hit a tree stump and ended upside down in the lake, seen in the background

below: Winner of the first two runnings of the Lurgan Park, Number 1 seed Bertie is seen here on the third running of the County Armagh event in 1982 in a one-off loan of John Burns super fit Escort, a Sydney Meeke built and prepared car

seconds and Haveron one second further back in third. The close action at the front was overshadowed somewhat by an accident when the throttle on the Ascona 400 of Sean Campbell and celebrity co-driver for the day, Downtown Radio presenter Lynda Jane, stuck open resulting in a crash with the car somersaulting and ending upside down in the Lake. The crew were quickly retrieved by spectators who were close by and they were all OK but a little shaken perhaps.

Although optimised for the Irish roads CIL 999's debut outing was actually not on tarmac at all but on a small Omagh Motor Club Sprint event at Moffett's Quarry near Drumquin where Bertie had planned to use the event as a shakedown for the Arnold Clark Scottish International Rally and to do some tyre testing on new Dunlop tyres. He may not have finished prominently in the results of the Sprint but it was a useful exercise in getting him used to the brand new car before going to Scotland. Joining him on the event would be several local fellow competitors including Hugh O'Brien, Robin Lyons and Ronnie McCartney.

Friends Bertie and Robin Lyons chatting before action got underway on the Ulster in 1982.

right top: Bertie and David Johnston on the Scottish Rally in 1982

bottom: Northern Ireland Rally Champion in the 1970s Robin Lyons from Castlederg County Tyrone had many tussles on the stages with Bertie at home and across the water, including here on the Scottish in his Lotus Sunbeam.

On the Scottish Rally, Bertie and co-driver David Johnston were lying ninth overall after a slow start but as Bertie's confidence grew with the new car and tyres he began to set more respectable times until, on an uphill stage start, a half shaft snapped. With his service crew too far away to offer immediate assistance he ran over time limit allowed to complete the stage, forcing his retirement.

A month after the Scottish the car at last was unleashed in its natural environment of closed tarmac road special stages on the Union Food Sligo Stages Rally organised by Connacht Motor Club. The event, run over some 150

miles of fast tarmac in 14 stages, had over 140 entries competing and although Bertie planned to use it as a warm up for the Ulster Rally, his previous good results and experience in Sligo meant that he went there with high hopes. And he came home with big smiles, and a fat prize money cheque of £1000 after he and David Johnston won the rally comfortably.

Two weeks later was the aforementioned Ulster Rally, that year sponsored by Belfast City Council. This was one rally Bertie had always wanted to win, having competed or been involved with it for 4 out of its previous 6 running's since its inaugural year in 1976. At that point in time he had been second on numerous International Rallies on the island of Ireland but he was yet to win one outright. Well, this was now his time to prove a point.

No one ever said it was going to be an easy ride, though. The competition was hot with top British and works entries from Per Eklund in the Team Toyota GB Celica and Malcolm Patrick in the Opel Ascona 400 plus a whole array of big names from all over Ireland such as Austin McHale and Brendan Fagan in Chevette HSRs, Ger Buckley and Ian Cathcart in Ascona 400s, also eventual Tarmac Championship winner that year John Coyne in a Lotus Sunbeam, and John Lyons in an Escort RS1800, amongst many others. The Ulster was not a full round of the British Open Championship that year, but it was as usual part of the Irish Tarmac Rally Championship, as it has been every single year since its inception several years earlier in 1978.

Very much a nonstop sprint event over a total route of

right top: Bertie on the 1982 Ulster en-route to his first international rally win

The only problem worthy of noting during the whole rally for the Fermanagh pair was on Stage 8 when the Escort glanced a rock at the side of the road on a stage in the Ballygawley area which resulted in a collapsed suspension strut which couldn't be changed by his service crew until service in Enniskillen two stages later. In an interview after the rally with Carsport, Bertie said *'The strut broke just a quarter of a mile into the stage and it handled like a barge after that'*

With the car having to be driven slower as a result of the damage, his lead was cut from around a minute to just 9 seconds, but he continued *'By now we were into Fermanagh and I felt I still had control of the rally. It wasn't so much that I had more knowledge of the roads because the others had pace notes too, but being back home gave me a feeling of confidence'*

Almost as quick as he had lost the seconds of that comfortable lead, he gained them back in the subsequent stages after service, to lead by over a minute come the Omagh rest halt at 4.30 am. *'I was able to build up my lead again and from the breakfast halt in Omagh it was really a case of keeping cool, driving smoothly and looking after the car'*

below: Per Eklund in the works Toyota Team GB Celica, who finished second.

some 480 miles, nearly half of which were on 26 special stages. It started at Belfast City Hall at 6pm on the Friday night and with over 23 hours before they would be back there for the champagne and very few long services or halts along the route (apart from a 1.5 hour halt in Omagh) it was truly a tough test for man and machine.

Having had numerous co-drivers in the previous few years, the Ulster saw Bertie team up once again with Austin Frazer. It was the first time since the summer of 1980 that he had sat with Bertie on an Irish closed road tarmac event.

So, to the competition itself. It was an al-

The 'note checking' Bertie mentions in the Carsport interview relates to the use of customised pace notes, which the organisers of the Ulster were using for the first time ever, in an attempt to eradicate pre-event practising by the drivers over the same stages in which they would later be competing, a problem which had beset Irish rallies at the time.

Pace notes involve the driver and co-driver travelling around the route beforehand at slow speeds, during a set period of hours or days known as reconnaissance, or 'recce'. During this recce period the crew make detailed notes of every straight, corner, crest and significant bump on the road, which the co-driver then reads back to the driver during the rally itself. It is a skilful operation requiring great concentration and understanding between the driver and co-driver.

most perfect outing for the Fisher & Frazer pairing as they led the rally from start to finish for Bertie recording his first international win. By just the second stage, he had established a lead of some 20 seconds which would only be increased as the rally progressed.

His lead was extended throughout the morning and early afternoon stages to such an extent that with a two and a half minute gap to the next competitor, Per Eklund in the Toyota Celica, he decided to ease off a bit and preserve the car, eventually finishing over a minute and a half from the Swede, but it wasn't entirely a stress free day of rallying as Bertie explained in a subsequent interview with Carsport *'I had concentrated my recce on the night stages as I reckoned it was more important to be sure of those but then I had run out of time and four of the last seven stages I had been over once but had not had time to check the notes. The other three I didn't see at all. On Orra Lodge I had the one big moment of the rally at the same place as Jimmy McRae and Brendan Fagan went off in 1980. I left two black tyre marks there – they went right up to the edge and Ian coming behind thought we were down in the bog somewhere.*

Can you just imagine it? One stage to go, a two minute lead and you put it off …'

But thankfully that didn't happen, and he cruised home comfortably. Third place went to fellow Fermanagh driver Ian Cathcart in the Opel Ascona 400, slotting in just 12 seconds behind Eklund.

When Bertie was asked about the competition on the Ulster, he went on to say *'I always reckoned John Lyons* was going to be the man I would have to beat. Then there was Per Eklund and one has to have a lot of respect for him, a top professional and world class driver.' As it happened, John Lyons was excluded for illegal recceing but allowed to start under appeal, although at the end of the day it didn't matter as he retired several stages in. 'The Lyons exclusion was a blow to the rally and when he was allowed to start under appeal I was determined to disregard him, but it didn't work out like that for there was no way I was going to let him beat me even if he was disqualified afterwards.'

This was Bertie's first finish on an all-tarmac Irish international rally since Ulster the previous year and as part of the same Carsport interview, he explained some of the reasons for his disinterest and hiatus from rallying at that time. 'I had lost all taste for tarmac rallying because of the illegal practising problem. It is something I don't do and there is no point in going to Galway, Donegal or Cork if you haven't had a good look at the stages. Carrying on just seemed a waste of time and money as far as I was concerned.

But the rally bug doesn't go away easily and I came back although it was originally my intention to do forest rallies across the water. When I heard the Ulster was going down the route of pacenotes I felt I had to do it … if only to prove a point to myself. I said I would do tarmac rallies again if pace notes were allowed and so I was committed.

I'm more convinced than ever now I was right. I mean I went to the Sligo Rally a fortnight before the Ulster mainly to get the car set up for tarmac again and play myself in a bit but I had to drive like a lunatic to win. Good driver and all that Vincent Bonner is, I don't think he would rate himself with Eklund. I could have accepted losing to Per but never to Vincent…'

After the highest of highs of winning his home Interna-

tional Rally, it was a full month before a revitalised Bertie again competed, this time on the 3 day Rothmans Manx International Rally.

Following his victory on the Ulster he went with high hopes, and he did not disappoint, finishing a fantastic third overall behind Jimmy McRae's Rothmans Ascona and Russell Brookes' Chevette. In a drama filled event he drove the absolute socks off the Escort to keep with his nearest competitors who included in their ranks no less than 14 World and European seeded drivers who kept the pace at a very high level.

Fisher and Frazer set their intentions clear from the start, setting fifth fastest time on the opening stage, followed by second fastest on the second stage. With some eight stages under their belt they were sitting in fifth when then they were dogged by a series of punctures including two on the one stage. With only one spare they were lucky to be able to obtain an extra wheel at the end of the stage from another competitor, John Morton, who surrendered his only spare to enable Bertie to continue.

Then, on the very next stage they had yet another puncture and had to drive out on a rim, but at the end once again a fellow competitor came to their rescue when Richie Heeley also lent them his only spare! After

right: Bertie celebrates his first international win with a champagne reception finish outside Belfast City Hall. From left, co-driver Austin Frazer, Belfast Lord Mayor Thomas William Sanderson Patton, winning driver Bertie Fisher, Clerk of the Course of the rally Robert Harkness from the Northern Ireland Motor Club.

all that drama, and despite all their time losses they still finished the day in seventh place overall.

Day two and another puncture ensued, followed by trouble with loose seat belt buckles, a problem which would persist until they were given a set of Willans belts from Terry Kaby whose Chevette had retired earlier in the event. Front and rear shock absorbers borrowed from Ari Vatanen's team after he retired following a massive crash had to be replaced and later, there were issues with the rear axle of the car which had been damaged while driving on the rim.

In order to solve the axle problem, Team Manager Sydney Meeke and his mechanics spent several hours through the night prior to the final day's rallying rebuilding a new axle for the Escort in Ian Corkill's garage from a variety of spares. They planned to fit it after the first service of the final day and it was duly installed along with new front struts.

With high temperatures and hot competition, tyre wear was the important chat of the day with the team running out of new rubber but Michelin, who had been supplying tyres to the Talbot team who were now out of the rally, came to the rescue to the Meeke team with the offer of a supply of tyres for the final days rallying. Despite all the problems encountered throughout the rally, Bertie and Austin glided through the last day to bring the car home in a brilliant 3rd Overall.

His result on the Manx made massive news delighting everyone in Fermanagh and in the wider rallying world in Ireland that he had done so well. It was possibly his

best result in an international to date, possibly outdoing the Ulster victory. The reception he got on the stages from the throngs of Irish spectators, and his new fans from further afield, was phenomenal, some of whom had specially chartered a plane in from Fermanagh after the first days action when they realised he was doing so well.

Despite the jubilation of the Manx in a stark illustration of how rallying is a sport of both highs and lows the following weekend saw Bertie record a non-finish on the Bushwhacker Rally after putting the car on its side on just the second stage.

It was a sad way to end his relationship with the Escort as that would be his last competitive event with it as a new Opel era beckoned in 1983.

The Meeke Connection

Post roll postmortem ! The first time Sydney Meeke helped Bertie and it rolled on from here

When Bertie Fisher started rallying in the late 1960s, it was an almost entirely different sport than rallying as we know it today. In those days teams would very often consist of just the driver and co-driver who carried everything they required to carry out minor repairs or, if they were lucky, they may have had one or two friends as mechanics – quite a contrast with today's professional teams on the International Rallying scene with their armies of mechanics and engineers deploying banks of computers not to mention the weather crews, catering teams and the myriad of other specialists who have to be organised with levels of planning which would not be amiss on a major military operation.

In Bertie's early days his father Tommy would have been one of his biggest supporters, backing him financially, acting as team anchor-man and lending a hand with a spanner when necessary but an incident in 1973 was to sow the seeds of change.

On that year's Circuit of Ireland when Bertie's Mexico had a rear quarter panel damaged in a roll, there was a postmortem of the damage at the side of the road. Amongst the company present was a County Tyrone man by the name of Sydney Meeke who weighed in elbow grease and a tub of Isopon and thus began a long lasting relationship between Bertie and Sydney which would see Sydney build, prepare and run many of Bertie's cars for the following 25 + years.

The two were in many ways a perfect match. Both were at similar stages of development – former Northern Ireland rally champion Meeke's fledgling rally car preparation centre and Bertie the up and coming driver and each

Three of Meeke's spanner men on the Donegal Rally in 1979. From left Gary Wilson, Norman Burns, George Crozier

The team, mid 1975, with chase car on left complete with spares and tyres at the ready. From left, Bob Clarke, Bertie Fisher, Derek Smyth, Sydney Meeke

spare parts which, if required, could be used to carry out roadside repairs or maintenance to the car in between stages. That pioneering level of professionalism which forced other

with a dogged determination to improve and succeed which often resulted in them introducing innovations not previously seen on the local scene in Ireland. One such innovation brought in by the Meeke team in the mid-1970s was that they were one of the first in Ireland to make use of chase cars on special stage rallies, i.e. cars which would be loaded up with at least one mechanic, supplies such as oil fuel and tyres, as well as a few

1st Grp. I Donegal International Rally
1975 - 1977.

Both these cars have been prepared and serviced by

SYDNEY MEEKE
THE BUSH — DUNGANNON

I can prepare your car to your specification to the same standard.

MASS ENGINES

Sydney Meeke Motorsport

Ford

Some of the rally cars recently prepared by Sydney Meeke Motorsport. Back row L.T.R. David Fraser, Hugh O'Brien, Flint McCullagh, Bertie Fisher, Davy Johnston, Vincent Bonner, Bertie Law, Alan Fraser Fraser and James McDaid. Middle row L.T.R. David Clarke, Gary Wilson, Robert McKeown and Gordon Thompson. Front Sidney Meeke and Ken McMillan.

NGK SPARK PLUGS

Ian Cuddy working on Bertie's Mk2 Escort CIL 999 towards his first international win on the Ulster in 1982

teams to raise their game, was a very commonplace thing right throughout Bertie's rallying career.

Initially the Meeke operation was employed by Bertie mainly for on event support but over time they became more and more involved in the preparation side of things and in 1975 undertook a complete rebuild of his car after he wrote it off in the Isle of Man.

In 1979 Bertie ordered CIL 999 from Sydney, the first car Sydney had built for Bertie from the ground up and by the early eighties he was a regular customer for Meeke's preparation operation.

That Bertie and Sydney seemed to have a natural rapport was a key ingredient in their success as preparing a rally car to meet a driv-er's specific demands is often not a straightforward exercise and requires a good relationship between all parties to know what really needs done. Mechanic, Ian Cuddy recalls one such incident when Bertie seemed to be getting over fussy about his seat

'One of the first jobs I ever had at Sydney's was to move Bertie's seat on CIL 999 and Bertie got in and he says I want it back ¾ inch, ½ inch up and so on and in those days you didn't just pull out the bolts and move it, it was a whole siege to adjust it, so Gary [Wilson]*, who was also working there at the time, said "Ah leave her as she is" and Bertie, who was in the office along with Sydney came out and Gary says "Come on Bertie, try that one there now", and he got into it, "That's dead on".'*

Of course the benefits in the relationship flowed both ways and with the 'Bush Performance Centre' decals and sun stripes on Bertie's cars, Sydney got a lot of attention from many people. Observing the successes Fisher had with Sydney Meeke as his main preparation man, many other drivers decided to avail of the Bush man's services and by the mid 80s, Sydney was also preparing cars for many other drivers including the Mantas of Billy Coleman and David Fraser, the Asconas of James McDaid and Vincent Bonner, and the Mark Two Escorts of Hugh O'Brien and John Burns.

While at one time Sydney had been very much the man to go to for Mark 2 Escort parts, by the mid eighties he had become the unofficial main agent for Opel preparation and, such was his and his team of mechanics expertise, that GMDS used Meeke's Bush workshop as a base for working on Jimmy McRae's and Russell Brookes' cars for pre-event preparation work and testing leading up to Irish tarmac events. As well as building several Mantas for Bertie, Meeke's team also built the body shell for one of Russell Brookes Andrews Heat for Hire Lightweight Manta 400s, ADZ 31.

Of course all this work put a lot of pressure on the spanner men who not only had to keep the cars going on events but in between had to get the cars fettled to give their peak performance and look in top shape.

Ian Cuddy, recalls many late hours spent in the workshop getting cars ready on time. *'There were plenty of late nights and all-nighters. You knew it was gonna be an all-nighter when coming near 12 o'clock Sydney would*

above: Mechanics work on the building of a Manta 400 in early 1983. This is one of two Mantas built at the time at the Bush, the two being Fishers and David Fraser's

right: The three GM Dealer Sport Mantas at Meeke's workshop before the 1985 Circuit of Ireland

head off into the town to get a Chinese' or as Norman Burns put it *'you could be walking out of the workshop over to Sydney's for breakfast along with a few of the other boys after a long spell in the workshop and you'd hear the birds tweeting and wonder whether they were tweeting going to bed or tweeting getting up!'*

But along with the hard work there was always plenty of banter and craic amongst everyone. Derek Smyth recalled that when he co-drove for Bertie on the Donegal Rally in 1975 everyone in the Meeke team called each other 'Hank'. He also remembered *'There were all sorts of little sayings you'd hear – one*

of my favourites that was used quite often by Sydney every time you asked a question was "As far as I know I couldn't tell ye". The fun and joking about took away any stress and anxiety

that there might have been. It allowed a break away from the importance of stage times and avoided there being much friction between team members when things were going tight. Everyone got on really well because of that.'

Although it was an in team joke, the name calling theme was obviously contagious, because if you watch the in car video footage from the incident on the Galway Rally in 1986 you can clearly hear Bertie's co-driver Austin Frazer say *"Jeepers well done Pete"*, commending Bertie on his having avoided a potentially dreadful accident. When asked what this was all about Austin remembered, *'Oh yes. On that rally everybody in the Sydney Meeke team called each other Pete. The mechanics, Sydney, everyone.'*

A spell with Meeke's was a valuable addition to any mechanics CV and many of them went on to work for even bigger teams on the

Hugh O'Brien and Bertie discussing team tactics at service on the Galway Rally in 1990

World and European scene. Norman Burns worked for Toyota Team Europe for 10 years before moving on to Ford's works team at M-Sport for 3 years and then set up his own preparation workshop. Wesley Emerson went on to work with Prodrive on the World and British scene for many years. Others also went on to work for such companies as Ford on the World and European circuit before setting up their own preparation firms. Ian Cuddy went on to own and run his own preparation setup and looked after most of Ian Greer's cars from the mid-1990s onward. Robbie McGurk is still a very active preparations expert while Adrian Kirkland works alongside Robbie on rallies and looks after his own customers. Brothers Graham and Peter Garvin both went on to

work on the GM Dealer Sport team through the late 1980s and onwards.

By the late 80s Sydney Meeke was supplying a complete rallying package to Bertie from initial building of the cars, to re-fettling them between rallies to providing on event support services and backup but the move away from GM products in 1988, initially to a rented Sierra and then to the BMW M3, saw a significant change in the relationship.

The Sierra, which was fully built in Ford's Motorsport division factory at Boreham was on loan from Boreham an arrangement which had come about as a result of a enquiry from Stuart Turner, head of Motorsport division at Ford at the time, asking if Bertie had intentions of making a full scale return to rallying

after just a few select events in 1987.

The deal, which covered the supply and usage of the car as well as kits of spares, did not include the running of the car, something Fisher had full responsibility for and which he delegated to the Meeke organisation. Upon unpacking the car after it arrived at the Bush, Wesley Emerson one of Meeke's mechanics remembers unpacking the spares package, only to find *'There was boxes and boxes and boxes of first aid kits, there was boxes and boxes of master cylinders. I remember all this stuff coming out and there wasn't a single suspension arm in any of it, we hadn't the right bits, but plenty of first aid kits.'*

The arrival of the BMW M3 from Prodrive the following year signalled a further loosening of the ties as the contract with Prodrive stipulated that the car had to go back to their Banbury headquarters after most events for checking and preparation for its next rally. This would have been a major expense until it was realised that Bertie's primary sponsor at the time, Alumac, regularly had lorries transporting their products from their Co. Armagh factory to England and, using a set of modified toes on a fork lift truck which could lift the car on and off the lorries, it was usually possible to hitch a free ride! Kieran McAnallen remembers *'The transporting of the car back and forward in itself in this manner was a substantial saving to the team, and this form of transit continued right through until the last Impreza. The car was always brought to our yard by some of Meeke's men, set up on to the lorry and then taken away by the same boys when it came back.'*

When the car was in Ireland it was looked after by the Meeke team under the supervision of usually one of two Prodrive engineers who had flown in from Banbury.

Following two successful years with the BMW, by 1991 Prodrive were focussing their attention on the Subaru Legacy and newly signed driver Colin McRae's campaign and with this in mind Bertie felt that they could not offer him the package he was looking for. He began to look around for alternatives with the result that for 1991 he campaigned an R.E.D. prepared car in a one off deal.

The new contract with R.E.D was a full package which negated any requirement for the Meeke team. When asked, Rory Kennedy, Bertie's co-driver at the time, remembered how this affected the team dynamics compared to previous years when Meeke's and Prodrive's joint efforts were very much to the fore

'The dynamic changed entirely because, about the time R.E.D came in. Meekes were doing the Spanish championship with the Corsas and Sydney was sort of evolving in that direction. When we had the BMW, Sydney maybe came to a few rallies to help out a bit but it was mostly Prodrive who looked after us. Dave Campion was our manager and Syd would have looked after logistics, and provided some men like Norman Burns to work alongside Prodrive mechanics such as Paul Howarth and Pete Holly. When R.E.D took over their team did everything.'

However winning combinations tend to keep coming back and the following year it

Long term Meeke mechanic Gary Wilson working with Bertie on the BMW on the Donegal Rally in 1989

was back to business with Fisher and Meeke with the arrival in early 1992 of a new Prodrive prepared Subaru Legacy to Sydney Meeke's Bush based stable was a big deal for everyone involved in the team, as Rory Kennedy explains

'The car came to Sydney's Workshop and we were all there the Saturday it arrived, discussing what was going to be done, and so on. Sydney was back on board again and the car was going to be run out of his place with Sydney being a sort of Team Leader but with Prodrive help. They would send over the same people every rally but essentially on our side we had Norman Burns, and maybe Robbie McGurk, Adrian Kirkland and a couple of Sydney's other men, all the time and of course Kris [Meeke] was there too, usually as the tyre man.'

Although at first sight the involvement of

Prodrive in the nineties might seem to mean Meeke operation's involvement to be less than in the days when they built, prepared and serviced cars, however this is only partly true. As rallying technology increased dramatically through the decade, so did the size and complexity of the on event support structure required and so while Meeke's role in Bertie's car preparation may have decreased, the size of the support function had escalated to take up much of the slack with mud note crews and weather crews feeding information back to a large team of mechanics and engineers in chase cars. To give an idea of the scale of things, in the 1994 Donegal Rally programme Plum Tyndall estimated that the Toughmac team's budget for the year was around 1/4 million pounds, a figure which has not been denied.

Bertie scrutinises the various tyre compounds available with a Pirelli tyre technician

One area where technology was moving very rapidly was tyres. Long gone were the days when Bertie and Brian Quinn would jump in the car and nip home to grab a set of slicks to try and put one over on the opposition. Now there were a choice of tyres for each stage and to keep on top of changeable Irish conditions, weather crews would drive the route just ahead of the rally, sending back advice on which tyres to use as Rory explains

'Weather crews are a very important aspect of the whole thing, because once you got that information and collated that, you could make a sensible tyre choice. Roads closed an hour before first car was due on a stage and so the mud notes crew were long gone by the times the competing crews were about to go from the tyre change spot to the stage. The weather crew were able to stay close to the stage and were able to give an up to date weather report before the final tyre choice was made. At that time there wouldn't have been any other teams that would have had as many people involved to that extent.' Michael Kirby, Sales and Marketing Manager at Subaru Ireland right throughout Bertie's time rallying Subarus elaborated.

'The 'Bertie Babes' as the crews were affectionately known, went to stage locations, took measurements of tarmac temperature with thermometer probes, and then radio or phoned in whether it was hot, damp, etc. This kind of thing was completely unheard of before.'

Long standing Meeke mechanic, Wesley Emerson, also elaborated 'We would have had every tyre available in the tyre van which would have been driven by Kris and each chase car and Kieran's Management vehicle all would also have had a stock of tyres, so you had every option and chance to put the right tyres on the car.'

And it was not only the internal team people who helped make the decisions. Very often Pirelli would send over a tyre technician and dedicated supply van to be available for the team and back up the event.

With tyres being so critical and the complexities of choosing the right ones, it was an area ripe for skulduggery and subterfuge with the various teams constantly seeking advantage over each other as Kieran McAnallen recounts in a story about Donegal in the early 90s.

'It was a partly wet but very changeable Saturday stages and the loop included Knockalla. We put Bertie out from Milford service and the decision was to send him out on any type of tyres at all from Milford until we got out to Kerrykeel where we would make a better decision on what tyres to choose for the Knockalla stage. Whilst doing this, Ian Cuddy had been noseying about and realised that other teams were listening in to our radios, and so we got the word not to relay any tyre information over radios. Brian Quinn, Sydney and I went out to the crossroads up to the top of the mountain to gauge what way the weather would go, and when we got there, despite there being a lot of black clouds we came to the conclusion it was going to stay dry provided the rally ran on time. When we were coming down off Knockalla into Kerrykeel we met Maggie McKinstry going up and she waved us down and since the traffic was serious she asked us in a hurry "What's it like boys, what's it like" and I said "We don't know, the traffic's that bad we never even got up next or near it Maggie".

So, anyhow, we came back down into the service at Kerrykeel, and Sydney went over and whispered to the mechanics to put on slicks. Just then rain started to spit on the windscreen and Bertie, doubting what I had advised, looked at me and asked me whether I wanted to drive, and I said "hold on Bertie there's no point in us doing a job if you're not going to listen to us" and the pair of boys went out to Knockalla and took 17 seconds out of everybody else'

As with every aspect of his team, Bertie took tyre choice very seriously. He blamed tyres for having lost the 1998 championship on the final round in Cork when there had been heavy rain and he felt he was at a disadvantage with using the Pirellis which he thought weren't as good in the wet as the Michelins used by other drivers. With the disappointment of his loss still raw, Bertie was very tempted to change supplier entirely, as Hugh O'Brien explained,

'Sometime soon after this, Bertie expressed his disappointment to Pirelli about their wet tyres and threatened to change to Michelin. Pirelli responded by offering to do a tyre test and full day of tyre testing ensued at Muckish in Donegal. Bertie had invited Michelin along as well and many types of tyre compound were tested whilst tyre technicians took pressure and temperature measurements as well as recording the times. As it transpired there wasn't an awful lot of difference in most of the tyres but towards the end of the test Pirelli produced an out and out wet tyre called the RS90. We had never heard of this tyre before – never even knew it existed. Half way through the stage, I said to Bertie "This is the best tyre we've been on yet", you could feel it in the car. We didn't even have to stop the watch this time, for it was a second a mile quicker than any of the other tyres we tested including the Michelins.'

This RS90 tyre proved to have an important part to play in the final outcome of the 1999 Circuit of Ireland, as Hugh relates.

'On the Circuit that next year we had a big battle with Nesbitt throughout and, coming up through Meath on the Sunday night, Sydney told me "go and have a closer look at the night stages because we are going to have to try and get in ahead of Nesbitt tonight." I went to the start of one of the stages just as the road closed car was about to go through and, since I was the last one in, I would have a good look at it, plus I could drive as if the road was closed or near enough. As it turned out on raised bits of road plenty of the road was dry but on all the parts where you really needed your tyre and on approach to junction and leaving junctions, the tight stuff where your tyre really counts, they were all still wet, so I went back to my professor and told Syd we would have to put on the RS90s'

So, armed with this most up to date information, they put Bertie on the RS90s and on the two stages he took an impressive 16 seconds off Nesbitt. Clearly such information was gold dust and, as in Donegal, had to be protected. At the very same service halt where the team had put the RS90s on the car, mechanic Wesley Emerson remembers that a rival crew were trying to see what tyres Bertie had put on but were foiled by a bit of quick thinking by the Toughmac team.

'Dave Leech from Prodrive who was working with Nesbitt at the time was slipping about trying to find out what tyre we were running so we got two space savers out of the chase cars and put them on to Bertie's car and he took the hint and drove off!

But even if they'd seen them it mightn't have mattered anyhow as to keep tyre choice secret we had used a code system and we had everything blanked out on the tyres – sometimes the mechanics changing the wheels didn't know what tyre we were running ourselves!'

With the plethora of vehicles required by the

Ready to rally on space savers!

over a year but the big one was in 1998 when the Toughmac Subaru Ireland Rally Team was launched. It was a fantastic professional set up, we really had two great years with Bertie in 1998 and 1999. The support we gave Bertie wasn't financial as such, but from our point of view it was an investment in cars and vehicles which were on loan for full seasons at a time, 1998 and 1999. We provided I'm sure around a dozen cars and vehicles for the Toughmac Team in total, including management vehicles, service cars, chase vehicles, vehicles for weather crew, we even had a motor home too.

When we got involved with Bertie, it redefined rallying and rally sponsorship in Ireland at that time. It was definitely a dominant team and raised the bar massively. It was super professional from both Toughmac and Subaru Ireland and it was the most professional team in Ireland at the time and the same level of

above and left: Neville Matthews, from Subaru Ireland standing with Kieran McAnallen, Bertie and Rory outside Subaru Ireland's premises in Dublin. Pictured are just some of the vehicles supplied on loan from Subaru Ireland to the Toughmac team.

various different elements of the team becoming a major drain on the budget it was a major coup when Subaru Ireland got involved with the team in the late nineties. Michael Kirby, then Sales and Marketing Manager at Subaru Ireland, provides an insight into Subaru Ireland's involvement with the Toughmac Rally team.

'The first association Subaru Ireland had with Bertie was in a small way on the front wing of the blue car in 1996. That went on for

attention to detail achieved has not been surpassed.'

Of course, like the early relationship with Sydney Meeke, the benefits from the relationship with Subaru flowed both ways as Michael explained

'In certain areas the awareness of Subaru was definitely heightened from our rallying. The Irish market was quite different to the UK market insofar as, while sales in the UK were predominantly to the farming community, in Ireland we had a different client base entirely because the farmers weren't interested in Subaru as we had no diesel engines at that time. So where we were getting our sales from as a result of rallying was largely where the rallies were based, for example in Cork, Kerry, Galway, Donegal, the dealers in those areas had great sales in WRX, Imprezas and rally Impreza look-a-likes and the accessory business also blossomed as a result also so that's where we would have got benefit from the rallying.'

Of course with all these different people and vehicles to co-ordinate communication was critical and given that many rallies were held in places where radio and mobile phone coverage was patchy this could be a problem but again the Toughmac team led the way by setting up a telecommunications repeater which ensured that Bertie and Rory could always be in touch with someone from the team even in mountainous regions. Team member Wesley Emerson explained how it worked.

'There were two radios, one worked just on an ordinary frequency and the other worked through a repeater. The repeater, hired from Victor Patterson communications, had to be in the highest possible place which was chosen from a map of the area bearing in mind the need to get a vehicle up which sometimes meant a very hairy drive – although in later years Bertie's helicopter was often brought in the day before a rally started to get the repeater up whatever the highest mountain was around the area which made it a bit easier. Although the repeater receiver was only in the management car they could relay all the messages to us, they could hear everything that was going on and it meant as a team you were now never out of reach of communication with the crew which gave us a clear advantage over other teams'.

Coming into the 1998 season, the sheer size and stature of the joint team of Sydney Meeke Prodrive, Subaru Ireland and Toughmac as well as the other numerous team members volunteering in different roles, had expanded to something similar to a works team. At its peak there were just shy of 20 people in the team, with additional bodies drafted in on events such as the weather crews and despite the nonstop action they all had to eat as Kieran recalls

'When it came to catering requirements, Emma and Gladys Fisher were usually the main people to look after the culinary necessities of the team, but on many occasions the late Carol Meeke, and Georgina Campion would be on hand to help as well. On occasion the barbecue would come out for some grilled goodness, other times it would be sandwiches

Gladys and Emma Fisher who were often present at service areas to create some culinary delights for the hungry team members.

and tea but whatever it was, the quality of the food provided by the Emma and Gladys team on events would be as good as you would get in the best hotel in town'

The chase car guys also got well looked after too according to Wesley Emerson.

'When we would land in to service, the rally car would often be there already so we would be straight out of the chase cars and working at it immediately with no time to eat – but afterwards when we would get back into the chase cars to head out, Emma would have made up wee lunch boxes for us with sandwiches, crisps, drinks, and all that. Between herself and Gladys they would always have made sure we were well looked after - they were very good that way.'

Team management responsibilities were taken on by Kieran and Sydney and they very often made decisions for Bertie in relation to various things including tyre choice as Kieran explains

'Management would have been a mixture of Sydney and myself over the years. Mechanical or technical would have been Sydney but if there was a major decision to be made there was a discussion. It would be a team decision mostly which no one person would have dictated. The team worked really well and the reason was because everyone was there to win and try to do the job as best they could, which they did all the time. Everybody stuck to the task they were given and didn't deviate or question it. In fact the team worked so well, I can't remember an incident when there was a bad feeling throughout all the years, no mat-

ter what happened.'

Administration and event planning within the team was largely carried out by Austin or Rory who as co-drivers would have been aware of all the logistics required as Kieran recalls 'You would have met at the Bush or a local hotel before the event as to who was doing what and then you went away with a clear instruction and then on the event Rory or Austin would have presented you with a schedule and task list.'

All in all, by the late 90s the Fisher / Meeke partnership had evolved from a quick helping hand with some Isopon into a true professional team in an amateur sport, with a full line of clothing stickers and posters, and one of the first Irish Rally Team websites in existence. It certainly raised the bar for other drivers and teams in Ireland and their professionalism shone through in every way.

Rory Kennedy sums it up

'It was a big team but it was local, everything was there. It showed the way the team had evolved to the point that every other team aspired to be like us, because this was the level or size of the team you had to be at to compete on a level playing field. Essentially it had all the size, stature and trappings of a works team. As always, our team then raised the bar, and set the standards for rallying in Ireland.'

Service Schedule

EVENT: AA Circuit Of Ireland Rally

DATE: 2nd - 5th April 1999

Rally Car Comp. No.	Registration No.	Crew	Call Sign
2	R 555 FEL	Bertie Fisher & Rory Kennedy	Rally Car

Crew No.	Vehicle	Personnel	Call Sign
Chase 1	99-D-6174	Ian Richardson & Wesley Emerson	Oscar 1
Chase 2	99-D-6198	Adrian Kirkland & S. Whitehead	Oscar 2
Tyre Van	UAZ 5326	Kris Meeke & T.B.A.	Oscar 3
Service Van	N906 ERV	Davy Lester & Andrew Meeke	Oscar 4
Management	99-D-6181	Kieran McAnallen & Sydney Meeke	Oscar 5
Supervision	Hire Vehicle	Paul Howarth & Karen Howarth	Oscar 6
Gravel Notes	RIL 3555	Mark Fisher & Gordon Noble	Oscar 7
Weather Crew	Hire Vehicle	Hugh O'Brien & Steven Kilpatrick	Oscar 8
Weather Crew	99-D-5551	Noel & Siobhan Behan	Oscar 9
Pirelli	S830 FUD	Dick Cormack & Dale Richardson	Oscar 10
Subaru Ireland	98-D-5552	Michael Kirby & Staff	Oscar 11

Bertie Fisher
Gobluck, Ballinamallard,
Co. Fermanagh, BT94 2LW.
Tel: 01365 388127
Fax: 01365 388371

Michael Kirby
Subaru Ireland, 65 Broomhill Road,
Tallaght, Dublin 24.
Tel: Dublin 452 0444
Telefax: 452 0415

Kieran McAnallen
Toughmac, 259 Battleford Road,
Benburb, Co. Tyrone, BT71 7NP.
Tel: 01861 548541
Fax: 01861 548548

above: Front page of 1999 Circuit of Ireland Service Schedule as devised by Rory Kennedy, includes a list of all of the vehicles in the team and the crew members assigned to each vehicle.

right: The Toughmac Team Service Schedules went into great detail including a tree level 'Team Structure' diagram

Toughmac / Subaru Rally Team
Team Structure

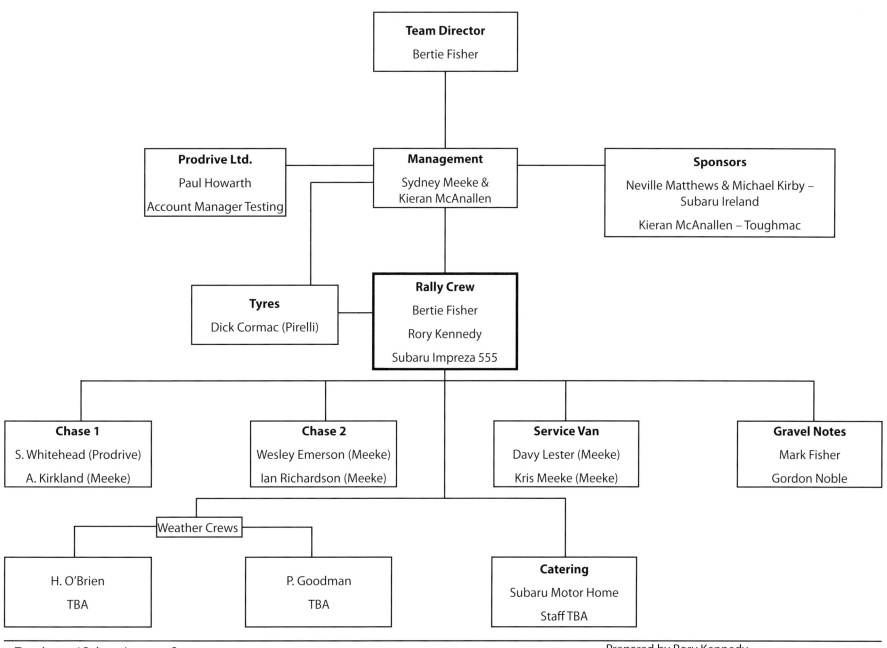

Toughmac / Subaru Impreza Sport

Prepared by Rory Kennedy

1983 - 1987

*The Opel Era, The Gold Card Year,
The 1-2-3 Year, The Gap Year,
Bertie's Big comeback*

By 1983 the Group 4 Escorts, Chevettes and so on which had dominated British Internationals in the mid to late 70s were getting tired and replacing them was a new breed of rally car – the Group B car.

Less restricted in terms of what engines they could use, and coupled with the introduction of the Audi Quattro and its four wheel drive system, rallying was going through a radical change. If Bertie wanted to stay competitive, it was time for him to upgrade and upgrade he did – to one of the numerous ultra-successful Opel Ascona 400s Jimmy McRae had been campaigning for the previous few years in Rothmans and Boelyn Cattini guises.

However before any stage action took place, Bertie's achievements in the previous year did not pass without notice as he was presented with the Northern Ireland Motorsport Personality of the Year Award for 1982 at the Association of Northern Ireland Car Club (ANICC) Awards being the clear winner in the poll which was carried out among the numerous ANICC member clubs and local motorsport journalists. A great accolade and end to a fantastic year.

And so on to the 1983 action. Bertie's first outing in the newly acquired Ascona was the Mintex Rally, the DeLacy Motor Club event and as always the first round of the British Open Rally Championship where a disappointing ninth place finish overall was followed up by the first round of the STP Irish Tarmac Rally Championship at Easter, the Rothmans Circuit of Ireland. Normally the Galway Rally was and still is the first round but in 1983 a sponsor could not be found in time and without that extra injection of money the rally obviously could not cover all the associated costs required to run it.

On the Circuit, there were many international and works entries, including Stig Blomqvist in the Audi Sport UK Quattro, Jimmy McRae and Henri Toivonen in the

right: In the 1985 Circuit of Ireland, due to the marathon but fast paced nature of the event, drivers had to pace themselves accordingly. In an interview with Sammy Hamill shortly before the rally, Bertie spoke about the pace required.

'Look at the first stage, it's 16 miles long and is the sort of place where your rally could come to a very abrupt end. If I drive that one the way I would like to and think about getting to the finish on Tuesday, I'm quite liable to drop a minute or more to someone who decides to take a flier. In my own mind I know that, in the end, the rally will probably be won by 10 minutes or more, but the psychological blow it would be to find yourself a minute down after one stage. It makes planning tactics very difficult indeed'

After several problems including a time consuming puncture Bertie dropped out of the battle for the lead between Russell Brooks and Jimmy McRae but his third overall made it a fantastic Opel 1-2-3 trio.

Rothmans Ascona 400s, Pentti Airikkala in the Evening Herald Lancia 037, Per Eklund in the Toyota Corolla GT, Russell Brookes and Terry Kaby in Chevette HSRs, and many more. While many of these entries were not around at the finish for one reason or another due to major offs or mechanical troubles or other problems, a fast steady Fisher lasted the marathon event to come home a well-deserved second place overall behind Brookes' Chevette, and some 13 minutes ahead of third placed McRae in the similar Ascona.

Despite a few minor niggles, it was obvious Bertie was getting used to the Ascona and Austin Frazer liked the new mount too *'It was roomier. It was longer; it felt longer, it took some time to adapt to it. It was a very competitive car in its day.'*

Following the success on the Circuit came disappointment with a non-finish on the Castrol Welsh International, the third round of the British Championship, and closer to home, The Lurgan Park Rally where on this one off occasion the co-driver was Fermanagh businessman George Deane whose Deane Public Works company would in later years sponsor Bertie. Following his second place the previous year and wins in 1980 and 1981 Bertie was the No.1 seed but during the rally the Ascona suffered misfire issues, and they had a spin which cost over 20 seconds, which may not seem like much but due to the short sharp sprint nature of the event too much to pull back leaving Bertie and George in a disappointing seventh overall 24 seconds off winner Kenny McKinstry.

The Arnold Clark Scottish International again brought a non-finish, this time resulting in serious damage to the car which presented a problem in so far it was only a few days to the Shell Donegal International Rally.

At the time Sydney Meeke was building several Mantas for customers including one which was being built for Bertie to drive later in the year but after the Scottish

left top: Finnish driver Pentti Airikkala in the Evening Herald Lancia 037 Group B car on the Circuit of Ireland in 1983

centre and below: Bertie and Austin in action in the Ascona on the '83 Circuit of Ireland.

right top: Working on the new Manta on the Donegal International side by side with the car of eventual winner Vincent Bonner who also used Meeke for his prep and on event servicing

Bertie's preparations for the event and the build-up of the new car ran dangerously close to the start of the rally, with the car only being finished at 3am on the morning of the start of the rally after there was a last minute dash to London for oil coolers which were held up in customs

Bertie was quoted in the 'Ballyraine Bugle' *'I woke the half of Ballinamallard at six o'clock this morning, it was my first run out in the new car and I did about five miles, it feels great, but I'll be happier with the first couple of stages under my belt'*

below: Fanad Strikes again! Bertie pictured here on the Knockalla stage shortly before he retired

accident, efforts were accelerated and all running gear where possible was taken from the Ascona and put into the new Manta as well as new Phase 3 engine.

The team started the Donegal International with high hopes but it was Austin McHale in the Chevette who got into an early lead with fastest times on the opening tests. But then disaster struck the Dubliner when the gearbox on his Chevette jammed and the car punctured costing him some 5 minutes and the lead.

Bertie now became the leader and although local Donegal hero Vincent Bonner was making some impressive stage times, it wasn't enough to match the Fermanagh man.

Day Two began in the same vein with Bertie building up a decent lead of around a minute and a half, until disaster struck – that Fanad jinx had bit again! Bertie's big Manta had argued with the scenery on Fanad, apparently clipping one side of the road and going off on the other.

Despite the damage which required some running repairs at the scene, Bertie was able to continue eventually, coming through the next stage, Knockalla, well down the running order though still going quickly – indeed too fast on one corner, having a massive spin, losing a further 20 seconds in the process.

He finished the stage and despite some efforts by his Service crew to repair the damages, the steering rack

seized up after Stage 19 and he was out of the rally on which Bonner went on to claim a well deserved and popular victory.

And so to the Ulster. Back in the British Rally Championship it attracted several high profile entries including Stig Blomqvist in the David Sutton prepared works Audi Quattro and Jimmy McRae in the Rothmans Opel Manta 400.

Stig, who was at the absolute top of his game at this time as team mate to Hannu Mikkola in the World Rally Championship Audi team, started the rally as hot favourite but Jimmy McRae was a long established Irish Tarmac expert with the new Manta 400, and Bertie wasn't far behind either. Throw in Harald Demuth in a second Audi,

left: Vincent Bonner and Seamus McGettigan who went on to become the first Donegal crew to win the Donegal Rally, after Bertie's retirement and Austin McHale's challenge for the lead came to an end when he had three punctures on the last stage, Atlantic Drive

Prior to the Ulster Rally given that Bertie had very little experience in the Manta to date, he needed to get a bit more seat time to get familiarised with the car's limits and possibilities. Rather than doing a full blown rally and potentially jeopardising having the car ready if he happened to crash the car or do something that left it unable to be ready in time for the Ulster Rally, he decided to have a shakedown doing 00 car duties on Day Two of the two-day Sligo Stages Rally.

Austin Frazer was interviewed in the week leading up to the rally and said *'Bertie had thought seriously about driving in the rally but he is such a competitive person by nature he would have ended up trying to win instead of simply giving the car a sensible shake-down'*

Per Eklund in a works Toyota, Russell Brookes and Terry Kaby in Chevette HSRs, Chris Lord in a Mazda and many more and you had a fantastic line up of many drivers who could have been victorious down the tight Ulster lanes. Twenty Five stages over 23 hours would bring the just shy of 100 entries through all six Northern Ireland counties.

Blomqvist immediately threw down the gauntlet with the fastest time on Stage One but on the way to Stage Two one of the Audi's fuel pumps began playing up. Initially it didn't hamper performance too much and by the time the crews reached Armagh for service after two more stages, Stig had increased the lead to 50 seconds

after McRae had brake problems and Fisher was unable to match the Swede's pace.

As the rally moved further west into Fermanagh county, Fisher was able to overhaul the brake stricken McRae into second, but Stig continued to dominate through the following stages until, on the start line of Stage 16 around Barnes' Gap area, the rear drive shaft of the big Audi broke and he was down to 2wd. This catapulted Fisher in to the lead by 26 seconds but, though he kept the lead for a few stages, a mighty effort by the David Sutton Team mechanics managed to fix the Audi of all its ailments and by the last few stages Stig had reclaimed the lead.

left: Celebrations at the finish of the Ulster Rally

right top: Audi works driver Stig Blomqvist in the big Audi Quattro on the Ulster Rally taking Audi's first international win on tarmac for the Quattro

right below: Winner of the Circuit of Ireland in the Andrews Heat for Hire Chevette HSR, Russell Brookes pictured here on the Ulster in the same year

As the rally began to reach its final leg, Austin Frazer has an interesting story about an incident involving Russell Brookes who –being at the top of his game – was not being best pleased at being lead by Fisher & Frazer.

'With a few stages to go, Stig was leading it, we were second, and Russell Brookes third. Russell hadn't been catching us and Bertie was driving quickly but he was holding back. With just a few stages to go we knew Russell wouldn't overtake us if we kept steady and there was no chance of catching Stig. So at the start of one of those closing stages, we had a bit of time at the control, and Russell came up my window of our car, and he said "I don't know what's up with you boys, which one of you is the chicken in here," And I said "Russell, we are not going

to be catching Stig, so you drive your rally and we'll drive our rally.'"

As it happens, Fisher and Frazer did drive their own rally, and finished comfortably second, some 1 minute 14 seconds behind Stig, and well ahead of Russell Brookes who finished some 4 minutes further back in third. McRae, who had all sorts of other problems since including fuel fumes, a puncture and a bent rear axle, battled on to finish nearly 8 minutes further back in fourth. An interesting statistic to note is that this was the first ever time an Audi had won an all tarmac event.

Overall though, this was a fantastic result for Bertie Fisher, he was very much the best of the rest and proved he was able to match and beat all the visiting crews from many foreign shores.

The next rally for Bertie was the Rothmans Manx International Rally on the Isle of Man, which also happened to be the next round of the Irish Tarmac and British Open Series. There he would not be only up against one Rothmans Manta like on Ulster but three – An all-star line-up of 1981 World Champion Finn Ari Vatanen, fellow Finn and former RAC winner Henri Toivonen, as well as the Scot Jimmy McRae.

From the start on Thursday, Bertie was immediately competitive just 33 seconds off leader Toivonen's pace over the 1st stage at Brandeywell. By the end of day one Bertie held 5th overall, way out of reach of the trio of Rothmans Mantas at the head of the pack but only 23 seconds behind Russell Brookes in 4th place.

Friday dawned and mechanical troubles for McRae and Brookes saw Bertie still in 5th, just 5 seconds behind Stig Blomqvist, but not for long. He managed to overhaul the Swede and, with McRae now out with half shaft failure, Bertie was up to third overall. For several stages he and Stig really battled it out, with almost identical times and by stage 31 the gap between them was 1 second.

left: Bertie was doing very well on the Manx up until he retired after an accident

But several stages on the Abbeylands stage it was all over when, on a tight first gear corner near the end of the stage Fisher's Manta under steered into a bank, and was too damaged to continue.

By all accounts, Bertie was the star of the week on the Isle of Man, another brilliant showing of pace to prove he could mix it with works drivers in a private team car, which unfortunately ended in an all too common Manx retirement.

A few weeks after the Manx was the Uniroyal Cork 20 Rally, the penultimate round of the Irish Tarmac Championship and again the outcome for Bertie was to be disappointment. Despite finishing the first day in 1st place 23 seconds ahead of Austin McHale, on day 2 he was once again caught out by the Manta's tendency to snap from oversteer to understeer, when on a tightening right-hander on the Musheramore stage the Manta under steered into a wall and was unable to continue. With Bertie out McHale went on to win the rally comfortably, his first International victory which also secured his first of five outright Tarmac Championships.

Understandably Bertie was disheartened considering this was the third retirement out of four rallies in the Manta due to under steering accidents. And it appeared the trend wasn't with the Fisher car alone. On the World scene Henri Toivonen and Ari Vatanen had also experienced problems with 'oversteer to sudden understeer' on numerous rallies resulting in a few nasty accidents.

downhill through the countdown boards, past the finish down into a dip with the road rising again to the stop car where the timekeepers were. There were about a dozen spectators standing around but the road was clear and everything looked OK as Bertie came down the hill, through the flying finish, and braked hard to stop at the time keeper's car.

However there were three or four local guys there and unfortunately one of them took a notion to run across the road into Bertie's path before he could get the car stopped. He was taken by ambulance to the hospital but didn't survive. People in general took it to be a dreadful accident and that's what it was really.'

The name of the spectator was Michael McKernan, a 29 year old diesel fitter from Eskra and a regular competitor on many events himself. He was also a regular member of Hugh O'Brien's service crew who had been leading the rally up to this point but organisers cancelled the remainder of the event after the accident.

Understandably, Bertie did no more rallying for the remainder of 1983 although as many pointed out, while it was a very sad occurrence, it was generally accepted as a freak accident which was made more poignant as it happened in a small tightly knit community of rallying people.

left: Bertie with the car in its new Shell Gold Card livery

right: Bertie Fisher, Austin Frazer and Sydney Meeke with the car at the Meeke workshop in its new Shell Gold Card livery and mechanics (L-R) Peter Garvin, Clive Grant, Ian Cuddy, Norman Burns and Graham Garvin. Journalist with the Belfast Telegraph and Carsport at the time, Sammy Hamill rumoured the deal to be worth £70,000, a huge amount at the time.

Austin Frazer recalls: *'It was a huge thing. It provided quite a substantial amount of funding to put together with the GM Dealership team we were all part of at that time.'*

Opel/GM also gave incentives to drivers at that time to be part of their GMDS team. Again Austin Frazer takes up the story, *'At that time drivers from the Three Provinces, of England Scotland and Northern Ireland got overall sponsorship from Opel through their local dealerships and we had a contract for several years. Each province had its own dedicated driver, Scotland had Jimmy McRae, England had Russell Brookes and Northern Ireland had Bertie. The deal was that Bertie owned the car and had his own private deal with Sydney on preparing the car but they were part of a team as such and got help with parts and such forth too.'*

Next up was the forests of Tyrone for the Bushwhacker and, perhaps due to the problems with the Manta, Bertie went back to using the Ascona 400. He was up against some hot competition from Ronnie McCartney, Robin Lyons, Bertie Law, Hugh O'Brien, and many more but after the first three stages he lay sixth albeit 12 seconds off the lead. Then on Stage 5, Lough Bradan, disaster struck an almighty blow for the team and for the local rally fraternity.

Standing at the finish line of the stage were a number of spectators including by chance Austin Frazer who for much of the year had sat with Bertie but, on this occasion, was acting as MSA Steward leaving old team mate from many years previous, Ernie Campbell to accompany Bertie this time.

Austin takes up the story:

'I was standing at the finish of that particular stage with two kids, my own and a neighbour's son. The cars approaching the finish came over a long crest and steep

1984 The Shell Gold Card Year

1984 dawned, same car, but different colour scheme and sponsors. After months of negotiations, a deal was struck with the main sponsor for the year, Shell Oils Gold Card, a credit card scheme launched by the Oil company around then for business users. It heavily influenced the colour scheme with a base colour of white, red and yellow lines in line with Shell's colours, and a distinctive golden roof and half covered bonnet. In fact, with the ex-

right: Bertie on his inaugural outing with the Shell Gold Card livery, the National Breakdown Rally

ception of a few small Pirelli, GM Dealer sport logos and a Sydney Meeke Motorsport thin banner, the car was totally covered in Shell Oils decals. This particular Shell Oils sponsorship of Fisher was a big deal at the time.

In an interview at the start of 1984, Bertie said *'I'm very happy with the deal. It is just about everything I could have hoped for and I'm very grateful to both Shell and GM for giving me the opportunity to have another crack at the Open Series'.* The deal was to compete on the full British Rally Championship, plus a few select Irish events of Bertie's choice.

In total, he would cover 12 events that year, half of them British Championship events, and the other half Irish events plus at the end of the year the RAC Rally.

That year's rallying started with the DeLacy Motor Club ran National Breakdown Rally the first round of the British Rally Championship.

Starting the event after several months of a layoff and bearing in mind this was the first time he had competed on a Forestry event in the Manta, re-acclimatisation was very much the story of the first day for Bertie. Through the early stages of the rally, which were only a few miles each in length Bertie made his way up the time sheets to reach into the top ten and eventually up to sixth, not far behind Per Eklund's Toyota Team GB Corolla. Just when Bertie thought Eklund's position was his for the taking, disaster struck. On the Staindale stage, coming up to a Y junction on the other end of a blind crest Bertie set the car up to take the junction. The car suddenly began to veer off its destined path, the back tyre had lost its grip and deflated almost immediately and ran sideways into a bog. With no spectators at hand, all the crew could do was wait some time before there was enough man power to get the car out.

The considerable time loss resulted in him being technically 'OTL' (Over Time Limit) and any attempts at a top

left: Action on the National Breakdown

Although Bertie had done numerous rallies in Scotland, Wales and other regions where the British Championship covered, his experience on the particular stages used in the championship was limited – a big disadvantage as Austin Frazer explains

'A lot of our competitors would have had the advantage of knowing the terrain. You couldn't recce those stages and despite all being on the GM dealer team, because we each had our own independent service team, there wasn't much sharing of information about things like the nature of the stage, the type of surface, what tyres you would use etc which all affected our confidence. The other guys would have been rallying those stages for years and years and would have known them well, particularly up in Yorkshire.

It took time to gain the confidence we needed and I remember on one lengthy stage in particular which we were doing twice on the National Breakdown Rally. The first time we were fairly cautious, and I would have taken a few notes on the map but second time round we were a minute quicker and you know it was just confidence. On a long rally you don't want to push your luck too quickly'

ten finish were out of the equation.

Two weeks after the National Breakdown was the Hills of Donegal Rally. With the 1984 priority being on the British Championship and with the Circuit of Ireland (the second round) coming up at Easter, Bertie headed to the Hills primarily for a tarmac test of the new Pirelli tyres he was using but he very nearly didn't get to compete in the rally at all after there was a delay in getting the Manta 400 back from a trade show in London.

Bertie waited patiently in Ballybofey on the car to arrive and when the car finally showed up some 45 minutes late, the organisers would only allow him to start at the very back of the field, No. 125!

Despite having to pass many slower competitors along the way Bertie's rally went like a dream. He set fastest time on all but the penultimate stage when he had a puncture which meant he drove on a flat for six miles. But the time lost was insufficient to drag him into the clutches of the chasing pack and the story of Bertie's rally was a last place start to a first place finish!

So, on to that important Rothmans Circuit of Ireland Rally. The quality of the entry list promised hot competition, and it showed in the first day's drama. Henri Toivonen, regarded at the time as the finest tarmac driver in the world, built up a lead on the first few stages with his Rothmans Porsche but disaster struck for the Finn on Stage 3, the first run through the Hamilton's Folly stage when he had two punctures handing the lead to Jimmy McRae in the Manta 400.

Jimmy led for several stages before hitting a bank and losing time. As the first day came to a close and the crews returned on their leg back to Belfast, Bertie Fisher was the new leader but others weren't far behind with German, Harald Demuth, in the Audi Quattro second, just 19 seconds adrift and Billy Coleman in another Manta was 11 seconds further back in third.

right top: Huge crowds came out to see Billy Coleman take his third Circuit of Ireland victory in the Dealer Opel Team Ireland Manta 400

middle: German Harald Demuth on the Circuit of Ireland in the works Audi Quattro

bottom: Rising star on the World scene, Henri Toivonen came to compete on the Circuit of Ireland in the Rothmans Porsche 911 SCRS

left top: Circuit of Ireland action through the scenic Sally Gap stage in the Wicklow mountains with helicopter carrying a camera was recording footage for nightly tv reports on RTÉ

left below: Bertie leaves a trail of dust behind the Manta as he slides round a corner on the Welsh International

below: Bertie tackles a hairpin on the Epynt Ranges on the Welsh

Day Two and Toivonen, recuperating from 37th place overall after his Day One disaster, was setting fastest times again and rocketing his way up the leader board.

Fisher still led, but then on Stage 20 came his turn for bad luck when a half shaft on the rear axle of the Manta broke, bringing his efforts to a sudden and terminal halt ending great effort from Bertie to lead so many World class crews in such a prestigious event as the Circuit.

With Easter having been late that year, just a week and a half after the Circuit of Ireland finished was Bertie's next outing, the Welsh. Bertie had done the Welsh twice before, the first time in 1975 in a Mark One RS 2000 and the second in 1983 in the Ascona so this time he was more familiar with the terrain, car and in a good team. He finished sixth overall, just six seconds behind Swede Per Eklund who was in the Toyota Team GB Corolla.

From the forest lanes of Wales to the tarmac lanes, where the next outing on Bertie's calendar was a Dungannon Motor Club event in Davagh Forest near Cookstown.

right: Bertie in typical Donegal terrain, pictured here on the Fanad stage

below: A bright evening heralded the start of the Scottish which ended with retirement from an event Bertie would prefer to forget.

Bertie was invited to the event by sponsor Alumac, owned by Kieran McAnallen, who would go on to be close friend and Sponsor of Bertie for many years. The rally was small in size in comparison to any of the larger events Bertie had been doing leading up to this event, but the competition was nonetheless very hot. Kenny McKinstry in an Escort, Pat Kirk in a Nissan 240 RS, Kenny Colbert in a Sunbeam Lotus and Sam McKinstry in another Escort were all punching in impressive times with Kenny and Pat within two seconds of Bertie at one point, but both of them faulted. Bertie finished the day 28 seconds ahead of Colbert with Sam McKinstry a further 4 seconds behind. At the prize giving in Dungannon afterwards, Bertie donated his £200 first prize winning money to the Special Care Schools in Killadeas and Dungannon. This shows the caring side of Bertie which perhaps was not often seen in the public limelight.

Following that local win it was back to the International Forestry events with the Lloyds Bowmaker Scottish International Rally, another round of the British Open series. He had been up to fifth at one point during the rally but a series of problems including a roll and then an oil leak resulted in a forced retirement. Bertie mentioned the Scottish as being the low point of his season. *'It was a disaster from start to finish and I believe things just have to get better from now on. Certainly I can't see how they could get worse…'*

Two weeks after the low point of the Scottish Bertie would be more at home with the familiar territory of the Shell Donegal International where there was strong opposition from the Mantas of Coleman, McHale and Collins, the previous year's winner Bonner in an Ascona

(Bertie's old car), Malcolm Wilson in the Audi Quattro, and British legend Roger Clark in a 4 wheel drive Sierra.

Though the competition was hot, the weather was not and it was particularly wet, the wettest Donegal ever witnessed at that point although the reintroduction of pace notes on a trial basis left crews more confident with the road conditions they would face along the considerable 375 mile route, with 225 stage miles on some 27 stages over the three long days.

With the car having got a bit of a battering on the Scottish International 10 days previously, it was a challenge for the Sydney Meeke team in the Bush, Co. Tyrone to get it fully fit and ready for the Donegal International Friday start in Letterkenny and it would be 5am of the morning of the start when the mechanics completed the final touches to the car.

For the first two days Bertie had an almost faultless rally, building up a comfortable lead that even a 15 seconds road penalty for catching the 00 car on stage 13 still left him with a comfortable lead of over half a minute. But the second run through his old nemesis Fanad Head was to undo all the good work when an off dropped

him down the field with an unbridgeable deficit to the leaders, especially after any chances of a comeback or snatch of a higher placing on Sunday's stages were put to rest when his Manta 400 punctured losing an additional 30 seconds.

At the end of the day Bertie finished a disappointed third some two and a half minutes behind Austin McHale who in turn trailed Billy Coleman by 31 seconds.

With the Rentatruck Ulster International Rally coming up at the end of July, and wanting to carry out additional Pirelli tyre testing on tarmac, Bertie decided to tackle the 2-day Sligo Rally the week before the Ulster.

Wary of the potential consequences of damaging the car and not having it ready for the Ulster which was a bigger priority for Bertie, Austin Frazer was quoted in the Belfast Telegraph *'While to all intents and purposes we are seeded No.1 and competing in Sligo, there will be no question of risking the car. Bertie is keen to put in some tyre testing and the best way to do it satisfactorily is in competitive conditions'.*

Unfortunately the rally was brought to an early close after a freak accident when Bertie Law's Chevette hit a milk churn by the roadside which in turn struck an elderly local spectator who later passed away due to the injuries he received. A late overnight meeting of rally or-

far left: Working on rear brakes on a wet and miserable Donegal International

left: Bertie flying high on the Ulster towards a 4th place overall, despite an accident

below: Bertie slithers sideways through a slalom of corners on the Donegal Rally

right: Audi works driver German Walter Röhrl came to the Ulster in the mighty 500bhp Short Wheel Base Quattro and blitzed the opposition

above: Spectators help extract Bertie from the scenery on the Ulster in '84

ganisers and stewards resulted in Sunday's stages being cancelled and the Day One results standing, a sad end to an enjoyable day of rallying. Bertie's performance during the rally gave him a boost of confidence leading up to the Ulster Rally the following weekend and with four days of a recce due to complete, there wouldn't be much time for relaxing before Ulster Rally mode started!

On the Ulster, the talk of the town was the new short wheel base Audi Quattro Sport, which had not been seen on the island of Ireland in action before. On this occasion it was piloted by Audi Works driver Walter Röhrl who, despite not having competed in Ireland before, obliterated the opposition with his aggressive fire spitting, 500 brake horse power German monster dominating the top spot on the leader board from start to finish to

win by over four minutes, with potentially much more in reserve if he had needed it.

For everyone else it was very much a case of who was the best of the rest. And the best of the rest was Russell Brookes in the Opel Manta 400 who was nip-n-tuck with GM team mate Jimmy McRae throughout. Bertie finished much further back in fourth, having had early brake troubles and then an accident on Stage 10 when he was caught out by the quick changing road conditions from dry to wet. Hitting standing water when slowing for a junction, the Manta slid off the road into a field and rolled on to its roof.

Although the damage was seemingly only cosmetic, by the time spectators got the car righted and the crew were able to continue, the time loss was considerable.

left: Action from the Manx

Up until that point Bertie had punched in several impressive times including a fastest overall on Stage 9, Marble Arch, by 6 seconds from Röhrl.

Despite the high attrition rate among the leading competitors with DNFs from Malcolm Wilson, Harald Demuth, Per Eklund, Austin McHale and Alan Johnston the time loss from the accident, which was well over five minutes, was too much to ever consider getting on the podium so it was a despondent Bertie who battled on to finish fourth.

Although it may not have been apparent to many at the time, Bertie's car actually was more seriously damaged than initially thought, and with several crashes during the car's 14 event history to date since the Donegal in 1983, Sydney Meeke's team decided to rebuild the car.

So with that 'fresh pair of heels' Bertie set off to his next rally which was the Rothmans Manx International Rally where he would face another all-star line-up over 49 stages. The usual British Championship regulars were joined by Hannu Mikkola in the same short wheel base Quattro as Röhrl used on the Ulster and Juha Kankkunen replaced the injured Henri Toivonen in the Rothmans Porsche 911 with Roger Clark doing '00 car' duties in a similar car.

However, despite their stellar billing, come the start neither of their efforts lasted long. Mikkola's Audi jammed in fourth gear on the fourth stage, and Kankkunen went out on the same stage after an initial skirmish with a bank and then later engine failure.

After that initial drama it was the Opel Mantas of Brookes and McRae in that order who led with only seconds between them, and Tony Pond in the ARG Rover Vitesse in third. Bertie Fisher was back in sixth, slowed by continuing brake problems with the Manta. The brake issue was a common problem with Mantas at the time and a new homologation clause was expected two weeks after the Manx to allow bigger brakes, and though Bertie had tested them coming up to the Manx they had to make do with the then currently homologated smaller brakes.

Despite the braking problems Bertie continued to push hard, reeling in and overhauling the big Rover of Pond who then dropped out of contention when he lost 2 minutes when a wheel disintegrated mid-stage. Up front, Brookes and McRae continued to have a ding-dong battle until Friday evening when Brookes crashed out on Tholt-y-Wil leaving McRae with a huge 11 minute margin over Bertie who, although now up into second

right: Tony Pond in the ARG, Daily Mirror backed Rover SD1 who finished in third on the Manx behind second placed Bertie

utes behind McRae, and far enough ahead of Pond in third to not have to push and lose his position with a mistake.

This second place finish on the Manx was undoubtedly Bertie's best result of the year and it meant he finished 5th overall in the championship helping secure the manufacturers championship for Opel – some consolation for a relatively lack lustre year overall.

Although not originally planned in Bertie's GMDS calendar schedule, Bertie decided to compete on the RAC Rally, his first ever World Rally Championship event, at the end of November and following on from the great Manx Rally result, a deal was done to do the rally.

With its traditional position of being the last round of the World Championship the RAC had attracted the absolute world's best rally teams and although Bertie and Austin would have competed with some of them in various British Championship rounds during the year, their relative inexperience at this level was reflected in their seeding at 37.

37 was probably not the best road positioning but nevertheless they soon got down to business on the mammoth 1600 mile event over four days which took competitors at that time right through England from near its borders with Wales right up to near the Scottish borders and back down to its base in Chester before doing a full day in Wales.

Given his lack of experience on the stages used, Bertie was probably never in with a chance for overall glory but he drove a steady sensible rally, 21st overall after the first

left: Bertie and Austin together on the RAC

Prior to the rally it became apparent that Bertie's usual co-driver at the time, Austin Frazer would not be able to spare the time required for the duration of the mammoth recce and rally so with Bertie being part of the GMDS setup, Russell Brookes' co-driver Mike Broad contacted his friend John Millington for the job.

On the Audi Sport Rally, the warm-up rally for the RAC, Bertie and John finished fourteenth overall.

Recently John reflected on his trial with Bertie saying: *'Unfortunately it did not work out partly because the car was so late arriving they had no time to wire in the 'poti' which I needed for reading the maps... I tried without it but it didn't work and I reckon I lost the RAC ride as a result. It was a pity I did not push harder to have it wired in, a valuable lesson for future years'*

However that wasn't the end of John's involvement with Bertie. *'I was a friend of Mike [Broad] so he offered me the job of chase car for Bertie & Austin [On the RAC], which I really enjoyed, sitting next to Sydney Meeke. We became good friends after this event and I ended up working for Bertie again later on when we ran his Sierra from RED, with Rory K co-driving for him'*

place, never really showed his true potential on this rally due to the chronic brake troubles.

In the closing stages of the event Bertie was to experience further car difficulties when a gearbox mounting broke requiring some road side servicing between stages costing some 40 seconds of stage times of a penalty, but he was far enough ahead of Pond for it to have been an issue. He did however punch in a few fastest times in the latter half of the rally and ended up staying in second place till the finish, albeit a huge 13 min-

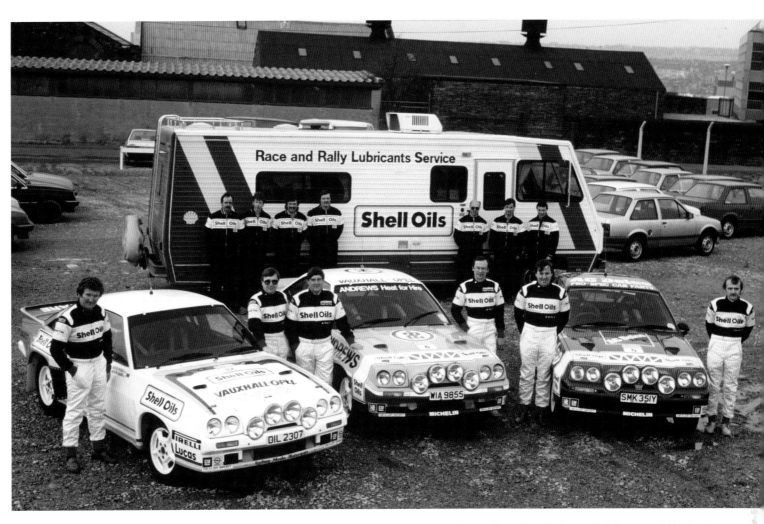

The GMDS supported team of L-R Bertie Fisher/ Austin Frazer, Russell Brookes and Mike Broad and Jimmy McRae and Ian Grindrod and the GMDS mechanics

day and steadily increasing the pace right to the end of the rally. There were a few minor but time consuming snags such as the car slipping off a quick release lifting jack while changing a puncture late in to the rally, losing them about 6 minutes. Sydney Meeke and his team of mechanics only had to carry out routine servicing and precautionary parts replacements including a back axle which was replaced when Bertie heard an unusual noise which subsequently turned out to be nothing more than mud on the brake callipers.

Bertie eventually completed the marathon event in a highly credible ninth position overall – the first driver from Northern Ireland to have finished in the top ten of a World event since Paddy Hopkirk.

Up front, Ari Vatanen took the top spot in the Peugeot

205 Turbo after a last day fight with Hannu Mikkola in the Audi where the lead changed several times in the space of the last leg.

Bertie's GMDS team mates Russell Brookes and Jimmy McRae finished 5th and 7th overall respectively, and as a team they were awarded the Trade Team Award for General Motors.

In an interview with Brian Patterson for Carsport after the rally, Bertie was quick to answer the critics who may have doubted his ability on gravel. *'I'll not tell you a word of a lie – I was fed up with all this chat about me in the forests. I knew, I was convinced within myself that I could drive well in the woods. I started this rally with only one thought in mind – to reach the finish. I started very cautiously, and worked up to a pace which suited me. I*

used Phil Collins' times as my personal yardstick, and I matched his times from the word go'.

Bertie continued 'I learnt a lot on this rally about the techniques of forestry driving, and certainly I was able to do things in the car at the end of the rally that would have had me on the roof had I tried them at the start'.

The RAC Rally would see the end of the rallying season for Bertie, and it wouldn't be long till the action resumed at the start of 1985.

1985 Steady as she goes

For the 1985 season, the Fisher team strategy was to build on the successes and lessons learned in '84 with the, same co-driver, same preparation and the same car, although a change of emphasis within Shell meant that it would run under the predominantly white livery of Shell Oils rather than the gold of Shell Gold Card. Still part of the GMDS team, the British Championship would be the priority with a few select Irish events added throughout the year. In an interview with Sammy Hamill

in The Belfast Telegraph at the start of 1985, Bertie explains his options *'Although my contract with GMDS and Shell is for the British Championship, I would like to keep my options open on the Tarmac series, particularly as the Circuit of Ireland and the Ulster International are rounds of both championships.'*

The first round of the British Championship was again the National Breakdown Rally where Bertie had been a non-finisher in 84. However with an extra year's experience of British and international rallying under his belt, Bertie was aiming for a decent result which, despite an early roll on Stage 4 and some gearbox selection problems later on in the rally, he duly achieved with a successful 5th Overall.

Back home, and with the Circuit of Ireland looming in April, Bertie made a last minute decision to tackle the Cavan National Rally as a pre-Circuit of Ireland tyre test All relatively routine except that for the first time in over 21/2 years Austin Frazer was not available to sit in the co-driver's seat for Bertie on an Irish Tarmac event.

When the first choice substitute, Davy Johnston, was unable to participate due to a family bereavement the next up was Rory Kennedy. Although they would not sit together for over another four years, their time together that day sowed the seeds for a close friendship, and a very successful partnership in rallying through all of the 1990s.

The event itself was made up of four stages looped three times giving competitors 92 stage miles to contend. And contend Bertie did in style. He dominated the rally to win with 3 and half minutes to spare from second

left: Being with Bertie on the Cavan rally was a bit of a shock for Rory as he explains:

'Bertie rang our house that Saturday and of course I wasn't there, but my father told him that I was definitely going to the Cavan rally the next day. With no mobile phones there was no way to contact us but my father assured him I would definitely be there OK

The first I knew of it was when I drove up to rally HQ at the Kilmore Hotel an hour before the start of the rally and I got chatting to Ian Cuddy, a mechanic in Sydney Meeke's team, who told me "Bertie's looking for you"

I asked Ian if he knew what he wanted and when he said it was because he was needing a co-driver, I was stunned and was wandering round in a state somewhere between shock and cloud nine. Then Bertie came up and said "Well, Are you ready to go?" – was I heck!

Here was me, a real rookie at the time, being asked to sit beside one of Irish rallying's superstars. It was like going to watch a Man United match and being asked to play! It was the chance of a lifetime and no way was I going to refuse

I quickly arranged for my girlfriend Paula to go with some friends to watch the rally while I tried to prepare himself for the day ahead. I got the loan of a racing helmet from someone but I used my own clothes rather than trying to find racing overalls, which were not mandatory at that time

Ready for action, we headed off towards the first stage, but with my head still buzzing from the excitement of the whole thing,

I promptly got us totally lost on the way with no clue as to where we were on the road section – not a good start! Fortunately, after a bit of gathering my thoughts together, I was able to get us back on track and, although we finally arrived at the start of the first stage late, in them days the timing system was a bit different and we weren't penalised

Once we got through the first stage I settled down and, once I got into it, I just felt this is where I should be and as the day went on I got more confident and things just got better and better

I was mad keen to impress or at least show Bertie I had what it took to be his co-driver and to be able to build up some rapport in the car between us. I'd like to think I'm pretty easy to get on with and on a rally, I don't call the shots, it's up to the driver to make the calls - and if he wants something, its up to me to try to make it happen to leave him free to get into the right frame of mind to do the job

I felt that I had brought a bit of that to the table in Cavan and that set the seed for our future relationship – and of course leading the rally from start to finish didn't do any harm and completed a fairy tale story!'

right: Bertie on the Sally Gap stage in the County Wicklow Mountain stages on the 1985 Circuit of Ireland

In the mid 80s the 'Circuit' attracted huge crowds with an estimated 1 million people turning out to watch in 1986

placed former British Junior International Alan Johnston in a Group A Toyota Corolla and could afford not to push to the extreme while still making it a worthwhile test for different types of tyre compound in anticipation for the Circuit of Ireland.

And so to the Rothmans Circuit of Ireland International Rally, headed from the start by Michele Mouton – the first time ever in its history the rally would be led by a lady driver – in her Audi Sport Quattro, similar to that used by Röhrl used on the Ulster the previous year.

Although Mouton started the rally as favourite, there were many other top seeds aiming for glory, including Malcolm Wilson and David Llewellyn in older model Audi Quattros, Per Eklund in a Toyota Supra, Billy Coleman and Frenchman Bernard Beguin in Rothmans Porsche 911s, Tony Pond in the Rover Vitesse SD1 and then a host of Mantas including those of Jimmy McRae, Russell Brookes, Austin McHale, Phil Collins and of course, Bertie plus many more top drivers and cars. With five days of action, covering 560 stage mile, and a total route mileage of 1500 miles, it would be a gruelling event for the 90 odd starters.

Despite the high speed nature of the event, due to it's marathon length drivers would have to pace themselves accordingly. Almost as soon as the rally had started its 52 stage run though, several of those top seeds were

side-lined with problems. Wilson's Quattro had a blown engine on Stage one and although Mouton's early pace was impressive with several fastest times, she retired the Quattro after stage 8 with hydraulic failure.

The big talking point of the event was the battle between McRae and Brookes in their similar Opel Manta 400s who, for two thirds of the rally, were so close that they often tied on times. Tensions heightened as the rally went on and there appeared to be a certain sense of awkwardness between the two drivers as it began to look like the two were going to keep driving as hard as they could right to the end, running the risk of a crash or mechanical problem dropping one or both of them out of contention and jeopardising important British Championship points.

To avoid such consequences, the GMDS Team Management ordered that Brookes should give way to McRae and both backed off as a result, although neither of them appeared to be happy with having to do so. The final results show McRae winning the rally by almost two minutes from Brookes with Bertie, who had suffered several problems including a time consuming puncture, finishing up third overall having managed to punch in several fastest times during the rally to make it a fantastic Opel 1-2-3 trio, a successful event for the GMDS team all round.

The results of the Circuit combined with the results of the National Breakdown where Russell Brookes finished 2nd, Bertie 5th and Jimmy McRae failed to finish, moved Bertie into second place overall in the British Champion-

left top: The top three finishing co-drivers on the Circuit of Ireland, pictured with Rothmans PR girls at the City Hall in Belfast. From left, Mike Broad, Ian Grindrod and Austin Frazer

below: Bertie's car sits in service during the event

ship – a fantastic bonus for Bertie going into the Shell Welsh International rally which would bring them up to the half-way point of the season. Despite this, Bertie's expectations for the event were not huge as they were back again to the loose surfaced stages where the Audi's four wheel drive and traction would give them a big advantage over the Opel. And so it turned out..

Bertie went off the road on the second running of one of the DYFI stages after beating Jimmy McRae's time by 10 seconds on the first run through. Although he was able to

continue, Bertie soon ran into more problems culminating in an 'off' on Waunmarteg which forced his retirement.

After a brief interlude back on the local scene when he won the Alumac Davagh Stages Rally, a short tarmac event through the single venue of Davagh forest, located between Cookstown and Omagh it was back on the British championship trail with the gravel stages of Scotland for the Lloyds Bowmaker Scottish International.

While it was one of the 4WD Audi Quattros which won the rally at the hands of Malcolm Wilson, the 2WD brigade put up a good fight with the remaining podium places filled by the Opel Mantas of Jimmy McRae and Russell Brookes with Bertie slotting into fourth, once again ahead of Tony Pond in the Rover Vitesse.

Two weeks after the Scottish rally was a rally a bit closer to home, the Shell Donegal International Rally. This rally was originally down on Bertie's contract calendar as one of several non-British Championship rallies he was

right top: Bertie raises clouds of dust on the gravel stages of the Welsh International Rally

below: Bertie relaxes at service, on the Lloyds Bowmaker Scottish International whilst catching up on the latest news of the day

considering competing on throughout the year, budget permitting.

However with the British series being Bertie's main priority in 1985, around this time a number of factors conspired to hamper him from being to compete the 3 day rally at the level required to run the Manta 400. Several weeks before the rally Bertie, in an interview with the *Belfast Telegraph*, explains some of the reasons '*I've costed out the price of going to Donegal and it will take over £7,000. That's a large slice to take out of a budget that is earmarked for the British Open Championship – and that price assumed the car comes back from Donegal in one piece, something it hasn't done in the past couple of years. I don't feel I can justify the costs and unless there is some support from the organisers or their sponsors, Irish Shell, I don't expect to be doing the rally.*'

Hinting at the interest of doing several European events, he continued, '*Apart from the financial side, there is a great deal more to be gained from reasonable results in Europe, when it's measured against even a win in Donegal.*'

So it looked like Bertie would not be doing the Donegal, but then, an 11th hour phone call from a certain County Armagh businessman offering to inject the needed funds to do the rally would save the day. That man was Kieran McAnallen of Alumac, and that phone call would be the formal beginnings of a 15 year sponsorship, an important business partnership and close personal friendship. Though Kieran had known Bertie for some time previously as fellow competitor and a long-time friend of the local rally fraternity, it was partly as a result of Bertie having come to compete on the Alumac sponsored Davagh Rally organised by Dungannon Motor Club for the previous two running's and giving all his winnings away from finishing top spot on both occasions, that spurred Kieran to make the call and as-

left top: Donegal Rally 1985 - Originally Number 2 but retired with mechanical issues, Tony Pond and Rob Arthur later ran as 007 car on what was the Metro 6R4's international debut on a tarmac event

centre and right: Bertie's inaugural rally carrying Alumac livery, the Donegal International in '85

bottom: Austin McHale sideways in his Opel Manta 400. He lost the rally by one second to Billy Coleman in the Rothmans Porsche 911

sist Bertie on his way. Additional funding would come from Dealer Opel Team Ireland who had been helping several competitors through their efforts in the Irish tarmac Championship for the previous few seasons, Austin McHale, Billy Coleman, Maria Moloney and Frank Fennell all previous beneficiaries of DOTI's assistance.

Bertie started the rally as one of the favourites, but there were others. Austin McHale in his similar Opel Manta 400, Billy Coleman in the Rothmans Porsche 911 were both there as was Englishman Tony Pond giving the ARG (Austin Rover Group) Metro 6R4 its international debut

On the rally itself, it did not quite go to plan for Bertie. Seeded at Number 13 because of the late entry, you would hope that the number would not be a bad omen of luck but as it happens on just the third stage he retired after the rear axle failed on the Manta 400. That was not the end of the weekend's rallying for Bertie though, as he would do Sweeper car, Car 008, for the remainder of the event in the subsequent two days. Pond's car also broke down and he too ran as a 00 but up front the big battle was between McHale and Coleman. So much of a battle was it that with just one stage remaining there were only 8 seconds between the two. Billy Coleman ended up winning after McHale overshot and Coleman grabbed a few of those seconds, the final winning margin, a mere one second!

left: Bertie at Lurgan park where the car retained its Alumac decals following the early retirement in Donegal

Stephen Finlay who would just a few years later go on to be one of Ireland and the UK's leading drivers. He was there in a Lotus Sunbeam and had finished a fantastic eighth overall.

It was back to familiar tarmac territory again for the British Midland Ulster International Rally, the penultimate round of the British Championship and also a round of the STP Irish Tarmac Championship. There was a huge entry with many overseas and works entries from Peugeot, Opel, Toyota, Austin Rover, and also the Irish debut of the S1 Audi Quattro, here in the hands of Michele Mouton. And though many of the crews fell by the wayside, including Moutons big Audi, Bertie drove a consistent rally despite being dogged with gear box problems early on Although a fresh gearbox was installed at service in Armagh it too caused trouble, losing fourth gear. Despite losing more time with a puncture on Glendun and a loose prop shaft late in to the rally adding to the tales of woe which had dropped him down as far as 12th place overall at one point, Bertie clawed his way back up to finish a steady 5th place overall and also win the Belfast Telegraph Award for top local finisher. The top four places ahead of him comprised GMDS team mates Russell Brookes and Jimmy McRae who made it an Opel 1-2, Finnish driver Mikael Sundstrom in the Peugeot 205 T16 in third and Welshman David Llewellyn in a works Audi Quattro fourth.

Since the inception of the rally Manta 400s it was widely known they were a heavy car and lighter less powerful cars were often more nimble and quicker than the

The following weekend saw Bertie's make his annual trip to the tight lanes of Lurgan for the Lurgan Park Rally where he finished a close second place to winner Kenny McKinstry with Austin McHale, Manta, and Fred Crawford, Escort, tied for third place.

His home rally the Lakeland stages followed a couple of weeks later. With regular co-driver Austin Frazer serving as Clerk of the Course, his place was taken by Opel Dealer and a supporter of the GMDS scheme Crawford Harkness the pair duly won the rally outright by 53 seconds over some 40 stage miles in total ahead of George Robinson in a Starlet with Alan Johnston third in his Toyota Corolla.

The rally wasn't entirely without its faults for Bertie as he had a puncture on an 11½ mile stage where he drove the last 6 miles of the stage on the flat. An interesting aside worth mentioning is that Bertie donated the class awards he won on the event to a 17 year old driver taking part in his very first event – County Tyrone man

right top : *right top :* Sideways action on the Ulster Rally

Dogged by gearbox problems on the event, at one stage on stage 3 the car stuck in neutral but Bertie's mechanical nous came to the rescue when he borrowed a penny from a nearby spectator with which he unscrewed the gearbox cover and managed to select and jam the gearbox into third gear to get him out of the stage and on to service

below: The three GMDS Mantas sit in service on the Ulster with Sydney Meeke keeping a close eye on the operations at Bertie's area

boaty, under-steering Mantas. To try and combat this disadvantage Bertie's GM team mates Russell Brookes and Jimmy McRae had been using Mantas with numerous modifications to reduce the weight of the original shells as well as changing their shells every few rallies since they started using Mantas in early 1984. Bertie on the other hand was still using his original shell which by this stage was getting quite tired so Sydney Meeke set about acquiring a shell and making modifications to make his own lightweight model of the Manta, specifically developed for the Irish tarmac stages.

The debut of this car, DIL 9482, would be the Tudor

left top: One of the many Audis who fell by the wayside on the Manx in 1985, here is French driver Michele Mouton with co-driver Fabrizia Pons in the Audi Quattro E2 which retired after an accident

Bertie fought his way back up the leader board, in to the top ten and eventually in to the top three.

Some would say this was one of his finest drives given the stature of the works and semi works car and driver combinations that finished below him in the top ten but the big talking point was the performance of the Audis.

For a team who were doing so well at World Rally Championship level and who were trying desperately to break the continuing successes of the Opels in British and Irish rallying, it was quite a disastrous event.

Michele Mouton's Audi Quattro S1 retired relatively early on after some chronic brake troubles, suspension and fuel pump problems and a huge time penalty, all topped off with an off on Stage 21.

Malcolm Wilson who, in his private older Quattro A1, had won every forestry round of the British Championship that year, was loaned a more powerful and newer short wheel base Quattro E1 for the Manx but he found it difficult to get to grips with the six speed box, lost a bonnet mid stage, lost some gears on his gearbox and, though he took the lead for a while, had a huge accident on Stage 21 ending in a burnt out car forcing retirement

David Llewellyn in his longer, older Quattro A2 had numerous small problems and his rally ended with a failed engine. There was a fourth Audi, German Harald Demuth, also in an A2 example Quattro but never really threatened the lead and finished in fourth, the only Audi UK driver to finish the Manx Rally, two years in a row!

Austin recollects this particular rally as one of his most

Webasto Manx International Rally, the final round of the British Championship, and Bertie's last rally of the year. The line-up of entries was a similar situation to the Ulster with many of the British and Irish Championship regulars as well as a select few big overseas entries. Despite the promise of all of the big entries, once again it was the Opels who triumphed at the top of the time sheets in a UK GMDS 1-2-3, With Russell Brookes taking top spot, Jimmy McRae a comfortable second and Bertie a further minute behind.

A good result eventually but on the first day of the rally it wouldn't have been a result many would have predicted. On the Injebreck stage, the misinterpretation of a pace note resulted in a skirmish with a bank costing some 90 seconds, a badly bent Track Control Arm and other cosmetic damage such as a bent wing and flapping loose bonnet, but able to continue. This, along with 1m 40s in road penalties, put him down as low as 24th place at one point but over the space of several days

right: Action from the Tudor Webasto Manx International Rally

al Rally in February and Bertie was there in his Manta 400 along with the usual STP Irish Tarmac Championship regulars such as Austin McHale and John Coyne in Mantas 400s, Cyril Bolton and Ian Donaldson in Metro 6R4s and Billy Coleman in a Rothmans Porsche 911 who was joined in the Rothmans team by someone more accustomed to the scorching heat of the dessert than Irish Tarmac Winter rallying – multiple desert rally winner and double winner of the Middle East Rally Championship Qatari Saeed Al Hajri, known as 'King of the Dunes'.

Given the conditions of some lying snow and patches of black ice as later shown quite clearly by the in car camera installed by RTÉ / UTV for the very first time in a car driven by Bertie, Saeed Al Hajri's eventual second place behind team mate Coleman in a Porsche 1-2 was a remarkable result.

Bertie's rally started out well but it was to no avail when he ended up stopping for some fourteen minutes mid stage on the Corkscrew stage in County Clare with electrical problems setting the stage for a stirring fight back which had progressed as far as 8th place on the Sunday when an event occurred which would not only put him out of the rally but would have ramifications for his whole future in rallying.

As rally cars had progressed through the years, from the sluggish boaty production Volvos of the 1950s, to the humble but nimble Mini special models of the 1960s, to the ultra-competitive rally pedigree Group1 & Group 4 Escorts of the 1970s and the bigger more powerful purpose built Group B Mantas and Quattros of

left: Following the lack of success of the numerous Audis on the Manx, Bertie brought the house down at the prize giving with his version of Pete Seegar's *Where have all the flowers gone?* reworked as *Where have all the Audis gone?*

Although it started as a joke in his and co-driver Austin Frazer's bedroom at their hotel, the joke ended up becoming something of a legend.

Austin takes up the story: *'After the champagne celebrations etc. at the finish control, we retired to our hotel to get cleaned up. I was tidying up books and maps and stuff and Bertie was lying in the bath where I could hear him singing away to himself*

I asked him what he was singing and he said "Wait to ye hear this… Where have all the Audis gone, long time passing. Where have all the Audis gone, long time ago. Bent and crashed them every one"'

Austin continues: *'He said "I wonder could I sing that at the prize giving" and I said "Not if you want to drive for Audi any time soon – better talk to the boss"*

Later at the prize giving there was the usual huge Irish contingent there who gave Bertie and me a great reception and after the awards were presented, Bertie, who'd spoken to the boss in the meantime started to sing the song and it went down very well with the audience and it was a big deal for Opel who got a lot of mileage out of it– but as you may notice, Bertie never drove an Audi afterwards! '

memorable rallies for so many reasons, but also a separate trivial one. *'I remember on the last day we had about two more stages to do and on a road section Bertie pulled over into a filling station, not to get petrol but to go into the shop. When he came out about 5 or 10 minutes later I said "what was that all about" and he said "I was on the phone to Gladys, and I told her to get in touch with Doreen* [Austin's wife]*, and hire a helicopter from St Angelo and come over to the prize giving". Unreal. And they did just that.'*

For him to be making such a plan during the rally, just for his wife and friend to come to the prize giving, shows how much it must have meant to him to have been nearing a third place finish on this rally whilst many of the more powerful teams faulted.

1986 - The Edge of Disaster

The International Tarmac season started as usual in Galway for the Clarenbridge Crystal Galway Internation-

the 1980s, speeds were increasing dramatically and many in the sport were beginning to express concern that these increases in speed were not being matched by advances in spectator safety.

With cars right on the limit hurtling past crowds of spectators within touching distance, all the elements were in place for a disaster which could threaten the very existence of the sport. As Bertie and Austin pushed to make up for lost time that Sunday, thanks to the advances with in car camera technology, everyone was given a taste of how simply such a disaster could occur – saved only by good luck and Bertie's remarkable skill.

Approaching a hairpin after a long, fast, flat out straight Bertie hit the brakes at over 100 mph, and his foot went straight to the floor as the Manta suffered complete brake failure.

Co-driver Austin Frazer recalls the incident vividly: *'I can picture it like it was yesterday. There were a lot of spectators out on the Sunday stages, they were packed, lining the sides of the roads and at some of the junctions they were standing in dangerous places. At the corner before the brakes failed where we had to take 90 left at a junction with the slip road blocked, maybe 10 deep with spectators – they weren't right up at the mouth of the junction but they definitely weren't sufficiently far back.*

After that junction there was another very long straight, followed by a hairpin right at a junction. This particular junction was locked into the inside of the route of the stage so the general public people didn't have access to it, but there was just a rope across it, and there was

a woman and three kids standing straight in line as we were coming down to it, at high speed.

As we approached the junction, I had my head down, calling the notes and I could feel Bertie hitting the brakes, and for a fraction of a second they caught and then the car just went forward. I looked up and the woman and three kids were just standing there with a wee bit of gap between where the kid nearest the road edge was and the grass verge or bank. He [Bertie] went for the gap, for there was no chance or no way of getting stopped and

right top: Leaving the start ramp at the Galway Rally 1986

below: 'King of the dunes' Qatar driver Saeed Al Hajri who on his very first ever drive on tarmac and in tricky icy conditions, finished second in the Rothmans Porsche 911 SCRS

left: Icy conditions on the Corkscrew Mountain stage – the rally attracted large number of spectators despite the inclement weather

tween the marshal's car and a wall and I had a go and got it through.'

Austin takes up the story again. *'We turned, came back to the junction, stopped and talked with the woman and kids for a few minutes to check on them. They were all alright, none of them had been touched, and I was all for getting back quickly onto the road again but Bertie said "No that's it, I couldn't drive after that". I think what hit him was if that brake failure had of been the previous corner, there would have been dozens killed, it really was scary.'*

They continued, still in shock and limping out to the end of the stage and pulled out of the rally shortly after.

we went straight through it, took the rope and all with us and eventually got the car stopped by coming down the gears.'

Bertie, in an interview with RTÉ after the incident, described what happened in his own words *'We were coming down a straight … well in excess of 100 mph, and normally at that sort of speed I would leave myself 75 – 100 yards for braking the car as it was very clean dry tarmac so I was braking very heavy and very late. When I braked, there was just a snap inside the car, a click like something broke and the pedal went straight to the floor.*

All I could see was a car and a lot of people in front of me, and I saw two small children, and I had my hand on the hand brake with the thought of spinning the car, but I feel if I had of spun it at that point I would've been out of control and would probably have hit some of the people. I just hoped that the children would move out of the way but they just seemed to freeze in their position. At the last minute I saw what I thought was enough of a gap be-

The incident might not have had quite the impact on the rally family in Ireland that it eventually did except for the afore-mentioned camera which RTÉ/UTV had fitted for the first time to a car driven by Bertie. Despite their shaken state Bertie and Austin were aware of the likely footage stored on the camera and the possibility of it being used to sensationalise the incident in a way that would be to the detriment of rallying. As such they held on to the camera until they had conferred with the Opel team management and it was only handed over on the basis that it would be used to promote spectator safety, a wish which came to fruition as the clip was incorporated into many safety briefings and films which undoubtedly helped raise awareness among organisers, competitors and spectators .

Bertie had many near misses and serious accidents over his time in the driver's seat, but this one scared him to such an extent that he would not compete on another Irish Tarmac Rally for some 16 months – as Austin says: *'It really hit him hard, more than he talked about, but he said to me "That's me out for the rest of the year. What I'd like to do now is Safety Officer on a few events and put my efforts into that". He probably hadn't lost his nerves but anyhow he took a year out and did quite a few events as Safety Officer.'*

In an interview with Michael Lyster for RTÉ's flagship weekend sports programme Sports Stadium the week before the Circuit of Ireland, Bertie spoke about his decision to quit rallying and about the accident. *'It was a horrifying incident and one which we were very lucky to get away with. I think if it were a junction crowded with spectators there just would have been nowhere to go because there were stone walls on both sides and the speeds were well in excess of 100 mph. It seemed to last for a long time even though it was probably over in a few seconds in total.'*

In an interview with the Irish Independent in May that year, Bertie jokingly said *'I haven't cancelled all of my motorsport magazines just yet.'* But on a more serious note, he continued, saying *'It's very difficult to say whether or not I will ever drive a rally again. I certainly won't at such a high level. But for now, I'm just determined to see that all marshals are properly educated for the job they have got to do. The fact that children were involved in the Galway incident really got to me. Imagine if I had killed them. I just wouldn't have been able to live with myself. The man who lost his life in the Bushwhacker accident was an experienced rally spectator. It took me an awful long time to get over his death. But, if the kids had died because they simply didn't know better, I just don't think I could have coped.'*

On the wider rally scene the close shave in Galway was not an isolated incident but part of a wider pattern as rallying struggled to readjust to the vastly higher speeds made possible by advancing technology. Internationally three spectators were killed and dozens injured when the Ford of Joaquim Santos left the road in March's Rally de Portugal and closer to home in the Circuit of Ireland at Easter another Ford RS200 driven by Kalli Grundel struck a boy who was walking on the middle of a stage.

Although the spectator was badly injured, fortunately the incident did not result in any fatalities but, when taken together with Bertie's incident in Galway and what was happening on the international arena, it alarmed Ireland's governing body of Motorsport, the then R.I.A.C enough to declare a two-month ban on rallying in Ireland to allow every one involved to take stock and seek solutions to the safety issues.

With the Donegal International being the first major rally after that ban, it was down to Clerk of the Course at that time, Matt Doherty, and his team of organisers to up

right: Bertie took the Galway accident so serious he decided to put the Manta up for sale as seen by this advert which was in Motoring News

Despite the advert the car was not sold and he went on to bigger and better things with it the following year

left: Back in action on the Lakelands Rally

the efforts of safety on the rally. Given Bertie's availability and the high profile nature about his Galway incident, Matt asked Bertie and Austin Frazer to drive the Chief Safety Control Car on behalf of the R.I.A.C.

Fisher and Frazer would, along with the 'Marshals flying squad', stop at different points along the route where they felt there needed to be something done about crowd control or extra marshals required and sort the problems out as they went round the route, in an attempt to bring home the message of rally spectator safety to the general public.

The Donegal Safety car run by Bertie and Austin was a success. The rally went ahead and finished without any major spectator incidents and by the time Bertie came away the confidence he had lost after Galway was at least partly restored and in the Donegal 87 programme he was quoted to have said after the 86 event *'If all rallies were run like this one I would have no hesitation in competing again'.*

And compete again he did, albeit not on closed tarmac road special stages for some time and his return, when it did come was a gradual and low key affair – at least as low key as his superstar status in Ireland would allow.

Sydney Meeke at this time was developing a new prototype rally car based on a heavily modified Ford Orion shell and as part of a campaign to publicise and show it off, he wanted someone to drive his rally version on the Lurgan Park Rally at the start of July. Given their close bonds Sydney asked Bertie and he obliged, wooing the fans in Lurgan Park in a tail happy fun outing.

Following this toe-in-the-water outing, by the start of September Bertie decided he was ready to compete on his first proper competitive outing in seven months, on his home rally the Lakeland Stages forestry event. Interviewed at a pre-event function, Bertie was quoted to have said *'I never said that I had retired from rallying… I'll just do events which don't take as much time away from home.'*

Since Austin Frazer was once again doing Clerk of the Course duties on this rally, Bertie required a stand in co-driver. On this occasion it was friend and client, County Tyrone businessman Freddie Patterson who stepped in. Bertie and Freddie won the rally outright with one minute and one second to spare from second placed man Kenny McKinstry, with Pat Kirk over half a minute further back in third.

1987 All Change

Following his break away from the stages for the most part of 1986 and having satisfied himself that the spectator safety question was being addressed, Bertie had been planning to come back in the Manta at the start of 1987 and with an almost certain deal done to be part of the usual GMDS setup for the coming year, things were looking good for Bertie's return but events in the wider rallying world were to throw everyone's plans into the bin.

Having facilitated the creation of some of the most spectacular racing machines ever seen, the group B rules were now recognised as being too loose, allowing the

right top: Sydney Meeke's prototype Orion at Lurgan

below: Part of the preparations for the Lurgan Park Rally are that drivers go around the route of the course on bicycle. Here Mikael Sundstrom and Bertie pose for a photo. Mikael was present in a full works Peugeot 205 T16, and by chance the exact car which Bertie would drive on the Millennium Motorsport Festival at Stormont in Belfast in 2000, his last public outing in a rally car

development of lightweight racers with stratospheric power outputs which simply were too fast to be allowed to compete in an environment where large numbers of spectators would be in close proximity.

Accidents such as that which claimed the life of Attilio Bettiga who passed away after injuries sustained in a crash in his Lancia 037 on the Tour de Corse in 1985, the Joaquim Santos accident in Portugal in 1986 and the deaths of Henri Toivonen and Sergi Cresto when their Lancia Delta S4 left the road in the 1986 Tour de Corse

and burst into flames when the fuel tank ruptured were demanding a major rethink.

Faced with threats to the very existence of rallying from numerous quarters – from concerned civil authorities to wary insurance companies – FISA felt they had no option but to ban group B from international competition from the start of the 1987 season to be replaced with group A which harked back to a previous and safer generation of rally cars.

Unfortunately for Bertie, although his Manta 400 had

left and right: Bertie and Austin's return to closed road special stage rallying was successful with immediate effect, with a comfortable outright victory on the Manx National Rally, an event Bertie would go on to win three times in all.

much more in common with these earlier generation cars than the turbo charged 4 wheel drive plastic skinned missiles that Group B had spawned, it was none-the-less homologated as a group B car and thus subject to the ban.

Although the ban had an immediate and blanket effect at the very top levels of international rallying, a step or two down from this level the effect was more patchy. Thus Group B cars would be banned from the British Championship but they would be allowed in the Irish Tarmac Championship apart from the three events shared with the British Championship – the Circuit of Ireland, the Ulster and the Manx – at short notice leaving many drivers, including Bertie, without a suitable car in which to compete at the top level across a full championship.

For the first few months of the year, Bertie considered switching to a Group A car but there were a distinct lack of suitable and affordable cars available. Added to that was the fact most of the top Group A cars capable of winning internationals in 1987 were not of the GM/Opel brand and Bertie had no desire to break the long links with GMDS. As far as he was concerned, why should he dish out some potentially £50,000 for an unproven car when his own Manta, which really had not done an awful lot of rallying in total, was still very much a car to be reckoned with, as he would soon prove!

As summer approached Bertie had his eyes set on the Donegal International Rally planning to use Manx National rally a month earlier as a warm up to get settled back in the groove.

Bertie had not competed on the Manx National event before, but having tackled the Manx International around half a dozen times in the previous 15 years with two 2nds and a 3rd place finish overall under his belt, he was well experienced on the islands roads as he explained in an interview with Carsport *'I've always enjoyed competing on the big Manx rally in September but the FISA regulations are going to keep me out of that. This is the next best thing'*

Despite the presence of a number of Group A Sierra Cosworths which had proved its pace when Jimmy McRae had driven one to victory in the Circuit of Ireland, Bertie went to the island with high hopes for a top 3 finish. These hopes were well founded as he drove a steady drive to dominate the rally, winning outright by nearly four minutes ahead of second placed Phil Collins in a Sierra and Malcolm Wilson in a Metro 6R4 in third.

As Austin Frazer points out though, Bertie's return to the special stages on the Manx National was not so

left: Donegal action and *right* a sudden end for Austin McHale's rally

When the Manta was prepared for Donegal it was thought that fitting the rear axle with a higher ratio crown wheel and pinion would be beneficial but by day two with Austin McHale closing in it was realised that this was a mistake and the team needed to revert to the normal setup and mechanic Norman Burns was sent back to the Meeke workshop to strip and rebuild the spare axle to the normal spec

Norman takes up the story:
'It was 9-30pm before I got to the Workshop and I had to get my brother to help me lift the axle out of the car. Stripping and rebuilding an axle isn't a straight forward job so it was into the wee small hours before I got the crown wheel and pinion re-installed. With any normal people being in their beds I was then faced with the problem of getting the heavy axle back into the car but I managed to lift it, without the half shafts, brake discs and callipers into the back of the estate car where I completed the build.
Shortly after I was back on the road heading for the Downings service before the first Sunday stage where we changed the axle in about 10 minutes and sent him on his way.
At the Prize Giving that night Bertie singled me out to say that 'only for one man, Norman Burns, I would not have won the Rally – his hard work and a sleepless night won the Donegal International Rally for me and the Whole Sydney Meeke team. Being quite an emotional person, needless to say it brought tears of joy to my eyes!'

much about a required morale boost as just wanting to get back into the swing of things again. *'I don't think there was any real drama about it, we won it by nearly 4 minutes. There wasn't any sign of a loss of confidence after Galway, he was driving fine.'*

So on to the longer challenge of the three day Shell Donegal International Rally. Bertie had competed on this rally six times in the previous 10 years (with three of those six ending in retirement due to mishaps on Fanad Head, a real bogey stage for Bertie) but a win had proved elusive and this year would prove no easier with a strong lineup including Billy Coleman in the Rothmans Racing BMW M3 and Austin McHale in his Opel Manta 400 amongst others.

However, just like on the Manx National, the Manta never missed a beat all weekend and the much anticipated showdown between the Mantas and Billy Coleman's Prodrive BMW M3 never really surfaced. On just the second stage Billy Coleman, whose M3 didn't have a particularly appropriate suspension set up for the rough and dusty surface, backed right off in an attempt to preserve the car. So slow was he that the hard charging McHale who was next on the road caught him not even half way through the 11 mile stage and with the dust could not get past allowing Bertie to bolt into a significant 30 second lead after those first two stages ahead of Donegal man John Connor in second with McHale two seconds further back and Coleman nearly a minute down in ninth. After the dust incident on Stage 2 McHale clawed back some time in the following few stages and

he and Bertie were now in a battle for supremacy – but not for long.

McHale's seat came loose on a stage due to a split floor pan and as well as losing a little bit of time on the stage he also picked up a 10 second road penalty when he had to stop to fix it so he could continue his attack, setting several fastest stage times but, as the second day ended, Bertie was content with the 38 second lead he still held.

Day Three was a disaster for McHale. With Bertie piling on the pressure with several stage wins, on the second run through the traditional Sunday stage of Atlantic Drive, a fuel pipe came loose on McHale's Manta causing fuel starvation and spilling fuel into the footwell. He lost some five minutes attempting to fix it sufficiently to limp onto the end of the stage where he was able to sort the problem out and clear up the petrol soaked footwell but on the very next stage just over a blind crest his rally ended in a head on collision with a wall.

won five years previously in 1982 and with his success in Donegal he was one of the favourites. Although it was a round of the British Championship, much to the delight of the local fans, the organisers opted to allow group B cars to run among the British Group A contenders including David Llewellyn and Sebastien Lindholm in Audi Quattros, as well as Jimmy McRae, Mark Lovell and Phil Collins in Ford Sierra Cosworths. With the Group B cars being allowed the field was further strengthened by regular British visitors in Mantas such as Russell Brookes and Pentti Airikkala as well as a host of Irish Manta drivers including Austin McHale and Stephen Finlay.

Due to Bertie's temporary retirement from rallying he lost his former FISA 'A' driver rating and so was now demoted to a 'B' costing him several places in seeding posi-

left top: The nostalgic Hamilton's Folly Long jump. Video footage shows Bertie as jumping the longest on this famous stretch of road

below: The Mantas of Bertie's and Austin McHale's sit side by side in one of the sheds at Fisher Engineering where Saturday morning service was held

This allowed Bertie to cruise home without anyone in particular to worry about behind, the winning margin between him and John Connor who finished second being over 6 minutes. Fellow Donegal man James McDaid finished third to make it an Opel Manta 1-2-3 finish.

This was Bertie's second international rally win and given his many previous ill-fated attempts in Donegal the win was a welcome and well-deserved one as reflected in Bertie's quote to the Donegal News the week after the rally *'That was something of a change for us ... once we came through Fanad I felt it was almost over'*

The next major event on the calendar was the British Midland Ulster International Rally, a rally Bertie had

tion, starting at Number 11. Whether this acted as a spur for Bertie is not clear but in the weeks leading up to the rally, in an interview with the Belfast Telegraph he admitted he had never worked so hard in the build up to a rally, increasing the number of reconnaissance runs over each stage, and even changing the pace note system they used saying *'Normally I wouldn't check a stage more than twice but this new system is different and we want to make sure it works as well as we think it should.'* Prior to the rally Bertie identified Russell Brookes was the man to beat, saying *'Anyone who is in front of Russell Brookes will be winning the Ulster Rally'*, but he also made it clear he would not be discounting the Sierras.

It was a wise move not to discount them for Mark Lovell, very much a force to be reckoned with at the time in his distinctive yellow British Telecom 'Radiopaging' Sierra Cosworth, would be the man to get in front and, despite all of the other leading and works entries present, Bertie seemed to be the only one who could challenge the Englishman's times.

The two fought hard for much of the first day, swapping the lead several times and after six stages Bertie was in the lead by just eight seconds as they took on Hamilton's Folly. A tricky stage through the hilly Co. Down countryside, Hamilton's Folly is well know for its famous jump where the faster cars get serious 'air time' and in his epic battle with Lovel in 1987 Bertie beat them all with a 'long jump record' which was caught on still and video camera and is still used today in nostalgic rally TV pro-

grammes. However his exuberance was to no avail as a spin on the same stage was to drop him seven seconds behind Lovell.

As the Ulster Rally's second day's stages started, Lovell gave it maximum attack and started to pull away from the field as despite the Saturday stages based around the Clogher Valley and Fermanagh being very much home territory for Bertie, their open fast nature gave the Fords, with their greater power and top speed, the advantage over the Mantas.

In a subsequent interview in Carsport, Bertie admitted that he realised by service in Omagh on the late Saturday morning he could not catch Lovell: *'The fight had gone out of me. I was accepting defeat and maybe if I had been fresher and more on the ball I would still have been trying to win. But it is all water under the bridge now. With hindsight I might have done several things differently and might have won. On the other hand I might not have finished.'* Bertie talked also about Lovell's per-

right: Mark Lovell's distinctive BT 'Radiopaging' Sierra Cosworth on the Ulster Rally in 1987

Lovell went on to win back to back Irish Tarmac Championships in Sierras in 1987 and 1988

left top and below: Bertie and Austin in the hired Group N Sierra in a one off drive on the Manx Rally

Despite Bertie's downbeat post-mortem of the rally, some would say this was one of Bertie's finest drives for, in finishing second, he beat a field sprinkled with stars and displaying a rare strength in depth, with third placed Jimmy McRae in the RED Sierra Cosworth finishing over a minute and a half behind.

The Tudor Webasto Manx International Rally was next up but it was back to the same rules as the Rothmans Circuit of Ireland meaning he could not take his Manta. Although he had said earlier that he would not be able to compete, when Sydney Meeke spotted an advert in Motoring News offering a Group N Sierra Cosworth for hire the game was back on.

A group N Sierra wouldn't have been Bertie's first choice of car but as he explained in an interview with Carsport *'For a start I didn't have an alternative choice. There was nothing else available and although I had reservations about driving a Group N car, I'm looking forward to it for this one event. I don't think I would consider doing a whole season in Group N but in the circumstances I think it was the right decision for this rally.'*

formance during the rally: *'There is no doubt that Mark drove well, brilliantly in fact. I was expecting him to make at least one major mistake but he never did. And at the pace we were going, that has to be some achievement.'*

Despite his acceptance that a win was out of reach Bertie still set several fastest times in the closing stages but it was not enough and Bertie finished the rally in a very credible second overall, 57 seconds behind at the end.

At the time it was a pragmatic decision because Group A was in its infancy with many of the cars constantly developing in terms of homologation and parts, therefore it would have been foolish to buy a new car which could be out of date just a few months down the line.

The Sierra which Bertie ended up hiring was a Cosworth built by Chris Mellors for the Peacocks of London team. While Sydney Meeke did the negotiating with the car owners (unlike many hire arrangements, the Meeke mechanics would be running the car on the Manx and Sydney had to travel to Mellors' Workshop to get familiarised with the Sierra), Bertie enquired with long term sponsor Shell Oils about continuing their support despite the, albeit temporary, change of car. In order to help Bertie familiarise himself with the Sierras, given the last Ford he drove competitively was five years previously on the Manx Rally in the Mark Two Escort he finished 3rd overall on the rally in, David Lindsay of Lindsay Ford stepped in and supplied a road going version of the Cosworth.

Despite the unfamiliar machinery the Fisher / Meeke team took a comfortable lead in the class for the first few days ahead of the Sierras of Simon Stubbings, Ken Skidmore, and Peruvian Raymon Ferreyros, as well as the Mercedes Benz 190E 2.3 of Russell Morgan but on Stage 34 they ended up retiring from the rally with fuel pressure problems leaving Russell Morgan in the Mercedes to win.

Despite his retirement, the Manx was nevertheless a useful taste of competition in a Sierra helping Bertie make his mind up on a replacement for the Mantas which were coming to the end of the road in International rallying although Bertie's would have hoped there was life in the old dog yet as it was back to the Manta for the two day Fitzpatrick-Silver Springs Cork 20 International.

The Cork 20 at that time was the penultimate round of the Irish Tarmac Championship and, even though Bertie had not competed on the Circuit of Ireland and retired

right top: The aftermath of the famous incident on the Cork 20 in 1987 where three of the major competitors went out on one corner – first Billy Coleman in the BMW M3, second Bertie in the Manta, and third Simon Davison's Sierra

below: The crashed BMW and Manta lie side by side in a County Cork farmyard after the accident on the Cork 20

from the Manx, his win in Donegal and second place on the Ulster left him with a good cushion at the top of the Tarmac Championship but cushions can all too quickly be yanked away in the unforgiving Irish boreens!

With heavy overnight rain it was a very wet slippy start

left: Bertie on the Carling Rally of the Lakes 1987.

This was his last ever rally in a Manta, and the end of a five year relationship with the GM brand.

Note the unusually plain livery on the car compared to the rest of the year when the car had more colourful Shell Oils stripes and decals.

to the rally stage 3, just 50 yards from the stage end, a 'K Left' which had become covered with slippery mud since the crews had recced the stage, brought a premature end to the rally for three leading drivers. Billy Coleman was first to park it in the hedge with Bertie tucking in beside him before Simon Davison arrived to crash into the side of Bertie's car. Although he was able to continue, limping the short distance to the end of the stage, he retired immediately due to broken electrics.

Austin McHale, who also got caught out on the same bend but got away with a bent axle, was instantly promoted to the lead where he stayed for all over the remainder of the rally finishing nearly 5 minutes ahead of Vincent Bonner in second

Despite the disappointment of the Cork retirement, Bertie actually still led the Tarmac Championship, but now by a very slight margin. By the last round, the Carling Rally of the Lakes based in Killarney there were a total of four drivers who had a chance of winning the championship, with Bertie on 38 points and Ulster Rally winner Mark Lovell, Cork Rally winner and 1986 reigning Tarmac Champion Austin McHale and Circuit of Ireland winner Jimmy McRae all within 4 points. All would be in Killarney apart from McRae but despite the hopes for a championship showdown, the rally ended tragically short after day one when a car driven by Willie O'Brien and co-driven by Sean Conlon mounted a wall near the end of Molls Gap, the last stage of the day and held in darkness. After hitting the wall the car went down a 20 foot drop into a lake and although Willie escaped and survived, Sean Conlon got disoriented in the dark and swam away from the car. Although they were both taken to hospital, Sean died from his injuries and the organisers called an end to the rally in respect to his passing.

By that point Bertie had already retired following various problems with his car culminating in a burst radiator. McHale, despite having punched some impressive times early on, was also being slowed with various car niggles leaving Lovell leading by over a minute at the end of the first day when the rally was declared over.

With Lovell's win and Bertie's retirement Lovell was declared the 1987 winner of the Irish Tarmac Championship.

The Mac Connection
The story of a friendship, a sponsorship, a partnership

When the Fisher name comes up in rallying circles the Toughmac brand name will often be in close attendance such is the public perception of the strength of the bond between Bertie and his main sponsor over a long period of his rallying career. However the connection between Bertie and the man behind Toughmac, County Armagh businessman Kieran McAnallen, was if anything, even stronger than the public appreciated.

Kieran, who himself was a keen clubman driver for many years, competing right across the island of Ireland and winning numerous class awards on various disciplines of motorsport, including special stage rallies and night navigations as well as sprints explains how he first met Bertie in the mid 70s.

'I started rallying in 1970, and at the start would have mainly been competing on Night Navs in the Dungannon/North Armagh/ Enniskillen area but after I'd got a bit of experience I started to do rallies like the Bushwhack-

Navigated by Brian Quinn, Kieran drifting his Mk2 Escort on the 1984 Circuit of Ireland

er and the Erne Safari and I think it was probably at one of those two events where I first met Bertie. At the time Colm and Brian Quinn from Castlecaulfield were doing a bit of co-driving for me and, with Brian being very friendly

with and having co-driven for Bertie, it sort of spurred on the initial contact between me and Bertie into a standing friendship.'

Bertie at the time was an enthusiastic young rally man as well as an up and coming busi-

ness man with a serious competitive spirit, and no matter how you would have met him, he would have left a lasting impression on you'

Kieran and Bertie kept in regular contact throughout the late 70s and early 80s and as well as meeting up at rallies they began to socialise outside the sport as Kieran recalls

'Through the early days of knowing Bertie I eventually got to meet all of his family and get introduced to them. Socially, you could not meet as nice a family let it be in rallying, business or whatever.'

As Kieran's friendship with Bertie grew through the early Eighties so did Kieran's Benburb based business Alumac to the point where in 1984 he was approached by the local Dungannon Motor Club of which he was a member to sponsor a single-venue event they were running at Davagh Forest Park near Cookstown. Kieran agreed and Alumac sponsored the event throughout its early years with Kieran's friendship with Bertie bringing him to the event for the first two years as an invited guest winning the event outright on both occasions in his Opel Manta 400.

In 1984, Kieran's young son Philip had taken seriously ill, lapsing into a coma and, in an effort to try to bring him out of it, the doctors attending Philip suggested to Kieran, his wife Phil, and family to talk to Phillip and play sounds of things he would be familiar with. They chatted to Philip about all manner of things including rallying and when Kieran told Bertie about this, he immediately arranged to visit Philip at the hospital where he spent a lot of time talking to him, assuring him all was well.

In a relatively short time Philip made a full recovery from his coma and Kieran and his family believed that Bertie's visit had played a significant part in this, resulting in a deepening and cementing of the relationship between Kieran and Bertie.

With Bertie's sights set firmly on the British Championship campaign during 1985, he hadn't committed to competing on any of the non-British Championship Internationals in Ireland such as Galway or Donegal. That said, the Donegal was a rally he had never won, having competed on it nearly ten times at that point since his first run in 1973, and while in 1985 he had ultra-competitive machinery capable of winning it, ultra-competitive machinery requires ultra-expensive budgets to run and with all the efforts focussed on the British Championship rounds, Donegal was simply not going to happen unless there was a cash injection.

Bertie with Kieran's young son Philip shortly after he came out of the coma

And so Kieran's involvement as sponsor began. Having heard that Bertie was keen to drive in Donegal but did not have the budget to do so, he approached Bertie to see if there might be a sponsorship opportunity and thus Bertie arrived at the start of the 1985 Donegal International in an Alumac decalled Manta.

However Bertie's rally did not go well and Kieran recalls with some amusement how on

Kieran in the Alumac liveried Manta in Donegal in 1985

the first day Bertie had to pull in to the side of a stage and retire due to a seized rear axle and his sponsor overtook him!

'We passed him, coming down to a cross-roads – he was parked up on the heather and we took time to stop with him to ask what the problem was and there was a fair bit of banter between driver and sponsor!'

Although the deal was initially only for the Donegal Rally, following Bertie's early retirement from the event he agreed to keep the Alumac livery on the car for Lurgan Park and,

feeling that the arrangement had worked well, Kieran continued to be involved later in the year when Bertie resumed action on the British Championship rounds of the Ulster and Manx. This time there was no Alumac livery on the car, since GMDS and Shell Oils were responsible for the sponsorship decals of their team cars on the British Championship events but Kieran recalls

'We came to a mutual agreement that we understood we couldn't advertise on the car but were still happy to be on board.'

After the much publicised incident on the Galway Rally in 1986, Bertie took a hiatus from special stage rallying until he made his come-back in May 1987 on the Manx National Rally followed a month later by the Shell Donegal Rally where Alumac decals reappeared on the car after both Shell Oils and GMDS relaxed their stance having seen the benefits the strong friendship between Bertie and Kieran could bring the team.

From then until Bertie's very last rally, Kieran continued his sponsorship in one way or an-

Celebrating the big comeback rally win on the Manx National in 1987. Back from left: Maxie Patton, Austin Frazer, Kieran McAnallen, Bertie Fisher, Dessie Sayers. Front: Nigel Frazer & Mark Fisher

other, but it was more than just a financial contribution to the cause. Kieran was often present lending his expertise in meetings involving Bertie's rally program whether with other sponsors such as Mobil , preparation firms such as Prodrive or the plethora of other companies and organisations whose abilities needed to be harnessed to give any chance of success on the international rally stages.

As with all good partnerships benefits flowed both ways as the Fisher-McAnallen partnership blossomed and the sponsorship gave Kieran's Alumac company great exposure as Kieran sums it up

'He helped build my business up big time. The Alumac name was spread wide because of the

rally sponsorship and any man who had an interest in motorsport would give us a chance if there was work to be done.'

This partnership paved the way for many business deals which grew out of the strength of their rally partnership, as Kieran recalls.

'Bertie often said the strongest structure ever put together was steel and glass if it was done right'

Although the two did not tender for contracts together they were happy to help each other in any way they could.

'Bertie would have introduced me to architects that he would have known and vice-versa and many of them liked to have us both on a job because the friendship and partner-

ship that we had would ensure things would run smoothly – we had a combination that worked extremely well in a difficult economic and political climate. We both introduced each other to many new jobs and those would have been strong introductions although it didn't guarantee we would get the job unless the price and service was right as well.'

In 1989 Alumac undertook a major £2 million+ investment, expanding their business to around double the factory floor area and setting up Ireland's first glass toughening plant able to meet the latest standards within the industry. Bertie took a big personal interest in this project and was very much hands on, keen to help out wherever he could as Kieran recalls

'Bertie helped me design and lay out the new factory, which his company also built. Additionally he designed and built unique customised storage racks, which proved very useful, and are still in operation to this day in the factory.'

This was not an isolated example of them advising each other in business, as Kieran points out,

'From the time I got involved in sponsorship up to the time of the accident, any expansion I was planning in my business, Bertie was heavily involved as an advisor just as I was in return to him because there were a lot of similarities in the two businesses.'

It was at the time of the expansion into the toughened glass business that the company, previously formally known as K. McAnallen Ltd. began trading under the three subsidiary brands, 'Alumac' which made aluminium windows, 'Glassmac' which was a wholesaler of standard glass and 'Toughmac' which produced and sold toughened safety glass, and from mid-1989 onward all of Bertie's cars would run with Toughmac branding.

Although Toughmac never owned any of Bertie's rally cars, the sponsorship of Bertie's rallying efforts was a major commitment as Kieran explains

'At the team's peak, without a doubt 75% or more of my company's marketing budget was spent on the rallying team and sometimes it wasn't an easy thing trying to persuade our accountants that this amount of expenditure on an annual basis was something worth doing. When it came to the annual accounts review every year, it was always questioned in relation to what we had spent on sponsorship on rallying, but I was always able to justify it on the basis that since becoming involved as a sponsor, the business had grown substantially and I concluded that much of this was due to the exposure Toughmac gained through rallying.'

However Kieran's involvement with Bertie's rallying exploits was not limited to writing cheques and in some ways the management and motivational expertise he brought to his role in the team's management was equally as important as Kieran explains

'I would go with Bertie to Prodrive or wherever to help negotiate deals for the car and package. The sponsorship deal came in the form of a number of different ways such as taking on the responsibility of providing the

Bertie and Kieran at the 1988 Circuit of Ireland scrutineering

service van, the transportation of the car back and forth from England, and the on-event accommodation and food expenses bills.'

Kieran's role as a motivator came into play at numerous times in the 1980s and 1990s when Bertie contemplated hanging up his helmet and stepping away from rallying at the top level for one reason or another and Kieran admits he would often have been the main driving force behind Bertie coming back to rallying time and time again

'There is no doubt he was pushed into doing events he wasn't planning on doing, but he wouldn't have taken much pushing for underneath it all he was always eager and didn't need dragging.'

And Kieran's motivational powers were readily acknowledged by Bertie. In an interview with *Carsport* in 1997 Bertie said

'We've had a great run together and Kieran has become more than a sponsor. I would never have won half the rallies without him – in fact I probably wouldn't have done half the rallies. He's the one on the phone asking if we are doing Donegal, are we going to Killarney, are we going to the Manx? I think he has enough enthusiasm for both of us. Whether its driving chase, doing mud notes, or whatever needs organising, he's there doing it on every event.'

Working so closely and intensely, with sometimes quick decisions to be made under pres-

Discussing tactics at service on the Donegal International in 1989

have to say Bertie listened, he took your advice and made the best use of it.'

Kieran finds it difficult to pick out specific highlights of their rallying partnership as

'They all stood out – it was just an absolute pleasure to be there and be part of it, the great camaraderie within the team and with other rally competitors'

Of course, to appreciate the highs you have to experience the lows, and Kieran recalled how he and Bertie dealt with it when an accident happened or things were going wrong

'If it was the case of him having crashed out of a rally the inquest would have lasted two or three minutes and you

sure you would think there would have been the occasional row or difference of opinion between the pair, but Kieran refutes this

'In the 20 odd years I knew Bertie well we never had a cross word. It was a sport in which you had to be serious about what you were doing, about what you were being told, about the advice you were being given, and I would

wouldn't have heard another thing of it other than maybe a resigned response like "Kieran, if we had all the money in China and ten new cars we still wouldn't win this championship' and with that he would have forgotten about it and looked forward to the next rally or the next championship'

In relation to Bertie's meticulous nature when

it came to his rallying, Kieran said .

'In rallying, Bertie was utterly meticulous in everything he did and everything had to be 100%. There was no 90% or 99%, it had to be 100%. He wanted everything to be just right and when something happened, whether it be a broken part or whatever, he always wanted to know what caused it so it could be corrected in the future.'

When asked to sum up his involvement with Bertie in rallying Kieran responded

'The long and short of it is I couldn't sum it up. Through my involvement in rallying as a sport, in clubs that organised rallies, all throughout the island of Ireland, and on the Isle of Man, which was the only rally we competed on outside of Ireland, I met and became very good friends with a lot of people and I put that down to being part of managing what was essentially the most successful and professional rally team on the island of Ireland.

You couldn't have asked for a better time. It was fabulous, enjoyable, a pleasure, no matter where or when or what it was. It was an honour and privilege to be involved with what would seem to be the most professional rally team in Ireland as sponsor, and to have been asked to be part of the management team'.

Given the long and rewarding relationship between Kieran and Bertie, when it was the turn of Bertie's son Mark to shine, just as Kieran had sponsored Bertie for many years, he also supported Mark's efforts.

As Kieran reflects.

'Bertie's aspirations for Mark were to promote him to the highest level possible, which would have been higher than even he had ever achieved. I started sponsoring Mark in the year 2000 when he won Group N in the Tarmac Championship using both cars from Prodrive and my own car, the Mitsubishi Evo. Indeed I can recall on the Manx in 2000 when Mark used my Evo, Bertie, Sammy Hamill and myself were spectating and on a particularly hairy crossroads where we were timing the cars. Mark, who was in this slightly dated Group N car, was up on Andrew Nesbitt, who was in a World Rally Car, and Bertie turned and said to me "We need to talk to this boy or you're gonna get this car back in a rolled up ball. I just said "Leave him alone" and I got the car back fine.'

Perhaps Kieran's enthusiasm to support Mark arose from the similarities he saw between the son and the father

'He had the same habits, same traits, same voice. He was Bertie Fisher Mark II and being in his 20s he was only going to get better. He had a great life in front of him, in both business and in motorsport.'

As the year 2000 drew to a close, at a small gathering over New Year's Eve Kieran and Bertie chatted over the future. Bertie talked about some major contracts Fisher Engineering hoped to win, the furthering of Mark's career into Peugeot's World Rally Team and the beginnings of Kris Meeke's journey up the rally ladder – there was much optimism in the air.

Though Bertie did not live to see it following the fateful events only three weeks later, many of the aspirations and goals he discussed with Kieran that New Year's Eve eventually came to fruition with the obvious sad exception of Mark's drive, although as a mark of respect no one took his place in the Peugeot WRC team that year.

Kieran's last conversation with Bertie took place on the evening before the accident, and it is something he remembers both vividly and poignantly

'While the conversation had the usual mix of business and rallying, it was of a relatively serious nature as we discussed the future of the business, with his firm in negotiations to secure their largest structural steel contract to date. Plans were being put in place for another large expansion of the factory to accommodate

Kieran with Bertie and Rory at the finish ramp of the Circuit of Ireland 1999, Bertie's last ever rally win

this contract and we discussed that in a lot of detail. The fact that he was sharing all this exclusive information with me and that he was seeking my advice in major decisions in his business means a lot to me and so it is a lasting memory which I will never forget.'

The untimely passing of Bertie, Mark and Emma left a huge void in Kieran's heart.

'It was a life changing event. Bertie and I spoke on the phone almost every day, and to this day I greatly miss the craic and times we would share together, be it socially, in rallying or in business. And while many of my friends tried to help me overcome the monumental loss, it was a gap in my life which was and still is impossible to fill'.

1988 · 1989

Sierra & M3 Years, the last of the Frazer years

With the exclusion of the Manta from point scoring in International championships, and the continued development of Group A cars, by the time 1988 came round Bertie felt the need to look for something new.

Despite Bertie having been almost entirely faithful to the GM brand (with the exception of a demo run in the Orion on the Lurgan Park in 1986) for the previous five seasons, Opel or Vauxhall didn't have a suitable car and so in the Autumn of 1987 he completed a deal to compete in a Ford Sierra Cosworth, D773 SVW, with a plan to compete on all of the British Championship rounds plus some Irish events not in the British Championship supported by continued sponsorship from Alumac, and Shell Oils in the guise of Gemini.

The car had been built by Ford's Motorsport division at Boreham who retained ownership of the car which came with kits of spares although, as had been the case with all of Bertie's cars for the previous 13 years, preparation of the car throughout the year would be by Sydney Meeke's Bush based team.

The deal came about after an enquiry from Stuart Turner, head of Motorsport division at Ford at the time, to find out if Bertie intended making a full scale return to rallying after the few select events he had undertaken in 1987.

Following an affirmative response from Fermanagh Bertie became part of Ford's plan to wrest back from Opel the dominance they had enjoyed in British Championships in the Seventies. Essentially Fisher would be one of a three car Ford team along with 1987 Champion Jimmy McRae and 1986 Champion Mark Lovell planning on making the manufacturers Championship Ford's once again. All in all it looked like an excellent package but looks can be deceiving as would become clear as the year unfolded.

right: Bertie and Austin with Kieran McAnallen, outside the Alumac factory and premises in Benburb, at the start of 1988

run in the car and seemed to indicate that the package was competitive although Bertie had identified a number of niggling problems with the car, especially with the brakes. The Meeke team worked hard to try and iron out the issues before the next round of the British Championship, the Circuit of Ireland at Easter, but even so, on the event Bertie still found the car hard to master.

It was Bertie's first Circuit of Ireland since 1985 but that didn't seem to hamper his performance as, for much of the rally, he lay in fourth overall and it would have been even better had he not suffered a string of minor problems including a 30 second road penalty as a result of lateness after a puncture, some misfire troubles, an overshoot and broken anti-roll bar. Pushing hard to try and get back into contention he had a huge spin on a particularly narrow section of road, forcing him to reverse some 300 yards up to the nearest turning spot at a junction, loosing further time as a result.

While at the front Jimmy McRae went on to win his sixth Circuit of Ireland, Bertie's rally ended on the final day when he went off the road on a narrow muddy tight right corner, overshooting into a gate pillar and causing enough damage to force his retirement. To add the final nail to a thoroughly frustrating event, as he sat at the side of the road where the crash happened watching the other competitors pass, along came Richard Hall whose Peugeot 205 GTi spun, clipping the rear of the Sierra to add to the damage – Austin Frazer was quoted in the Fermanagh Herald as saying *'He didn't even stop to give us his insurance details!'*

Bertie's debut with D773 SVW was the Cartel International in England in mid-February. This rally (formerly known as the Mintex then National Breakdown, was run in the mainly Yorkshire based forest stages which would have been familiar to Bertie having competed on the event before. With that familiarity he was immediately competitive even though it was his first rally in the new car and he was up against not only the other Fords but many other big entries including Pentti Airikkala out in his new Mitsubishi Starion, David Llewellyn in an Audi 200 Quattro, Kalle Grundel in a Peugeot 309 GTi, Louise Aitken Walker in a 205 GTi and Malcolm Wilson in an Astra GTE.

After 24 stages under the drivers' belts, Llewellyn and McRae were out, Llewellyn with a mechanical and McRae in a crash. Bertie, despite some chronic brake troubles throughout the rally, had been up as high as third place overall behind Airikkala and Aitken Walker but his success came to a sudden end though after he hit a log at the side of the track and was unable to continue. Despite the retirement, it was an interesting first

above: Journalist Sammy Hamill and Bertie at Circuit of Ireland scrutineering

right top: Bertie travels through a tree lined narrow section on the Rothmans Circuit of Ireland, watched by crowds of eager spectators enjoying a sunny Easter weekend's sport

below: Bertie's first finish of the year, on the Fram Welsh International

The third round of the British Championship was the Fram Filters Welsh Rally and this proved to be yet another disappointing run for Bertie who still was not comfortable with the car, finishing in 12th place overall.

Adding to the disappointment as Gary Wilson, one of Meeke's mechanics, points out was the fact that many of the problems were recurring issues which the team didn't seem to be able to sort out: *'Head gaskets were a problem and the brakes were just not good enough, and Bertie had to have the best'*

Norman Burns, also part of the Meeke set up, says Bertie also struggled with the engine response on the

turbo charged Sierra. *'He found the car very hard to drive because there was a huge amount of turbo lag with it, which he had never come across before – the turbo just came in very aggressively and he wouldn't have been used to that in a rally car.'*

While the British Midland Scottish Rally was initially part of the plan for the year, Bertie decided instead to compete on the more familiar territory of the Shell Donegal International where he could try and build some confidence in the car – if he could not do well with it on home soil in a rally he had won just the previous year, he could not do well at all.

Amongst the opposition in Donegal this year was Mark Lovell in a Sierra as well as Vincent Bonner and Pat Kirk in Manta 400s. But it was James Cullen in his somewhat out dated Ascona 400 who raised the most eyebrows on the first day of the rally. On home territory Cullen, was consistently punching in faster times than the much fresher and more powerful Sierra Cosworth of Works driver Lovell right through the rally. Unfortunately his heroics were hampered by a considerable time loss of around 1m 40s on the sixth stage when he was blocked by Phil Collins' stricken Sierra which had come to a halt.

Despite a protest by his co-driver Ellen Morgan to get a 'scratch' time, the time loss stood and Cullen eventually finished in second behind Lovell by around the amount of time he had lost in the incident.

In the race for overall honours it was obvious these two were out by themselves with Bertie finding it hard to eke out a steady third place by a narrow margin from Vincent Bonner in fourth driving Bertie's old Manta 400. Nevertheless it was Bertie's best result to that point in 1988 and, as it would turn out, the whole year.

Two weeks after Donegal was the Lurgan Park Rally and Bertie, after his frustrations all year so far in the Sierra, decided to try something completely different and hired a

left top: Bertie and Austin flying high towards their best result of the year, a 3rd overall on the Shell Donegal International

middle: James Cullen drove the proverbial socks off the ex-Fisher & Bonner Opel Ascona 400 on the Donegal Rally to finish second ahead of Bertie in third

bottom: Kieran McAnallen inspects the Sierra in service on the Shell Donegal Rally

Note the size and space taken up by in-car camera equipment. A mammoth amount compared to todays in car camera systems

John Price Metro 6R4, Q630 BFQ.

Bertie had never driven a 6R4 before this rally, nor even tested one properly so it is perhaps not entirely surprising that his rally was over almost as quick as it had started when he ploughed the car into a tree on the first stage to make it game over at Lurgan.

Bertie and Austin's string of bad luck continued on the Ulster Rally four weeks later where a blown turbo charger stopped them on Stage 5.

It would be a month and a half before Bertie would compete again, on the Manx International – could it have been possible that he could have a trouble free rally to end the year on a high note? Unfortunately, no was the answer.

right top: Bertie hired a John Price Metro 6R4 on what was very much a one-off outing on the Lurgan Park in 1988 which ended badly *(below)*

Although he was doing very well on the first few stages, matching some of the drivers in the front group of competitors including Phil Collins in a similar Sierra, the oil pressure light had started flashing from as early as the second stage. The car was kept running by adding extra oil at the end of every stage but then on Stage 7 the

water temperature gauge soared and he was forced to stop altogether due to a head gasket failure.

Reflecting on what had been a disappointing year in an interview with *Carsport*, Bertie outlined his discomfort with the Group A Sierra *'It was never half the car that the Opel Manta was. Even on the Manx where I was doing well before the head gasket failed, I never felt entirely comfortable – not the way I had done in the Manta. The Sierra doesn't ride the bumps as well and although I thought I finally mastered the technique of using the turbo, I never had the same confidence in the car that I had with the Opel.'*

He summed up the year as *'... one of those seasons I'd rather forget'.*

On the assumption the Sierra would not be around the following year, he was asked about his choice of car for 1989, to which he responded

'The fact that it would have to be Group A to do the Circuit of Ireland and the Manx International makes it difficult. With the other tarmac rounds still being open to Group B cars like the Manta next season there is the possibility of doing events like Galway, Donegal, etc. but I haven't made up my mind and obviously it would have a lot to do with whether Alumac and Shell would be prepared to continue their sponsorship'.

Continue their sponsorship they did although with Kieran McAnallen choosing to promote the Toughmac division of the company rather than Alumac – a branding which would remain a feature of Bertie's cars from then on.

With a new car on the horizon, it heralded the beginning of a two year period in which Bertie Fisher and Austin McHale would wage many a battles over the Irish stages in their very similar cars – Prodrive supplied BMW M3s.

left: Bertie trying hard on the Ulster *(top)* and the Manx *(middle and bottom)* but his efforts on both rallies were to no avail as both ended when mechanical gremlins intervened

1989

While choosing the optimum car may still have been a difficulty, for some time Bertie had been eyeing up BMW's M3. With the emergence of 4WD turbo-charged cars it may have struggled on forestry stages but its nimble chassis and responsive naturally aspirated engine made it popular on tarmac based championships all across Europe.

With their continental roots the ex-works rally cars were all left hand drive which was at odds with Bertie's preference for sitting on the right so he persuaded Prodrive, the company responsible for the preparation of all of the Rothmans Rally M3s and the most recent official BMW

The BMW M3 Bertie bought in 1989 from Prodrive was an already successful car having won several major rallies including:-

right top: the Manx Rally in 1988 with Patrick Snijers at the wheel

below: the World Rally Championship round the Tour De Corse in 1987 in the hands of Bernard Beguin

left above: Bertie and Austin Frazer on their debut in the M3 finished 6th overall on the Circuit of Ireland behind Jimmy McRae *(bottom)* who scored a record seventh victory in 1989 with Rob Arthur co-driving

above: a fast sweeping corner on the Isle of Man

right: Bertie coming sideways into a tight hairpin towards his second Manx National win

racing M3s, to convert one of the ex-works shells to right hand drive.

This deal for the BMW M3 heralded the beginning of a long lasting partnership with the Banbury based firm who would, for much of the remainder of Bertie's rally career, supply and maintain his subsequent cars.

The car, GXI 9427 complete with most of its works parts was scheduled to arrive in time for the 1989 BIF Circuit of Ireland although it was missing a high ratio steering rack which at the time was not available for RHD versions of the car. However help was on hand when local firm, Crossen Engineering in Castlereagh, stepped in and re-engineered the existing rack in order to have the car ready in time for the rally.

Being his first rally with the car, Bertie wasn't expecting a huge result and finished sixth overall, concentrating on learning the car and getting to the finish. The car did prove to be quite reliable with few major problems but he did notice it twitchy over the Donegal bumps and he wasn't quite able to match the pace of the various Ford Sierra Cosworths which dominated the rally, taking the top five places with Jimmy McRae notching up his record seventh win on the Circuit followed home by Russell Brookes in second, Mark Lovell third, Gwyndaf Evans fourth and Austin McHale fifth.

With his eyes set on the Shell Donegal International in June, Bertie decided to take part on a warm up rally, the Manx National Rally in May which he had won on his last appearance two years previously. And just like before he won with a considerable time to spare, over 3 min-

utes in total although this time Rory Kennedy sat in the left seat for the first time since his one off on the Cavan Rally in 1985. Bertie had first approached Rory about a more regular co-driving role in Galway in February when the pair had teamed up to act as gravel crew for Hugh O'Brien as Rory recalls it *'At that time he told me it looked like Austin wanted to take a back seat and he definitely wasn't going to be available for Donegal. He said if I was going to be available for it, we would talk later in the year, so the Manx National was really a precursor to the Donegal and a chance to familiarise ourselves with each other. The week before the Manx we sat down and went over the sort of notes that Bertie used and generally made a big effort to plan and prepare everything right which paid off as we won the rally quite convincingly in the M3 BMW – they were the machine to have at the time, an incredible bit of kit, one of the most iconic rally cars of all time and one of my favourites.'*

With the win on the Isle of Man under their belts, Bertie and Rory went to the Shell Donegal Rally with high hopes where they were immediately in a battle with David Llewellyn who was there in a works Toyota Team GB Celica GT Four. At the end of Day one Llewellyn led by a scant margin of 9 seconds from Fisher with McHale a few further back in third. Bertie's M3 had some troubles with the brakes sticking on although he was still pushing hard no matter how hard he tried it seemed like there was nothing he could do as Llewellyn steam rolled the field in the more powerful four wheel drive Toyota, punching in a series of fastest times in the particularly damp conditions that persisted throughout the weekend.

When McHale went off the road on Knockalla and out of the rally he was no longer a threat and so Bertie eased off to stay in a comfortable second place. Rory summed the rally up by saying *'We pushed him [Llewellyn] hard a good bit of the rally, and ended up second behind him but it was as good as we could have hoped for at that*

left top: Welshman David Llewellyn on his way to winning the 1989 Donegal Rally in his Toyota GB Celica GT Four

below far left: Bertie tackles a wet tight tricky section on the Donegal

below left: Cars? Drivers? – all the same to Meeke mechanic Norman Burns as he applies running repairs to Bertie's hand

Opposite right On the Lurgan Park rally Bertie's co-driver was UTV sports reporter Jacqui Berkley who has some vivid memories of the day:–

'I'm not sure how it came about. I was working as a sports reporter in the UTV sports department at the time but my features were very much covering family sports and the more unusual and upcoming sports rather than the cut and thrust of high profile ones. I can only guess organisers understood how far out of my comfort zone taking part in a proper rally with probably the best driver at that time would take me!

'I took my responsibilities as navigator very seriously, going over the race course in the park over and over again the night before in preparation. I remember at Lurgan Park on the Saturday it was hot and very noisy. I was introduced to the Fisher family- Bertie's wife and children and others. They were delightful- very welcoming and friendly, making tea and barbecuing at their caravan. I was put into a white boiler suit and handed a helmet. All very exciting. Up until then I hadn't met my driver but I was getting on like a house on fire with his entourage. Then Bertie arrived and we were off on a test run. He did ask me if I'd done anything like this before - but he knew the answer! And I have never experienced anything like it- I was centrifugally impaled back in my seat as Bertie roared into action and took to the back roads like the proverbial bat out of hell. I quite literally couldn't speak when we arrived back - the camera crew was waiting to hear my experience but I couldn't get a word out - I was petrified!

The actual rally paled in comparison – we went fast, I tried to navigate – so much for my prep- we got muddled and we ended up way down the leader board – but that didn't matter, I always felt Bertie had made his mark with me on the trial run – and he knew it. Bertie was a man of few words, but was quietly in charge throughout. Totally fearless but oh so focused and totally sure of his considerable skills. I will never forget those couple of hours – the fear out on the road, nor the love and support he had from his lovely family- a very random day! I often think of them and our brief meeting'

time because Llewellyn's car was one of the new first generation Four Wheel drive cars, works team, Toyota GB and all that.'

A few weeks after the Donegal was the Lurgan Park Rally where Bertie, despite having Rory Kennedy's name on the side of the car as navigator, would be joined by Ulster Television presenter Jacqui Berkeley. Bertie was well used to the park, having been involved in all of the rallies there to date, which helped compensate for a few initial navigational inaccuracies which dropped them down the leader board but with Rory Kennedy there to keep Jacqui on track throughout the rally they clawed their way back to eventually finish second overall.

The final three rallies of the year in Bertie's program saw the return of Austin Frazer to the co-driver's chair for a last hurrah but unfortunately he didn't bring any stores of good luck with him.

By this stage Austin, now a very experienced co-driver, felt it was nearing his time to hang up the helmet but not before he would complete the remainder of the season. *'The time had come, and I was finding it increasingly difficult to get time off work. Previously I was able to find decent time off work, especially in the Opel days because of a clause in working terms and conditions that if you competed in international sport you could get free time off. But then with a whole reshuffle in management I fin-*

place overall, having been dogged with problems with a new ECU which changed the car's throttle response. As a result of that combined with the at times slippy wet conditions, the car was a handful and they ended up going off the road at a hairpin and getting stuck in a ditch losing several minutes and dropping to 14th place overall.

Bertie was never really on top form during this rally, but nevertheless clawed back much of his lost time in the subsequent stages with two fastest times in the closing stages of the already decided rally to finish fourth overall behind overall winner Gwyndaf Evans in the Sierra who had over half a minute to spare from Russell Brookes in a similar Sierra in second and David Llewellyn in the Celica third.

With a broken gearbox eliminating the M3 early on the 5th stage the Tudor Webasto Manx International served as little more than a footnote to the final rally of the year, the Carling Rally of the Lakes based in Killarney.

Although Bertie had not originally planned going to the rally, his results throughout the year, albeit not sounding particularly impressive with a 6th, 2nd, 4th and non-finish, were enough to leave him in with a shot at clinching the Irish Tarmac Championship outright if the results ran in his favour. Amongst the main challengers in the rally were Russell Brookes in the Sierra Cosworth (who was also aiming to wrap up the Tarmac Championship which he led coming into the final round), and James Cullen in an Opel Manta 400 who had previously proved his competitiveness with his fantastic second in Donegal the previous year.

left top: Gwyndaf Evans won the British Midland Ulster Rally in 1989 in the distinctively coloured Sierra Cosworth which Bertie had campaigned the previous year. This was the first international win for the 'Welsh Wizard'

below: Selection of competitors take part in a fun event before the Ulster Rally. From left, Ian Grindrod, Malcolm Wilson, Louise Aitken Walker, Ellen Morgan, Bertie Fisher, Plum Tyndall

ished up with pharmacy responsibilities for two hospitals and it was taking up a lot of my time so that I hadn't any spare left. The rallying was also getting more and more competitive and I was still organising events in our own club – you could go on but one way or another my time had come, it was taking up too much of my life and really I felt I had my fill.'

The British Midland Ulster International Rally, a month after the Lurgan Park resulted in a disappointing fourth

Despite still just getting to grips with an uprated engine which had been installed before the Manx, the rally started off well with Bertie blasting up the Molls Gap stage between Killarney and Kenmare to set fastest time one second ahead of Brookes.

Fine margins were the order of the day at the head of the field and over the next two loops of stages the leader board would change twice with initially Cullen in the lead and then Brookes. On the second loop of stages round Caragh Lake and as the rally descended into early afternoon December darkness, Fisher began to lose time with the spotlights on the M3 which were vibrating so hard it was difficult to see properly at high speeds so it was easier to ease off a little and rely on the car's standard headlights.

Then, due to what would eventually be diagnosed as a faulty crankshaft sensor, the BMW's engine died completely on the road section after the Churchtown stage. It took a considerable time to get the car going again and when he got to the start of the next stage, Caragh Lake, the car's engine died again. Although they got it going again after another long delay they were OTL when they got back to Killarney and as a result were excluded by organisers. The rally was eventually won by Russell Brookes who finished with over 3 minutes to spare from Cullen and Phil Collins in an Escort a further three and a half minutes back in third.

Apart from a one off outing on the Cavan Rally in 1992, this would be Bertie's final rally with Austin Frazer as co-driver and It was not a particularly fitting note on which to end to what had been a long and fruitful partnership. Austin recalls the end of the rally well:

'After the rally, Bertie said "Do you mean to tell me this is the last time you'll be taking that suit off?' and I said "it is", and he said "Have you your mind made up?" and I told him "I had" for I'd decided some six months before that I was retiring and that it wasn't just a decision I had made there and then.'

Bertie was undoubtedly disappointed to see this 12 year driver – co-driver relationship end in a non-finish in Killarney especially for Austin when you consider that he had won every single international tarmac rally in the British Isles with the exception of the Lakes rally, the one missing from his mantelpiece. But all good things must come to an end and the pair certainly had plenty of good times throughout their partnership including two international wins and multiple smaller rally wins.

When Austin, who at the time of his last rally with Bertie was 50 years of age, was asked how he would sum up his time in rallying, he said

'It was a great experience. I had the 12 years with CB [Cahal Curley], they were totally different to the 12 years with Bertie, different circumstances, two totally different characters, and Cathal would fly off the handle very quickly, could be hot headed, while Bertie was more calm and collected. I have been very fortunate to have sat with these two very good, competitive drivers for over a 25 year period, because they both took it seriously, tried to leave no stone unturned, and you were able to develop a good working relationship with them, and even though they were two different temperaments, I would have been flexible enough to work with both of them and say

what I thought and for them to take that on board.'

As he looked back on this time with Bertie, several rallies and years sprang into Austin's mind as he considered his memorable moments, 'That Manx in 1985, the 1-2-3, that's one that immediately comes to mind. The one in Galway too with the very near accident, and subsequent to that, his year out and helping improve safety on rallies in general. The Ulster in 1982 was also good.'

Of course someone as deeply involved in a sport as Austin was in rallying never really retires and this was not the very last of his outings in the rally world, not by a long shot.

He would later compete in the Northern Ireland Navigational Championship as driver along with his son Nigel and he took a keen interest in Historic Rallying, taking part as co-driver in the Monte Carlo Rally in 1990 with Frank Fennell in a Riley 1.5, and the following year with Frank again in a Sunbeam Rapier. He also tackled the Pirelli Marathon event, a six day race across Europe, with Donal McBride in an MGC one year and then in an Austin Healy 3000 the following year (finishing third overall in the event out of around 150 competitors in total) and in between times he also took part in the Irish Historic Tarmac Championship with fellow Fermanagh man Mervyn Johnston in a Mini Cooper for several years up to 1996.

His involvement with rally organising also continued for many years with Chairmanship of the T.R.O.A (Tarmac Rally Organisers Association) the group responsible for the running of the Irish Tarmac Rally Championship. That is a position he has now stepped down from as he has from the post of President of the Donegal Motor Club but he is still President (and active member) of the Enniskillen Motor Club committee, over 50 years after he originally helped set the club up in 1964.

right: Austin Frazer, Bertie's main co-driver for 12 years, decided to hang up his helmet in 1989 although he and Bertie retained their close friendship.

Austin remembers Bertie asking him what he was going to do in his spare and he said he was considering playing some golf, to which Bertie, according to Austin, said *"Play Golf !? You mean to hit a wee white ball up and down a field?"* but about three years later, in the early 90s, Bertie himself took up golf joining a society set up in the late 80s or early 90s called the 'Rally Golfers Society', mainly made up of retired rally men. The society still meets today for a round of golf, a meal and a reminisce every year.

below: Bertie and friends at a charity golf event at Castle Coole in the 1990s. From left, Tom Graydon, Brian Doran Northern Bank Manager, Bertie Fisher, George Deane

The Prodrive Connection

Bertie's new Prodrive perepared Legacy sits outside their premises in Banbury, England in early 1992

It was autumn 1987 and Bertie had been rallying Sydney Meeke prepared Opel Manta 400s for some 4 years at that point, albeit including a hiatus from tarmac rallying for 15 months. With Group B on the way out, the Manta was coming near the end of its development potential and Bertie began to consider the various Group A (which was coming to the fore) options available for 1988 one of which was a Group A BMW M3 rally car prepared and run by Prodrive.

At the time Prodrive, formerly called David Richards Autosport, were a Silverstone-based company mainly involved in preparing and running BMW M3 cars for the BTCC and Rothmans Porsches & Metro 6R4s for the Rothmans Rally team on the World, European and local scene. While the M3 would have been an ideal car for Bertie for 1988, he believed it was too expensive for his budget – and even if it had been, at that time Prodrive were not in a position to sell cars. In the end he rallied a Ford Sierra Cosworth on loan from Ford for a year but it would prove to be a very unsuccessful year with, in Bertie's terms, no decent results.

Enter Dave Campion, one of the first people to join Prodrive and the driving force who helped the company transition to supplying and preparing customer cars.

In an interview with Dave and Paul Howarth, Prodrive's head engineer for many years, they gave their thoughts on the company's relationship with Bertie.

Dave started by giving a background on how he was involved and how the team evolved with his guidance: *'I was initially responsible for workshops and all things that were associated with car builds and rebuilds, component rebuilds, etc. When we moved to a new site in Banbury I was responsible for setting up the workshop and many other things. So I had worked in just about every side of Prodrive at one stage or the other for a number of years. When we started to get enquiries about rally and race cars, it occurred to me that although Dave Richards Autosport was a rallying and racing team running their own cars, we were missing a trick. I came very much from a commercial background, trained as an apprentice and worked my way through to a service*

172

manager in the ordinary automotive industry, and I thought we should consider operating in the customer sector as a way of enhancing the business.'

Although the company was reluctant at first to sell the former works rally cars, they eventually came round to Dave's way of thinking. *'They were completely stripped and rebuilt, right down to the point of taking the shell, stripping it, jigging it, refurnishing it, repainting it and then building it up again, not with all new parts but with the same rebuilt parts we used on our own programmes.'*

This is when the beginning of the long-lasting Fisher-Toughmac-Prodrive relationship took hold, one which would last until the very last rally car Bertie owned. Dave explains the first contact he had with Bertie around the beginning of 1989 and how they dealt together. *'I was approached by Bertie who called and asked what could we offer. He gave me a list of his requirements and asked me to quote him. Most clients would then come back to you and say "how can we reduce the price without reducing the content' but you never got that with Bertie, ever. You would show him how it all added up and then he would consider the budget, we would both make a commitment to do whatever was agreed and I loved it because that's the way I like to work. He never asked for something for nothing. Dealing with Bertie right from day one was a good experience'*

Elaborating on how easy he gelled with Bertie from the word go, Dave said

'You couldn't help but take to him, you didn't have to agree with him on everything, you could discuss with him, but all those conversations were always so easy, and as a consequence we got into this rhythm of 'That's where work is, That's where pleasure is, never the two shall meet' and that's why it was a pleasure to do business with him. When at his house or our house it was always fun to socialise with him and his family, there are very few people I've found in this world that you can do that with.'

After Bertie won the 1990 Tarmac Championship in the Prodrive prepared BMW the attention turned to getting a new car. Around that time Prodrive's new flagship car was the Group A Legacy being used in the British Championship by Colin McRae and though that was the car Bertie had his sights set on,

there were only a limited number of shells available and financially it probably was not feasible for Bertie at the time as Dave Campion explained *'He asked "what I could offer", I told him and he replied "OK, That doesn't suit my budget for the next year", and he went off and did something else.'*

The something else was to throw his hat in with R.E.D. for a year, rallying a Sierra Cosworth, but at the end of the year Bertie was back at Banbury and a deal was done whereby he would have a Legacy as soon as one was available.

Kieran McAnallen recalls how the projected costs for each years' rallying were worked out, *'He sat down and did a budget plan for every event, and at our annual budget meeting at the start of each year, so he would tell you this*

Bertie's Prodrive prepared '555' Impreza sits at a test set up by Prodrive in Donegal in late 1998 where Bruno Thiry was also present helping Proddrive set up the new WRC Impreza for Irish tartmac specs

Dave Campion and Bertie in Donegal 1996

is how much it's going to cost, this is what we are thinking of doing (It was always we!), do we agree that we are putting this together and that we want to fund it to the level that is suitable?'

And so shortly before the Circuit of Ireland in 1992 Bertie and Prodrive were back in business. *'The temporary separation never affected our relationship at all. He came back to me six months later and said "Right, What can you do for me now?" I explained the situation and showed him what was possible with a Subaru and he said "OK we'll do that". That was typical of the straight forward business relationship we had all the way through.'*

With Bertie always wanting as good a spec car as he could afford, the question came up as to how similar Bertie's cars were to the works cars Prodrive ran to which Dave responded *'The specs used to vary slightly. In Legacy days, a Legacy was a Legacy. It didn't matter who drove it or where it came from, or*

where it was going. But in later years development started to ramp up on the works cars and we would normally be 2 or 3 months behind the works team, although you also have to bear in mind that if you were rallying in Ireland the car was always a different spec. If we found something that worked well on one car, we would transfer it to other cars, if customers were prepared to pay for it.'

Bertie kept the ultra-successful Legacy until the start of 1994 when a Group A Subaru Impreza Rally car became available. It was Prodrive Impreza Chassis Number 1, a former works car having been driven by Markku Alen on the 1000 Lakes Rally in 1993, and was debuted by Bertie on the Welsh International Rally.

For a privateer team to have a Prodrive prepared Group A Subaru Impreza in 1994 was something of a rarity and at the time Bertie acquired L444 MCA, there were only two other privately run Prodrive Imprezas in existence – Pierro Liatti ran one in the Italian Championship and Tonny Harhianto had received one in Indonesia at the start of the summer in 94.

I asked Rory Kennedy how Bertie had got into such a privileged position and he explained the changing relationship with

Prodrive as the years went on, *'The team were valued customers of Prodrive for we brought a lot of other customers to Prodrive from Ireland as well. The Toughmac team set the standard and then others came along and wanted the same type of setup. In fact we ended up ambassadors/guinea pigs for Prodrive in many ways.'*

As the years rolled on, the Toughmac-Prodrive relationship continued to develop, the successes continued, and behind the scenes Dave and Bertie had a unique relationship as they had got to be close friends. Dave explains some of Bertie's traits, in and out of business. *'You knew where you stood all the time. Very very determined, sometimes verging on the selfish, but you always knew where you stood, always, and a more fun person to go out with you would struggle to find.*

On the business side, at Prodrive we had our own standards and had established our own way of working. Bertie did not change that but working and co-operating with him confirmed to us that our standards were correct and helped us be successful in what we did. Anybody sent from Prodrive that worked with or came in to contact with Bertie always wanted to go back.

Without a doubt, he inspired me. I thought I was good at my job, and I still think I was good at my job, and I still think I behave properly in life but that man could certainly be an inspiration.'

Paul Howarth, who for many years was Chief Engineer at Prodrive and worked on every car Prodrive supplied Bertie with had this to say

RAC in 1999 including top left the whole Prodrive Allstars team including Bertie and Mark Fisher's crews as well as other European crews

Rally car homologation spec with a semi-automatic gearbox. Paul Howarth explains the special gearbox which was unlike anything seen on any Group A car in Ireland before. *'As part of the homologation for the car it was fitted with an aluminium flywheel which was homologated with the auto shift system which was only being tested by us at that time. Bertie preferred manual, but at the same time wanted to take advantage of the aluminium flywheel which gave us better driveability. if it was scrutineered we had to prove it was part of the system and that it worked in auto shift mode. So we fitted the kit so you could make the auto shift mode operational or like Bertie did leave it off and use the manual shift.'*

During this period, the Prodrive-Toughmac relationship was really in full swing. Dave explained what happened between rallies. *'Normally the cars would come back [to Prodrive] every time. It was not a complete rebuild every*

about Bertie's forethought and professionalism. *'I think to be fair, early on Bertie recognised how to win rallies and championships. You really needed to focus on the details and if you then get people of the quality of Kieran, Sydney Meeke and the others involved the way Bertie did, it inevitably leads to outstanding results. As an example Bertie spent a considerable amount of time understanding the tyres. We would always ensure that he had maximum choices for every single stage and you would often see Bertie on the right tyre when others struggled, That wasn't by chance, but by collating the best information available in the seconds you have to make a decision – information from the numerous weather crews, gravel crews, Pirelli engineers etc – all brought together at the right moment to make sure*

the right decision was made'

In 1995, L444 MCA was replaced by L555 FEL, and Bertie used this Impreza until the Circuit of Ireland 1997. In terms of results, it was Bertie's most successful Impreza, and probably the most fondly remembered.

The car, a Prodrive test car originally registered as L408 FUD, came to Bertie before the Circuit of Ireland in 1995 when it had previously been in the World

Bertie's brand new 555 Impreza, the last ever to be built by Prodrive and the only ever 555 built by Prodrive specifically for a customer, sits outside Sydney Meekes workshop upon arrival in late 1997

Bertie chatting during service at the Manx National Rally in 1992 with Prodrive technician Martin Spurrell

time, it was scheduled on mileage, engines would normally get what we would call an intermediate inspection so we would get a camera and look inside and do physical checks on cylinder leak downs and compression test, that sort of thing. The box would invariably come out, the clutch would be inspected and adjusted, the gearbox would be partially opened up, as a norm, and then fully stripped at the appropriate mileage. Bertie wasn't particularly hard on anything from memory.'

Cars being cars though, things didn't always go 100%, and Dave gave an insight as to how they dealt with things when there was something that went wrong mechanically with the cars, no matter how minor. 'It was never forgotten about. It was always investigated, and there was always a report sent back to Bertie with what was found. If it by chance was our fault, we paid for it, if it was an act of the rally gods, he would pay for it – that was how we dealt with every customer.'

And of course after a crash, there was also the benching aspect, which Paul Howarth explained. 'Any time Bertie would have an accident, when the cars came back to Prodrive they were benched measured by default and always returned to their original spec.

Post-event, Bertie's car would go through a post-event set down (check set up). The typical message from Bertie post-event was always to leave no stone unturned and this included prep for the next event – focus on the detail and you get the outcome.'

Of course even if they were always striving for the best, the reputation or history of some particular events always gave cause for extra concern. The Manx was an example of such a rally where things seemed to go wrong mechanically more often than not for Bertie, Dave recalls 'The Manx was a nightmare rally. Engine went pop one year, gearbox another, for no real reason to be honest, but for some reason Bertie never had a lot of luck on the Manx. We would always go there with that in mind as far as pre-event work was concerned, - Manx was always a hard event for us.'

Through all the times that Prodrive were involved with Bertie, Sydney Meeke's men were there too in a relationship Dave acknowledges as unique among Prodrive customers. 'I always had the greatest respect for Sydney and his boys to the point that when his team got smaller, we used to employ some of the boys that worked from his team on a contract basis – Wesley, Robbie and the others, and they progressed on to the World Rally Championship where they did a lot of work for me on the Allstars team. There was always a dialogue between Sydney and me and the relationship was always good.

When Bertie first said he wanted the cars to come back to Prodrive between rallies, and that he wanted Sydney to look after it on events, I think he was expecting a little bit of opposition from me, because up to that point we had never done anything like it before.

I said, OK just explain to me how you see this working, and when he explained how it would operate, I said I don't have a problem with it –

but had anyone else in the world suggested it I suspect I would have refused. It was all down to his integrity and I knew how he operated and I didn't expect or anticipate any trouble. There was never any bickering over who had to do what, and it just worked.

To Bertie's competitors, our relationship worked so well they couldn't imagine how we weren't giving some special assistance to Bertie, and that created a few problems for me as it was suggested as developments became available we were letting Bertie have them on an exclusive basis. They would say "Well he's got X, Y, Z, why haven't we got it!?"… I would tell them what was available and it was always up to them to say if they would like a particular development or not. Some customers looked after their own cars but Bertie came to us and for sure there was a certain advantage in having the car looked after at Prodrive as it was automatically 1st in the queue! But it was never a prerequisite that if you wanted to have the latest upgrades you HAD to bring it to me, that's not how it worked. If you wanted it you could have it.'

Of course it wasn't all work and no play even in the middle of a tense rally as Dave recalls a story about the 1996 Rally of the Lakes where Bertie decided it would be good for the team to break out of the intense pressure for a few hours by going to see Riverdance; 'Bertie decided we should all go to watch Riverdance in Millstreet but it was a real short time between when the rally finished for the day and the start of the show. Bertie was well known in the Royal and when, with us all sitting in the mini-

bus waiting, someone was sent to find him, there he was wandering around in the Royal Hotel, basically cooking his own supper in his overalls so that we could get to Riverdance! But that's sort of the way he operated. On the one side, things need to get done. I've got out of my rally car, I'm hungry, I'm going out for the evening, I need to eat, Boom! Then he had the character and the charisma to carry all sorts of things off.'

In 1997 Bertie sold L555 FEL and though he did very little more rallying for the rest of the year, he did get a unique new car from Prodrive for the 1998 and 1999 seasons. Dave explained just how unique it was.

'That was the only car that was ever built directly for a customer. The normal way we operated at that time was that the World Rally Team cars were built from bare shells we got direct from the factory taking them off the line and shipped to us before they were sealed or painted etc. and at the end of the Group A time as we went into World Rally Car era we ended up with a spare Group A shell! It was the very last Impreza ever built and I have to tell you it took a fair bit of working through the system but we persevered A) Because it was Bertie and B) Because it made good business sense at the time – if it didn't make good business sense it wouldn't have happened. It was

R555 FEL sits in Prodrive in between rallies for a rebuild

the only customer car that had not come via the factory team and the only car we ever built and sold on a new shell.'

And it wasn't just the nature of the background to how the car came about that was unique. Dave suggested it was also the ultimate spec Group A Impreza ever built. *'Without a doubt. That car was built to the latest Group A regulations at that time, so it could have gone anywhere in the world to compete and being the last Group A car to be built it would influence its resale value throughout its life. Build time wise, that car would also have taken around 600 hours for the body shell plus 350 hours of build time for all the gear.*

Throughout the time he used this car, as with previous years, Bertie made full use of all the services and support we were able to give him. He was the only one that took full advantage of it, he was the flagship customer of Prodrive in Ireland at that time without a doubt and to a certain extent that caused the relationship to be misunderstood at times by others.

At Prodrive we were in a position to see how other customers went about their rallying and when you saw other people with the same machinery having trouble then you had to question, as they did, why the Toughmac team was not having those problems and I am of the opinion that it was because Bertie's setup was well organised and professionally operated.'

Elaborating on this, Dave praised the professionalism from everyone in the whole Toughmac team down through the years. *'As time went on the rapport between Bertie, myself, Prodrive and the Toughmac Team was* very successful, sometimes you would wonder why? I would like to think there was professionalism all the way down the line, Sydney and the boys always behaved professionally, Bertie was the leading light who set it up professionally, we were professional because that was our job, that's what we did, that's how we earned our living and if we weren't professional then we were going to make a hash of it.'

After 1999 Bertie wanted to concentrate on Mark's rally career and so he scaled back his own rallying. The Cork 20 in 1999 would be the last time Prodrive prepared and ran a car owned by Bertie, but Bertie did rally with Prodrive one more time, and it was an event which Dave worked hard to broker a deal for as he explains *'It's probably the only rally I ever talked Bertie into, and it was the best thing I ever did. We already had a deal with Bertie to provide a package for Mark on the RAC in 1999. I was in a lucky position that I had another car which had just enough mileage left to do the RAC before it was scheduled to be totally rebuilt for sale and I was in a position to do an attractive deal for Bertie to do the RAC.'*

Although it was due a rebuild, the car was an absolutely top level spec car, as Dave said, *'The car Bertie drove on the RAC was so up to date, a full works spec car, that you couldn't buy it as it was still in the hands of the World Championship team and it hadn't even got its first rebuild yet.'*

Given subsequent events this is a deal which Dave now looks back on with particular fondness *'I felt this more so since his and Mark's demise, that one was very much from the heart.*

He'd set up the deal for Mark and then out of the wood work I gave him this opportunity for a second car. I think that was the only event they had rallied together at that level. I just had a feeling in my heart at that time that somehow we have got to make this happen. Where was profit line in this? I just felt justified that it needed to happen as a thank you for the amount of business we had done over the years and the amount we might do in the future!'

To sum up working with Bertie, Dave mused *'Drivers can sometimes be fickle but Bertie by and large didn't have off days – some days were better than others but he didn't make too many mistakes. We visited the odd field here and there but nothing on a regular basis, so, I treasure it if you like the overall ambience of my relationship with Bertie in particular, there weren't many other drivers I've had as strong a personal relationship with as I had with Bertie.*

The way he conducted himself in life, in his Family, in his business, in his Rallying, you could use that as a model as confirmation in a way I have done quite a lot of things since I have known Bertie. But yes, I will remember Bertie as a role model, of how any successful person should lead their life, and it doesn't matter what they do, be it a businessman, community person , rally driver.'

A cartoon by Jim Bamber specially commissioned by Dave Campion
for Bertie's 50th birthday in 2000

1990 - 1991

The first of the Prodrive Years, the first big Tarmac successes and the RED year

Throughout Ireland there are pockets where rallying attracts remarkable levels of support and in these areas you find high concentrations of teams, organisers and enthusiasts, often across several generations of a family who are involved or interested in the sport in one way or another. Donegal is one such area and one of the many rally-faithful is Rory Kennedy. The son of Jim Kennedy who was involved at the time of setting up the Donegal Motor Club in the early 70s, Rory grew up very much with rallying in his blood and when he was old enough to get a licence he began co-driving for local Donegal based drivers such as James Cullen, James McDaid and Vincent Bonner, as well as drivers from slightly further afield such as Robin Lyons of Castlederg.

It was while Rory was co-driving for Robin Lyons that he got an opportunity to co-drive for Bertie in the 1985 Cavan rally, an opportunity he grabbed with both hands. This successful outing (they won the rally) obviously sowed a seed, for when Austin Frazer decided to hang up his helmet at the end of 1989 Bertie approached Rory to ask him to become his regular co-driver , a role he held until Bertie's last rally on the Monaghan Stages Rally in 2000 by which time the pair had taken 20 International Tarmac Wins and Four Tarmac Championships.

But back to the 1990 Tarmac Championship season which was shaping up for some fierce competition between the BMW M3s of Bertie and Austin McHale fighting the bit out to reign supreme on Irish Tar. *'It was really an iconic year. It was like the two heavyweights, Foreman and Ali, McHale and Fisher in their Prodrive BMW's on every rally – fantastic.'* recalls Rory.

The first round of the Seven Round series was the traditionally February run Lydon House Galway International Rally and while Fisher had been using his M3 for nearly a year and had become well accustomed to it, McHale

Bertie and Rory sideways in the BMW M3 in front of a large crowd towards their first of six wins on the Rally of the Lakes and their first Tarmac Championship

left: Rory checking over notes with team assistant and mud notes man Brian Quinn on the Galway Rally in 1990

was competing in his car for the very first time.

In an interview for TV before the rally Bertie predicted close competition between himself and McHale *'Certainly when we have had similar cars in the past there have been some very good battles and I think this will be no exception'* but as the rally got underway Bertie's extra experience in his Bavarian product was noticeable as he pulled out a lead of almost a minute after the first loop of four stages from McHale, who was getting acclimatised to the six speed gearbox and noisy clutch of his recently acquired Prodrive ex-works car.

The rally's Number 1 Seeding (due to FISA B seeding) was Kenny McKinstry who in a previously Manx Group N winning Group N Sierra Cosworth was the best of the rest with some reasonable stage times in the first loop of stages but gradually increasing gearbox gremlins and transmission troubles put him completely out of the rally late into the first day's stages.

The second loop was a different story altogether for Bertie. An off into a potato field when he aqua planed on the ultra-wet Galway roads had already cost him some 90 seconds to McHale when the M3 began to suffer electrical problems initially leaving it down on power before bringing it to a complete halt. Rory takes the story from here *'She finally died and gave up outside a farm house but fortunately the farmer had a tractor battery that was that big it had two ropes on it for lifting. Initially we took it round the front but couldn't find the battery under the bonnet as the BMW, being a new generation of car, only had a tiny wee battery in the boot. But anyway we put the farmers' battery into the boot along with it, put the jump leads on both batteries, fired her up and away she went.'*

The incident cost them over five minutes, leaving them battling back in seventh place overall although at the front of the field McHale was having his own problems with a loose alternator lead.

As day two dawned McHale had a misfire early on but a faulty sensor was soon replaced and he was back in full flow again, while Bertie and Rory continued to make their way up the field setting seventeen fastest times in a row. However although their gallant charge netted them a second place, it wasn't enough to catch McHale who won comfortably. Bertie, interviewed by RPM Motorsport's Alan 'Plum' Tyndall at the end of the year said *'The gap gave Austin enough of a cushion that he could really learn to drive the car without too much pressure from behind'.* but it was a good taster for the Fisher-McHale battles which would light up the Tarmac Championship year.

Onto the second round of the Irish Tarmac championship, the three day B.I.F Circuit of Ireland Rally which

right top: The low winter sun catches the rear end of the BMW on the winter Galway International in 1990

middle: Bertie and Rory manoeuvre the Bavarian product around the narrow mucky Galway lanes

bottom: Jim Bamber's take on the battery incident on Galway 1990

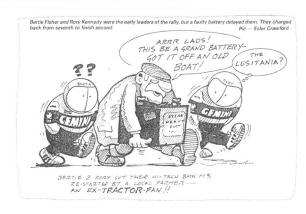

Bertie Fisher and Rory Kennedy were the early leaders of the rally, but a faulty battery delayed them. They charged back from seventh to finish second. Pic – Esler Crawford

attracted several big guns from the British Rally Championship, which the 'Circuit was part of then, including Dai Llewellyn in a works Team Toyota GB Celica GT-Four, Malcolm Wilson in a works Q8 Mike Little prepared Sierra and Colin McRae in an RED Sierra. By the end of the event these three would fill the leader board in this order, Llewellyn winning his second Circuit of Ireland ahead of the other two British Championship contenders with Fisher and McHale battling it out in their two M3s to be the best of the rest.

But before the action event got under way there was controversy, as an MSA appointed steward questioned the eligibility of Fisher and McHale's Right hand drive M3s. Despite the UAC backing the drivers, the MSA steward had other ideas leaving Fisher and McHale fuming to the extent that Bertie said he would not start with potential exclusion hanging over him. After much discussion, phone calls and meetings, the Steward finally backed down and both drivers were allowed to start without fear of disqualification.

With the first days stages almost entirely in the North, Fisher was in familiar territory and he held onto fourth place for the whole first leg while McHale after a brief sojourn down as low as eighth after problems, moved up the field to settle in fifth. But as the crews headed south for the second days stages they were entering McHale's home turf and he began to reel Bertie back in as Rory explains: *'With it being a southern based Circuit, although we were very strong in the North as usual, McHale was playing the auld game and once he got down south to*

right: Bertie and Rory slide the M3 sideways on the Circuit of Ireland, while some spectators take an unusual vantage point on a digger bucket

the Sally Gap and his home stages he was on it. Even though we were going as quickly as we could, he was closing in on us and we were under pressure.'

Eventually the pressure would tell and on a stage near Killkenny City, Bertie let the M3's tail slide too wide and overshot, hitting a telegraph pole and damaging the suspension so badly he had to retire at the end of the stage. After Bertie's retirement McHale held fourth comfortably to the end, meanwhile McRae was making a name for himself as he held on to third place despite being slowed by several brushes with walls and scenery.

Expectations of a battle royal between the M3 mount-ed crews on the Shell Donegal Rally were high with the presence of previous winner Jimmy McRae in a 20-valve adding spice to the mix.

As events unfolded though the brain in McRae's Audi malfunctioned and it was withdrawn from the entry, hours before the start leaving the wild card action to be provided by local man and 1983 Donegal Rally winner, Vincent Bonner who, in an ageing and some would say out-dated Opel Manta 400, surprised everyone with some very quick stage times. So impressive were they that for a period of the first day and overnight he held the overall lead until an over exuberant jump resulted

left: Action from Donegal as Vincent Bonner *(right top)* threw down the gauntlet to Bertie *(far left top / right bottom)* and Austin McHale *(far left bottom)* all yump high for outright glory

When asked if Vincent Bonner had the beating of Fisher and McHale that weekend Rory said

'It's one of them things you'll never know. He was right on top form at the time, mad to do well, really driving out of his skin and right on it. He was a huge concern for us early on and it was just an unfortunate thing that when he went over that big jump that the rotor arm broke on his Manta and put him out of contention completely. Had that not happened I think he would have been there or thereabouts, I mean he's another iconic Donegal name and he's been some driver over the years'

right: Bertie and Rory on a charge on the British Midland Ulster Rally

in a broken rotor arm on the Manta which dropped him out of contention leaving the two M3s to duke it out. Over the 160 stage miles driven during the three days of rallying Bertie was ahead by a scant 1 second but a time penalty on a road section between stages due to a botched tyre change resulted in a further 10 seconds being added to Bertie's time dropping him behind overall winner McHale by 9 seconds with James Cullen two minutes further back in third.

With the year nearly half over, it was looking likely that unless Bertie had several maximums he had a very slim outside chance of clinching the championship, but on they continued to the British Midland Ulster Rally where the final leader board echoed the previous year's Donegal rally with David Llewellyn and Phil Short taking the win in the Team Toyota GB Celica GT-Four ahead of Bertie in the M3. While the final winning margin on this occasion was over two minutes, that margin is not an accurate reflection of the competition that weekend.

As the rally got underway, a several-week spell of hot sunny weather was replaced by cold damp conditions putting the two-wheel-drive Sierras of Wilson, McRae, and Evans and the M3s of McHale, Fisher and Middleton at a disadvantage to the four wheel drive Toyota Celica of Llewellyn who initially pulled away, building up a lead of a few minutes over McHale in second. However all was to change on the seventh stage where McHale's differential failed forcing his retirement and both Llewellyn and McRae slid off on the same slippy corner dropping Llewellyn back into the clutches of the chasing pack and

McRae, who had inherited 2nd when McHale retired, even further back leaving Llewellyn with a narrow lead over Wilson who had been maintaining a steady if slightly lower pace throughout the day.

Day two dawned, on the first stage of the morning Wilson took the lead by over a minute after Llewellyn clipped a rock, and was forced to change a wheel, costing him two minutes. Although Wilson extended his lead on the following stages, by Stage 15 his rally was over after the rear cross-member on the Sierra broke and nothing could be done to repair it.

On the same stage McRae had an off and as a result punctured a wheel, all of which cost over seven minutes, putting him completely out of contention leaving Llewellyn with a comfortable lead which he retained till the end.

Meanwhile Bertie was having his own troubles struggling with new high revving engine from Germany in the M3 which was short on bottom end power needed for steady progress on the slippery roads and as a result his tyres were quickly shredding. Despite this, the second day's stages around his home territory as well as the drier roads helped him keep a constant pace and when the Sierras began to retire, Bertie made his way up the leader board from a miserable fourth overall to eventually finish a more credible second overall. Graham Middleton in another M3 was third.

And so, to The Manx International which was a part of multiple championships as Rory Kennedy explains. *'In those days, because the Manx was a coefficient 20 European Championship rally as well as being rounds of the British and Irish Championships, you had competitors there with high FIA seeding's who were running ahead of us down at Number 19 because we weren't seeded.'*

Despite the disappointingly low seeding Bertie, Rory and the rest of the team put everything they had into preparations for the event to a level they had never previously had as Rory explains:

'With our championship being tits up after a non-finish and two second places, we went to the Manx with a huge amount of pre-rally preparation and effort already put into it. We had never won it before but this year we planned to pull out all the stops and everything was done with the car to squeeze every last ounce out of it.

Mentally the preparation was enormous. Unlike modern day rallying where there's usually only three passes allowed, in those days the Manx was an open recce event, you could recce as long as you wanted, even 3 weeks before the rally and we made full use of that. All aspects of preparation, recce, tyres (Pirelli), set ups from Prodrive, everything was looked at.'

As the rally started Bertie and Rory jumped into an almost immediate lead despite having obstacles such as, passing slower runners along the route! Despite those little headaches and the strength of the opposition they were in a league of their own for much of the rally.

At the end of the second day with some ten stages left, Fisher and Kennedy were 32 seconds ahead of Russell Brookes in his Sierra. Surely they could hold it together and cruise home for their first Manx win?

Rory takes up the story

'On the final day, we had done two or three stages and between stages we stopped to change tyres leaving us a bit tight on time so we couldn't waste time getting to the start of the following stage. We came round this corner, not on the door handles but doing 60 mph or thereabouts and there was a service van doing a three point turn in the middle of the road. We took evasive action to avoid hitting him, and hit a high kerb at the side of the big footpath. We didn't bust the wheel but we bent it to such an extent that the steering was a bit skewed.

Although we hadn't time to do anything there and then, we figured we could get a proper look before we started the stage as at that time you were permitted to change a tyre before the start of a stage if you had a puncture or a problem by asking the timekeeper who would extend your times in the time control.'

Having received permission from the marshal present at the control for an extra five minutes to allow them to change the wheel, Bertie and Rory carried on with the job at hand.

'We started to change the wheel ourselves to make sure we stayed within the rules when Russell Brookes, having come up past us and seeing what we were doing, got to the start line and started to kick up a fuss with the timekeepers. He argued that we should be started the stage not realising that we were allowed to change a tyre and the whole thing got into a bit of a tizzy.'

Of course while all this was going on the clocks were still running and, unknown to Bertie and Rory at the time, during all the frenzy Russell Brookes's actual start

right: Bertie and Rory on the Manx which they led all the way right until the last day as Rory recalls

'We were right in the hunt but because we were 19th on the road due to all the FIA A and B seeds being in front of us, if you passed somebody out on the stage, come the start of the next stage, they had to go in front of you again because of the way the timing system operated

The rally went perfectly, a copybook rally. Although we had a couple of indiscretions into the sheugh, luck was on our side and we were pushing really hard as was everyone – on the famous 12 mile St Mark's stage on the last day there was us, Colin McRae, Russell Brookes, James Cullen and, I think, Gwyndaf Evans, all finished the stage on identical times which is remarkable but it shows how much everybody was trying and pushing and how tight the event was that we were all in a position where we could do that.'

time had elapsed and he was controversially issued a new one.

When Bertie and Rory did eventually get going, just a few miles into the stage Bertie cut a corner and hit a stone or a kerb damaging the suspension strut and flattened the wheel. With still around 10 miles of the stage to go on a flat wheel they finished the stage but dropped about 50 seconds allowing Brookes in to the lead.

Rory takes up the story again

'With four or five more stages still to do, we had to get the car sorted out but also go out and give it our all. Considering that all the way up to this point we had been in the lead which gave us great motivation and kept us fully focussed. But then when this happened, the bubble completely burst, we'd lost the lead and our motivation is at Zero. But with Colin McRae only some 15 seconds behind and closing we had to try and get fired up again to go out and push as hard as we could.

Testimony to Bertie, full credit, he went out and was able to do it, and respond again and it's always a great measure of a sportsman in the way he responds to adversity.'

For Bertie to be able to hold Colin McRae was a big thing bearing in mind how fast McRae was at that time but hold him he did to get across the line in second place.

Despite the great second place, as the rally ended, and as they faced the crowds at the podium finish, deep down Bertie and Rory were hurting.

'At this point we had demoted ourselves to the fact that we lost the rally, we beat ourselves, it was in our hands and we lost it, we let it slip through our fingers, we grasped defeat from the draws of victory, all these sort of things.'

However as the inquests got under way, especially about the events at *that* stage start it began to emerge

left: Images from the Manx 1990.

top: The stage after the controversial wheel change where the M3 hit a rock and punctured

middle: The tyreless M3 arrives at a subsequent time control

bottom: A demoted Bertie and Rory put on a brave face for the huge crowds at the finish of the rally

that Russell Brookes hadn't started the stage on his correct start time. When this revelation came to light, there was much consideration among the team as to whether it would be a good or bad decision to raise a query as Rory explains

'It was their thinking that if we broke the rules, others would have no hesitation in pointing this out to the organisers about us, so if he broke the rules, it was our right to point it out. Finally, the query was written, as to why Brookes didn't start the stage on time, which if it was upheld would result in a penalty of five minutes.

Now, Bertie had never protested against anyone in his career up to that, and he didn't want to bring his own integrity into question – to be regarded as unsportsmanlike or a poor loser with sour grapes creating bad feeling and animosity with Brookes. It was totally alien to him to do that and he had no intention of going down that road as it was very important to him and I think the hardest thing Bertie had to do that weekend was sign that query form.'

Given the final results were not yet published, the team were well within their rights to lodge a query and after it was lodged, the organisers duly penalised Brookes with a penalty of five minutes pushing him down the leader board with Bertie going straight to 1st place.

The query and its initial outcome was very popular amongst the rally fans, as Rory continues

'Of course half of Ireland was there and they all wanted us to win the rally. I think it was even just that Bertie had never won the Manx which was in its glory days at the time – we'd done everything we could and deserved the win and to have it snatched away in such a manner would be a travesty.

That's not to say we were discounting Brookes for at this time he was at the top of his game – he'd won British Championships and done the World Championship and

right (top & bottom): Russell Brookes on the Manx in 1990.

middle: There were many hard triers on the Manx that year including Colin McRae (middle), showing some serious damage to the rear of the car.

always been very strangely emotional thinking that Bertie never got to win the rally he always wanted to win and when I got the win at the end it brought me right back – 1990 was really the one that got away.'

The penultimate round of the Tarmac Championship was October's Cork 20 as usual in October and despite Bertie's lack lustre performance throughout the year, Austin McHale had also had his bad days which resulted in Bertie heading to Cork with a 10 point lead in the championship.

Initially it was neck and neck as Bertie took the first stage by only a handful of seconds, but on the tricky mountainous Mullaghanish test he got his M3 out of line over a series of crests, catching grass at the side of the road and clipping a rock in the process. In an interview for *Carsport* Bertie explained the consequences of his error. *'I soon realised I had a front wheel puncture, the same wheel, incidentally, as the Manx, and although I knew I was going to lose a chunk of time to Austin there wasn't a real problem in driving the car.'*

But worse was to come as the ill handling car ran wide further down the stage on a tightening right-hander and hit another rock. *'It snapped the wishbone and the car just nosed down into the ditch. That was that. There was no real damage to the car except for the front spoiler and once they had changed the wishbone it was driving again. In fact we went back and looked at the spot where we got the puncture. It was a rock right on the edge of the road but covered up by the grass. We didn't see it when we were recceing the stage, otherwise it would have been*

his team, RED, were one of the top preparation teams in the business with direct links with Ford, backed by big sponsors such as Havoline.'

And Rory was right not to discount them as the Brookes team mustered all their resources and convinced the Stewards to overturn the penalty. Given Bertie's initial reluctance to raise a query at all, the Toughmac camp, had already made a decision not to carry on with subsequent protests if there was an overturned penalty, *'Although we had the option of protesting, we decided not to, and so we walked away, with our heads held high but underneath we were devastated.'*

Bertie was quoted to have said of all the rallies he competed in, it was his highest high and his lowest low. He had led from stage one of a rally he had never won before and this would've been the most important win of his career to date.

Rory reflects *'Looking back now I did the Manx rally many times after 1990, and finally won it in 2008 with Mark Higgins. That was an iconic day for me for it had*

in the notes. It was unfortunate but that's the way it goes.'

Austin McHale and co-driver Dermot O'Gorman were then able to cruise to a comfortable win which, with Bertie scoring no points, meant that if McHale finished in the top four on the final rally of the championship, December's Carling Rally of the Lakes he would be champion no matter what Bertie did as Rory Kennedy recalls *'We went to Killarney with an outside chance of winning the championship, but we thought we would go anyway and keep him* [McHale] *honest and try to win a rally.'*

top: Bertie and Rory took a late win on the Rally of the Lakes to clinch their first of four championships together'

below: The Bolshikhs in their similar BMW M3

At The Rally of the lakes Brian Quinn was doing Mud note duties for Bertie and as the Bolshikhs didn't have a mud notes crew he decided to help them out as Brian explains:

'It was decided that when we were doing the mud notes for Bertie we would sort the Russians out as well. I was given a set of their notes but they were all in Russian but I could make out the numbers from which I could gauge the distances and structure of the notes. So I did Bertie's notes and then transcribed the information that I had from his across on to the Russian notes and then tried to explain to the Russian co-driver what I was trying to get through. It seemed to work because the Bolshikh boys went seriously quick and gave Bertie a tough time on that rally

One other thing I could remember about the Bolshikhs was they were seriously fond of Guinness – if there was any stop or a delay and there was a pub close at hand one of them would be away like blazes to get a Guinness even though he was driving.'

Although the fight for the championship was between Fisher and McHale, the entry of Russian brothers, Nickolay and Igor Bolshikh provided stern competition as they proved from the start that they were not there just for fun with some impressive stage times.

Despite treacherous icy conditions which played havoc with the organisers trying to work around stages which had to be cancelled, the rally continued on. McHale led the rally outright after the first loop but by the end of day one he had dropped to fourth behind Bertie and the Russians who led on stage times but had incurred a ten second penalty which put them back to second place overall.

McHale attacked hard at the start of Day Two and managed to pull back time on Fisher but then on the second running of Cods Head, disaster for the Dubliner. The differential on his M3 gave way, causing almost instant retirement at the side of the road catapulting Fisher into the lead of the championship. *'We realised the champi-*

onship was there for the taking and debated should we back off and let Bolshikh win the rally, or keep the foot down and try to take the win ourselves. On the one hand we knew the championship was ours for the taking but against that we hadn't won a rally together that year, and had the Bolshikhs coming like troopers behind us. Eventually we decided to continue pushing hard which

worked well as we won the rally and the championship. It was tremendous.'

The win with some 20 seconds to spare over the Bolshikh Brothers in second and Bill Connolly in his Manta in third signalled Bertie's long awaited first Tarmac Championship – what a way to end the year!

It was a popular win and even a disappointed Austin McHale whose cruel luck had allowed Bertie to snatch the championship admits *'I didn't begrudge it to him because it was his first championship. Right from the very start of the year it was the big battle between two identical cars, two teams much the same, and it was nice to see one of them win the championship anyway.'*

1991 The R.E.D year

Fresh from success in 1990 and wanting to continue in the same manner for 1991, Bertie considered his options.

Having sold the M3 at the start of the year to Bill Connolly, as the season got underway he was still without a car. Prodrive had supplied and prepared the BMWs he had been driving for the last few years and he would have liked to continue the relationship if they could supply a car which would satisfy his requirements, ideally one of the Group A Legacys which Prodrive were putting out in the World and British Championships.

Prodrive had just signed rising star Colin McRae to drive the Legacy in the British Championship in the Rothmans colours and Bertie was hoping to get in there, to drive another car alongside McRae, but Rory Kennedy recalls

left top: Bertie and Rory with their trophy along with runners up, the Bolshikh brothers and Joe Scally, owner of the Royal Hotel in Killarney

Dave Campion, the representative from Prodrive who was responsible for looking after Bertie's and the Bolshikh's cars has cause to remember the post event party as he recalls

'Bertie and I organised dinner at Gaby's and we took all the Russians, the boys that I had over there and Bertie's and Sydney's lot too. Towards the end of the meal, Bertie said "What … What are we going to do about the bill? … What about we split it in half, are you happy with that?'

'I said I was – which was true until we actually went to pay it! The Russians in particular had got carried away with everything from the menu and the bill was well over £1000 – bloody hell I've never in all my life paid a restaurant bill like that one, but we both looked at one another and said "well we've done a deal so we'll stand over it" but I can't deny we were well stung!'

below: News of the Championship win, as featured in Carsport

'There were all sorts of rumours that there might be a car for Bertie but I think the truth of the matter was that Prodrive only had one Group A car capable of winning, and McRae had it, but they also had a Group N car as well. and in a bit of an11th hour arrangement Bertie hired the car to do the Talkland International Rally in late February but a Group N Legacy in them days wasn't much to be writing home about for it wasn't much better than a road car.'

Regardless of that lack of optimism from Rory in relation to the Group N car, they did set equal fastest time on the very first stage but later in the rally, the car had to be retired with mechanical problems.

Unhappy with what Prodrive could offer him, after the rally Bertie went looking elsewhere for other options to compete with on the remainder of what was his priority now in rallying, the Irish Tarmac Championship.

There was Toyota with the Circuit of Ireland and Ulster rally winning GT-Four Celica, or there was the Ford Sierra Sapphire Cosworth which a number of British companies were preparing for rallying. One such company was R.E.D (Rally Engineering Development), whose representative had approached Bertie at the end of the Talkland Rally regarding what they might be able to offer to him.

From that point things moved quickly as Rory explains. *'Because Prodrive had nothing else to offer him, the day after the Talkland Rally, Bertie went to meet RED. He rang me that night and said "There will be a fella called John*

right: Bertie's one and only outing in a Prodrive prepared Group N Legacy on the Talkland in 1991

He and Rory retired after numerous mechanical problems including the gearbox

Millington who will be ringing you later on – you and him sort it out" simple as that! So, John Millington, who is one of the head men now in the Ford World Rally Team, rang me a few days later and explained that the first outing would be West Cork.'

Thus Bertie's new mount for the remainder of the 1991 season was the RED prepared Sierra Sapphire Cosworth E28 JWK, the first Four-Wheel-Drive Ford ever to win an International Rally on the Manx in 1990 – yes, ironically it was the same car which Russell Brookes had driven the previous year when a road penalty incurred by Brookes was overturned to snatch victory from Bertie on the Isle of Man!

The first event to be tackled, the West Cork Rally, was planned primarily as a shakedown for the upcoming Circuit of Ireland and Bertie started the rally well as he and Rory moved into an early lead but their efforts came to nought when they suffered a puncture early on a stage

as Rory takes up the story *'At the time we'd only done 3 miles and with another 10 miles to go in the stage we had to stop. We jumped out, changed the wheel and were back on our way only dropping 1 min 40 – unheard of as you would have allowed three minutes for a flat wheel – which left us still in contention.'*

Trying to make up the time lost with the puncture, Bertie pushed even harder – too hard as it would turn out, for shortly after he had a massive accident when he lost control over a jump. The crash was considerable leaving the car in a mess and even getting out of the car safely and off the road was a challenge as Rory recalls

'We ended up on our side at the side of the road and the belts came up over the torso and I got the wildest shot in the groin leaving me winded. The car was down on my side and I remember Bertie putting his foot down over me onto the door bar before he opened his belts and just walked out through the windscreen like he was walking through a door. People were asking me was I alright and I couldn't say anything. Of course there was a bit of a panic to get me out before I managed to gasp "No, no leave me alone, I'm OK."'

While Bertie and Rory were able to walk away they were well shaken and were glad to accept a little liquid sustenance, courtesy of a local farmer, to calm their nerves after the fright of the accident!

With a written off car and the Circuit of Ireland starting less than two weeks the pressure was on but RED rose to the challenge as Rory explains *'This was our very first event with RED who basically came along and said "Hmm, We'll have to have a rethink about this… This wasn't part of the plan at all, writing this yoke off!" Anyway, we headed off home and Bertie asked RED if they could re-shell the car for the Circuit of Ireland which they did and we got the car back for the Circuit on time.'*

The 60th anniversary running of the Circuit of Ireland

left: Trying to catch someone isn't always the best of ideas.

Bertie *(top)* tried to catch John Price's Metro 6R4 *(middle)* on the West Cork Rally in 1991 and paid the price *(bottom)*

below: Bertie pictured at the Circuit of Ireland with nephew Alastair who would ensure the Fisher name stayed at the forefront in rallying in the 2000s

attracted a scant entry list of only 40 although what it lacked in size it made up in quality, with Colin McRae in the Prodrive Subaru Legacy RS heading a field that included Austin McHale and Bill Connolly in M3s, and a whole host of Sierras driven by James Cullen, Kenny McKinstry, Richard Smyth, Bertie, and visiting drivers Dave Maslen and Bob Fowden.

As the event got underway Bertie took an early lead after the Nutts Corner stage but once they got out on to the real roads McRae proved to be in a class of his own surging away from 'best of the rest' winner Bertie some four and a half minutes behind.

This was still a good result as given the lack of testing Bertie's Sierra had previous to the rally, the car was unpredictable and not set up right for the bumpy Irish stages which were a big talking point of the rally, with Fisher quoted to have said that the Glen of Imaal stage in Wicklow was the worst stage he had driven in his 22 year career.

At the Gemini Oils Donegal Rally there was another McRae to do battle with, but it was not Colin but father Jimmy who was present in a Sierra Cosworth although he never really got on the pace to threaten the lead and it was left to James Cullen to provide Bertie's nearest challenge.

Although Bertie led comfortably through the first day on the second day it was a different scenario, when he and Rory adopted a more defensive strategy which didn't work well for them as Rory explains

above: Bertie sliding sideways through a hairpin on the Circuit of Ireland

right top: Like Father Like Son – Colin takes has a cup of tea with and takes tips from father Jimmy as he becomes the second King of the Circuit from the McRae clan.

below: Colin McRae in the Subaru Legacy RS was unstoppable on the Circuit of Ireland in 1991

'There is a complete difference between an attacking and defensive mind set – when you're attacking you're doing your own thing, fully focussed and clear but when you're defending you're reacting to the other guy and

left: Donegal action with James Cullen *(top)* and Bertie *(below)*

Rory Kennedy reflects on the Fanad accident that took them out of the 1991 rally

'We went to Fanad in defensive mode and we were flying along the road when, not long after the start of the stage we came round this corner and up a straight when this wee cat ran out on the road, slithered out and then ran back in again. With it catching my attention, it just momentarily broke my concentration. The road went about a Four Right which I should have called but I got flustered and muttered "blehpelp emm Fo..Ri emm Fou..." By the time we got to the corner I was only getting myself back together and it was too late as I only was saying the corner at the corner and we sailed straight off the road'

That momentary lapse in concentration would haunt Rory for many years after as he was ribbed by his rally colleagues about the year of the cat!

I put my hand up, I made a mistake and I share a fairly heavy responsibility for that accident by not calling the note in time – but on the other hand everybody in the rally knew the corner as we had done the Fanad stage a hundred times

I don't know if Bertie had any sort of phobia about the Fanad stage. We would often have a laugh when we were going through the stage during recce because we do Fanad every year in different configurations and he would often make some funny or sarcastic remark on it but we didn't dwell too much on it. If you dwell on the negatives you'll never get anything positive'

because you're thinking about what he's doing it's easy to loose concentration and make mistakes and it effects the whole team.'

One of the day's stages was Fanad, a stage renowned for bringing Bertie bad luck and 1991 would be no different as a mistake between him and Rory with the pace notes sent them off the road and out of the rally leaving local man James Cullen, with Ellen Morgan co-driving in the Sierra Cosworth to claim a win. Followed home by Frank Meagher in second and Vincent Bonner in third, Cullen's well deserved win was only the second time a Donegal man had won his home international.

A week after Donegal, Bertie took time out from the Tarmac Championship to take part on the Burmah

Lurgan Park Rally. A rally which he had won on its first two runnings some 10 and 11 years previously but he would have his work cut out for him this time with English visitor and former works driver Tony Pond over in a Metro 6R4 at the Park. And so it proved as Pond won by some 24 seconds from Bertie with the undisputed 'King of the Park' Kenny McKinstry third in a Group N Sierra.

A whole month later was the British Midland Ulster Rally, a big one for Bertie who had not won the 'Ulster' in the nine years since he had beaten Per Eklund, Terry Kaby etc. in his MkII Escort in 1982. Obviously he wanted to win it again, but a certain flying Scotsman stood in Bertie's way and by the end of the first day Colin McRae, had built up a lead of 37 seconds.

As day two dawned, McRae's seemingly unstoppable charge faltered as on the way to Dungannon for the early Saturday morning stages his gearbox broke en route. Despite road penalties for late arrival at service, he pulled out a further 22 seconds on the first stage of the morning on Fisher. Bertie's first fastest time of the rally came on the Brantry Wood stage, a long and twisty 13 miler up tracks which at times would have to be widened and improved to be described as lanes!

McRae suffered a puncture but pulled back time on several following stages before the rally moved into Fisher country around Ballinamallard and Bertie could pile on the pressure. Unfortunately fans were deprived of a battle royal when further mechanical issues forced McRae's retirement leaving Bertie to cruise home and win ahead of Russell Brookes who drove steady throughout with few problems to finish second and four other Sierras to make it a Sierra top 6 line-up at the finish.

The victory was even sweeter for Bertie and Rory in that they convincingly beat Russell Brookes in the same car which Brookes had driven on the infamous Manx Rally the previous year – true Karma!

above: Bertie coming through a busy junction on the Ulster Rally

right top: Bertie in a moment of reflection at service in Gortin on the Ulster Rally

middle: Bertie and Rory take the winning spoils for the cameras on the finish ramp with a representative of event sponsor British Midland

bottom: Bertie beat Russell in Russell's old car !

left top: Bertie's outing on the Manx in 1991 didn't last long, retiring at the start of just the second stage with transmission troubles

bottom: The fire-spitting Sierra coming sideways into a junction on the Cork 20 Rally

below: Bertie chatting with James Cullen at the Ulster

given the high probability of breaking their cars in the attempt. But it hardly mattered to Bertie as he would barely be given the chance for any real action anyway as his transmission failed at the start of stage two.

Talking point of the weekend was Francois Chatriot, McRae's Subaru team mate who, with very little experience of the Isle of Man lanes (normally essential on a rally of that calibre) crashed heavily early on shortening the car by several feet in the process, but battled on to eventually finish second overall and pick up the 'Star of the Rally' award for his efforts. Third home was Brookes in his Sierra followed by Cullen in fourth, Mikael Sundstrom in a Mazda fifth, Dave Metcalfe in a Nova in sixth. Slotted in seventh was Frank Meagher who had kept up a good constant top 10 slot all weekend.

Another non-finish for Bertie followed on the Cork 20 Rally when a turbo oil pipe leak forced his retirement while leading the event. With the Group N championship wrapped up with four wins already, Kenny McKinstry used an ex-Al Hajri GpA Sierra in Cork to try for an outright win which, with Fisher gone, he achieved at a canter ahead of Bill Connolly in his M3 and Donal O'Donovan third in a 2 Litre Escort.

This was McKinstry's first international rally victory and it vaulted him to the top of the Tarmac Championship tables, although five drivers could potentially have secured the Dunlop Tarmac Championship going into the last round at the start of December in Killarney for the Gleneagle Hotel Rally of the Lakes.

The Manx Rally followed and the British stars were out in force again. Colin McRae in the Prodrive Legacy was once again in a class of his own, and most of the other top drivers including Brookes, Fisher and Co made conscious decisions not to even try to keep up with him

Come the rally and for various reasons most of the other Championship contenders were not present but Bertie was and he led throughout all of the rally, to win convincingly by nearly three minutes ahead of Kenny second who pushed the Russian Bolshikh brothers into third, just 16 seconds further back in third in their BMW M3.

Despite Bertie's win on the Killarney Rally of the Lakes with Kenny McKinstry taking second place, it wasn't enough and Bertie finished up second overall in the Tarmac Championship, 15 points behind McKinstry and 10 in front of Bill Connolly driving Bertie's old BMW M3.

right top: Bertie and Rory celebrate their second win of the year on the Rally of the Lakes in December

bottom: Low flying in Killarney

1992 - 1993

The Legacy years

As the 1992 season got underway with the Claren-bridge Crystal Galway International Rally in Febru-ary Bertie still had the same Sierra with which he had won the Gleneagle Hotel Rally of the Lakes some two months previously although Sydney Meeke was now back on board looking after the car rather than RED.

Although Bertie's package was still competitive, his op-position in the Tarmac Championship had not been idle with Austin McHale having acquired a Toyota Celica GT4 and Kenny McKinstry a new Prodrive prepared Subaru Legacy RS backed by Kaliber.

That Bertie was still running the Sierra was not a case that he was settled with the car but rather that he was still keen to get his hands on one of the Prodrive pre-pared Subaru Legacy's which were in short supply al-though given they had sold one of their cars to Kenny McKinstry and another to County Antrim car breaker Eddie Torrens, the time was bound to be coming pretty soon when one would be available.

As the crews set out to tackle the 22 stages in the County Galway area, it was really anyone's rally. Bertie, with experience and rally wins under his belt in the Si-erra had the confidence and knowledge of what his car was capable of, but would the newer Asian high-tech specs and performance of the Toyotas and Subarus be too much for the Ford?

On the first day it looked like experience would hold the upper hand as Bertie pulled out a comfortable lead over McKinstry whose Legacy had lost steering power assistance on stage 8 and Austin McHale whose Celica GT4 was impeded by brake issues caused by faulty sen-sors in the transmission system as he took time to ac-climatise to the car.

It wasn't all plain sailing for Bertie though as he suffered severe back pain throughout the rally following an ac-

right: Bertie and Rory corner in style on the Burmah Rally in Lurgan Park 1992

left: With a Legacy on the way, Bertie and Rory squeezed one more event in 1992 out of the Sierra, and competed on the stone-walled, low lying stages of the Galway rally

cident at Silverstone while judging a Shell scholarship Award.

Day Two opened with treacherous conditions leading to Bertie having two slight off on losing time to McKinstry although Kenny had his own issues with a turbo boost problem and a misfire. The two had several fastest times apiece for the first few stages of the day with Bertie maintaining his lead but on Stage 16 it all changed.

Rory Kennedy explained what happened. *'Just a few stages from the end we went over a big jump and when we landed the track control arm broke nearly putting us off on the following square right. We got to the end of the stage, and after messing about with the chase car we got it fixed and got going again'*

The Meeke service crew worked hard on the Ford, but Bertie would end up some nine minutes late for the next stage, which meant 90 seconds in road penalties. Despite this all but finishing Fisher's chance of a win in the West, they battled on, plagued by several problems resulting from the incident, but there was more drama to come, as Rory said. *'Sitting on the start line of the last stage, the Dyke Road spectator stage, Bertie revved hard, sidestepped the clutch and broke 1st gear, but luckily we had enough gears left to just get through the stage and still finish second but he'd had a sickner with the car.'*

With that 'sickner' as Rory put it, of the Galway Rally behind them, the time came to change, and soon after, the Sierra was sold to make way for a Legacy from Prodrive,

above: Bertie with Frank Meagher

Frank who went on to win the 1992 Circuit of Ireland event died a year after Bertie in a tragic testing accident in March 2002

right: Bertie's debut in the Legacy on the Circuit of Ireland was short lived as he went out with engine troubles

H187 GUD, the car McRae used to win the British Championship the year before and which was delivered just before the Circuit which would be Bertie and Rory's debut in the car.

With the Circuit of Ireland being dropped from the British Open Series in 1992 there were no British or foreign crews among the favourites and, released from the strictures of the British series, the rally would revert to a more traditional longer route which proved to be a major factor in the outcome. One by one the new cars with their hi-tech gadgets and gizmos fell by the wayside leaving Frank Meagher and Michael Maher with their older Sierra to be crowned Circuit Champions.

The reasons for the big guns demise? Bertie had been in contention for the lead early on but on just the seventh stage the Subaru's engine went on to three cylinders and it was all over for them. McHale's Celica had a blown head gasket on the third day of the rally while the clutch on McKinstry's Legacy failed on the final night and despite being supplied a replacement clutch from Bertie's team to get them going, it came to nothing as a blown turbo put them completely out of the rally just a few stages later.

County Down man David Greer finished second, some seven minutes behind in another Sierra with Dublin based Derek Smith in a 2.4 Escort Mk2 in third and Niall

Maguire fourth in another Escort.

Only having covered some six and a half full stages so far in the Legacy, Bertie was keen to get more stage mileage under his belt so following the Circuit of Ireland he embarked on an intensive run of three rallies in the Irish national Championship to gain experience in the car and get it set up to his liking.

The first was the Carlow Stages Rally where although the rally was curtailed due to the death of a competitor (co-driver Jim Dunne who succumbed to injuries sustained when George McCarron's Opel Manta left the road), the final results show Bertie having won by over a minute from Eddie Torrens in a similar Subaru Legacy.

Just a week later was the Monaghan Stages Rally where, seeded at 105 due to being a late entry, Bertie won the rally with over a minute and a half to spare from second place Armagh man Andrew Nesbitt in a Metro 6R4.

Finally two weeks later was the Cavan Stages Rally where the tables were turned after the Legacy suffered problems with an intermittent intercooler switch sensor, and gear selection issues and Nesbitt took the win by 12 seconds.

So keen was Bertie to get the car set up properly that in the brief break between the Monaghan and Cavan rallies, he entered the Manx National Rally on the Isle of Man. It was Bertie's third time doing the rally, having won on his previous two visits in 1987 and 1989 and this time would be no different as he dominated over the 120 stage miles to finish over two minutes ahead of John Price from Wales in a Metro 6R4 in second place.

Three victories in as many weeks brought a massively increased level of confidence in the car and the team in general to take back to the Dunlop Tarmac Championship at the Shell Donegal Rally in June where a win by

left top: Frank Meagher and Michael Maher in their Sierra

below: celebrating victory

right clockwise from top left: Bertie and Rory on the Carlow; Monaghan; Manx National Rallies: Cavan winner, Andrew Nesbitt in his Metro 6R4.

The Cavan Stages rally was the first time in several years Rory was not able to sit with Bertie, but it provided some amusement.

'I was going away on holidays on the day of the Cavan Rally. Enter Austin Frazer for the Cavan Rally. And of course true to form, they went to that rally, and then what happened to them? They got beat! So of course I had great pleasure in teasing Bertie that some boy in a wee Metro had beat him'

Rory explained the purpose of going to do these events.

'Those rallies were used to get the car set up - Bertie felt it was a bit wandery and it took a while to get the right tarmac set up for him. When Prodrive brought out a new car they would come to Ireland to do some testing and develop a 'Basic Irish Set up'. So when you got the car it would have been in that 'Basic Irish Set up', which you would then adjust to suit yourself – every driver's setup is different'

'We were still getting the car set up to Bertie's liking in the Isle of Man. We went there, and the car wasn't initially great but as time went on through the event we got it better and finally by the end of the rally it was perfect, we'd found the ideal setup and went on to win that rally, 2nd time for me, 3rd time for Bertie.'

left top: Bertie flying high on a misty Muckish stage jump

below left: Bertie celebrating his second win in Donegal

below: Bertie cosies up to fellow Subaru buddy Kenny McKinstry

over five minutes from Austin McHale who said he was simply unable to match the pace of the Subaru, showed that the promise shown was not empty!

Just six days after the champagne was sprayed in Donegal was the Burmah Lurgan Park Rally where the undisputed 'King of the Park' Kenny McKinstry made up for his disappointing Donegal finish by winning the event for the fifth time,

14 seconds ahead of Bertie who after the seven short runs through the town park, was unable to match the Banbridge man's pace. Kenny also picked up a consider-able £2,500 in prize money for the win. Kenny Colbert from County Tyrone finished third in his Metro 6R4.

A whole month after Lurgan was 'The Elbow' spon-sored Ulster Rally. While the Circuit of Ireland had been removed from the Mobil 1 / Top Gear British Open Championship, the Ulster Rally remained part of it and its championship status brought with it some strong opposition including rising superstar Colin McRae in the Subaru Legacy.

Bertie had won the Ulster Rally the previous year in the Sierra and had no plans to give up the title easily. He was fastest on several stages on Day One and despite some misfire problems and a puncture he finished Day One in just behind McRae.

Then disaster. As day two dawned – or rather just be-fore it dawned – Bertie, dazzled in the half light by the glare of his light pod reflecting off a white washed wall, ran off the road. It wasn't a major impact but unfortu-nately a fence post had punctured the radiator and al-though Bertie and Rory were able to make it out of the stage, the engine was overheating and they were forced to retire to avoid irreparable damage.

With Bertie's exit from the rally, Colin McRae totally dominated from the front winning with a staggering eleven minute margin over David Greer in second and Frank Meagher in third, both in Sierras.

In contrast with the frenetic start to the year there was

a full 6 week break between the Ulster and the Manx in September. Once again Bertie would be up against 1991 Manx winner Colin McRae in the Rothmans Prodrive Subaru Legacy RS amongst other top line entries including Kenny McKinstry in his Kaliber sponsored Legacy, Patrick Snijers in a Castrol Sierra Cosworth, Frank Meagher in an older Sierra Cosworth, and many others.

Bertie and Rory leapt into the lead on the first night's stages raising a few eyebrows in the process as Rory says. *'We were going really well, pushing hard and getting progressively faster. Some of the British drivers were surprised and didn't expect us to be in the lead early on. Bertie really showed how good a driver he really was, competing against Colin McRae who nobody could touch at the time'*

Given where Colin McRae was in his career at that point and where he was destined to go, it was a big deal leading a rally where he was in a similar car. But the lead would soon evaporate. A fierce attack back by McRae, plus a series of problems including a broken brake pipe, a tyre puncture and later a broken turbo, culminated in Bertie and Rory dropping back to second behind McRae where they eventually finished overall.

Bertie, in an interview for *Carsport* at the time told of how hard he was pushing as the rally unfolded.

'I had a great run over those early stages. I had a good rhythm going but I was right on the limit and taking every last ounce out of the car. There was no margin for error.

Colin had been 23 seconds faster over the Curraghs earlier in the day and I wasn't surprised when he took 11 off me. I knew he was going to come back at me and that was the stage to do it. There are a lot of square corners and better throttle response of his car is worth at least a second each time.'

Bertie's Subaru wasn't the only one to suffer turbo prob-

lems as Kenny McKinstry's Legacy suffered the same issue and as a result of the time taken to fit a new one, incurred time penalties which, added to time lost due to a puncture, meant that while Kenny was going hard he was too far back to realistically get any higher than third place overall.

In the end, the rally finished with a Subaru 1-2-3 podium, with Colin McRae arriving back on the finish ramp at Douglas promenade some 7 minutes in front of Fisher, with Kenny McKinstry rounding off the podium, over 2 minutes further back in third.

Any disappointment from Manx and Ulster Rallies had to be set aside as the team headed south for the penultimate round of the Dunlop Tarmac Championship, the Fitzpatrick Hotels Cork 20 Rally at the start of October.

With non-finishes in 1980, 1983, 1987, 1990 and 1991, almost all related to crashes, Cork 20 was a kind of a bogey rally for Bertie, but as some of the leading rally and championship contenders began to fall by the way side things began to look up. On the fast but slippy Cork stages Frank Meagher went off the road and into a field followed by early leader Kenny McKinstry in his Kaliber Subaru Legacy who went off the road, hitting a wall and out of the rally completely. David Greer, who started the rally on equal championship points with Kenny McKinstry, hit some rocks on Stage 9, presumed to have been placed there by vandals, and although he was able to continue, he was out of contention.

Bertie came across the same rocks but saw them just in time and managed to avoid them and his subsequent efforts for the remainder of the rally consisted of a second day cruise in the Toughmac Legacy with a winning gap of over three and a half minutes from nearest rival Austin McHale. The Dubliner had suffered a series of problems with his Tom Hogan Motors Toyota Celica GT4 including a puncture which led to a driveshaft failure,

ners would finish or be well up in the top ten, it did not look likely that Bertie would have been able to win the Dunlop Tarmac Championship, but his fortune (and others misfortune) in Cork meant that the Championship standings had been turned on their head to the extent that Bertie only had to finish in the top five in the final round in Killarney, the Rally of the Lakes, to win the Championship outright with only Frank Meagher in a position to challenge should Bertie retire from the rally, but that didn't happen.

The top four finishers in Killarney were the same four as in Cork, with Fisher winning comfortably ahead of Austin McHale's Celica, David Greer third and Enda Nolan both in Sierra. The Belgian Dominique Bruynell in a BMW M3, made up for the lack of presence of the Bolshikh's (who had written off their M3 in a pre-event test) by finishing fifth, and Frank Meagher who had been up as high as third at one stage when a heavy landing after a jump damaged his suspension before a later puncture and road penalties, resulted in a sixth overall finish.

left top: Bertie en-route to his first ever win on the Cork 20 International in 1992

below: Bertie and Rory made it three in a row wins on the Rally of the Lakes in three different cars, BMW, Ford and Subaru

This was the last year the Lakes rally was run in December, changing to a summer date thereafter. When Rory Kennedy was asked which he thought Bertie preferred he was ambivalent

"It didn't matter because we could win in the summer or the winter although the winter Killarney was really our party piece. It was the end of the season, going there having done all the others during the year. 1992 wasn't unusual We went there, full on it with a winning formula, with everything just spot on"

but held a steady second with Enda Nolan co-driven by TV presenter Michael Lyster in their Sierra, in third.

Going into Cork, on the assumption all of the top run-

1993

Just two months after the last rally car went over the Killarney Rally of the Lakes finish ramp and they said goodbye to the 1992 Tarmac Championship, the new season was back in full swing as usual in early February for the first round of the 1993 Championship, the Galway International.

The list of challengers for the honours in Galway had not changed much from the last few rounds of the 1992 Championship although after Austin McHale's disappointing first full season in the ex Carlos Sainz Toyota Celica GT-Four he was hoping to release more of its potential after a series of changes over the winter to the engine as well as changing to Pirelli tyres from Dunlop.

McHale's hopes were realised with a triumphant win in Galway, his first Tarmac Championship round win in exactly two years, the previous win coming in Galway in 1991.

Kenny McKinstry, who had been leading up to the start of day two, was pipped for the win after the persistent McHale kept nibbling away at his lead to finally overcome the Subaru in the final few stages.

For the new season Bertie had changed oil supplier, changing from Shell to sign up with Mobil 1 just before Galway, but it failed to bring him good fortune as he suffered problems with a turbo as well as several punctures which cost him around three to four minutes demoting him out of contention and towards the bottom end of the top five positions. As well as the direct time loss they cost, the niggling problems seemed to sap Bertie's motivation which wasn't helped by the discovery that a change of gearbox as a precaution after the puncture

right top: Team tactics and some last minute mud note checking in the motor home, on the Galway Rally

below: Bertie on his first rally of the year in the West on the Galway International

left: Bertie and Rory fought on the Circuit of Ireland with Kenny McKinstry in a similar Subaru Legacy for the lead until Bertie faulted

had left him with an inoperative centre differential. As Bertie summed it up in an interview with *Carsport* shortly after the rally, saying *'It cost about four minutes in time lost in the stage and road penalties plus about another minute in motivation – once it had happened I couldn't get myself fired up again.'*

However, despite the lack of motivation he managed to overhaul Frank Meagher and Enda Nolan on the Sunday to finish in third overall.

The Circuit of Ireland Rally held on Easter weekend was a fascinating prospect with any number of potential winners, and indeed during the rally there were several leaders. With much of the first days stage mileage in

his home county, Down and the others in Lurgan Park where he was an expert, Kenny McKinstry had led the rally early through Day One and overnight into Day Two, at which point he held a lead of a minute over Bertie in second who in turn held a minute over third placed McHale.

McKinstry's comfortable lead evaporated when his driver's seat came loose on the opening test on Day Two allowing Bertie to take the lead but, as the rally progressed into McHale territory through the Wicklow mountain stages of Aughavannagh and Sally Gap, he began to charge and almost grabbed first spot but for a spin on one of the day's final stages leaving Bertie in the lead after two days hard rallying.

However Bertie's lead would not last as on the first stage of the 'Sunday Run' stages in the Waterford area he crashed the Legacy heavily and the reason for the crash gives an insight into the fine margins in top level rallying. Kieran McAnallen who had been doing mud notes crew along with Brian Quinn explains:

'The section where he went off was a blind crest followed by a quite gravelly corner a little further on. When Brian and I had looked at it we were wondering whether to put a caution on it or not and we decided no, that there was enough distance to the corner, but when Bertie did the stage they jumped high and long and landed on the gravel and had no chance of getting stopped, just slid straight on into the bank.'

The impact burst the radiator which would normally signal instant retirement, for fear of the car seizing without any water to cool the engine but when Rory got on the radio to Prodrive engineer Paul Howarth he assured them they could continue if they followed his guidelines as Paul explains 'There's a bit of a trick with the Subaru engine – although it would lock up very easily being an aluminium block you could just let it cool off then see if it will start again. This is something I saw in Indonesia quite a few times so I told Rory to keep the engine turned off, wait a few minutes and restart.'

As Rory recalls Bertie was quite reluctant but said he'd give it a try if it meant they could continue in the rally. 'On Paul's advice we drove on as best as we could but

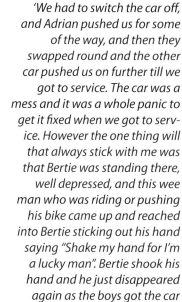

right top: Bertie takes the shortest route back to service after the incident

below: The Meeke & Prodrive mechanics work frantically to fix the car in the following service

Once Bertie and Rory got the car out of the stage, the two chase cars, one being driven by Ian Cuddy and the other by Adrian Kirkland, took turns to push the car to the following service.

'We had to switch the car off, and Adrian pushed us for some of the way, and then they swapped round and the other car pushed us on further till we got to service. The car was a mess and it was a whole panic to get it fixed when we got to service. However the one thing will that always stick with me was that Bertie was standing there, well depressed, and this wee man who was riding or pushing his bike came up and reached into Bertie sticking out his hand saying "Shake my hand for I'm a lucky man". Bertie shook his hand and he just disappeared again as the boys got the car fixed and, while we didn't win the rally fair enough, we done alright!'

then she stopped down the road and we thought she had seized. We got on the radio again to Paul, and he assured us to not worry about it as the engine would shut down before it would seize, so we waited a wee while and started her up again and on we went but we lost over five

engine troubles.

There was now such a gap between McHale and Fisher that all Austin had to do was cruise home, but given that the final leg of the rally through Monday night into Tuesday with a total of 140 stage miles over the 12 stages still remaining, 'cruise' is a wholly inappropriate term for the task McHale faced.

As around half of the original 80+ Good Friday starters pulled into the finish at Newcastle in County Down on Easter Tuesday afternoon after having completed 420 stage miles Austin had completed the five day route with a massive six minute margin over Bertie's Legacy, struggling to make up for lost time after his accident but happy to be home a further fourteen minutes ahead of third placed James Cullen in his Escort Cosworth Group N car.

minutes limping out of the stage.'

As day three closed, McHale led, with Kenny McKinstry two minutes back in second and Fisher a further 5 minutes back in third.

Day Four, Monday, and as the competitors progressed onwards from Tipperary, through Clare and up to Galway McHale continued to lead and it was McKinstry's turn for bad luck as the Legacy ground to a terminal halt with

The Carling Rally of the Lakes based in Killarney was next, only five months after its last running due to its shift to the May bank holiday weekend. This move, seen almost as essential by the organisers, allowed for all of the stages to be ran in complete daylight, without continuing into stages of darkness towards the end of the first or second day. This cleared up potential logistical problems, safety issues and costs for competitors not having to purchase special lamp pods for their cars and special lights for servicing. It also made for a generally warmer and more pleasant spectating experience and with it being a bank holiday weekend, brought the people out in their droves.

Austin McHale, fresh from his victories in Galway and on the Circuit was expected to do well but when a burst

right: Bertie and Rory won once again on the Carling Rally of the Lakes, the first time it ran as a 'summer' event

hydraulic pipe on the very first stage resulted in penalties which dropped him out of contention to tenth overall, Fisher and Kennedy were left in a class of their own. They went on to dominate the rally, leading from the first stage to the finish, Bertie's fourth win in succession in the County Kerry round. At no point during the rally was his lead in danger, which was in the end over four minutes from his nearest challenger, second place finisher James Cullen whose Group N Escort Cosworth went through several gearboxes throughout the weekend. Belgian visitor Domonique Bruynell rounded off the podium in his BMW M3.

With the Tarmac Championship half over already, go-

ing into the Shell Donegal Rally in June, Austin McHale held a marginal lead after two maximums and the poor result in Killarney, but Bertie with a 1st, 2nd and 3rd was within striking distance should Austin have any more disappointing runs – which is exactly what happened in Donegal as McHale retired on the first day with mechanical problems.

Bertie had jumped into an immediate lead of 13 seconds after the first stage and by the end of the day the gap to second place man Kenny McKinstry was still only 18 seconds. It was looking tight for the remainder of the rally, but a gamble made on a single tyre choice on the very wet Saturday afternoon of the rally proved to be a

major turning point.

Given the unpredictable weather patterns around the stages in the Portsalon, Lough Swilly and Milford area, it could be incredibly wet where a service was located but a few miles away the road would be bone dry. That was the case in 1993 on the Donegal, when it was pouring rain at a permitted road side tyre change near Kerrykeel en-route to do the Knockalla stage and wets seemed to be the obvious choice. While Kenny had made the choice to stay with wets, Bertie, partly on the guidance of Pirelli's Any Hallam, and Chase/Weather Crew Kieran McAnallen and Sydney Meeke who had gone out to the stages to scout out the weather and road conditions, took the gamble on slick tyres. It was a gamble that paid off as the end of that stage and the following two stages were dry and Bertie doubled his lead over McKinstry.

With a comfortable lead built up, even though there were signs of a failing turbo on the Toughmac-Mobil 1 Legacy, it wasn't enough to harm Bertie's lead, which he held right to the end of the rally, when the final margin between he and Kenny was just over two minutes. Winner of the rally two years previous in a Sierra Cosworth, James Cullen in his Group N Escort Cosworth was in third, four minutes behind McKinstry. This was Bertie's third win in the North West, and his fifth international in twelve months. He was really on top form.

Over a month after the Shell Donegal International

left top: Bertie and Rory travel through a scenic coastal stage on the Donegal Rally in June

below: Kenny McKinstry was Bertie's main challenger on the Donegal Rally in 1993 where Bertie edged ahead because of a single tyre choice which was an all important factor with the unpredictable weather

right: images from the Donegal Rally in 1993 including:-

top left: An unusual shale and seashell lined stage on Malin Head,

top right: team tactics with Andy Hallam of Pirelli, Sydney, Kieran, Bertie and Brian Quinn

middle left: Colin McRae on motorbike chatting with Bertie and Rory outside Rally HQ

Rally was the Village Homes Ulster Rally. Being a round of the British Open Championship as well as the Dunlop Irish Tarmac Championship, the event attracted some top quality entries from Britain and Europe for the many local crews who competed on it every year to measure themselves against.

Amongst the leading visitors were Richard Burns and Alister McRae in Elonex Subaru Legacy's, David Llewellyn in a works Vauxhall Astra GSI, with Gwyndaf Evans, Rob-

bie Head and Malcolm Wilson in Escort Cosworths.

Wilson, who from the late 90s until the mid-2010s ran the official works Ford WRC team and now runs the leading privateer Ford team in the World Rally Championship had been having a lack lustre year in the British Championship up to that point in 1993 but everything went right for him on the Ulster which he dominated to give the Michelin Pilot Escort Cosworth its maiden win on the British Open Series.

left: Malcolm Wilson gave the Michelin Pilot Escort a successful pilot run in Ireland by dominating the 1993 Ulster Rally to take his first Ulster rally win.

Bertie had a relatively disappointing run. The only spare gearboxes Prodrive had brought to the event were the electronically controlled versions for the Elonex cars which they were looking after. As such when his Legacy became troubled with gear selection issues, there was little he could do only battle on regardless. The issue, which had been a recurring and worsening problem throughout the year, had cropped up again despite the gearbox having been sent back earlier in the week to Prodrive for a complete overhaul.

The end of the first day rallying which had seen the retirement of Richard Burns, caught out by shiny tar on an approach to a downhill junction and crashing out of the rally saw Bertie in fourth, with Austin McHale second behind Wilson and Kenny McKinstry right behind him by one second in third.

A very early and very wet start to Day Two dawned and with Burns out of the rally Prodrive were able to modify one of their spare gearboxes to suit Fisher's car improving his chances which improved further when, on the early morning stages around Dungannon, McHale had an accident when his brake pedal snapped as his Celica approached a tricky left hand bend at over 100mph and he had little choice but to head straight on into a bank. The car, while not entirely mangled, was retrievable but he retired shortly later, afraid of the same brake pedal issue recurring.

right: Images from the Ulster Rally

top: Mechanics working on the Legacy on the Main Street in Aughnacloy County Tyrone, a popular service halt for the Ulster Rally after the early Saturday morning stages in the area

middle: Bertie slides around a very wet Ulster lane

bottom: Former World Champion boxer Barry McGuigan who competed on a few rallies around this time gets in on the act and plays for the cameras

Kenny McKinstry also had a gearbox issue which together with a bad tyre choice meant he slipped back moving Fisher up to second And it was there he finished

Even contest: Bertie Fisher and Barry McGuigan indulge in a light-hearted 'trial of strength' before the start of the Village Homes Ulster Rally — but out on the road former World featherweight boxing champion Barry will be hard pushed to keep up with Tarmac rally champion Fisher.
Picture by Trevor Martin

left: Future British World Rally Champion Richard Burns took the Elonex Subaru Legacy to a win on the Isle of Man after it looked like eventual second place finisher Kenny McKinstry could have taken the win until a time costly mistake.

the first Irish winner of the famous Isle of Man rally. He had maintained an overnight lead of 40 seconds from Richard Burns who, in the Elonex Subaru Legacy, only had to finish to secure the British Championship and in the process become the youngest person ever to win it. A simple mistake on the second day however cost McKinstry most of his lead and allowed Burns to pounce and take the lead, a lead which he would hold to the end of the rally. In the end McKinstry finished second, a minute behind Burns, with Robbie Head in an Escort Cosworth third and Frank Meagher fourth in a Sierra.

As for Bertie? Well, despite not feeling well and having to see a doctor during the rally, he had started well but then got caught out on a left-hander and the car hit a wall, bounced across the road, climbed the bank and ended up on its nose, breaking a steering arm. Although

ahead of the Elonex Subaru Legacy of McRae in third with McKinstry in fourth.

After Bertie's near miss on the Manx in 1990, for a time in 1993 it looked too like Kenny McKinstry would be

they were able to continue, the delay of changing the arm resulted in 2 minutes of road penalties, dropping him to 18th overall. With time loss from the accident, and later brake problems causing other excursions off the road, Bertie retired from the rally after he put the car in a ditch backwards.

In an interview shortly after for *Carsport*, Bertie said:

'I was able to get it back on the road without much delay but three or four corners later the same thing happened again and this time we couldn't get it out. There were no spectators around and it took five minutes or so to get enough people to lift the front out of the ditch.'

A disappointed Bertie actually resigned himself to the thought that he may never win the Isle of Man based event, which unfortunately turned out to be an accurate prophecy *'I knew there and then I wasn't destined - ever - to win the Manx so I pulled out at the end of the stage. Maybe if I had been feeling better I would have carried on but there just didn't seem to be any point in prolonging the agony.'*

I asked Rory Kennedy about the high number of Manx non-finishes and the several close ones but never managing to finish first. He said, *'He loved the rally, and would have loved to win but he never could manage it. It was like reaching for something that was just a wee bit out of reach, not being fit to get it but coming very close on a lot of times.'*

Despite the disappointment of the Manx, with his string of excellent results throughout the rest of the year when

the points had been calculated, Bertie had won his third Dunlop Irish Tarmac Rally Championship with a round to spare. He had secured the championship already comfortably with two wins, two seconds and a third, and so he did not go to the new final round, the Cork 20

right top: Bertie having a splashing time on the Manx,

below: Showing some battle scars after an indiscretion with some Isle of Man scenery

Giving Back
Bertie the Clubman, teacher and promoter

above: Even when in semi retirement in 1986 Bertie didn't entirely stay away from the special stages, teaming up with Austin Frazer in Spectator Control car for the organisers of the Donegal International

While Bertie was first and foremost a competing driver, he was always aware of the fun and enjoyment rallying had given him and thus, when the opportunity arose, he was always willing to put something back. Whether you needed a clubman to help out on events at the local motor club, someone to co-ordinate groups to organise and improve the safety of rallying at the highest level, someone to promote and sponsor events, someone to lend up and coming drivers a helping hand or promote initiatives to get more people involved in the sport, if Bertie could help, he would.

At the Enniskillen MC 25th Anniversary Dinner: Back L-R Austin Frazer, Pat McCourt, Ron Neely, Bertie Fisher, Mervyn Johnston Front L-R Gladys Fisher, Sylvia Johnston, Cahal Curley, Doreen Frazer

On the safety front, having been involved in one fatal accident and, due to his skill and good fortune, just avoiding a potentially much worse one, Bertie was acutely aware of the risks of high speed motor sport with hordes of fans in close proximity. As such, after everything came to a head following serious accidents both abroad and closer to home in Ireland in 1986 Bertie played a key role in developing and introducing new safety measures, getting involved at first hand when he and Austin Frazer drove the Chief Safety Con-trol Car on behalf of the R.I.A.C. at the 1986 Donegal International Rally.

Improving safety was also a factor in his desire to give competitors a louder voice in the planning and running events and in 1995 he was instrumental in the setting up of the I.R.C.A (Irish Rally Competitors Association) which sought to influence governing bodies to avoid overly obtuse rules being introduced and to act as a co-ordinating body when there needed to be collective agreement between competitors on the general aspects of the sport. Having high profile personalities like Bertie at its core, the I.R.C.A was a great platform from which issues that needed addressing could be aired. As Kieran McAnallen, who was initially Chairman of the I.R.C.A, recalls *'As a result of a meeting of the top competitors within Irish rallying, it was decided to set up a representative body of competitors to liaise with the governing bodies, i.e. M.S.A/T.R.O.A, etc. I was honoured to be asked by Bertie and fellow competitors to take chairmanship of this body. My position allowed me to sit in on meetings of the T.R.O.A, and M.S.A, plus others as a representative of the I.R.C.A. Bertie, like many others, travelled the length and breadth of Ireland to attend meetings and many positive outcomes were achieved.'*

However not all Bertie's non-competitive contribution was so high profile and he was happy to help promote grass roots activity such as when, during a break between rallies in 1999, he took time out to help launch the new Rally School Ireland centre just outside Scotstown in deepest rural County Monaghan. The Minister for Regional Development in the Republic at the time Chris Flood TD was present to officially open it. Amongst the drivers present to help Mr Flood open it in style were Bertie, Andrew Nesbitt and Niall Maguire, who drove their respective cars for demonstration runs around the purpose built track which would be and still is used for groups of people to come and learn the basics of what rallying is all about.

Another important involvement by Bertie at the grass roots level of Irish Rallying was by helping to launch and financially support the Irish Tarmac Rally Supporters Club. A brainchild of Matt Doherty, an ex Clerk of the Course of the Donegal International Rally and an organising stalwart in the North West of the country, who had initially approached several drivers early in 1987 including Bertie with a view to putting their weight behind an initiative to give Irish rallying the rejuvenated kick start it needed, the two month ban was imposed on stage events in Ireland in 1986 as safety measures were re-evaluated as previously discussed.

In terms of sponsoring events Fisher Engineering had always been willing to help out but In the year 2000 Bertie was to get involved on a whole new level which demonstrated the connections he had and the respect in which they held him when the T.R.O.A (Tarmac Rally Organisers Association) who are responsible for the running of the Irish Tarmac Rally Championship were left in a tricky situation when the Galway International, the Circuit of Ireland and the Ulster Rally dropped out of the series.

This resulted in a huge void that needed filling, not only in order to keep the Tarmac Championship healthy but also due to the fact that there was not to be a single round of the Championship planned to be held in Northern Ireland that year. When the T.R.O.A asked Enniskillen Motor Club could they help, Bertie stepped in with a suggestion of a single venue, one day rally based around the Cavan-Fermanagh border on a road, but with access from The Quinn Group's yards near Derrylin

on the north side of the border avoiding the need for road closing orders as the mountain road was a private road with rights of access held by the Quinn Group.

Given the long-time close ties Fisher Engineering had with the Quinn Group Bertie approached Sean Quinn who recalls *'I was more than welcoming for it to happen when Bertie approached me, and we would like to think we are a community based company what with our proud association in the area given my father and grandfather grew up here, so as far as we and the local community were concerned, anything like the rally which brought a bit of life, a bit of investment and a bit of enjoyment to the area was more than welcome, and sure that's life and society isn't it, you never try to block progress if people want to enjoy themselves.'*

With Sean's agreement the fledgling idea

Bertie and Sean Quinn at the launch of the Summit Rally

was put into motion and would eventually go on to be called the 'Summit 2000 Rally'.

Bertie threw himself in to organising the event, getting several motor clubs involved and engaging rally veteran Austin Frazer as Event Director.

The Summit 2000 Rally was very much billed as a cross-border, cross community supported event and, with Fisher Engineering as the event's main sponsors, it was able to attract support from the NI Millennium Company, Fermanagh District Council and UTV. All the event needed for a final polish were some superstar headline acts which duly appeared in the form of former world champions Stig Blomqvist and Hannu Mikkola.

Dave Campion of Prodrive, recalls how Hannu Mikkola came to be there.

'I felt that needed to happen for Bertie and Prodrive. Bertie had asked me "Could you get a star name to come across to the Summit Rally" and by some mischance some time previously, I had arrived at a test where we were doing some testing with a Group N car and Hannu was at the same venue driving a Mark 2 Escort for David Sutton. I have known Hannu for long enough and we got chatting over a coffee. He had never driven a Group N car and asked if he could have a go. I couldn't get him out of it! He said "Bloody hell, that was good fun, bit different to these things (referring to the Escort). I would really like to try a proper World Rally Car at some stage' and I said "Well if the opportunity comes up you're more than welcome". Shortly afterwards Bertie rang me and he told me about what it was he was trying to do and I said I would have a look and see. The trouble is the cost of running a WRC car per kilometre would blow your head off so it wasn't an easy thing to do, but I had a car and a load of tyres and I managed to con some tyres out of Pirelli and then heard that Hannu was coming to the UK to do a PR thing the week before and I rang him and I said "You said you wanted to try a World Rally Car, there's a rally for charity in Northern Ireland, would you be prepared to do that" He said "Hmm yeah maybe". I said "You are not going to get paid for it but it won't cost you anything" so he said "Yeah I'll do it if I can take Number 1 Son as a co-driver". I said "Has he got a licence?" He said "He can have". I said "So long as he turns up with a li-

cence I think everything else can be fixed". So I rang Bertie and told him. The only person in Prodrive who knew we were not getting paid at the end of it was me, and my justification was we had taken a lot of money from Ireland, Bertie and others and this was a "Thank you very much". David Richards respected Bertie for all the same reasons that the rest of us do.'

The event itself was a huge success, with thousands of spectators coming out to see the day's rallying. The rally was initially won on times by Derek McGarrity but an alleged infringement of the technical regulations meant he was excluded from the results, when the Subaru WRC he was driving was deemed to be underweight by the eligibility scrutineers. Andrew Nesbitt thus inherited the win in his Subaru Impreza WRC, with Austin McHale second in his Toyota Corolla WRC, Daniel Doherty third, Stig Blomqvist fourth, and Mark Fisher rounding off the top five in Kieran McAnallen's Mitsubishi Evo Group N car. Kieran's Evo was also used for pre-event stage setup by Bertie and Austin Frazer.

After the day's stages had ended with a Champagne finish, the prize giving was held at the Slieve Russell Hotel where it was eventually declared that in excess of £40,000 been raised which was distributed to local charities – a remarkable achievement given the often loss making nature of organising rallies!

In addition to his support for the sport in general, Bertie was also keen to support up and coming young drivers

And Bertie's influence wouldn't end even after he passed away.

On New Years Eve 2000-2001, Kieran McAnallen was out at a private gathering with his wife Phil, Bertie and Gladys and a discussion ensued about Kris Meeke, one of the two sons of Sydney Meeke who for many years prepared and helped run Bertie's rally cars.

'Bertie said he would love to get him a rally car. He said he had been in touch with Gerry McGarrity and asked him to help look for Mark's old Peugeot and that Bertie wanted to do this for the late Carol Meeke, Kris's mother, who had recently passed away. Bertie asked me if I would share the costs of getting Kris up and going as he felt he had potential, of which I agreed.' Kieran recalls.

Naturally with the horror of the accident on the 21st January, everyone forgot about the plan until the following Saturday afternoon when Kieran was relaxing at home and he remembered what Bertie and he had discussed *'It was like a white light flashing in to my eyes and I felt I had to do something about this to fulfil Bertie's wishes.'*

At this time, Kris was working at Malcolm Wilson's company M-Sport in Cumbria and wasn't aware of the plans which were afoot for him to get his foot onto the rallying ladder but, having approached a few fellow rally competitors with a view to contributing towards the fund, Kieran also visited Sydney to gain his permission as well as Gerry McGarrity, who had looked after Mark's rallying efforts previously.

Gerry, initially reluctant to get involved due to the huge loss he felt after his great friend Mark's passing, eventually agreed to become

Kris Meeke, 2009 IRC champion

part of the plan to get Kris on his feet. *'Gerry set about looking for a car and off to England he went. After looking at several cars which didn't fit the suitable bill, he knocked on the door of Peugeot UK HQ in Coventry with whom he had a relationship having worked with them running Mark Fisher's cars.'* Kieran continued.

Peugeot had a new shell but they were reluctant to sell it as they wanted to place it in a museum. However they eventually agreed to sell it after a number of phone calls were made to both Stella Bowles and Mick Linford who were part responsible for the running of Peugeot's Motorsport division. Gerry landed home with the new shell and set about preparing it for some rallying.

Kieran and Gerry then approached Gordon Noble, who had sat with Mark for the latter part of his career and knew the ins and outs of the UK rallying scene although he too was initially reluctant until Kieran applied his considerable persuasive powers.

Thus with the package put together and Gerry running the operation Kris set out on a yearlong championship, winning the first rally but with limited success for the remainder of the year.

As Kieran reflects fondly *'Although that was the end of my involvement in Kris's rallying, he later went on to bigger and better things and it's nice to think that a part of Bertie's legacy lives on in that success.'*

1965
1975
1985
1995
2005

228

1994 · 1997

The Blue 555 Subaru

With the Legacy coming near the end of its development potential as it was replaced in the WRC (World Rally Championship) by the new Group A Subaru Imprezas being used by Prodrive, Bertie's plans for 1994 included the acquisition one of the new cars, although with limited availability from Prodrive he would have to wait a few months before he could get his hands on one.

As such Bertie started his campaign to retain the Dunlop Tarmac Championship using the same trusty Legacy he had driven for the previous two seasons with little changed on the car since 1993.

On the first round of the championship, the Statoil Galway International Rally, there were a number of potential winning crews including amongst many others, Bertie and Rory, Austin McHale and Dermot O'Gorman in their Celica, new boys to the Tarmac club Stephen Finlay and Dessie Wilson in their new Michelin Pilot Escort, and Kenny McKinstry and Robbie Philpott who in their usual Kaliber backed Legacy jumped into the lead after just the first stage by nineteen seconds!

They continued to dominate throughout the first day to take a lead of over a minute into day two when despite two punctures on the same stage continued to win the rally outright. Bertie, while never threatening McKinstry's lead throughout the rally, had been going along comfortably in second place until, on the penultimate stage, he put the car off the road into a field and out of the rally as he hit a pole in the process.

That promoted Austin McHale to second, and that is where he finished in the Celica, 46 seconds behind McKinstry, ten seconds in front of third place finisher Stephen Finlay in the Michelin Pilot Escort. Given that it was his first competitive outing in the car, it was an exemplary drive by Finlay having competed in Sierras over the previous few years.

right: Bertie and Rory who in 1997 took their second Circuit of Ireland victory in three years

The Galway Rally in 1994 would be the last time Bertie would competitively drive the Legacy and, with the Impreza almost ready at Prodrive, attention turned to the next rally. On the Tarmac Championship calendar this would have been the Circuit of Ireland but this time Bertie decided to opt out with a suggestion that he was unhappy at the type of pace note system used on the rally given as a reason why. For this particular Circuit the

supplied pacenotes had been prepared by Russell Brookes, who used a system a little bit different from the one that many of the Irish crews would have been used to, giving rise to many complaints from local competitors..

So instead of the Circuit of Ireland Bertie followed the example of several other Irish drivers and headed to the forests of Wales to debut the car on the Welsh Rally, held in March, that year two weeks before the Circuit of Ireland.

Competing in both the British and Irish Championships throughout the year in the Michelin Pilot Ford Escort Cosworth Stephen Finlay was there with the Welsh being a round of the British Championship, but so was Tarmac contender Austin McHale in his Toyota Celica GT-Four.

Bertie's car, L444 MCA, was a first generation of Impreza, the shell being Prodrive Impreza Chassis 001 which was used first by Markku Alen on the 1000 Lakes Rally in 1993. It bore the first personalised registration of several that Bertie would use with the MCA being related to the fact Kieran McAnallen was one of the main sponsors together with Mobil 1, the oil company getting more involved with funding Bertie's rallying exploits in 1994.

That outing in Wales was one of only four full gravel rallies Bertie competed on in all of the 1990s (excluding Lurgan Park) but he had won numerous gravel rallies in the past so, although he wouldn't have been expected to be top of the time-sheets, he could not be discounted.

After the first day he was in 6th place, just 14 seconds off McHale's Celica but then McHale overshot at a junc-

left top: Bertie on his last ever outing in the Legacy, the Galway Rally 1994'

below: From left Messrs Fisher, McHale, O'Gorman, Kennedy and Finlay inspect the layout of the Dyke Road spectator stage on the Sunday morning of the Galway Rally

right: A rare outing on gravel for Bertie and Rory on the Welsh, Rory explains why they decided to enter

'There was a bit of a desire for a change of scenery on our part because around then we seemed to be doing the same events year in, year out, and we thought, what with all the big teams and manufacturers being in Wales that year for the BRC, we would go a slightly different direction that year and give it a go.

Also with Prodrive already going to Wales with other drivers it was easy for us to go along as well seeing they already had all their men and equipment there.

Even though it was effectively a one off and a lot of the parts on the gravel spec car would have been different from the Tarmac one, because of the strong relationship we had with Prodrive they would have just given us the parts for the rally, and then would have used them again for other drivers as there would have been a lot of interchanging of parts with other drivers within the Prodrive stable and every month there was a different rally they had cars at.'

right below: Rally of Wales 1994, Stephen Finlay drifts the Michelin Pilot Escort to his first International rally victory

tion to drop him back to eventually finish 6 seconds behind Bertie, who came home in 5th overall behind fellow Northern Irishman Stephen Finlay who took the overall honours. Not that Bertie considered it a bad result in his first time out in a new car and on his first gravel rally in many years.

Having opted out of doing the Circuit of Ireland, Bertie's next rally was the Rally of the Lakes based in Killarney. Rory remembers this rally well as one of total dominance. *'It was a great rally in the Mobil 1 car – we didn't win, we blitzed the opposition!'* Fisher had made it five in a row in Killarney in the new, blue, Subaru and with

left: Action from the Rally of the Lakes including bottom left The top cars lined up at the end of Day One

those five wins came a new record, breaking Billy Coleman's former record of four.

A first stage blast and fastest time up Molls Gap gave him a 19 second lead almost before the rally was properly underway. Despite Stephen Finlay pushing hard towards the end of the first day, Bertie still had a good enough cushion to remain ahead of everyone else. Next day Finlay's Escort started to consistently jump out of seventh gear and this, followed shortly after by a broken driveshaft, meant Finlay would have to be happy with second with McKinstry moving ahead of McHale to finish third with the latter fourth.

The Shell Donegal Rally followed in June and featured many of the usual favourites. Bertie led after the first stage but not very far behind were McKinstry and Finlay. McKinstry then took the lead after Stage Two, Bertie losing a few seconds having spun his car but by stage three he was back in the lead again after McKinstry lost three minutes following a serious brush with the scenery which damaged his steering and suspension.

The second loop was a repeat of the first three stages and this time Finlay was flying, eventually finishing the day just eight seconds behind Fisher.

Day two and Finlay kept piling the pressure on Bertie, taking the lead after the first stage of the day before Bertie blasted round Fanad and Knockalla to regain the lead by a mere five seconds at service. It was perhaps the level of pressure that caused Bertie to slide the Toughmac-Mobil 1 Impreza off the road on a muddy part of the following stage, getting stuck atop a fencing post for around

9 minutes in the process as Bertie explained in an interview with *Carsport,* *'It was a tight corner over a crest and I had it cautioned in my pace notes. It was no problem the first time around but mud had been dragged onto the road from the first run through the stage and when I hit it the car under-steered off the road. I still didn't think we had done any real damage until we tried to get the car out and that's when I discovered the fence post we'd hit was mounted in concrete. It was jammed under the sump and the car wouldn't move. Rory had to run for nearly a mile to fetch spectators to lift the car off it. There was no damage to the car but the whole thing cost us the best part of ten minutes.'*

They continued on, albeit way down the leader board, by that point having lost any realistic chance of winning the rally outright. With Finlay now holding a margin of some 3 and a half minutes over his nearest rival, Kenny McKinstry in the Kaliber Legacy, the County Tyrone man could afford to relax cruising to a comfortable win with McKinstry in second, Peadar Hurson in a Metro 6R4 third. Ian Greer fourth in a Celica GT-Four and Bertie slotting in

right: Bertie coming round one of the fast 'fresh air drop' Knockalla mountain hairpins on the Donegal Rally in 1994

probably not achievable though, with three rounds remaining, not impossible.

Malcolm Wilson in the Michelin Pilot backed Escort convincingly made it back to back victories on the Stena Sealink Line Ulster Rally, dominantly setting fastest times on 16 of the 19 stages, with team mate Stephen Finlay second. Kenny McKinstry third and future world champion Tommi Makinen fourth in a Nissan Sunny GTi. Unfortunately for Bertie he had rolled the Impreza on just the first stage of the rally, having to get the car back on its wheels with the help of spectators. He finished the stage, with not a huge lot of time loss overall, but then on the following road section the car's oil light came on, and wary in case it would seize the engine, they stopped. Game Over on the Ulster.

Wilson won again on the Manx, with Kenny McKinstry second this time and Dieter Depping in an Escort Cosworth finishing third. Next Irish finishers were Finlay who had a disastrous rally to eventually finish 7th and Meagher in 8th who had steering, turbo and electronics problems throughout. Bertie did not have a good rally on the Manx this year either. He had been up to second on Day One, nearly 20 seconds behind leader Wilson, but a small road penalty, then a puncture, meant they lost considerable time. Then on Stage sixteen the Toughmac-Mobil 1 car stopped with transmission and clutch failure. Game Over again.

There were several potential Dunlop Tarmac Championship winners going into the final round of the series on the Cork 20, but barring remarkably unlikely po-

fifth overall, nearly 30 seconds down on Greer, making it one of his more disappointing Donegal's as there was little he could do after Saturday's excursion and subsequent time loss while retrieving the stricken Subaru.

With the Tarmac Championship half over, Stephen Finlay was leading with Kenny McKinstry in second and Bertie a distant third so an overall championship win was

left top: Future four times World Rally Champion Tommi Makinen was on the Ulster Rally in 1994 in his Nissan Motorsport Europe Nissan Sunny

left below: Bertie splashing the Impreza through a Ford on the Manx International

below: A stage One roll on the Ulster put Bertie out of the Ulster Rally after his engine oil light subsequently came on and he pulled out for fear of seizing the engine

dium combinations only Finlay or McKinstry had a realistic chance of taking the laurels. With only a faint mathematical chance of the championship honours, Bertie was happy to let the other two fight for a championship showdown, trying to pick up what points he could, and maybe capitalise on someone's mistakes, and that's exactly what happened as Finlay built up around a 20 second margin over McKinstry on the first few loops of stages

However his ascendancy would not last as he dramatically crashed out on stage eight against a concrete bridge parapet, robbing him of a potentially fantastic climax to a great season.

That left champion-elect Kenny McKinstry, who had played second fiddle on so many occasions, with a comfortable lead of over a minute after the first day over Bertie and, while the lead fluctuated over day two, in the end McKinstry won by some 44 seconds over Bertie to secure his second tarmac championship.

1995

For Bertie Fisher, 1995 would end up being a very different year's rallying to that of the previous few years. Gone was the big Tarmac Championship campaign and instead he decided to select a few key rallies he wanted to compete on. As an example, three years previous between the months of April and June Bertie had competed on a total of seven rallies, while this year he would only compete on two in the same period.

As well as the new strategy for the year was a new car. With L444 MCA having been sold on by Prodrive, he

bought another similar Impreza.

As he set off to tackle his first event, the AA Circuit of Ireland Rally, gone was the major Mobil 1 sponsorship from the previous few seasons and it was back to mainly Toughmac livery across the striking Blue coloured Impreza, with additional funding and help from Subaru Ireland and Pirelli. .

That year's Galway winner, Tipperary man Frank Meagher (would end up becoming Dunlop Tarmac Champion that year), was one of the favourites for the Circuit but also in contention was Stephen Finlay in the Michelin Pilot Escort Cosworth, back with a vengeance after his Cork crash as well as Liam O'Callaghan and Andrew Nesbitt who were in ST185 Celica GT-Fours. Add in to the mix 1993 National Rally Champion Ian Greer in an older ST165 Celicas, David Greer in an Escort Cosworth, and many more and you had a top entry for the four day marathon on which Bertie would try out a number of new ideas.

right: Tarmac Championship leader going into the final round Stephen Finlay crashed his Michelin Pilot Escort Cosworth heavily

One such idea was the video recording of their recce so that he and Rory could watch it over and over again and check any particular sections they wanted to re-examine the notes from.

Bertie was quoted in *Carsport* after the rally to have said *'It was useful. It helped me get each stage into my focus, reminding me of different features, dangerous bits, road surfaces ... things like that. I don't think it made me any quicker, just safer.'* while Rory said *'It was really good because after you had done the recce, when you went back to the hotel, you maybe had plenty of time to spend, work and change your notes again if they needed tweaking.'*

While nowadays it is the norm for competitors to buy a DVD with a video of the stages of most current events, at the time this was a pioneering concept bringing a heightened sense of professionalism not previously seen in Irish competitions.

On the car itself, being an ex-Prodrive test car it was fitted with some of the latest parts available from Prodrive,

including an aluminium flywheel which brought with it as part of the homologation standards the new and developmental paddle shift system behind the steering wheel. Though this was present in the car, Bertie opted out from using it and instead used the standard H pattern dog box he would have been used to on many of his previous cars.

And so to the rally itself. For Bertie Fisher and the Toughmac Team, with the exception of one poor tyre choice that made the car hard to handle until corrected, it was essentially otherwise a flawless rally throughout and Bertie's lead was never threatened over the whole four days. As a driver this was Bertie's 18th time competing on the prestigious Easter event (with half of them being non-finishes) and this was no doubt the sweetest of all, coming home top of the time sheets on the Circuit for the very first time. In not one of the 34 stages did the newer model '555' Impreza have any major mechanical or other technical issues, and he came home with a winning margin of 1 minute and 45 seconds.

What of Fisher's other competitors and the many leading entries? Early on Stephen Finlay had a big accident on stage three but he continued, and throughout the rally he rattled up half of the fastest stage times to come back heroically to finish ahead of Frank Meagher, who had held a constant second place for much of the rally.

James Leckey, driving the old Subaru Legacy in which Bertie had won the 1992 and 1993 tarmac championships, put in an amazing performance that at one point saw him in joint second place overall, before he crashed

left: Tipperary driver Frank Meagher who won the Tarmac Championship in 1995 in the Lombard & Ulster Escort Cosworth, is pictured here at the Adare Castle Spectator Special stage in County Limerick on the Circuit of Ireland.

According to the time sheets Meagher finished 61 seconds behind Stephen Finlay but some 60 seconds of this gap was down to a ridiculous rule which came into force on this event which stated that if a driver hit a cone on the spectator stage they would be penalised with a one minute penalty – although privately both drivers disregarded this as their long journey came to a final and dramatic conclusion at the final stage at Bangor Castle on Easter Monday with only one 'real' second separating them.

right: Images from Bertie's first Circuit of Ireland win including

top right: The winning Team of (L–R): Bertie, Rory, Paul Howarth (Prodrive), Brian Quinn, Sydney Meeke, Robbie McGurk, John Archer, Adrian Kirkland, Jimmy Murray, Kris Meeke, Wesley Emerson, Barry Meeke

bottom right: Bertie, surrounded by media at the finish ramp in Bangor on Easter Monday takes time out to receive a special phone call from his father Tommy who couldn't be present due to an illness, to congratulate him on the good news

left: Bertie travels through the scenic Atlantic Drive stage of the Donegal Rally

was a sweet weekend overall.

With an air of confidence about him after his Circuit of Ireland win, you would have thought the natural thing to do come the May bank holiday weekend would be to head for County Kerry for the Killarney Rally of the Lakes. However, with Fisher Engineering's expansion limiting the time Bertie could devote to rallying allied to his desire to do some international rallies he had not competed on before, for the first time since 1988 he decided to give the rally a miss.

And so Bertie's next rally, his second of the year, would be a whole two months later on the Shell Donegal International Rally.

the car on the Sunday stages.

This win really meant a lot to Bertie, and indeed Rory Kennedy too. *'First time we ever won the Circuit – the five months out of the game after Cork seemed to have done him the world of good – let him recharge the batteries and refocus so it was one of them fantastic moments that was tremendous for the whole team. What can you say, it's all about the competition on the day, and I think we led all the way.'*

Though many of Bertie's family and friends were present in Bangor to celebrate with him at the finish of the rally, his parents were unable to make it due to his father Tommy having just come out of hospital, but as Bertie and Rory sat atop the Impreza and spraying the champagne in victory, a phone call came in on his mobile from Ballinamallard and it was his folks at home looking to congratulate him. A sweet moment in what

On the Circuit of Ireland the car had borne the plate L408 FUD but by Donegal a personalised registration L555 FEL had been obtained, the FEL referring to Fisher Engineering Limited and the 555 referring to the new model of Impreza which took its name from one of the cigarette brands of the Subaru World Rally Team sponsor, British American Tobacco.

While others such as Austin McHale and David Greer fell by the way side with troubles, Donegal developed into a dingdong battle between Bertie and Donegal man James Cullen in his Yorkie sponsored, Mike Little (MLP) prepared Ford Escort Cosworth. Although they shared fastest stage times throughout the three days, Bertie had snatched an early lead at the start of the rally which meandered between 10 and 20 seconds for much of the first day and a half but half way through day two the Subaru punctured on the High Glen stage and again on the following Gortnabrad. With Bertie's lead gone and Cullen now in the lead, Bertie wanted to retaliate but a noise from the transmission was giving cause for concern. A precautionary gearbox and clutch change at service in Milford in a record (at that time) 17 minutes put paid to any worries and on the following loops Bertie pushed really hard to pull back the difference to initially go level and then take the lead by 5 seconds at the end of day two.

Day three and the fight was on again, with Cullen eating away at Fisher's lead to arrive into the final stage with just 8 seconds of a gap, but Cullen's effort wasn't enough and Bertie pulled away on the final stage to win the rally outright by 15 seconds and secure his fourth win in Donegal.

Following on from this great Donegal win was a performance from lower down the scale on the Burmah Lurgan Park Rally, an event which Bertie had not done since 1992 leaving him a little rusty on the specialised event – a unaffordable luxury as every second counts in the park. Paul Howarth, chief engineer for Prodrive on the event, said *'I think it was damp in the morning and because it was slippy through the trees he didn't have a lot of confidence. At lunchtime on the event he told me he was just gonna go home!'* He didn't go home, but neither did he really regain his normal composure and finished in third behind winner David Greer and second placed Frank Meagher, both in Ford Escort Cosworths.

The next event saw a return to form on the Ulster rally where, as the rally was a round of the Mobil 1 / Top Gear British Rally Championship, the entry dominated by top

right: The top three finishers in Donegal (L-R) Pat Moloughney, Frank Meagher, Bertie Fisher, Rory Kennedy, James Cullen, Ellen Morgan

below: Alister McRae seeded No. 1 in the works Formula 2 Nissan Sunny

class British and European drivers in both works and privateer F2 cars. These cars were ultra-competitive high revving normally front wheel drive rockets, but they simply did not have top end speed and performance to match the 4 x 4 Group A cars and Bertie and Rory returned to their winning ways with an almost entirely dominant performance where they claimed the fastest times on all bar one of the stages.

A somewhat subdued second placed finisher Stephen Finlay in the Michelin pilot Escort Cosworth admitted he couldn't keep up to Bertie's pace, the final winning margin being a minute and half. A further two minutes back, Liam O'Callaghan finished off the podium with his Toyota Celica GT-Four.

Hugh O'Brien who was doing mud notes for Bertie on the Ulster recalls a great story about Bertie's determination to beat Finlay on one particular stage even if he didn't need to do so to stay ahead of him overall. *'We were out that morning doing notes and both Bertie and Stephen Finlay, maybe one of the best to come out of this country, were driving well. As the night dropped Bertie was relaxed ahead of Finlay maybe 15 or 20 seconds in it – enough of a margin that he didn't need to be riding the horse close to the tail. However when we did the notes for what we call 'Finlay's stage', the one that started in Stephens backyard in Ballygawley, Bertie started questioning me heavily about what it was like and then asked me to go over it again and do all the cuts. I tried to reassure him he didn't need to be doing that but he insisted. When you're going into the stage at 5 in the morning you could do the right hand cuts that they couldn't do when they would be doing recce so I went into it, did all the cuts and with those sharper notes to my knowledge he beat Finlay by 10 or 15 seconds and he was happy then as he just wanted to beat him on his own doorstep.'*

After the Ulster Rally win, Bertie's Tarmac Championship results read 'tackled three, won three', and so with the optimism and confidence that brought could he follow up with a win on the Isle of Man for his first Manx International win? It's fair to say Bertie never had a better chance of winning the Manx Rally than that year, with there being no other serious Group A contenders present apart from Frank Meagher in the Escort Cosworth, with the main opposition coming as on the Ulster in the form

left top: In the slippery lanes of Lurgan Park

middle: Bertie and other fellow competitors in jovial form during the Ulster Rally in 1995. From L to R, Andrew Nesbitt, Stephen Finlay, Bertie Fisher, Liam O'Callaghan, James O'Brien

bottom: Bertie yumps to his third of four wins on the Ulster Rally

of the many F2 cars.

Bertie started the rally well, settling into a steady lead and after day one he comfortably led the rally, well over a minute ahead of second placed Gwyndaf Evans in the Ford Escort RS2000 F2 car. Day Two and Bertie had extended his lead but then, in one of the very rare occurrences when any of his Subarus ever let him down mechanically to the point of retirement, the Impreza's gearbox gave up on the ominous sounding Stage 13.

They were able to have made it back to service with the help of a service chase crew who had to use their front bumper to provide some high speed 'assistance' the stricken car but, although the crew repaired the gearbox, Bertie decided the recovery had stepped beyond the rules and pulled out on the way to the next stage.

For eventual winner of the Manx Frank Meagher, who had made a terrible start with turbo troubles and a puncture demoting him to the lower end of the top 20 before making up time throughout and then jumping into the lead after Bertie's retirement, it was a dream come true as he crossed the finish line of the last stage to become the first Irish winner of the event since Cahal Curley, some 21 years earlier. All of the remaining top ten finishers behind Meagher were F2 or Group N cars, Welsh Wizard Gwyndaf Evans coming home second in his screaming Escort RS 2000 while Alister McRae was third in a Nissan Sunny.

Meagher followed up on the magnificent Manx win to win on the last round of the Championship on the Cork 20 Rally and with it secure his first and only Tarmac Championship. Despite the three wins during the year, Bertie opted out of Cork as he was behind Meagher on points and it would have been unlikely for him to win the championship outright if Meagher finished in any of the top places.

opposite right: Bertie's Manx in three pictures

The decision to retire was one Bertie took himself to avoid putting the organisers in an awkward position as he explained in an interview with *Carsport*

'We were able to freewheel to the end of the stage, but it all took time, maybe ten minutes, and when the chase car crew had a look they realised there was nothing they could do except try to get me back to the service halt. The input shaft to the gearbox had broken and it was going to be a full gearbox change to fix it. I won't try to pretend Rory and I got the car back under our own steam. The chase car pushed us up the hills and eventually we made it back to Douglas. The initial reaction was to get the gearbox changed and carry on; we were back to ninth at this point and with the car healthy again it seemed worthwhile to get going once more. In fact that's what we did and we were out of service and heading for the next stage when I changed my mind

After all the hassle there had been on the Ulster Rally with the British championship people I didn't want to get involved in any dispute with the Manx organisers. I've always had a good relationship with them and I didn't want to put them in a position of having to exclude me for receiving outside help. I know it happens all the time that people get outside help and get away with it - in many ways it is all part of rallying- but in the circumstances I felt the right thing to do was pull out.'

1996

It may have been a long time coming but this year saw Bertie score his first ever win in the West on the Statoil Galway International Rally, which he led from just the second stage although it wasn't an easy ride as he was constantly under pressure from the charging James Cullen in his Escort Cosworth. Leader after the first stage Frank Meagher damaged his exhaust and bodywork after a spin and then a blown turbo put him out of contention entirely. Bertie had his own troubles on the very first stage when a spin into a bank caused a crumpled bumper to burn against the exhaust and put fumes into the cockpit but it was never enough to put him out of contention at that early stage. James Cullen had two spins in terrible conditions including torrential rain downpours and lost some time, nevertheless he was never too far away from Fisher, finishing the first day only sixteen seconds adrift.

On Sunday Cullen went for broke with a joint fastest time on the opening spectator stage and rumoured unofficial faster mid stage times on the following stage but, perhaps trying too hard, went wide on a muddy corner and shattered a wheel.

Although Cullen's charge for the lead was over, he finished a minute back from Fisher in a very credible second place, three and a half minutes ahead of Liam O'Callaghan in the Toyota Celica ST205.

So, with top Tarmac Championship points for Bertie in the West it was onto the second round, the AA Circuit of Ireland held over Easter weekend where things would not go just as well for Bertie. Despite leading early on, Bertie had quite a disaster of a rally. An accident on the Friday on a section of the Devil's Elbow border stage cost him around a minute which he never really recovered from although it didn't stop him trying! It was a case of throw everything you have at the remainder of the

left top: Galway Rally 1996 where Bertie and Rory took their first win in the West,

below: The fire spitting Yorkie Escort Cosworth of James Cullen threatened Fisher's position as leader until a time costly accident which shattered a wheel.
Rory Kennedy shared some thoughts on Cullen

'James Cullen was just a good a driver as anyone – if you read Colin McRae's book, he spoke well about James, mentioning how good a driver and underfunded he was and it was good to see him recognised in that way. I could see right from the start how quick he was and Bertie saw it too.'

event taking a flat out aggressive approach to driving to recover any time that could be clawed back, but despite coming to within 40 seconds of the lead after the second days action, it didn't pay off. A second accident on the Sunday travelling through the Lough na Fooey stage in Connemara where the Subaru came over a blind crest in the wrong line too fast and hit the top of a stone wall causing damage to the steering and suspension with another puncture and more time loss.

Then a third and final disastrous accident on one of Mondays stages where he came round a corner too fast, spun and hit a telegraph pole which was snapped with the impact. Although Bertie and Rory were able to continue and drive of the stage it was with a smashed wheel and a car twisted out of line.

All the meanwhile Stephen Finlay, in the Malcolm Wilson Motorsport (MWM) Sport Escort Cosworth, had been having a seemingly faultless rally and although he had wrangles with tyre choice at times and clipped a bank once, it never really fazed as he went on to win his second Circuit in just three years. Behind Finlay, Andrew Nesbitt finished nearly three minutes back in second in his Toyota Celica ST185 and Liam O'Callaghan just over a further minute back in third in a fresher model of the same car with Bertie, after all his spins, punctures and various problems throughout the four day rally, battling on to the end, slotting into fourth 15 seconds off O'Callaghan.

A month later was the Carling Rally of the Lakes and it

was very much a case of back to winning ways for Bertie, but this one was a little bit special as there were several records he broke that weekend which still stand today. The win was his sixth out of six attempts on the event, winning every year he was there from 1990 till 1996 and, in the process of claiming the victory, he broke the ten minute barrier for the full original longer version of the

Right top: A battle-scarred Subaru limping through Tardree near Antrim town

Wesley Emerson, one of the Meeke team mechanics, recalls working at the car after the third accident on the Monday. *'He came out of that stage with the back wheel hanging out of her. Robbie and I were in a chase car not far from the finish at one of the main roundabouts near Antrim town, and when the car pulled up we were shouting to the van get this out, get that out, whatever we needed to fix the back left corner – we were that busy trying to get the back wheel on to her what we hadn't realised was that the front right corner of the car had taken a thump as well until the car arrived at service in Saintfield!*

That was the type of driver Bertie was – he always seemed to get the car to you, two wheels on it, three wheels on it, he would get her out of the stage. You wouldn't be allowed to do that kind of thing now though, it would be instant retirement.'

below: After Fisher's demise on the Circuit of Ireland, Stephen Finlay took his distinctive orange striped Malcolm Wilson Motorsport prepared Escort Cosworth to a second win on the event

Molls Gap stage.

out of us. After getting over the shock Bertie's attitude was "Well, we'll have to see about this". So then we pushed hard and the next time through that same stage he only took 7 seconds off us, and then directly after that – and this goes to show the kind of driver Bertie was and the kind the other boys weren't – we went and did a spectators stage in around the castle grounds outside Millstreet, and in 2 miles we took 4 seconds back. And you think, he drove 14 miles up Gortnegane and beat us by 7, and we drove 2 miles around this and took 4 back just to keep him in check.'

Despite Bertie's fight back O'Callaghan took a small lead into the overnight stop and with his confidence of extending his lead over the Ulsterman on the first of Sunday's stages where O'Callaghan claimed he knew 'The secret to the gap' things were looking tight for Bertie.

But O'Callaghan's confidence was misplaced as Bertie set fastest time over the gap, in the process breaking the ten minute mark on the full (currently unused) version of the stage. As Rory recalls *'We went up the gap that next morning, and took 7 or 8 seconds off him* [Liam]. *We didn't quite retake the lead but we had reeled him right in and we got him on the next stage and then we went on to win the rally from there.'*

So, what of that the promised challenge from O'Callaghan and why was Fisher faster on Sunday's opening test? Some said Liam was caught out on the wrong tyres but there may be more to this…

Breaking tradition entirely, Fisher and the whole Toughmac team decided on the Saturday that once

left top: Carling Rally of the Lakes

below: County Corkman Liam O'Callaghan in the Esso Ultron Toyota Celica GT4 maintained he knew 'the secret to the gap' in order to reach ahead of Bertie and claim his first Rally of the Lakes win, but Bertie beat him well that weekend to take his sixth win in Killarney

The victory was however far from a walk over with Liam O'Callaghan from Kanturk in County Cork in his Esso Ultron Toyota Celica Gt-Four providing strong opposition. Fisher took a small lead after the first stage but O'Callaghan set a blinder of a time on the Gortnegane stage to take the top spot. Rory Kennedy recalls the day's battle royale well *'Liam started doing unbelievable times including on one stage – I think it was Gortnegane – where we were gobsmacked when he took 14 seconds*

right top: Bertie and Rory blast up the 'Gap' towards their record sixth win in the Kingdom of Kerry

below: Bertie celebrates his emphatic sixth win on the Rally of the Lakes with Left to right Billy Coleman, Dave Campion (Prodrive) and Roger Clark

the day's rallying was over, rather than follow the usual routine of restaurant, hotel and early night, to instead go to the 'Riverdance' show at the Green Glens Arena in Millstreet County Cork. Rory elaborates *'We brought all of the team, and Prodrive and the other guests they had with them too. It was a tremendous show, and we all came back to Killarney afterwards buzzing about it.*

Really, if you think of what we did that night, we got totally disconnected from the rally – it took all of the pressure and stress of the event away, then we came back and we got up the next morning, completely recharged.'

Whether or not as a direct consequence of the team's break from the rally fraternity that night, Fisher was a different driver on the Sunday and, even though O'Callaghan did punch in a few fastest times, Bertie upped the pace again to take the last three stages and

complete the route 27 seconds ahead of O'Callaghan with James Cullen a further two and a half minutes back in third.

Bertie's record of six wins in Killarney which he achieved that year is something probably unlikely to

be broken any time soon.

June time and the traditional Shell Donegal International was next on the calendar for Bertie who was now the Tarmac Championship leader with two maximums

to his credit. There he would be up against the usual suspects in Cullen, McHale as well as Andrew Nesbitt, the Armagh man who had been progressing well for the previous year in his Interko-Philip White Tyres Toyota Celica GT-Four.

The first of three days saw a tight leg which finished with Bertie in the lead by a scant six seconds over Nesbitt, and Bertie was quoted in *Carsport* to have said *'It doesn't add up to much but six in front is better than six behind'*. Cullen, who was having problems with intermittent intercom problems meaning he could not hear the notes co-driver Ellen Morgan was reiterating to him, had lost time with spins and a stall, but was still only 13 seconds off the lead in third.

Day Two and Bertie faulted. On a wet Atlantic Drive cor-

right: Armagh man Andrew Nesbitt took his first international rally win in Donegal that year in his Celica GT4

ner, the Impreza went in to a ditch and although he was able to retrieve it, he lost around 40 seconds and the lead. However Nesbitt, who had led after Bertie's ditch visit, then had mechanical problems on the second run over Atlantic Drive allowing James Cullen to emerge as the third leader of the rally.

Cullen extended his lead initially but on the faster open stages Nesbitt fought back to regain the lead. Fisher meanwhile had two punctures on the rear of the Subaru after he hit a rock on Fanad, dropping a minute which, given the unrelenting pace at the top meant that a win in the North West that year was looking unlikely.

With Fisher resigned to not winning he left Nesbitt and Cullen to battle on the final day, with Nesbitt emerging to win his first international by 29 seconds from local man Cullen and Bertie a further 1m 45 back in third.

A full month later was the Stena Line Ulster Rally and Bertie had grounds for expecting more success than on his last outing in Donegal as there were virtually no other Group A contenders to challenge him with only Eamonn Boland in the Hertz Escort Cosworth in the same class as Bertie's Impreza in the top ten entries. Instead the field was dominated by Formula 2 cars from the Mobil1-Top Gear British Rally Championship classes, top entries including Alister McRae, Gwyndaf Evans, Harri Rovanpera, Alan O Reille, Robbie Head among others. However, regardless of the paucity of Group A cars, the times by the F2 cars on the opening stage were certainly enough to make Bertie sit up and take notice, with Robbie Head and Alan O Reille both taking fastest stage times in their

the Ulster, three minutes ahead of Head's F2 Megane Kit Car with 1989 Ulster Rally winner Gwyndaf Evans in the Escort RS2000 F2 car a further three minutes back in third.

With the second victory of the season in the bag, Bertie went to the Isle of Man for his last outing of the year on the Manx International Rally with a certain optimism and spring in his step. And just like the Ulster Rally all of the usual British Championship contenders in the Formula 2 cars were present, but setting the Manx apart from the Ulster was the inclusion of the event in the European Rally Championship, the top classes of which stuck to roughly the same regulations as the Irish Tarmac Championship. Thus alongside the F2 opposition were a number of Group A mounted crews to contend with. Amongst those European Championship entrants were Alexander Potapov in the Impreza 555 and Kurt Gottlicher in the Escort Cosworth but the star attraction was Toyota works driver Armin Schwarz, over in the works Celica GT-Four.

Bertie was quoted in *Carsport* before the rally to have said *'I wanted some good opposition but I wasn't thinking of anyone this good!'*

As the rally got underway, Bertie built up a lead of 5 seconds over Schwarz over the first six stages – not a huge lead, but it reassured Bertie that he could compete toe-to-toe with the Toyota works driver and he drove the point home as he opened the gap by another 20 seconds on the last stage of the day.

Bertie's streak of stage wins continued on day two, holding the lead despite a single stage win by Schwarz,

left: Bertie won the Ulster in 1996 amongst a Formula 2 dominated rally. Here was one of the leading entries, Frenchman Alain O Reille (nicknamed 'Alan O'Reilly') by some locals in the Renault Megane Kit Car.

works Renault Meganes. After this wake-up call Bertie got down to business and made the leader board his own, setting a string of sixteen successive fastest stage times. Although he did have one little skirmish on the early Saturday morning stages, where he caught the back of the Impreza on the Brantry Lough stage, obliterating three concrete posts and tearing his back bumper off, the damage was only superficial an he was able to continue at undiminished pace to take his fourth victory on

but on stage 10 things started to go wrong for Fisher as the engine lost power on the latter part of the stage.

He still managed to finish the stage a few seconds quicker than Schwarz, but the problems persisted forcing retirement after the following service as Paul Howarth of Prodrive explained *'The engine problem was a broken value due to an over rev on the down shift. It happened on occasions with different engines, but for Bertie it was a rare occurrence.'*

Bertie summed up what happened in an interview for Carsport.

right top : Toyota works driver Armin Schwarz in the Celica GT4 took a comfortable win in the Manx Rally- Bertie *(below)* tried many times to win this event and some say 1996 was his best chance at a win but engine troubles put him out, When Paul Howarth of Prodrive was asked whether he thought Bertie had the beating of Schwarz that weekend. He made some interesting points about drivers and the various championships they competed in

'Definitely. When it comes to grades of drivers, top grade is 0 seconds lost per kilometre, i.e. the fastest driver, and then there is Grade 2, 1 second per km slower, and there's Grade 3 etc, etc.

At that time when drivers went to do World Championship events they did high speed recces in proper recce cars but they could only do it 5 times and you could go to a new event and expect you were going to be on about the same pace. It's a bit like when Kankkunen went to the Manx, when all of a sudden it levelled the playing field a bit.

Armin Schwarz was probably Grade 2, and he maybe did the recce 20 times so Bertie's experience on the Manx got him up to that extra level, but if Bertie had gone to Germany and tried a similar event that he had not been on before, he wouldn't have been on the same pace as those boys.'

'We radioed the chase car and told them what had happened. There was service after the stage and I was still hoping it was going to be something simple that could be fixed quickly. I didn't even want to think it was a serious problem. They worked on the car in service and got the engine firing on four cylinders again and we headed for the next stage. But 100 yards down the road it cut out again and wouldn't re-start. That was it, all over. Sydney Meeke pulled out the plug on the dead cylinder and there was a fragment of metal on the tip of it. A piston must have come up and hit it. Sickening when you think that I haven't had an engine problem with a Subaru since the first time I drove one on the Circuit of Ireland in 1992. Why now? It's just my Manx luck! When was the last time I retired from a rally? The 1995 Manx? The time before that? The 1994 Manx? And the time before that? The 1993 Manx?

"I'm just not meant to win this rally...."'

An amazing statistic which Bertie alluded to in this

interview is that this was in fact his ***eighth*** retirement in the 10 years in a row he had tackled the Isle of Man event between 1987 and 1996. Given how well they were doing on this occasion against a full works driver, it was a demoralising blow to Bertie, Rory and the whole Toughmac / Sydney Meeke team. It was the highest of highs and the lowest of lows, and it would be Bertie's last ever stab at the Isle of Man classic, due partly to the demoralisation from that loss, but also due to changing class regulations of the British Rally Championship, which were aimed at pushing Group A cars like Bertie's further back from the limelight in the British Championship events demoting them to a separate 'Trophy Rally'. Many did not think was fair or justified, believing that the fastest man home should win the rally outright, rather than being declared winner of a second, lesser important section within the rally.

With Bertie retired from the rally Schwarz cruised to a four and a half minute win over Mark Higgins in his Nissan Sunny GTI with Kurt Gottlicher in the Escort Cosworth, over eight and a half minutes further back in third.

Despite the disappointment on the Isle of Man, his Galway win at the start meant that the Manx was the only round of the Irish Tarmac Championship where his name had not appeared on the victors roll at some point and with a fourth (at that time) Tarmac Championship in the bag it had been a successful year.

1997

Although 96 had been a successful year, that very success was to play a role in Bertie only taking part in a vastly reduced program for 97.

Some insight into his probable thinking in 97 can be gleaned from an interview he did for a Donegal Rally programme in 1994. *'I've done most of the things I wanted to do in Irish rallying and it would only be a matter of doing them all over again just for the sake of it. I would really rather try something different and I have been looking at various options on the continent. The Tour of Ypres was one possibility; I've been to Belgium once before for the Haspengouw Rally and did quite well but that was over 10 years ago, and I'd like to try it again. There is also an offer to go to the Rally of the Lebanon and one or two other things I've been considering.'*

By 1997 he had ticked even more boxes in respect to the Irish rally scene leaving the option of looking abroad as the only way to progress in the sport and there is some evidence that he gave this option some serious consideration in that he attended a few foreign rallies with Prodrive who were already running cars in the events but for once it would appear that Bertie was daunted by the level of commitment he saw would be necessary – not in absolute terms but in terms of how he had to balance his commitments to rallying with the demands of Fisher Engineering which, with the advent of the Celtic Tiger, was on a roller coaster ride of expansion.

By the late 90s Rory Kennedy had become not only Bertie's co-driver but a close friend and he recalls Bertie's struggle to keep the right balance between rallying and business

'You had Bertie Fisher the rally driver and you had Bertie Fisher the businessman running a huge business and whose growth rate was incredible. In his own words, the business became a monster – and you need to keep feeding a monster once you've created it. He couldn't step back from it because at that time there was so much going on in terms of the stuff they were involved with such as Quinn's Cement factories, Intel in Dublin, The Odyssey, the Waterfront Hall and some of the biggest shopping centres in Ireland. Of course his brothers Ernie and Ivan were involved and there were a lot of very good and dependable people working for them there at Fishers but at the end of the day he was the top man responsible for the major decisions and deals brokered.'

In the end his one and only tarmac championship outing in 1997 came on the AA Circuit of Ireland at Easter time.

Having won the rally two years previously, Bertie knew what it took to win this rally and he put that knowledge to good use to make it one of his better Circuits.

With an opening leg taking the competing crews

from the rally's main headquarters in Bangor, County Down down to Tallaght in County Dublin, it was a relatively long route on the first day. As the miles accumulated Bertie jumped in to a comfortable lead while others around him succumbed to problems, some more serious than others.

The rally's first major victim was Andrew Nesbitt who, although second fastest on the opening spectator stage at Bangor Castle, crashed his Celica GT-Four on the following stage after getting out of shape over a series of bumps and

going off at the next corner. Another of the main contenders Austin McHale in his similar car, dropped down the leader board after losing two minutes due to a problem with the car's throttle cable while in another Toyota Liam O'Callaghan had engine troubles due to a leaking oil pipe.

Day One ended with Bertie and Rory a minute and a half to spare from Stephen Murphy in an Escort WRC, with Eamonn Boland less than 20 seconds back in third and James Cullen a few more seconds further back in fourth.

Day Two and the rally was in to McHale territory, through the Wicklow mountain stages of Sally Gap and Aughavannagh but after some of the stage times were scrapped due to timing errors, McHale's fastest time on Sally Gap meant nothing, as Fisher extended his lead by the end of the day to almost 2 and a half minutes from new second place man James Cullen in the Wrangler Escort Cosworth after having overtaken Murphy and Boland.

right: Bertie dominated the 1997 Circuit of Ireland, seen here (top) jumping over a bridge in the Wicklow Mountain stages and (below) on the tight mucky Sweathouse stage in County Tyrone

The Third Day saw a run of stages along a route from the rally's second headquarters based at Tallaght in County Dublin, heading West through Mullingar and on to Sligo, before it headed Eastward again to the main headquarters in Bangor, County Down. McHale had made his way back up the leader board to eventually end up second by the end of the day, but there was little any of them could do about the man in front.

The final day saw Bertie's faultless run conclude as he arrived at the finish over three minutes ahead of second placed Austin McHale with James Cullen in third, 35 seconds adrift of McHale.

Although to all intents and purposes it was a faultless rally for Bertie an interesting occurrence on the fourth day shows the fine margins between winning and losing in rallying. While sitting in the passage control of one of the final stages, the gruelling Sweat House stage in the Brantry area near Dungannon, Bertie got a tap on the window from a young female spectator who was there with her father, to warn him before starting the stage that he had a puncture which could only be heard when Bertie's and Austin McHale's cars had been turned

off to avoid overheating while waiting for the start of the stage. Bertie and Rory were able to change the wheel and proceed without penalty but who knows what would have happened saving the girl's timely intervention? According to Rory. *'It was remarkable that the girl and her father heard the hissing and pointed it out when they did – you chat about bad luck and you chat about good luck, but Fate was definitely smiling down on Bertie that day!'*

With everything going so swimmingly in his favour on the Circuit it was with some irony therefore that Bertie didn't do an awful lot of rallying in the year 1997, with 'The Circuit' being the last time Bertie competitively drove the ultra-competitive and ultra-successful L555 FEL Impreza which brought him seven international wins and a fourth tarmac championship, and so for the remainder of the year he did not actually own a rally car which he could compete in at the top level of Irish Tarmac Rallying.

Despite this the sports attraction was still strong for Bertie and later in the year he was enticed back after some pressure from long term sponsor Kieran McAnallen although witnessing Austin McHale's revived success on the Tarmac Championship that year may also have played a big part, but whatever the reason, by all accounts it seemed Bertie wanted to be back behind the wheel of a car again.

On the ALMC Rally that summer, a Leinster province based round of the Irish National Rally Championship series, Bertie tried out one of the Prodrive 'Allstars Team' Impreza 555s, P161 EUD. The Allstars team, a subsidiary of Prodrive who both built, prepared and looked after cars for customers, had built many cars for British and European drivers and this particular car, a Left Hand Drive Group A car, had been built for European rallies.

The major difference between this event and his last

left: Bertie and Rory spray the champagne at Bangor Promenade, victorious on their second Circuit of Ireland victory in three years

rally on the Circuit was that this was more an experiment than a full competitive outing. With the new WRC Subaru Imprezas making headway in the 1997 World Rally Championship in the hands of Scot Colin McRae and Italian Pierro Liatti, Bertie felt that If he was going to come back the following year he would want to have the latest technology. However his preference for right hand drive would prove a major stumbling block as Prodrive did not seem interested in providing the car in any configuration other than left hand drive as

Paul Howarth of Prodrive explains *'We were just about to launch the new 2 door car and we were fairly adamant that we wouldn't be going down the route of converting to RHD. You could have got away with it, but it was going to be much more complex to design the car than the Group A car, the BMW or Legacy which were quite easy to convert'*

So with only Left Hand Drive guise WRC cars available from Prodrive, Bertie wanted to see how he could adapt to rallying a car in Left Hand Drive, as Rory Kennedy says *'For younger drivers it's an easier adaptation to go from right to left but for someone who had driven Right Hand Drive all their life it was a big change'* .

But the Left Hand Drive really wasn't a success. Bertie felt it a particular strain on his arm, and he found gear changes a hassle. On the event itself his old adversary Austin McHale won with Bertie a creditable but very sore 2nd.

After the lack lustre ALMC event Bertie was in no doubt that buying a LHD WRC car would be of no benefit to him

regardless of the newer technology and so he turned his not inconsiderable persuasive powers on Prodrive to convince them to build him a car with right hand drive as close to WRC spec as possible.

It was a big ask but eventually Prodrive acquiesced and a deal was done for the new car late in 1997, R 555 FEL, a car which, given its unique top level spec, convinced Bertie he could win again and was ready to contend another full Tarmac championship.

Paul Howarth explained just how unique this car was. *'It was probably the ultimate spec Group A Impreza, it had the best suspension, the best engine, and it was also the lightest Group A shell to date, you name it, every attention to detail was followed… chassis 061, what a car!'*

It was a strange coincidence that as R 555 FEL was the last ever 555 shell to be build by Prodrive, Bertie had competed in both the first ever and the last ever 555 shells to have been built by Prodrive!

right: Bertie on a one off outing in a Left hooker 555 on the ALMC Rally.

Also one-off was the particular colour scheme and Toughmac livery on the car, never to be repeated on any of Bertie's subsequent cars

Making His Mark
Mark Fisher

by Andrew Bushe

If Bertie Fisher had achieved greatness in rallying and business, there was no question his son Mark was enroute to achieve the same, but sadly we never got to see how far this talented young man could have gone in both his sport and in the family engineering firm.

There was no questioning the support that Bertie Fisher had built up in the rallying fraternity, but there was a special magic about Mark. His sense of fun and kindness had people rallying around him and, like his father, he had an ambition to do the thing right, and to do it the right way.

Mark's early forays into competition were in night navigation events as a co-driver, debuting in 1990. With drivers such as Paul Moore and Harry Cathcart, young Fisher was learning his skills, and learning well with results as high as fourth overall. Growing up in the Fisher household however, the natural ambition was a foray into stage rallying, but Bertie was insistent that he completed his Structural Engineering degree in the University of Ulster before he took to the stages seriously.

Lodging in Belfast, naturally he had friends in the rally scene, and it was with one friend, Davy Patterson, that he co-drove on the Townparks forestry stage rally in a Talbot Sunbeam. Now anybody that knows 'Davy P' will understand that it quickly turned into quite an adventure!

'Mark and I were pals when he came up to university in Belfast and we'd often hook up when he was free to spend a night out on the town in Belfast, sometimes going indoor karting which was always super competitive but, as with any Fisher, always good clean & fair racing. Mark was always busy between studies and work and rallies but he had a few handy side-lines he did for spare cash, making and selling alloy parts for rally cars in his spare time!

One thing I always noticed with Mark, just like Bertie, despite his busy lifestyle, he would call in with me or my mum and dad, just for a cup of tea and a social friendly chat, with no agenda or motive other than being a genuinely good guy. He caught me by surprise one day just before I left to go and drive in the

Arctic Rally, calling into the house with a very thoughtful gift of a pair of racing boot over-shoes to keep my feet warm! That was the kind of mindful and genuine friend Mark was.

Mark was never shy of trying anything to do with motorsport, driving, navigating, going in service cars or just spectating for fun.

On the one time he co-drove for me in a 1600 Sunbeam on the Townparks rally he kept me in the rally with his tenacity. We had been dicing with Stephen "Weavey" Whitford all day in a similar Sunbeam and with two stages to go in the Tardree forest we were under pressure and took the famous Tardree jumps flat out. On landing the Springalex steering wheel broke off completely and we spun into the trees in 4th gear without hitting anything!!

I thought it was game over, but Mark had other plans. He told me to wait as he ran 2km to the stage finish and arrived back with a pair of Vise Grips to clamp onto the column and use as a Heath Robinson handlebars style steering device. We somehow managed to clear the stage and the last stage, and the Road Section back through Antrim to the finish on time, so finished the rally without steering wheel and partied in Antrim with no idea how it all ended up or how we got home.

I knew Bertie well, and it was always clear to me the "black cat, black kitten" scenario – Mark was just like his father in every way. A great, honest and fair guy in Sport, Business, Family and socially. Mark and Bertie set high standards in everything they did and to get close to those standards would be high attainment for anyone.'

Mark had a keen interest in rallying from an early age as this picture of him lending a hand at the 1990 Manx international shows.

It was clear that Mark's interest in rallying was not just a passing phase, and when he was home in Ballinamallard he used to call into Gerry McGarrity's work-shops on the main street in nearby Irvinestown.

At that time Gerry was running Kevin O'Kane in the Irish Forestry series amongst others and Gerry recalls *'He used to ring me up or call round to see if he could go to the events and service with us and it would always be forty questions, whatever you did. "Why are doing that? Why are you doing this?" – over and over again-questions! Kevin used to say to him "If I was to do it all over again I would listen to your man, but I'm too old to re-programme" and I remember years later on events, it was comical as Mark would re-quote things that Kevin said back then.'*

In 1994 Mark entered his first rallies, and not surprisingly Gerry acquired and looked after the car, an ex Harry Cathcart Suzuki Swift. The machine nicknamed "JAP" after the last letters of its registration brought Mark to a class win on the Quinton Stages, and second in class on the Woodpecker Stages, and these gravel rallies would feature strongly in years to come as Gerry continues *'He realised early on that you needed to be good on the gravel as well as the tarmac, and he saw that he could shortcut the learning time by drawing on my experience. He wasn't the best driver at the start, but he made himself what he was at the end, he really wanted it, never gave up and never forgot anything that you did for him'*

Ravens Rock, Mark's first Irish Tarmac rally for which he borrowed the services of Rory Kennedy

regional final, which some found surprising, at the time, as he was little known, compared to 24 year Stephen Whitford, who had already made quite a name for himself with giant-killing acts in Talbot Sunbeam's. *'I already knew Mark at that stage'* said Stephen. *'He was living just off University Street in Belfast at the time, and we would often meet for a bit of craic especially between the rallies, and this continued right up through the Micra and Seat days. We became big rivals, but bigger friends. We were opposites in many ways but always got on like a house on fire.'*

Mark had put a huge effort into his presentation for that Shell Scholarship regional final and he carried that same level of preparation through to the Shell Scholarship final at Croft Race Circuit in England where he became a joint winner with Mike Brown.

The emphasis on his studies was set in stone but when Mark completed his exams, the Swift was sold at the end of 1994 and the 22 year old entered the Nissan Micra Challenge half way through the season with a car run by McRae Motorsport. The Ravens Rock Rally was the fourth of seven rounds, and Mark with co-driver for the day Rory Kennedy, finished a fine second to Englishman Dave Pattison, in 21st place overall in the 1300cc Micra.

In five rallies in the Micra in 1995 he took three class wins and two second places, one of these being a fine Micra round win on the Trackrod Rally in Yorkshire, just before the Shell Scholarship finals at that time.

Mark had won the ANICC Northern Ireland

Stephen remembers *'At the time there were a few people that were annoyed that I didn't get the Scholarship, and it was just after that there was a petition went round at the end of the Lakeland Rally, to say that he didn't deserve the prize, that I should have got it. I had finished well up in the Sunbeam that day. I think ninth overall and won the class, and at the prize-giving I felt that I had to had to make an apology, even though I had nothing to do with the petition and this at a local event to Mark! He knew me well enough though to know that I wasn't behind this, and I didn't begrudge him the scholarship. It actually made me more determined to get out there and the rivalry started in the Micra's in 1996'*

It was first blood to Whitford on the Somerset Stages, with Mark and co-driver Chris Wood in their McRae Motorsport run car dropping from fourth to twelfth after a five minute penalty was applied for Mark failing to remove his helmet on a road section. It was fifth place on round two at Millbrook for Mark, but round three was in Donegal, and, with the base for the Micra effort at Gerry McGarrity's work-shops near home, he was keen to win. Former Donegal winning co-driver Dermot O'Gorman took to the hot-seat for the event, and they claimed a victory which was much enjoyed by Bertie at the finish.

Further results started to come, second on the McRae Stage to the experienced Geoff Jones, and another victory – this time on the loose on the Woodpecker Stages, with Clive Jenkins taking up the role of reading the maps. Finally a fourth on the final Cambrian

Bertie congratulates Mark on his Micra victory at the Donegal Rally in 1996

round, netted Mark third place in the series, and first Junior netting £5600 in prize money.

The decision was made to tackle the WRC Rally GB in the Micra – Rory Kennedy braving the co-driver's seat, and brave was the word in what was an incredibly snowy event. Gerry McGarrity once again prepped the little Nissan and he recalls *'Even at that stage, Mark was thinking ahead, and from day one was thinking about the WRC, getting to know the stages that would be used in future years. I'll never forget how before that event he rang me and said he knew an auld boy locally who had snow chains and would I go and get them before leaving for the boat, as they would fit the Hi-Ace van we were using. I went away up to this farm, lifted these old rusty chains, and*

the first thing Mark asked me when we met up was "Did you get the chains OK?" Sure enough the snow just came in blizzards, service vans (including the works Ford one) were getting stuck everywhere but when I put the old chains on, I was able to bomb along at 80mph in the snow! As soon as he came to the end of stage or into service he'd joke and ask me "what about the chains?"' In the event Mark and Rory ended up 52nd overall and 3rd in class, despite spending 14 minutes stuck in a fire-break on stage four.

For 1997 the Micras were pushed up to 100 brake horse power and featured a limited slip diff in their new 'Performance' specification, and Mark tackled the challenge once again with Clive Jenkins as co-driver for the season.

Action fron the 1997 Donegal Rally with co-driver Clive Jenkins

Round one was the North Humberside Rally based in Hull and second place was a good start behind a new challenger in the shape of another young Fermanagh driver, Niall McShea. The result was replicated on round two- the Plains Rally in Wales before an eventful third round in Donegal for both drivers ended in retirement for Niall and third for Mark. It was then back to the forests and the Quinton Stages where again McShea headed Fisher home to claim the title but the Fisher team proved their pace with a win on the final Trackrod round, after a great race between the two Fermanagh hot-shots.

'At this stage Bertie could see what we were doing, what the programme was, and he never interfered. He was 100% backing us, but he did warn us if we did something wrong that would be the end of it' said Gerry.

At this point Seat was heavily involved in rallying and the Seat Super Six competition was an opportunity for six drivers to compete in identical 150 bhp very mildly modified Ibiza's. Mike Brown, Olly Clark, Mark Perrot, Wayne Sisson, Stephen Whitford and Mark were the six selected from twelve finalists at a shoot-out in the Silverstone Driving Centre. *'Mark and me were different'* Whitford remembers *'We both had a good assessment, through the archery, skid pan and driving assessment with Gwyndaf Evans but on the media side of things he was second to none. He was so professional in whatever he did and I remember him in the suit and tie for the presentation.*

He trained hard, and worked hard in everything he did and he made himself into a good driver – *his approach was at all times the best he possibly could do, whereas sometimes I lacked that.*

He brought that same work ethic to the business where he often worked to 11 or 12 at nights although he would take a day or two before the rallies to switch off work mode and get into the right frame of mind for the rally.'

The season promised much, though the cars often didn't withstand the punishment that these six rapid drivers threw at them, and drive-shafts were to prove a weak link. A consistent approach by Mark netted him second places on the Bournemouth Winter, North Humberside, Sligo, Trackrod rallies and second place in the series to Mike Brown, who claimed a kit car drive in the following year's British Championship. Mark's second place secured him a WRC Rally GB run in his Seat Super Six car, but the car simply wasn't up to the punishment and, in an event fraught with mechanical dramas it was a struggle just to get to the finish! For the RAC Mark was accompanied by Rory Kennedy as Gordon Noble, who had sat alongside throughout the 1998 season in a partnership that was to continue to the end, came down with a bout of shingles.

'I had been gravel noting with Mark for Bertie, and we did a number of events including Galway, Killarney, Cork and Donegal. I suppose it was from there really that I was asked to sit in the Seat Super 6. It was a good year, with some good finishes, but he was always conscious that the car was fragile' said Gordon.

An outing on the Galloway Hills Rally at the

end of 1998 in a Group N Evo 3 hired from Terry Harryman' gave Mark a taste of four wheel drive as he finished third behind Jock Armstrong, and winner (and dad!) Bertie in the silver Toughmac Impreza.

Come1999 and the focus was to be on the new Peugeot 106 Super Cup, co-ordinated by the enthusiastic Stella Boyles. With a 206 WRC prize drive at stake, this was to become the mecca of one-make series and what an entry it attracted!

Gerry McGarrity reflects *'We felt we had to win a one make series and this had to be the year but, boy was it going to be difficult.*

I remember Mark knocking on my door and he really was up to high dough! He had the latest list of registered drivers in his hand and was reading down them. Marcus Dodd was on the list, and Mark was getting all agitated demanding "How we gonna beat Marcus Dodd?"

"We can beat him" I replied abruptly and shut the door on him, much to his surprise. But it did the trick and when I opened it a few seconds later he said "you're right, you're right!"'

It was a challenge just to get the cars all built for the first round at the Silverstone Rallysprint course in March, and an early fourth behind Martin Sansom, Kevin Furber, and a very quick driver from Oldcastle, Co. Meath – Rory Galligan started the year soundly. For Gordon the hard work had just started to try and win this prize. *'There were early teething problems with the 106, but Gerry was onto sorting those very quickly. Mark would always analyse everything, and I know from my side the prepa-*

McRae Forestry stages rally 1998, round five of the Seat Super Six series

ration was always meticulous, with a lot of homework done before the rallies. The whole team tried to leave no stone unturned as we set off for the rounds.'

Despite the preparation, round two in Somerset turned out unlucky as, swerving to avoid a crashed car on stage two, Mark clipped a wheel and broke the steering arm in the 106, so a score was dropped.

As such it was with a renewed determination that the team tackled round three the Millbrook Stages – around the famous vehicle proving ground. While third place might not have seemed a dream out come, but behind winner Dave Pattison and runner up Martin Sansom it was an excellent result, as both of these driver's had previous experience of the venue, Martin actually having won there

before in a Darrian. *'I remember on that rally we had an in-car camera system in the car'* explained co-driver Gordon Noble. *'It was quite a bulky recorder, but Mark had the idea to watch our in car footage between loops for the repeat stages. It definitely helped and we were quite pleased with the result that day.'* Mark was always thinking ahead and the in-car camera concept was to develop further as Gerry McGarrity explains. *'I had a guy – Charlie McGuicken – call in with me to the garage, and he was fitting tiny micro security cameras to a shop in the town. I was chatting to Mark about this and he insisted that I give him Charlie's number. It wasn't long before the cameras where being mounted on brackets that Mark had made for the car. It meant that he could watch the rallies afterwards and keep a log of*

Mark and co-driver Gordon Noble on a wet Knockalla stage on the Donegal International Rally in 1999

all the stages used for future events. That was the start of Micro-Cam and the in-car boom in rallying here.'

It was Martin who was proving to be the big threat in the series, not Marcus Dodd or Niall McShea (who also tried the 106 Cup). A win on round four the Kerridge National, in the Welsh forests, demonstrated that Sansom was a force on both surfaces, and for Mark and Gordon, second place was hard earned. It nearly slipped away, quite literally! The clutch on the 106 was slipping badly by the service at the Royal Welsh show-ground in Builth Wells, and the only remedy was flour and coke. Indeed they got through twenty bottles of the stuff as they poured it onto the plate, drying off the oil leaking from a faulty crank oil seal. 'I promised Gordon I would have a glass of coke if we

made the end!' Mark said at the time, for the Carsport magazine report.

The time was right for a foray into four wheel drive again for the Donegal International, where Mark and Gordon took a hired Prodrive Group N Impreza to a fine 11th overall and comfortable Group N win, a sign of things to come! 'That was a great event, although we had a huge moment on the final stage in fifth gear and nearly lost the whole thing! The incident resulted in a funny moment afterwards when we had stopped on the last road section near Buncrana – I think for an ice-cream – and Bertie came over to us, and said "well done Gordy for keeping it all under control especially as I didn't insure that yoke!" – If only he knew what we had just got away with!'

But despite this diversion the focus had to

be kept on the Super 106 Cup, the hottest one-make series of all time, and next it was back to the forests for the ATS Coracle Stages, where Mark turned the tables on rival Sansom to take a decisive win, with Marcus Dodd in the runner up spot.

After a test on the Sligo Stages where he was 13th overall in the little 1600cc car, it was the Ulster International. The heat was really on both figuratively and literally as a heat-wave was causing the tar to melt and playing havoc with the 106s. "I remember that rally really was something. There were about thirty 106 Cup runners at that time, and it was just the most competitive thing. The speed was excellent on that rally and I remember many stages where everything just clicked. We clocked into over-night Parc Ferme in the lead, and there had been a few casualties on that first day" said Gordon.

Amongst the casualties were Sansom, who had a minor off and broke the steering, and Dodd who went through a fence, but the race that weekend was between Fisher and Galligan and the race was on with only 12 seconds separating them when they clocked into the brief over-night halt in Belfast.

Day two and Rory was putting up a formidable challenge, but Mark was soon to strike trouble on the Sweathouse stage near Dungannon. The gear linkage broke, and he had to jam the car into third gear, dropping to third over the next couple of stages. To add to the injury, when Gerry went to the Peugeot parts truck to get a spare linkage, the last one

right: Action from the Ulster Rally 1999

1999 Network Q RAC rally where for the first time Mark put one over on his father beating him by some four and a half minutes.

had just been taken by the Galligan team! Had they caught wind of the Fisher cars malady? For Gerry it was time for makeshift repairs *'We had no option but to weld the one we had in position, but we knew it probably wouldn't last. Sure enough it broke, and we had to arrange for one to be brought from Roy Nixon's breakers to Ballygawley roundabout where it was fitted at the road-side.'*

As the rally continued Mark fought his way back to second as Paul Wedgebury crashed on the penultimate stage but heading into the final stage at Tardree the rally looked to be going to Galligan until he rung the centre out of his clutch 300 yards from the finish of the stage and had to be pushed by another car along the final road section. He was ex-

cluded by the organisers who had witnessed this, handing the win to Mark and Gordon, but the tension at the finish was tangible, and Galligan was in no mood to talk to Mark. He had driven a great rally and felt cheated to have lost it on the final road section, overlooking the fact that Mark had suffered his own ill luck with the gear linkage. The series was so heated there was a Senna and Prost esk feel about it, not helped by media hype. *'Mark was annoyed about it and wanted to talk to Rory, but he didn't answer Mark's call on the Monday after the event, so it was never fixed. Mark never held it against him, and Rory told me at Mark's funeral, that he wished that he had spoken with Mark about it'* said Gerry.

Next up was Flanders, where they won the

prize for the best turned out car in the Cup, which was a big thing for the McGarrity team. It was a neutral playing ground with several stages containing big cuts. One such cut had taken out the sump on the recce car and, as a result, Gerry set the 106 a few inches higher than the opposition which initially worried Mark. However, with the higher ride height, he was able to take the 100 mph cuts flat out on the shakedown – a big turning point in him always believing what Gerry doing with the car.

Mark started the rally on equal points with Martin Sansom who had a huge off through a fence and into a tennis court on stage one before heroically climbing back to second in his battered 106, behind Mark and Gordon, who took the front after Galligan, Pattison and Andy Burnell had all led at one stage.

'That was a great win' said Gordon *'and again I remember great speed all weekend. We had an adventure on the recce, with a 106 GTI lent to us by Pat Burns. It ended up in a field at one point, the poor car got an awful hard time, and we had to pull the grass out of the front bumper, change a puncture and fix the sump. We were staying in this village and the guy we were staying with really celebrated the win with us. He had a purple London Taxi and he insisted in taking us and collecting us from the prize-giving in it!'*

Onto the final round, the Bulldog Rally, and the pressure was on although it was almost over before it started with the unlucky Sansom rolling down a 30 foot bank on stage one into retirement. However despite the opposition's misfortune, it was to be no dream day for the Fisher team, as Mark struck power steering trouble before a piece of the fuel tank was ripped off, rendering the team OTL.

In spite of the 106 arriving on the end of a tow rope at the finish ramp, Mark was declared victor in the 106 cup to claim the grand prize of the 206 WRC drive.

'Bertie was on the event, and very proud of Mark's achievement. He had realised at this stage what we were doing and how far Mark could go' said Gerry.

Bertie had entered the RAC Rally in a WRC Impreza, and finished in a steady 21st overall, but for the first time, was eclipsed by Mark who took a fine 17th place, setting many top fifteen times along the way in his first rally in left hand drive.

'He was determined to do that rally' said Gerry. *'The only car Prodrive had was one that Freddy Dor had rolled badly in Sweet Lamb that year, and they said they hadn't time to fix it, so Mark phoned me and told me I was heading to Prodrive to help fix this car! He would ring me for a quick progress report every day at mid-morning, and he always was quite hard to hear. It must have been because Bertie was in the room next to him, and he didn't want him to hear him!'*

2000 was looking like an epic year with Mark entering the WRC in the Peugeot 206 WRC on the Acropolis and RAC events, although in the event the prize drive didn't glitter as it should have!

To keep up the 4wd experience Mark and Gordon tackled a series of events close to home with Kieran McAnallen kindly lending him his Group N Mitsubishi Evo 5 to tackle Monaghan as a testing exercise. Despite Kieran's gesture the event was far from an easy run out.

Gordon recalls *'There was a panic the night before the rally when Gerry had to change the gearbox and I remember Mark calling into the garage at 6am to find Gerry sleeping underneath the rally car, having worked all night.'*

On the rally itself they had a turbo pipe come off into the first stage, dropping many minutes locating the problem, but recovered to set top four times all day.

Next up was Killarney and a deal was struck to drive a 2 door Prodrive Group N Impreza. Mark dominated the category, taking a seven minute win and coming in 7th overall, with the pace-notes being called by Gordon who recalls *'On the Saturday night Bertie gave us a warning to take it easy and conserve our big Group N lead. However we were racing Davy Greer in his Group A Celica and we wanted to stay ahead of him. I remember we*

The lows and highs of rallying:
above; a recalitrant car in Monaghan and *below;* Mark and Gordon Noble celebrating their win in Group N and 7th overall in the Rally of the Lakes in 2000

came round this fast corner on Lough Allua, with a high speed drift, and there was Bertie, Kieran and Sammy Hamill peering out of the hedge. As soon as we reached the end of the stage the phone rang, and it was Bertie to give us a telling off! We turned our phones off after that and raced on to the finish to beat Davy!'

On the Acropolis in his first outing in a works car

Then the Summit 2000- a unique round of the Irish Tarmac Championship, run along the private roads of Sean Quinn's quarry, with a rally forum at Fisher Engineering the night before. Mark had tested at the venue before, but it didn't take away from an amazing result – 5th overall in the Group N Evo 5, with Stephen Murphy, Hugh Dunne, Ian Greer, Davy Greer and Hannu Mikkola all behind in Group A machines.

Gordon again *'For that event we made two sets of notes, one ordinary set and one for the fog, with markers in and more distances. It turned out a very foggy start and we had an exceptional time on the first stage, about fifth fastest. The stages got slippier for every stage, but Mark was driving brilliantly and he always managed to miss hitting anything. There was great speed that day.'*

Despite the excellent results, all this activity

was really a build up to the first WRC event, the Acropolis, with three days testing at Ales-France and Chateau De Lastours. The Acropolis was tough- really tough and sadly Mark and Gordon were early casualties. A small off on stage one was only a prelude to the stage two drama when they hit a large rock and broke a front ball-joint leaving them to limp to the end of the stage before the drive-shaft broke forcing their retirement exhausted and dejected. As Gordon explains *'It was disappointing, but in the back of our heads we felt that the RAC would be the place. One memory of that rally was going out spectating the next day. Mark felt in the recce that there were two jumps together that could be cleared if taken flat. The first few cars all backed right off and went down gears, then Colin McRae came in the Focus and proved Mark right! He famously took them flat out and cleared them. That is a good memory.'*

The relationship with Peugeot UK was still healthy, and Mark was lent the ex Sundstrom Group B Peugeot 205 T16 for the Millennium Motorsport Festival at Stormont, and Justin Dale's 106 Maxi for the Lurgan Park Rally. Carsport's Pat Burns sat with Mark in Lurgan and has great memories of him.

'I first got to know Mark while he was in Canada finishing his degree in Engineering. He wrote a few pieces about rallying in Canada as he visited some events while he was out there. I got to co-drive for him in Lurgan Park in 1998 and 1999 in a Seat Ibiza Cup Car. By this stage I was doing some PR and marketing for Mark and we got on really well together. In 2000, we got the loan of Justin Dale's works 106 Maxi kit car for Lurgan Park and were confident of a good run up against Niall McShea and John McIlroy in the Citroen Saxo. It poured really heavily the night before the rally and it was very slippery. We spun on the first stage, the car stalled and we dropped almost 20 seconds to Niall. We pulled 6 or 7 of them back during the rally and set fastest two wheel drive car on a couple of the stages once they

Manx 2000: 2nd overall and 1st in Group N on the Manx Trophy Rally wrapped Group N Tarmac championship. This car, owned by Kieran McAnallen, is the only car to have been driven in competition by both Bertie and Mark

had dried out.

I remember sitting in the car between stages and Mark studying the list of previous winners and saying to me that "the boss won it in 1982 so we will have to win it in 2002, twenty years after him."

Just three days before he died, I had lunch with Mark who was hoping to land a seat with Prodrive in the USA as he was over there a fair bit with work. I was working on the proposal at the time and Mark was actually designing part of the roof of our house which we were replacing at the time. Mark never got to see the roof finished and the

Prodrive USA drive went to Mark Lovell who was sadly killed on a rally in Oregon in 2003.'

Back to 2000 and more four-wheel drive experience was clocked up in a Group A Impreza hired from Kenny McKinstry on the Enterprise

Amazingly Mark and Gordon made the start ramp of the Network Q RAC Rally in a pristine looking 206 WRC

Printing Rally in Swansea, where they finished second to Marcus Dodd before heading to the Isle of Man with Kieran McAnallen's Evo 5 for the Manx Trophy Rally, a round of the Irish Tarmac Championship.

Second overall and first in Group N, behind Andrew Nesbitt in his WRC to wrap up the Group N Tarmac Title was an amazing result as they again punched above their weight. *'That event stood out'* says Gordon. *'We were setting fastest times in the dark and I think even Andrew Nesbitt was surprised. Definitely one of the highlights.'*

Another second place was netted on the Bulldog Rally in the McKinstry Group A Impreza, despite a poor seeding causing them to catch Steve Petch on a stage. Before the event, on a Sweet Lamb test, a young Kris Meeke got his first sample of 4WD rallying as he sat in for a run with Mark. *'He was there that day to test his 106 Cup car, after winning a Silverstone Rally School competition that Mark had ad-vised him to enter. That was the start of another rally career!'* quipped Gordon.

Next up was testing the 206 WRC in Wales for the RAC Rally, and Mark didn't forget his friends from the past. *'We always kept in touch, he wouldn't forget you and he rung me up and asked me if I wanted to go for two days testing with him in the 206'* said Stephen Whitford. *'It was great, and of course I said yes.'*

On another day of testing, this time just before the rally there was real drama, Mark putting the car onto its roof in the forest, and it took an all-nighter in the local body-shop to get it ready for the rally.

Gordon recounts the story *'The initial testing had gone well with a lot of work done, but when the car came back just before the rally it didn't feel right at all, Mark describing it 'handling like a grizzly bear'. On the night before the rally I went to a rally driver's ball with Corrado Provera, Jean Pierre Nicolas and Mick Linford from Peugeot while Mark and Gerry, who should have been there, decided to have one last go at sorting the car on a test road above Cardiff.*

I was having my dinner when the phone rang. It was Mark, and I asked how it went. "Don't tell anyone but I've rolled it". It was bad enough, the roof was well down, and they set to find a local panel beater to help them. They worked all night and by the next day when the car was returned to the service park it was still an all-out race. Indeed we had to cut across the grass from service just to make the start ramp in time – it was that close!'

The rally itself was a litany of mechanical problems as a broken front wishbone on stage two followed by gearbox problems, and eventually a water pipe being rubbed through by the bottom engine pulley forced retirement. *'The engine had lost water, and it eventually just seized at the time control into the service park. We were pushed in and that*

Mark in action on the Network Q RAC Rally, which would be Mark's last ever rally

was to be the last time I stepped out of a rally car with Mark. We were gutted afterwards, we thought that was going to be our rally to show our speed, but not one clean stage did we get. Afterwards though Corrada Provera came over and apologised to us, and mentioned that he would do something for us in a WRC the following year. They had been impressed with Mark, and his demeanour. Mark had taken French lessons just so that he could speak to the team. In 2001 we went to the Autosport show and signed with Peugeot UK for the Formula Rally series which replaced the BRC that year in the 106 Maxi. so although it wasn't the best end to 2000 it was looking promising for 2001, but it wasn't to be.'

Mark had really left his mark in more ways than one, and the out-pouring of emotion showed how well-liked and how many friends he had. In his short time in rallying he had touched many. *'Mark had so many attributes'* said Gordon. *'He had speed, he was clever, he was good at PR and had engineering skills to boot. His determination was well above normal, and he demanded the highest level. We were all prepared to give that and everyone wanted to achieve so much at the time. There was an implicit trust between Mark, Gerry and myself and it really was a very special time for all of us. We will all miss him both as a rally driver, and a special friend in our lives'.*

1998 - 2000

The Final Years, the new Silver Subaru

Before the 1998 season kicked off in proper fashion, Bertie spent a day testing the new car over Muckish Mountain in County Donegal, an old now unused Donegal International Rally stage where he could fire the car at all the humps bumps, yumps and straights, one of Donegal's trickier stages had to throw at the new silver bullet.

The 1998 season proper got underway with the first round of The Toshiba Equium Irish Tarmac Rally Championship, the Statoil Galway International Rally, held in February and that year celebrating the Galway Motor Club's 25th running one of the most prestigious events of the Irish Rally calendar.

As part of the celebrations the route incorporated some of the most classic of old Circuit of Ireland stages in the Connemara region with Service at Maam Cross which unfortunately gave rise to a phenomena not often seen in that part of the world – gridlock!

As thousands of cars converged on the junction it was chaos for competitors, organisers, spectators, and locals alike. As a result the rally was delayed and it very nearly meant the cancellation of the Lough na Fooey stage as crews found it hard to get into the access road leading to the start.

Fisher led the event from the start, going into an immediate lead of some 36 seconds after Austin McHale in his Tom Hogan Motors backed Toyota Celica GT-Four had problems on the first stage with a windscreen wiper. It was typically wet in the West that year, very wet, meaning working wipers were a must and McHale was forced to slow down allowing Paul Harris to initially slot in to second behind Fisher. Seeded behind McHale, Bertie actually caught and overtook him on the stage but once out of the stage the wipers were fixed restoring the Dubliner, originally from Louisburg County Mayo, and his Celica to full song again and ready to battle it

right: Bertie jumps high and long on the famous Hamilton's Fully jump on the 1998 Circuit of Ireland rally

left: Bertie on the Galway Rally travelling through the rural Connemara

out with Bertie as McHale made his way up the leader board from 7th place overall.

With the stages being straight and fast in many places, the 'bogey' times were however beaten by Bertie and Austin on around half of the day's nine stages hampering McHale's chances of reeling Bertie in.

Although both had overshoots and spins on the Saturday the gap between them remained steady.

Come Sunday morning however and McHale began to up the ante taking some nine seconds out of Bertie's lead on the first stage of the day, the short Dyke Road Spectator Stage. The pressure continued and Bertie was pushing as hard as he dared until on SS13 Tiaquinn, he slid the new silver Subaru too wide on a junction, hitting a wall and a pillar and deranging the rear suspension and allowing McHale to take the lead by 45 seconds.

Wesley Emerson, one of the Meeke mechanics who was on chase car duties that weekend recalls following Bertie as he came out of the stage. *'We could see that the*

car was crabbing down the road. Based on what we could see from driving behind we called on the team radio to the van at service to get out all parts we thought might be required to get the car back going again – a rear trailing arm, rear lateral links, rear hub etc. But we were really just guessing based on what we could see out of the windscreen of the chase car and when we got into the service and looked underneath, everything looked intact. Lateral links were OK, trailing link OK, hub OK, strut OK. Looked up, and she had broken the cross member. I don't know if it was fate but that particular rally was the first time we had ever carried a spare rear cross member!'

A flurry of activity ensued as the Meeke and Prodrive mechanics went about changing the broken rear cross member to get Bertie out of service on time, but with only three stages to go to the finish of the rally, a last chance re-grasp of the lead was all but impossible and McHale took the win on the prestigious West of Ireland event for the sixth time in his career, with a margin of just over a minute from Fisher.

Behind the two big Tarmac Titans, Andrew Nesbitt in the Cross Refrigeration secured third place in another Celica GT4, ahead of Eamonn Boland in his new Ford Escort WRC.

So first blood of the Tarmac Championship to McHale. Would Fisher get his own back on the second round, the AA Circuit of Ireland Rally?

Initially the answer appeared to be Yes but then, just over one day after Bertie Fisher and Rory had sprayed

'Because of the handling problems on the first day we decided to change the steering rack on the car which was a big job. On the Saturday morning the road section from the Parc Ferme in Bangor to the stages down near Ballygawley took the rally near our workshop at the Bush so we diverted Bertie there to use the 2 post lift.'

Though changing the rack seemed good at the time it was fortunate that they had taken the car to the workshop as, they encountered problems putting the new rack in and almost ran out of time but Robbie McGurk, who was servicing for Tony Kearns in a Group N Impreza that weekend, came to the rescue when Wesley and the lads needed him most. *'By the time we got the chase cars packed up again Bertie was already away, and when we got to the Ballygawley roundabout, which was not far from where the first stage that morning was, Robbie was there and already had Bertie's car jacked up for us. We landed and all we had to do was fit the tyres he needed and away on he went, still on time!'*

the champagne under the winners arch at the finish of the rally at Bangor Promenade on Easter Monday, confident they had won the rally outright by 19 seconds, the title was suddenly and cruelly stripped from their clutches after a meeting of UAC and MSA stewards on Easter Tuesday.

The special meeting was held in relation to a 20 second penalty imposed on Austin McHale on the eighth stage on the first day at a time control, and so when that penalty was overturned and the time taken off the total stage times, Austin McHale and Brian Murphy were then declared the new winners of the rally title award by a mere **one second**.

Rory Kennedy explained the nature of the original penalty. *'He didn't arrive early to a control but he actually just crossed the arrival board by a fraction and somebody decided to penalise him for doing that. Now, technically, that may have been correct, but unless all the distances and signs at the control were set up perfectly how could you apply a penalty for such a small infringement?'*

And indeed McHale argued that the control had not been set up properly and was both hurt yet at the same time motivated by what he saw as an unreasonable penalty *'To get penalised way back at the start of the rally for something like that, and then with it hanging over you for the rest of the rally, you just felt like you had the whole club and everything against you, but really it just made everybody in the team more determined.'*

A few days earlier when the rally started and progressed, the leader board was showing a very different picture.

On the opening spectators stage at Bangor Castle, three top drivers tied and an amazing **nine** drivers beat the bogey on the next, before Greer and McHale began to stretch their legs with Ian Greer leading after the first loop of stages by a narrow margin. But on the next loop Greer's fight was all over, a blown turbo and subsequent time loss dropping him out of the picture and handing McHale the lead until the disputed penalty on the sixth stage knocked him back.

Where was Bertie amongst this?

Following advice from the mud notes crew, the team had taken precautionary measures such as fitting smaller brakes which would be easier to get to operating temperature in preparation for the snow-capped stages in County Antrim. The modifications slowed Bertie down on the stages that weren't as badly affected but as the rally moved north they began to pay off and with Greer's time loss and McHale's penalty, Bertie found himself leading the rally after the first day by a narrow 8 seconds from the unhappy McHale.

left: The Circuit passed by many landmarks including The Crosskeys Inn, Co. Antrim, 'the oldest thatch pub in Ireland'

Come day two and McHale was on a real charge as the crews embarked on a route which would take them from Bangor to Tallaght in Country Dublin. He had made his way up to second with the bit between his teeth when an intermittently failing intercom meant a misheard pace note which cost him some 30 seconds after a spin and a stall.

As the cars progressed South towards service at Mullingar, Bertie extended his lead to almost a minute over Armagh man Nesbitt with McHale not far behind. Following a poor tyre choice and several further spins, McHale began to lose more time leaving Bertie and Rory

clear at the top as the rally crews prepared for an overnight halt in Tallaght on Saturday, with Nesbitt, his nearest challenger, adrift by over 2 minutes.

Into the third day's action where the Tallaght to Tallaght route was right in the heart of McHale territory – if there was a fight to be had, this is where it would be….

A quick blast round the Tallaght Square Shopping Centre car park saw McHale shave a second back before the first proper stage where Fisher was fastest. The subsequent stages saw a real charge from the Dubliner, making up 22 seconds over the next three stages, regaining his second place, before eating a further 11 seconds out of Fisher's lead on the second run over the same stages. By the time the crews pulled back into Tallaght for an overnight halt, while the gap had been significantly narrowed it looked like only a big problem or mistake from Fisher would allow McHale back into the reckoning.

Day Four, the final leg home from Tallaght County Dublin to Bangor County Down, saw a vintage Fisher-McHale battle. For Bertie, in a comfortable lead with three quarters of the rally over it was all about preserving the car and getting her home safely while for Austin, still motivated by the penalty hanging over him, it was simply a case of all-out attack to pull back what time he could over the remaining 65 stage miles.

On the first stage of the day near Ardee in County Louth they were equal fastest, McHale the victor on the next two by a total of 11 seconds. Three stages down, five more to go and the McHale express was firing on all cylinders, making further time up on the following stage, especially after a time-costly overshoot by Fisher, saw the gap narrow between the two to around a minute, including the penalty.

'As we pulled out of Dublin on the Sunday heading North, Bertie was a couple of minutes ahead of us and we were making up great time, pulling it back and pulling it back until it all came down to the wire on the last stage on Monday.' said Austin recalling the event.

Fisher retaliated after his mistake, setting fastest on the next stage by four seconds but McHale made five back on the next to arrive into the final service at Newry, with it all to play for over the final two stages.

The penultimate stage saw McHale was right on it again and set the fastest time leaving a gap of either 25 or 45 seconds (depending on the outcome of the dispute over the penalty) at the start of the last stage, the 18 mile Begney Hill test in County Down which would witness the culmination of this nail biting duel.

Austin recalls this last stage vividly *'Going into the stage we were 25 seconds behind Bertie without the penalty and so if we went for it, we had everything to gain and nothing to lose so we really went for it.'*

The continuing erratic weather meant that tyre choice was both very difficult and critical and both McHale and Fisher planned to use intermediates in place of the cut slicks they had been running on previous stages. However planning is one thing, but in rallying the smallest of thing can scatter the best laid plans and such was the case as the two teams prepared for the showdown.

The service regulations at that time allowed the use of chase cars to assist in the supply of tyres, fuel and parts for road side servicing and updates and, while Fisher got his tyres changed before the stage OK, McHale's chase crew were late and as a result he had to go to the arrival control of the stage without the new rubber on the car.

Austin recalls *'It was one of those Easter weekends where the weather was totally unpredictable and tyre choice was difficult. Bertie had changed onto intermediates while I didn't get a fresh set in time from my team so we were stuck on our old slicks which we had to change from back to front because the fronts had been bald and showing the canvas on the inside.'*

Ahead of the competitors on the stage were problems out of their control, as the officials tried to deal with the huge number of spectators who had come to witness the showdown it would be a full hour before the stage got underway by which time the earlier tyre choices had become redundant due to the ever changing weather.

Bertie first on the road, was no sooner started when he realised he was on the wrong tyres for the stage, struggling with intermediate tyres on the dry roads. By the end of the stage, the tyres were almost completely shot, and he had lost considerable time. McHale, second on the road, meanwhile was having a ball, his 'wrong' tyre

choice being right inadvertently, and he finished the stage 26 seconds faster than Fisher, and as a result brought the final gap after all 35 stages were complete to 19 seconds including the penalty.

Austin recalls the final stage *'By the time we eventually started the stage it had dried out but I'll always remember when we got towards the last few miles of the stage there had been heavy hailstones and I felt that any advantage we had gained up to that point we would then lose it back in the last three or four miles.'*

As they arrived back in Bangor both crews felt they had a claim on the crown which naturally resulted in some tension. In Austin's own words, *'So by times we had won the rally by a second as far as we were concerned but it was the only time with Bertie that I ever had words, saying that as far as we were concerned we had won the rally, but anyway while he was announced winner at the finish obviously it eventually went the other way in the end.'*

Although tensions were high Rory Kennedy was keen to point out that *'McHale's gripe was with the organisers, not with us and we had no gripe with him whatsoever – yes we would have won the rally, and we felt we were the just winners of the rally when we went over the ramp but as McHale felt very strongly that he was hard done by and he had every right to stand up for himself and follow it up. I admire him for his tenacity even if it was a cruel blow for Bertie, me and all the rest of the Toughmac Team'*

Rory described Bertie as being *'scundered'* over the de-

cision, an assessment Bertie confirmed In a preview of the following years Circuit of Ireland in *Carsport* when he said *'Certainly I was angry and disappointed at the way the whole thing was handled but I had no argument with Austin and as the only avenue open to me was to lodge a protest against him, rather than against the organisers or the stewards, I wasn't prepared to do that. But it is all behind us now, maybe not forgotten, but in the past. It will have no bearing on this year's rally. We start with a clean slate on Good Friday'*

Putting the disappointment of the first two rounds of the Tarmac Championship behind him, Bertie set his sights on the Gleneagle Hotel / Ordnance Survey Rally of the Lakes Killarney, held just two weeks after the Circuit due to Easter falling late that year. Bertie went to with high hopes as a six times winner of the event, the undisputed King of Kerry, but with all the usual Tarmac Championship regulars present and vying for top spot it was not going to be easy.

The media hype following the Circuit of Ireland was not helping matters either as Rory Kennedy remembers *'It*

Gap stage. A tough, at times narrow and twisty and then frighteningly fast stage with rocks protruding from many of its hundreds of corners, it can catch out even the best and 1998 would prove to be no different. Just a few miles in to the stage, Bertie took a bend too tight, clipping a rock on the front left corner, instantly puncturing the rubber and causing the rapid deflation of the tyre on the rim. Given the length of the stage, it would have been a tough choice as to whether to stop and change the tyre or struggle on but it never got as far as being an issue for, at a tight right-hander shortly after, the car under steered off the road and rolled into the bog below where it remained until the Meeke and Prodrive men arrived on the scene after the stage was over to overturn and haul the car out

With Bertie out McHale seemed to have the event at his mercy until a suspension problem on stage 14 exacerbated by time penalties incurred when his service crew ran over time with the repair promoted surprise package James Leckey & George Millar in their CabelTel Subaru Impreza 555, whose best result up to then had been 4th on the Circuit of Ireland in 1995, to the top step of the podium. They were followed by McHale in second with the steady Andrew Nesbitt finishing third overall for the third time that season.

With three rounds over Bertie, with two 2nd places and a non-finish, lay third in the championship, Nesbitt with three 3rds second overall and Austin McHale way out in front with two 1sts and a 2nd.

Due to rule changes which prevented 'full-house'

left top: A first stage bog excursion put an end to Bertie's hopes for a seventh win on the Lakes.

Surveying the damage on the nearside are Bertie, Hugh O'Brien, Kieran and Philip McAnallen while on the far side of the car is Kris Meeke

below: James Leckey took his first and only international rally win on the Rally of the Lakes in 1998, which happened to coincide with his 40th birthday!

was all dressed up 'In the Red corner' and 'In the Blue corner' going to Killarney, as if there was terrible animosity between the drivers, which there wasn't. Don't forget, it wasn't between the drivers that the problem was, it was between the driver and organisers.'

The first stage of the rally was as usual the famous Molls

Group A specification cars such as Fisher's or McHale's, running on the main part of either the Manx, or the Ulster Rallies, both Fisher and McHale opted out which meant that, McHale was going to be hard to beat in what was left of the 1998 season, the Donegal international and the Cork 20.

Any thoughts Bertie had of closing the gap in Donegal went out the window when following an underestimation of the severity of a corner during the recce he rolled his Impreza on the third stage of the event, Letterleague.

The rally was won by Andrew Nesbitt in his second Donegal win in three years in the same car, leading home second placed Austin McHale by over a minute.

Due to his decision not to go to the Ulster or the Manx Rallies, Bertie's next outing would be a whole two and a half months after Donegal, in early October for the Cork 20 International Rally.

Before the rally Bertie said that he would be taking it easy and would be happy enough with even a finish given the disappointments during the year, and it showed. Despite Austin McHale being a non-start and two of the pre-event favourites, Andrew Nesbitt and Eamonn Boland crashing out on 'shiny tar' on the first stage on Sunday, Bertie completed the rally in second place overall after a relatively lack lustre performance, 1 minute and 13 seconds behind winner Ian Greer in the Toyota Celica GT-Four.

At the finishing ramp of the rally, at the Tivoli docks on the outskirts of Cork City, Bertie warmly congratulated Ian on his first Tarmac Championship rally win, but Aus-

right top: After a swift exit on just stage 3 of the rally, Bertie and Rory are seen here out and about spectating the Donegal Rally stages. Also pictured behind is Mark Fisher and Maurice 'Mo' Hamilton

below: Despite never having been on the Donegal Rally before, Finnish driver Jarmo Kytolehto was number 1 seed in the North West that weekend in his Formula 2 Vauxhall Astra kit car

tin McHale had already been officially declared the 1998 Tarmac Champion, for the fifth time in his career, just before the Manx International Rally was held weeks earlier as, with none of the Tarmac Championship contenders. competing on the Island, McHale's lead in the championship was unassailable.

Overall the 1998 Tarmac Championship turned out to be a disappointing year for the Toughmac team, with

left: Bertie and Rory ended the disappoing 1998 on a high note by taking victory on the one off outing to the gravel event Galloway Hills Rally in Scotland

three 2nd places and 2 non-finishes so for a bit of end of season fun Bertie decided to do something completely different, and the Toughmac team decamped from Ireland to the Galloway Forest Hills Rally in Scotland.

Rory Kennedy remembers how the outing came about. *'We had such a poor year and so we decided to do the Galloway Hills, almost as a last minute thing, bit of craic, end of season and all that, hadn't done the forests before in that car, and he wanted to get a good run in her. Now, you might think it was rare going doing that wee short rally, but anyway, over we went, Bertie and myself and Sydney and Kieran in the jeep and the boys brought the car over.'*

However there was a second reason for Bertie's interest in the Rally – his son Mark would be doing it in a hired Mitsubishi Evo Group N car and, giving a flavour of how Bertie saw things panning out in the future, he wanted to go and keep an eye on things.

Given that Bertie's car was set up for Tarmac it might have seemed a problem to switch to forestry settings but because of the scale of the Prodrive operation it was not difficult as Paul Howarth of Prodrive explained *'We were able to do it easily because it was a factory operated car. We were running the All Stars team at the time then, which would convert cars backwards and forward all the time and it was just a straightforward conversion. The gravel spec parts came as part of the support package Bertie had. It wasn't that difficult to swap the suspension because in some ways an Irish car was quite similar to a gravel spec car anyway although there would have also been different diff settings, different discs, etc.'*

As the day of the rally dawned things did not get off to an auspicious start only to turn in the teams favour later in the day as Rory recalls

'On the morning of the rally it was a real frosty morning, the stages were slippy and everybody was saying how dangerous it was, but for whatever reason the car wouldn't start outside the hotel. There we were, turning the car over and she wouldn't go with Bertie looking at the weather and saying "Of course she doesn't want to go, look at them conditions!"

Well anyway, she eventually started up and despite only having the organisers notes and all, we had great craic, great rally, great bit of fun, sliding around and that. Murray Grierson who was with Prodrive at the time in a Subaru was a bit of a hotshot there and was doing quite well but we weren't that far behind him with only a couple of seconds between us going into the last stage where he went off and we went on to win.'

This was Bertie's first forestry rally win in over 13 years with the previous win coming on the Fermanagh based Lakelands stages, in 1986 during his period of semi-retirement. What a great positive way to end what was a disappointing season overall. Jock Armstrong was second in another Impreza splitting father from son Mark in third.

right: Bertie on a very wet dark Galway Rally stage with the unusual sight of the lamp pods on the bonnet

This was Bertie's second win in the West

1999

The 1999 started off with a bang for Bertie and the Toughmac team with a strong showing in Galway where they finished the Statoil Galway International Rally one minute and 43 seconds clear of the 2nd place 'Taranto de Pol' Toyota Celica GT-Four pair of Ian Greer and Dean Beckett. Greer, a former National Rally Champion, had been in the lead of the rally in his new 'ST-205' model Celica GT-Four up until the last 2 stages of Saturday when a relatively innocuous looking crash with little bodywork damage damaged the suspension of his Celica after which he eased off a little on the Sunday stages around Gort to settle for second position overall. Eamonn Boland finished Third overall in his Hertz Escort WRC. And what of Austin McHale, Bertie's main opponent in 1998? The six times Galway and 5 times Irish Tarmac Champion was warming tyres up for SS1 when his transmission blew and was forced immediately to retire.

The win in Galway gave Bertie not only a head start over one of his main rivals in the Toshiba Tarmac Championship but also a re-found sense of confidence, since this was his first Tarmac win in 22 months and he was quoted in *Carsport* after the event *'When your last big*

win is almost two years ago you get a big kick out of finishing in front again.'

On to Easter and the second round of the Toshiba Tarmac Championship, the AA Circuit Of Ireland Rally. There would be all the usual Tarmac Championship contenders present, including controversial 1998 winner Austin McHale, but his rally was over on Day One when Good Friday was a not so Good a Friday for McHale. Approaching a very tight hairpin surrounded by spectators, he hit the brakes on the Celica hard he lost control, going backwards through a hedge, and falling about 15-20ft. down a steep ditch to land on his roof. There were no injuries, thankfully, but he was out of the rally.

After McHale's early departure, the main contenders at the top of the time sheets were Bertie Fisher and Andrew Nesbitt, both in Impreza 555s who engaged in a titanic struggle throughout the remainder of the weekend.

Andrew had a slight early advantage over Bertie on the Friday over the stages situated around his home territory in South Armagh and, as the crews arrived into service at Newry, Nesbitt held a slim lead of just 6 seconds.

That advantage, however small it may have been, was still a help and Nesbitt carried the lead of the rally right until the last day when Bertie, who had ben setting a string of multiple fastest times on the Sunday and who started to really pile on the pressure in the dark stages on Sunday night to take a narrow 4 second lead in to the rally's final few stages but it could still go either way as Rory Kennedy takes up the story

'If I remember there were 7 seconds between us for 2 or 3 days, and we could never get under that threshold, it would go up to 10 and down to 7, up to 8 and down to 7. Although it seemed we couldn't get below the threshold of 7seconds, I always personally felt we still could beat him – it's always great to be able to have the mental strength like that in your head especially if there's a bit

left top: Bertie and Rory pop the champagne at the finish ramp of the Galway Rally at Eyre Square in the city.

below: There were huge crowds in attendance as Bertie rocketed to victory down the narrow stone-walled tracks of rural County Galway

right: Selection of images from the Circuit of Ireland.

top left: leader for much of the event Armagh man Andrew Nesbitt

top right: Bertie and Austin shake hands before the start of the rally

middle: Ian Greer and Bertie in jovial form at service in Hilltown

bottom left: The whin bushes were out in bloom at Easter as Bertie blasts through the countryside in the silver Bullet

bottom right: Jumping for joy - Celebrations in Bangor with 1st, 2nd and 3rd crews

Bertie travelling round one of many meandering bends on the scenic Cods Head Stage on the rally of the Lakes

of banter going on – and once we got to the night time stages we really pushed hard, exceptionally hard.

The whole dynamic changed, daylight to darkness, tyre choice and everything else. It was a beautiful evening in County Louth through the Dundalk and Carlingford area and we really pushed until we got the lead, and once we got it, we weren't going to let it go again.'

Then, Armagh man Nesbitt, who had lost some time with gearbox problems on the Sunday, had a devastating puncture on one of the final stages on Monday, Buck's Head, which would see him losing 37 seconds to Bertie who was then able to cruise home ahead of Nesbit in second and Ian Greer in third to a record-breaking 20th Tarmac championship victory.

The win gave Bertie a solid lead in the Toshiba Equium Tarmac Rally Championship as the crews headed south to Killarney for the Rally of the Lakes but this outing to the third round of the series would not prove as fruitful for Bertie as the first two. In a repeat of 1998, Bertie picked up a puncture on the classic Molls Gap test and, although this time he managed to keep the car on the road, it cost him over a minute leaving him way down the leader board. With that disappointment behind him Bertie set about regaining some seconds Frank Meagher, Austin McHale, Ian Greer who were all in the mix but, despite a fastest time on Stage 3, it all came to nothing when the Toughmac Impreza suffered power steering failure on Stage 9. The spray from leaking hot oil from the power steering unit pipe in turn caused a fire on the exhaust manifold and with no power steering the car was a real handful as he dropped back to be passed on the stage by Ian Greer and losing around another minute.

Although Bertie regained nearly a minute from leader Greer's time on the second day's action, overall victory was no longer a realistic outcome and the best he could hope for being to bag a few points for the Tarmac Championship which he did, eventually finishing in 5th place overall.

Winner was the impressive Ian Greer from Hillsborough County Down who, despite having broken a prop shaft during the rally and having to borrow one from another competitor, took a great win ahead of second placed finisher, the ever steady Eamonn Boland, while rounding off the podium was Austin McHale.

A very wet weekend in the North West for the Shell Donegal International Rally, saw another disappointing fifth place finish overall for Bertie, having had a considerable time loss on the Kindrum stage on the second day of the three day event. He started the rally well and on the Saturday was having a dingdong battle with Ian Greer but then he hit a rock and punctured a wheel in the process. With the car somewhat less controllable the Subaru slid into a ditch and with little man power around, there was an estimated time loss of around 15 minutes before he got back on to the road again.

Rory explains what happened in detail. *'Nemesis again! Everybody that does the Donegal Rally knows about that particular rock that sits out on the Kindrum stage*

right: The Killarney Rally of the Lakes went through some scenic locations throughout County Kerry

and the Cork-Kerry borders including the Tim Healy Pass. Unusually on this occasion there was time to enjoy the scenery as the stage had been cancelled so it was a drive through

so we were watching for it and thought we were out far enough, but we needed as much of the road as we could and he went in a fraction and I felt him just nip it on my side. He got round the next corner but at the next one, he turned in, and went straight off the road, and got stuck in a sheugh – guaranteed if we hadn't got caught out we would have had the lead because we were flying'.

Although they gained a few seconds later in the rally here and there it wasn't enough to gain back many places and they eventually finishing ten minutes behind local winner of the event James Cullen. Driving a Wrangler / Tony Kelly Cars Subaru Impreza 555 hired from McKinstry motorsport, it was Cullen and co-driver by Ellen Morgan's second victory on the Donegal Rally 8 years after their first win.

It was a great win for James but the big talking point of the rally was the exclusion of Ian Greer and Dean Beckett in a Toyota Celica GT4. After being weighed by scrutineers in a random weighing test at the service area at Barnesmore Gap after the first stage on the Friday, his Taranto de Pol Toyota Celica GT4 was found to be shy of the minimum weight allowed by FIA regulations for Group A cars. Ian, who had been leading the rally on Day One and Day Two, continued under appeal to finish third overall on stage times but the result was struck out after a stewards meeting later. His car was not the only car found to be underweight, Paul Harris' Subaru too was shy of the minimum weight but he decided not to continue and not to contest it.

With the Ulster and Manx event organisers going down the route of leaning toward the British Championship regulations and therefore excluding Group A cars from the main section of the rallies, Bertie decided not to tackle either, instead holding out till the Cork 20 Rally at the start of October, but to break up the three and a half month gap he visited the Lurgan Park Rally in mid-August.

Only having competed in the park once in the past six years, Bertie was perhaps a little rusty on the disciplines required for this specialist, mainly tarmac based, event

consisting of a series of quick sprints through the tricky tree lined avenues of Lurgan Park where every second is vital. After a spin (which he continuing it into a quick '360'. to lose only six or seven seconds) Bertie trailed in fifth overall twenty six seconds behind winner, Welsh Wizard Gwyndaf Evans in a Seat Cordoba WRC, who had a comfortable (in Lurgan Park terms) eleven seconds

one had been used on Irish tarmac, it wasn't going to be an easy weekend.

As the rally got underway Ian Greer and Frank Meagher were locked together in tight tussle for the lead with the lead changing hands several times until the seventh stage when Meagher damaged the steering and suspension on his Escort WRC after he went off the road due to a brake problem. Though he lost some time, he was able to continue, he was out of the hunt for overall victory finished fourth overall after the two days. Meagher's incident left Ian Greer with a comfortable lead over Andrew Nesbitt with Bertie taking things steady in third, not wanting to jeopardise the potential championship victory by pushing too hard.

Day Two dawned and though Bertie punched in a fastest time, Greer retaliated on the next before it all went wrong for Bertie on Stage 15, Mount Uniacke as Rory explains:- *'Almost at the end of the stage, there was a complete lapse of concentration on what wasn't even a difficult corner, just an ordinary medium range corner and we went straight off the road and into the hedge and got stuck in the sheugh. There wasn't anybody about so I ran up the road to slow down the next car while Bertie was up on the bonnet, trying to kick the windscreen out of her as it was shattered and you couldn't have seen a thing if we'd managed to get going.'*

However, getting out of the ditch and on their way with no one around to help them out of the ditch wasn't going to happen and so they radioed the team for help.

left: Bertie made a return visit to the tree lined Lurgan Park for the first time in a few years in 1999. The incredibly fast paced nature of the event punishes the slightest of mistakes and a spin was a big contributor to his lack lustre fifth place overall in the end, albeit only 20 seconds behind leader Gwyndaf Evans

margin over Belgian visitor Patrick Snijers in an Escort WRC with Denis Biggerstaff in a Metro 6R4 third and Derek McGarrity in an Impreza 555 fourth.

Coming in to the rally, both Evans and Snijers were former winners of the rally, three wins in all between them, so they were no rookies to the specialised nature of the Park.

And so it was back to the Tarmac championship for the Cork 20. Despite Bertie's disappointing results on the last two rounds, going into the final round on the Cork 20 International he held a healthy lead of 14 points on Ian Greer Following Greer's exclusion from the results of the Donegal Rally, which meant if Bertie finished anywhere in the top three or four places overall, he would secure a record fifth championship. However the 'ifs' in rallying are never small and with both Ian Greer and Andrew Nesbitt on top form, the latter out in a Subaru WRC, the first time

right top: Bertie and Rory may have been having a splashing time in the lead of the Cork 20 but disaster struck with an overshoot on Day Two, the aftermath was all too clear to see *below*

Wesley Emerson, a mechanic in the team at the time takes up the story *'We were sitting in our chase car at the end of the stage waiting on him to come but when we got the call that he was off and stuck we had to go looking for him. We ran up into the stage and though we were knackered by the time we got there, we manoeuvred him out and got him heading the right way in the direction of the stage.'*

But all the efforts were in vain. By the time they had been recovered out of the ditch and were ready to complete the stage, they were OTL, and with it (assuming Ian Greer would finish) their hopes of clinching their fifth Tarmac Championship of the 1990s had been shattered.

left: Selection of images from the RAC in 1999

So close, and yet, so far away. After the accident, it was a disappointing but sharp exit for home for the Toughmac team, having felt the devastation and knock on effects of the accident, which they knew probably shouldn't have happened on such a simple piece of road.

Ian Greer did go on to win the rally, his second Cork victory, and with it secured his first Tarmac Championship outright, while just seventeen seconds back, Andrew Nesbit's second place was enough to see him promoted to second in the Tarmac Championship.

The Cork 20 Rally in 1999 was the last rally on which Bertie drove the R555 FEL Silver Impreza, and the car was sold on to County Carlow man Stephen Murphy. It would also be the last ever Tarmac Championship round Bertie competed on, deciding that the following year he would concentrate on the career of son Mark who was progressing through the ranks of Peugeot and by 2000 was on the verge of getting his first full WRC seat with Peugeot in 2001.

To try and shake off the disappointment of Cork and end 1999 on a high note, Bertie took up a chance to go the Rally of Great Britain in a Prodrive-prepared Subaru Impreza WRC in what was essentially a two-car team, with Mark in another car.

Dave Campion of Prodrive explains *'He'd set up the deal for Mark to do the rally in a WRC run by ourselves and then out of the wood work another car became available and I gave him an opportunity to use it – I think that was the only event they had rallied together at that level.'*

As Rory recalls. *'That rally was simply for fun. Mark was*

right and above: Bertie slides sideways on the gravel rally the Network-Q RAC, the last round of the WRC and Bertie's last rally outside the island of Ireland

coming of age then and to be honest the focus was really on him, with Bertie's thing being kind of second which wasn't the most ideal way to be rallying but with the disappointments during the year between one thing and another Bertie thought he might do this rally just for the craic. It was still a bit rare to do a rally like that at such short notice but Bertie was very unpredictable, he would arrange stuff sometimes and I'd go "Where the **** did this come from!?' Even though we had a lot of time to chat about things, at times he was so unpredictable it was unbelievable.'

The Rally of GB of in 1999 was the first and only time Bertie ever drove competitively in a WRC car and in an interview with the *Belfast Telegraph* Bertie admitted that it had taken some getting used to. *'It was the first time I have driven a left-hand-drive WRC Subaru with this paddle gear-change. It was quite difficult at first but I got used to it as the rally went on and felt reasonably comfortable towards the end but it was such a rough rally and several of the stages were real car breakers. There was little you*

it every now and again and he took the notion that Monaghan was the one he wanted to do.'

On the day he finished second overall behind Niall Maguire in what for Bertie, was a fairly lack-lustre performance. Although there were various factors which contributed to the poor perform-ance, including a wrong tyre choice and a spin on the second stage due to an oil spill on the road, more than anything Bertie was just a little rusty, having not competed on an Irish Tarmac rally for a full six months previously.

Monaghan was Bertie's last pub-lic outing in a rally car other than a brief outing at the Millennium Motorsport Festival at Stormont in Bel-fast, where he drove the Peugeot 205 T16 Group B car in a demonstration run up the hill as he decided that for the rest of the year at least he would con-centrate on Mark's rally career, whose hard work over several years paid off when Peugeot offered him a full works drive for two selected WRC rallies, the Rally Greece and the Rally GB to see how he would per-form at the top level.

Both outings in the works-supported 206 WRC were blighted with various problems and he never really got underway properly in either but Peugeot had seen enough potential in the young Fisher that a month and a half later at the Autosport show Mark's dream became a reality when he was signed up with Peugeot for a full works drive in the World Rally Championship for that year.

The following week Bertie and his family, Gladys,

left: Bertie and Rory on their final competitive outing together on the Monaghan Stages Rally in 2000

could do except try to get through without wrecking the car.'

Bertie had competed on the rally once before, way back in 1984 when it was known as the RAC Rally and on that occasion had finished a very credible 9th overall. On this occasion with the challenge of an unfamiliar car and perhaps with one eye on what Mark was doing he finished 21st overall although in the event that was enough to win the top privateer award – a small consolation in an otherwise disap-pointing end to the season.

2000

Having shifted his priorities to developing Mark's career Bertie only competed in one rally in 2000, the Monaghan Stages Rally, which he entered, as Rory explains *'just purely for fun – it's hard to let go when you've been at the top competing and you like to do*

Mark, Emma and Roy headed off in Bertie's helicopter to Ashford Castle County Mayo to celebrate Gladys's birthday and no doubt Mark's success. On the return journey, just a few miles from home, at around 3pm on the afternoon of Sunday 21st January 2001, all their plans, hopes and dreams came crashing down as the helicopter got into difficulty and fell into a copse of trees.

Son Mark and Daughter Emma died at the scene and, although he survived the initial impact, some 30 hours later Bertie passed away in hospital from his injuries never having recovered consciousness.

Gladys and Roy survived but were too seriously in-jured to attend the funeral of Bertie, Mark and Emma in Ballinamallard on Thursday 25th January when thousands crammed into Ballinamallard despite the horribly cold and wet weather to pay tribute to a Fermanagh hero and his family.

Bertie Fisher, born 21st March 1950, died 22nd January 2001. A legend of rallying, A hero of rallying, A king of Rallying. King Fisher, we salute you.

right: Bertie drives the ex works Peugeot 205 T16in what was his last ever public outing, at the Millennium Motorsport Show at Stormont in Belfast

The Fisher Foundation

Established in 2003 by Fisher Engineering, the Fisher Foundation serves as a permanent memorial to the lives of Bertie, Mark and Emma Fisher who died following a tragic helicopter accident in 2001. The Foundation seeks to commemorate Bertie and Mark's interest in rallying and Emma's commitment to Christian service overseas by supporting those involved in these areas today.

The Fisher Foundation is administered by the Fermanagh Trust, County Fermanagh's community foundation. It is one of a number of funds administered by the Trust in its support of community and voluntary endeavour. Over £300,000 has been awarded by the Fisher Foundation since it was established. Young people have been supported via bursary awards towards carrying out voluntary work overseas. Support has also been given to motor clubs and other relevant organisa-tions to improve safety standards at rally events.

Since 2003 over 400 young volunteers from Fermanagh representing a wide range of organisation including The Leprosy Mission, Trocaire and the Church Mission Society Ireland have been awarded grants to help fund various development programmes. The Fisher Foundation aims to provide much needed financial resources to help organisations and volunteers who give their time to assist so many excellent and much needed projects right across the world. The projects that have been carried out including illness/ physical disability programmes, help for women and children, education initiatives etc are of worthy benefit not only to those affected in many countries but also in terms of personal development for our young people.

The continued support of motorsport safety initiatives is at the heart of the Foundation in recognition of Bertie's long established interest in this particular aspect. Safety in rallying was always of paramount importance to the three times Ulster Rally winner and during the 1980s he became increasingly aware of the need for improvement in safety standards at Irish rallies. To highlight the urgency in addressing the problem, Bertie, already one of the top Irish drivers withdrew from competi-tive rallying in 1986 to enable him to assist event organisers in the promotion and implementation of improved safety standards.

Each year the Fisher Foundation supports a range of initiatives, each promoting the continued development of safety in motor sport. This may include the cost of relevant training for voluntary officials and marshals or support of the purchase of appropriate safety equipment. Previous recipients include those organising rallying events such as 'The Circuit of Ireland' which received support for safety training for marshals and volunteers. Also supported were Motorsport Ireland who used their grant to host a national training weekend for rescue vehicles at Mondello Park. 70 participants ranging from first responder rescue crews to paramedics and doctors were involved in the programme which included lectures and practical demonstrations with opportunities for all to experience potential scenarios that may be faced by those attending a motor sport incident. In addition the Foundation has supported the development and upgrading of rally rescue vehicles for clubs across Ireland.

Appendix 1: Snapshots of Bertie

The journey to compile the information for this book has been a long one, and throughout my research and the many interviews I carried out, I picked up many inspiring thoughts and quotes about Bertie Fisher, but there are three recurring words that continually stand out – professionalism, integrity and honesty, and it is with those three admirable traits that Bertie became the most successful of privateer drivers from the island of Ireland, a true professional in an amateur sport. He continually pushed Irish rallying from one level to another right throughout his career, whether it was with pioneering the use of chase cars in the 1970s, highlighting spectator safety to the masses after his accidents in the 1980s, or enviably raising the bar of standards for Irish rally teams to aspire to in the 1990s.

Though it would have been an impossible task to speak to everyone who ever had any dealings with Bertie, I feel the following collection of excerpts from interviews carried out by myself, submissions of tributes sent to me and to the bertiefisher.com website, and from quotes in publications I uncovered in my research along the journey to create this book summarise people's experience of the man and pay fitting homage to the legend of Bertie Fisher, the rally King, King Fisher.

Bill Adair

The first time I met Bertie was in Finlay Engineering Ballygawley in the drawing office. He was erecting another new factory for the late John Finlay (Stephen's father) and it soon became obvious that one thing we had in common was a passion for engineering and motorsport. This was further compounded by a very young Stephen Finlay who found every reason in the world to get us in to one of their many gravel quarries. Bertie worked and played hard and was extremely determined. Bertie held a position in motorsport here, a mantle that no one has come close to taking over and I consider myself privileged to have been a very small part it!

Norman Burns, former Meeke mechanic

People may well use a lot of different words to describe or show their friendship or affection for Bertie, the two words that have been with me for many years are Honesty and Commitment.

As a young lad he was the first Rally Driver I was involved with in the Bush Performance Centre. As the years passed and he moved on in his rallying career, you could easily tell the nature of the man.

Honesty was at the forefront and the commitment ran deep, Bertie grew with the company and committed himself to bring further success to the company, with the success it gave him the resources to commit to his rally career, which gave him the platform to strengthen the Fisher name. All of which was done with honesty and commitment. Fond Memories Always

Andrew Bushe, Writer / Journalist

Bertie was a hero growing up, the iconic image of him in the Manta 400, that for me was the car- the Shell liveried Manta- so spiritedly driven, always trying hard. I still remember as a kid of 6, being allowed to stay up late to watch the rallies on UTV. It's a vivid childhood memory of his amazing save in Galway 1986, the Manta over Hamilton's Folly jump in 1987 and watching him out on the Circuit of Ireland stages, though I'll be the first to admit I was more of a McRae and Brookes fan.

As someone starting out in rallying, and beginning in motorsport journalism with Carsport magazine and RPM, I got to know Mark better than Bertie, and it was the junior Fisher who I admired the most. Mark would always answer his phone to me, as I wrote up the 106 Cup reports, and his enthusiasm and encouragement was infectious. As a student starting rallying, with little money, he also gave me a few of his second-hand tyres, as I headed for the Lakeland Rally, and the next time I phoned him up it was one of the first things he asked about. I also remember (vaguely!) a nights partying after the ATS Coracle Stages, in a hotel with Paul Crossen, Seamus Donnelly and his crew and Mark all in full flight. It was some nights craic, and Mark right in the middle of it, pulling pints at the bar at one stage, and taking pictures of it all! The 1999 106 Cup win was a special achievement, and for me to later achieve success rallying Mark's old 106 Cup car, with who else but Gerry helping in the preparation was a great honour, and a special time in my life. I really think that Mark would have gone far in rallying and in business, and the "King Fisher" title could have been later attributed to this extremely likeable young driver, a role model for the young up and coming drivers of today.

Dave Campion, former head of Prodrive teams and friend

Bertie was: Husband, Father, Business man, Rally driver, Friend.

Bertie applied himself to all of these tasks with the same underlying focus that was Bertie Fisher, a man of application, determination and generous spirit.

The best person I have ever had the opportunity to conduct business with, a demanding person to deliver too, the fairest person to debate with.

He had character that could only be applauded and admired in all elements of his life. The way in which he conducted himself was an inspiration to me and others.

As a friend you could not ask for better, our relationship was born out of business, nor-

mally a dangerous situation, but business and friendship remained separate and never crossed the line.

Every day something makes me think of Bertie, he will always be remembered by Georgie and I.

Billy Coleman, rally driver (excerpt from Carsport)

I could never say a word against Bertie Fisher. Such a fine driver, his results speak for themselves, and a fine man in every way. Everything about Bertie was totally above board

Ian Cuddy, former Meeke mechanic

He gave you the credit, when it was due. If you were good at your job, he wouldn't try to tell you your job, he would give you the trust and credit that you knew how to fix the car for him. There's a lot of other drivers that would try and tell you how to fix the car, he didn't do that, he just walked away and let you work at it.

James Cullen, rally driver (excerpt from Tarmac Titan DVD)

He was the person who set the standards for so many things not just in rallying but also for the way you should live your life, in his business, and family. He knew how to enjoy himself, and if there was a way to do it right it was the Fisher way

Cathal Curley, rally driver (excerpt from Tarmac Titan DVD)

When I retired in the late 70s or early 80s Bertie was just coming on the scene and I watched him at the time and I thought when that guy gets up and gets going right he's going to be a force to be reckoned with. I have great admiration for the way he approached his rallying. He is one of the few people in rallying who to my knowledge anyway has never fallen out with anyone in rallying, either a competitor or an organiser or an official. Bertie was really the gentleman of all sections of rallying be it a fellow competitor or whoever. He didn't have an enemy in the world

Fr. Brian D'Arcy & Canon Paul Koey tributes to the Fisher family

Fr. Brian D'Arcy, Rector of St. Gabriel's Retreat in the Graan outside Enniskillen, is a well-known author, a country and western enthusiast, newspaper columnist, and has his own weekly radio show on BBC Radio Ulster. Though he spent many years in Dublin, he is a native of Fermanagh, and knew Bertie and his family on a close personal level, as he did Tommy for many years previous.

"Bertie was just one of those men who was a God around here. You heard his name on the radio and you were as proud as punch of him, proud as punch of Bertie Fisher from Fermanagh doing all of these wonderful things and leading championships, you'd be rooting for him."

Fr. Brian was also impressed by Bertie's successes away from the stages, in the way he helped bring together communities and bridge gaps. "Bertie did an awful lot for local people and local businesses. He crossed borders, he crossed businesses, he did everything. He wasn't a politician, he wasn't anything else, but he used sport to unite people. For example, when a young Catholic rally driver Brian McGrath up the road from here was killed, the first man in the Church was Bertie Fisher that day. I had anointed Brian on the road, and he was coming from a rally when he was killed on the road that night. I'd been at the funeral mass and Bertie Fisher was there representing the rally fraternity. Bertie deserves great credit for being a great ecumenical worker."

Fr. Brian explained how from his ties with the Fishers that after the accident there were many occasions he was humbled to be asked to attend, including the funeral, and the re-opening of the factory. "The first morning back after Bertie's death and the factory reopened, the family asked me and the local Church of Ireland Minister Canon Hoey to say a prayer together before they opened the factory at seven o'clock on a Monday morning and I will never forget it, it was a January Monday morning."

As a businessman Bertie led the local community and did more for the area than you would perhaps initially think. "Bertie obviously as a businessman had to be involved in some sort of politics, and that's grand, but it was the right kind of politics, the kind of politics that puts bread on tables. Sean Quinn and Bertie, for example, were two men of a similar era, one a good footballer, one a good racing driver and best of friends. They worked through each other, and those two men did a lot for this area and continue to do so. You don't forget people like that. The biggest thing that anyone does is give employment to an area which nobody else wants to recognise as anything. That's why he and Sean Quinn were terrific guys who had the ability to see that a small place was as deserving of employment as Belfast or Dublin and so they stayed in their own area. Sean Quinn and Mark were also terrific friends. Sean often told me that Mark was one of the greatest losses, he said he had the best head he ever come across on a cub. A big compliment from Sean Quinn."

Fr. Brian then talked about how the integrity Bertie had as a businessman carried across to leadership qualities as a sportsman. "That's what makes the man, that's what makes a sportsman, that's how you find the character that becomes the top sportsman and a decent leader... there's nobody more so than Cormac McAnallen as an example of that, a leader on and off the field willing to take risks as a leader and having the dedication that you need in life to be a success and Bertie had that in, I'll just use the word, barrowfulls, since his father started making wheelbarrows."

Fr. Brian continued to explain what he felt were Bertie's admirable sportsmanship qualities. "If you don't prepare you're going to fail but even if you do plan and prepare, sport being sport there's no guarantee you're going to win. You can train your whole life, but a fella can go up and pull a hamstring in ten minutes... but if the luck's with you, the luck is with you. Sometimes you make your own luck, and I think this was Bertie's biggest thing – to win with absolute dignity and lose with absolute respect."

Summing up Bertie, Fr. Brian said, "I'd like Bertie to be remembered as a wonderful sportsman, a fantastic businessman, but most of all a most generous family man who is still remembered in good stead across the world through the Fisher Foundation and has saved lives through the Motor Foundation"

The Reverend Canon Paul Hoey, who moved to Magheracross Parish as rector in 1990, im-mediately became familiar with the Fishers, and as Tommy was nominator in the church, he was the very first person he met when he arrived. Very soon he realised how important the Fishers were to Ballinamallard and to the wider parish "No family has done more for Ballinamallard. It would not be the place that it is but for the Fisher family. When Tommy came back from the war having spent time as a Prisoner of War, he started his own small engineering business and even up to the point when it had become a much bigger company, you could bring the smallest of jobs to Tommy and it wouldn't have been a problem"

As Canon Hoey points out, Tommy and wife Elsie were also great parish people. "Tommy and Elsie involved in everything; from lunch club for the seniors, to the vestry committees, and they never missed church. They had their finger in every pie with regard to church and parish life"

As time went on, Canon Hoey got to know the wider Fisher family but Bertie's high profile never got in the way of his commitment to church and parish "Bertie was a quiet, modest character, much the same as his father, and he did lots of things behind the scenes." When it came to church time, Canon Hoey said "Bertie's own family often came to church from different directions in different cars but always made it on time and all waited to come in together, with Bertie usually leading the way."

"They were a great family, they brought people together, they gave pleasure in lots of different ways."

Talking about Bertie's own family at the time of the accident, Canon Hoey said "Each of them in their own way touched the lives of those who knew them. To my mind they shared 2 great things in common:1 was their humility. In spite of all their successes and achievements in life they never saw themselves as anything other than ordinary people, and the good they done for others was all done quietly. The second was their ability to make anyone they met feel important and part of their lives."

Being the parish rector from 1990 until 2003, Canon Hoey conducted the funeral service for Bertie, Mark and Emma, and as he pointed out there had never and has never been as large a scale funeral in the parish.

On the evening of the accident, Canon Hoey was due to preach at a church in Portadown that night when he got the phone call to alert him of the sad news and he had to inform the minister in Portadown he needed to return back to Fermanagh urgently to attend the vigil at the Erne Hospital.

Given the expected scale of the funerals, Canon Hoey remembers "The Church parishioners and local community along with other friends and colleagues of the Fishers all took leading roles in putting up marquees, street barriers, parking, logistics etc."

At the service the week after the accident, Canon Hoey recalls "The place was absolutely packed, and everyone was in awe, shocked, everyone gathering as a family, giving support to the Fishers. This catastrophe really united people in grief"

"It's hard to believe that is coming 15 years since the tragedy but they are still remembered like its yesterday due to the lasting legacy whereby they gave a lot of people a lot of pleasure during their lives"

"When you mention Bertie Fisher you see a lot of smiling faces. They just remember him something like themselves, insofar as Bertie never lost the common touch, and he saw himself as one of them and who made them feel good about themselves. I think the word I'm looking for is people, they were always about helping, supporting, encouraging people."

As time had passed after the tragedy, and when Fisher Foundation was being created, Canon Hoey was invited, as rector of the parish to serve as a trustee for the charity. He, along with Fr Brian D'Arcy, were responsible for the development of the missionary and overseas aspect of the charitable works, something Emma Fisher was already deeply involved in as Canon Hoey said. "She actually wasn't long back from a year long trip to India when the tragedy occurred. There she had worked with lepers and had told us stories about how she helped lepers who walked on roads with no shoes and remarked jokingly that if she had half the tyres her dad had used up on rally cars she could have made shoes for them all."

Elaborating on Emma, Cannon Hoey reflects "She had a very open faith, very up front, while the others had a solid faith but buried it a bit further down."

"Emma had a very different personality to her dad in some respects but was outgoing and bubbly while Bertie was quietly working in background, and when releasing grants from the Fisher Foundation we are always kept in mind what Emma would have done because she always took the lead on that kind of thing".

"Her heart certainly lay in helping disabilities from her own faith perspective, and indeed at home she was involved in fund raising and helping others to go fund raising"

"She could have done a whole lot of things in life but she found great contentment in her charitable work."

"I think faith pulled the family through quite strongly after the tragedy, and I will never forget Tommy's reaction when I broke the sad news to him. So typical of Tommy, he said "I knew when Bertie had not been in to see me I knew that something was wrong". Weak physically but fresh in mind"

"Ultimately though, Tommy was devastated after, and essentially he lost the will to live with a broken heart"

In summary, Canon Hoey remembers Bertie Mark and Emma as "Well, I have different memories of all of them but mostly I remember them as a family, a family who did things together as they were doing on the day of the accident"

"I have a photo on my wall of Bertie in competition attire smiling, and this is how I remember him, a man who took all his success in his stride and never went overboard"

George Deane, sponsor, business client, and friend

I started my career in Killadeas in Fermanagh in 1967 when I bought my first digger and I first knew Bertie in those days from the business side of things. In those days diggers broke down regularly so Tommy Fisher did all my repairs. Any time I'd be over at their yard Mrs. Fisher would be out with the tea and bread and it was just like home. That's when Bertie appeared for although he was in college at the time, when he was around home and if there was a breakdown he would come out to fix it and do the welding for me along with Tommy.

It took a while but over the years I got to know Bertie personally and we would have gone out for a drink occasionally. In the 1970s when I started a bit of rallying as well in Escorts and Minis in the club rallies where Bertie would have been involved, and from that we moved on till he became one of my best friends. He then asked me just for fun if I wanted to sit with him for a rally so we sat together on the Lurgan Park in 83 and I still have the crystal on my dresser at home. Then we went down to Castlederg to do a rally together but they wouldn't let me do it because I didn't have the licence. When he took up the rallying seriously and wanted a bit of sponsoring, I wouldn't have been giving him much but he used to put the digger logo of my firm on his car. The team he had built up around him with his sponsors and so on was second to none, there was no body to touch him and it was so well organised.

Then what brought us closer together still was when he supported me in running a very successful charity dance for cancer research. In later years we started golfing then and that took us out a lot but we also went out for a drink too.

I still have one of Bertie's last race suits which, when Gladys gave it to me because she was friendly with my wife, it was like a million pounds and I cherish this dearly.

There are no words for what he means to me, he was my number 1, my hero, like a brother, and I miss him every day.

Colm Doherty

While competing as a co-driver on the Circuit of Ireland back in the early '90s, I was both surprised & impressed to encounter Bertie the morning after he retired from the rally with terminal engine problems. Approaching a time control in deepest Tipperary, I saw that it was manned by Bertie, who courteously took my time card, smiled at me and wished us luck for the rest of the event.

It was a true mark of the man, who never forgot his clubman roots, that he chose to stay & serve the sport rather than rush home in a sulk. He was a class act, as a competitor and as a human being. It was a privilege to meet him, and to witness his artistry at the wheel of every car he drove.

Wesley Emerson, former Meeke mechanic

I would remember him as the one man I worked for that would bring the car to you no matter what shape it was in, it might have had square wheels but he would get it out of the stage. He would have expected miracles, and got them.

Enniskillen Motor Club, where Bertie was a former member, chairman, organiser, event sponsor, etc

Bertie had a massive influence on rallying throughout Ireland and beyond, and Enniskillen Motor Club were proud to have him as a club member. He inspired so many to become involved in the sport through his personality and his achievements. His dedication to the sport was unquestioned and selfless. When brake failure led to a dramatic accident on the Galway International Rally in 1986 it was only Bertie's skills and reaction that averted disaster. He was so affected by the incident that he sacrificed his own rally career, retiring from competition for a year and dedicating himself to improving safety issues. The results of the changes he instigated are still felt today 30 years later, and some rally spectators undoubtedly owe their lives to his

efforts. This personal sacrifice to benefit others was typical of his character and one of the reasons that he will be remembered with admiration and affection not just in his home county but much further afield.

Stephen Finlay, rally driver and friend

I always had a great interest in cars from a very young age. When I was only knee high I was wrecking around my father's quarries, pits and block yards in old bangers. Then as I got a little older and could manage to see over the steering wheel without props, I raced stock cars in Fivemiletown because I didn't need a licence for that.

The first time I met Bertie was in 1981 when as a young teenager my father took me to a sprint at St. Angelo Airport. My father was involved with St. Angelo because he did a lot of flying there. Fishers had built the first hangar at the airport and he got to know Bertie through that.

On the day of the sprint my father was chatting with Bertie when he offered to give me a run alongside him around the airfield in the Monte Carlo Escort. I can still remember the excitement I felt, a dream come true! Before we set off he was showing me all the gauges and instruments in the car but at the stage they were all alien to me. When we went for the run round it was just fabulous and I was even more hooked!

My father then also used Fishers for the steelwork for a few of the factories he was building and I would frequently see Bertie coming in and out of the yards. There was always a business association between my father (John) and Bertie but I never thought that one day I would be competing with him in rallying!

Fast forward a few years... I did my first rally at Nutts Corner, a small multi-surface event and my next event was the Lakelands in Fermanagh. Bertie won the Lakelands and when we went to the prize giving, as usual I was trying to hide from the media but Bertie announced on stage to everyone that he was giving his prize to me and to watch out for me in future rallies. I have never forgotten that!

We had connected right from the beginning but little did I know that he was about to become a much bigger part of my life! At the age of 18 I lost my father and Bertie was not only a friend but he then became a father figure to me as well. He had such charisma about him and I always aspired to him. He drove me on and encouraged me whether it be in rallying or business.

Bertie was a great ambassador to Irish Motorsport and the bravest of the brave, especially on Tarmac. I think the only way you could beat Bertie was when he would over think things, which he did from time to time. When Bertie was rallying it kept me at it but when he was gone I lost the hunger for it a bit and it just wasn't the same.

We would have spoken a lot about business and when he supplied steel frame buildings to various jobs I would have been supplying the hollow core slabs to the same jobs, the two things worked together.

We would bounce ideas of each other and ended up speaking each day on the phone as friends, I still miss that. He was my inspiration and my mentor.

Bertie became a huge part of my life, we had the same hobbies, went on holiday together, socialised together and played golf together...

sometimes badly! Bertie, Gladys & their family were always a joy to be around.

Bertie was one of a kind, I knew it and so did everyone that knew him. I remember the many times we laughed, travelled, rallied and celebrated together. He was a friend and a father figure to me and to say he is still missed is an understatement. This tribute comes from a place where he left his mark on.

Alastair Fisher, rally driver, nephew of Bertie

My memories of Uncle Bertie's rallying exploits relate back to the famous Group A Subaru Impreza days, namely L555 FEL and R555 FEL. I mainly recall iconic events like The Circuit of Ireland and The Donegal International Rally, standing in Milford mart watching the mechanics go to work or on my dad's shoulders during the hustle and bustle of a street service on The Circuit of Ireland. I have a great memory of all the family at Uncle Bertie's house during Christmas 1998 when we were all brought out to the courtyard where Uncle Bertie opened one of the garage doors and resting inside was the silver Toughmac Impreza R555 FEL. The car was in absolute immaculate condition with the silver paint work shining, fresh from the factory. I can remember saying that the car was far too nice to rally and Uncle Bertie just laughed and said, "That's what she's for". Looking back, being one of the first people to see the car was something special as it went on to be one of Uncle Bertie's most memorable Toughmac livered cars. During the following 1999 season I remember travelling to watch what I know now as a typical Galway rally, Uncle Bertie in the silver Impreza blasting through the foggy and muddy conditions with the Subaru crack-

ing and banging out of sight which was that iconic sound we all loved. I also travelled to the AA Circuit of Ireland that year with Granda and Granny Fisher where we watched Uncle Bertie and Rory Kennedy spray champagne at the finish ramp in Bangor.

Like many families involved in motorsport, it was in the blood and undoubtedly Uncle Bertie's career inspired me to give rallying a go. My first event was in 2004 when dad and I went to a closed circuit sprint at Nutt's Corner where we ran dual entry in a Vauxhall Nova and I competed in the Juniors finishing 3rd in my class. I passed my driving test at 17 and competed on my first stage rally, my local event the 2005 Lakeland Stages in a Suzuki Swift, with dad co-driving. My rallying career snowballed from there!

During my career I have been extremely fortunate to have had the opportunity to compete both at home and abroad and experience the thrills and spills along the way. I have been privileged to have had both of Uncle Bertie's and Mark's co-drivers, Rory Kennedy and Gordon Noble, in the co-driver's seat on numerous occasions. Furthermore, I have also built up a strong relationship with Mark's mentor Gerry McGarrity over the years as he also prepared my cars. No matter where I compete, Uncle Bertie is always mentioned and everyone's respect for him and old stories are greatly received. I feel privileged to be able to carry the Fisher name on my side window and I hope to be able to continue to do so for many years to come.

Ivan Fisher, youngest brother

My relationship with Bertie is easily summed up, he spoiled me with one hand and was strict but fair with the other.

I have many memories growing up as Bertie's youngest brother, I will share just a few.

Bertie had bought what was at the time a proper racing kart chassis minus the engine from a local karting enthusiast and Church of Ireland minister, the Rev. McMurray Taylor.

Dad had a grey Ferguson tractor that was mainly used for testing trailer rams and general towing jobs around the yard etc. I was brave and foolish enough, at Bertie's request, to let him tow me around the yard in the kart with him driving the tractor. The track stretched from what we called the front street, down the entry, into the bottom yard and up to the top yard and back. I can assure you not the longest special stage in the world but with loads of Cautions and Don't Cuts.

After a few laps and with growing confidence and increasing speed the BIG accident happened at the Sq Left Don't Cut into the bottom yard. It was a Don't Cut because the big water tank for cooling the steel was on the inside of the corner, however I drifted out wide on the rope and collided with about fifty cow cubicles that had just been neatly stacked in bundles against the wall of the bottom workshop!!! Not looking behind just at that time Bertie continued towing me, scattering the cubicles everywhere. When we stopped I wasn't really hurt but I saw Mum coming down the yard so I started to cry and that got me off the hook; boy did she give Bertie some telling off!

The night of my wedding when the party was over we went to pay the dance band, only to be told that Bertie had already thanked and paid them. Later that night when Hazel and I were leaving the hotel heading off on honeymoon, just as the car drove off, Bertie opened the back door and pushed an envelope of cash into my pocket. His exact words were,

"Have a good time and a few drinks on me." (I can assure you we did both and had cash home in the envelope; no I didn't give it back to him!)

The last conversation we had was a phone call. The weekend of the accident it was Bertie and Gladys's weekend to have my Mum as Dad was in hospital, Bertie asked me to go over to their house and stay with Mum, which I did. He rang me on the Sunday morning to enquire about mum, he told me approximately what time to expect them home, to keep the fire going and switch on the red landing marker light at the hangar.

I was just back from leaving Mum to the nursing home when the house phone rang, it was George Deane, a close friend of Bertie's, enquiring if they were home yet. He said he would call with me in a few minutes. I knew that second by his tone that something was wrong, I remember going outside and walking around seeing the fog low on the lake. George arrived minutes later, he had heard at the Golf Club there had been a helicopter accident in the Monea area, he gradually broke the news to me as we headed to the Erne Hospital. I can remember clearly, just as we turned into the hospital him saying; Bertie, Gladys and Roy are still alive but Mark and Emma died at the scene.

Bertie, Mark and Emma, your presence in life enriched us all.

Austin Frazer, Co-driver to Bertie 1977 - 1989 and friend (inc excerpt from Tarmac Titan DVD)

Whenever you're doing those sort of rallies with somebody, it's almost like a family thing with the mechanics and so on where you could be away from home for 5 or 6 days. He was very good to work with, very competitive minded. He was a great guy – very, very competitive in anything he did. We built up a bond that can't be replaced or forgotten

Andy Kallam, Pirelli (excerpt from Carsport)

We worked with Bertie since 1983, and have always thought of him and the family as such wonderful people. Bertie was responsible for almost all our success in Ireland. He helped us so much with development, he knew instantly what tyres would work for Ireland and what was good for Irish tarmac rallying. It was always a pleasure to work with him.

Sammy Hamill, Journalist and friend (excerpt from Belfast Telegraph / Carsport, written in Jan 2001)

Bertie was one in a million

Bertie Fisher was a special person. Not because he was one of the greatest Irish rally drivers of all time - which he was.

Not just because he was an outstanding businessman who had built the family firm into one of the leading steel construction companies in the UK - which he did.

Not even because he was a proud and devoted family man - which he was.

No, the single most abiding quality I remember was his integrity.

What you saw was what you got, a straightforward, open and honest man who lived his life by a simple code - treat other people as you would have them treat you.

He may have been a millionaire, with his beautiful Palladian-style home right on the shores of Lough Erne, his Squirrel helicopter, his £200,000 rally cars and the other trappings of wealth, but he and his wife Gladys never forgot where they came from, their humble beginnings - nor were their children, Mark, Emma and Roy, allowed to forget either.

He may have lived a fast and hectic life but his feet were always on the ground, firmly rooted in family values, good sense and civility.

When you remember that some of his fiercest rivals in Irish rallying, like Andrew Nesbitt, Stephen Finlay and Austin McHale, went straight to the hospital when they heard about the awful accident, and maintained a vigil there along with his close friends like sponsor Kieran McAnallen, engineer Sydney Meeke and co-drivers Austin Frazer and Rory Kennedy, you can begin to understand what type of person Bertie Fisher was.

He was held in the highest esteem, almost awe, by friend and foe alike.

He was my friend for more than 25 years during which I wrote thousands of words about him and reported on his rally career in a professional capacity but was also welcomed into his family circle where I was privileged to share in his successes, his disappointments and his thoughts.

A generous, funny - often unintentionally so - competitive, thoughtful and modest man, just thinking about him evokes so many memories.

Like the first of his three Circuit of Ireland victories when, soaked in champagne and still sitting on the roof of his Subaru Impreza with the media clamouring around him for interviews, he grabbed a mobile phone to ring his father Tommy who was at home recovering from an operation.

Like the bitter disappointment of winning and then losing hours later, on a protest, the Manx International in the Isle of Man where his dashing driving style had made him a folk hero even though he never did succeed there.

Like the second of four Ulster Rally successes nearly a year later when we all went out to dinner and, as the party swung, he remarked: "This almost makes up for the Manx ... almost." That Isle of Man defeat hurt so much.

Like the day we competed together for a bit of fun on his home Lakeland Rally and dropped the Ford Escort RS1800 into a ditch because he was too busy waving to spectators to get round the corner.

Like his BMW M3 performing tyre-smoking pirouettes under the finish area floodlights on a cold frosty December night in Killarney after he had recorded the first of his six wins on the Rally of the Lakes. He loved Killarney.

Like the night he went on stage at the prize ceremony in the Lido in Douglas to sing his version of "Where have all the flowers gone" - "Where have all the Audis gone" - after he and his Opel team-mates Jimmy McRae and Russell Brookes had crushed their much-vaunted German rivals. It brought the house down.

But the memories extend well beyond his rally triumphs and tribulations. We shared so many good days, some of them in the very helicopter which was to end his life along with those of Mark and Emma.

I will never forget flying over Mount Rushden where he had conceived the Millennium Summit Rally and hung on as he dropped the Squirrel in to land under the blades of the giant wind turbines which dominate the landscape above Derrylin. I had sweaty palms but it was no bother to Bertie.

On the other hand he really put himself under pressure organising a huge BBQ & rally show which he put on inside the Fisher Engineering complex on the eve of the Summit event.

Still, the unstinting effort was well worthwhile - he raised £40,000 that night for local charities. That was a side of his character that he didn't strive to publicise.

And speak to Phillip McAnallen who was in a coma when Bertie came to the hospital to talk to him and play tapes of the sound of his rally car.

Another of his schemes for helping the Ballinamallard community was to bring the Ulster Rally into the village for a breakfast stop over a number of years - Gladys and her friends provided the bacon baps, the proceeds of which went to the church restoration fund. We used to joke they could have built a new church never mind put a new roof on the existing one with the money they raised.

Fisher Engineering may have become a hugely successful company under Bertie's stewardship, being involved in the construction of such landmark buildings as Castlecourt, the Waterfront Hall and the Odyssey Arena, but around Fermanagh they have built everything from farm gates to cow sheds.

I remember when the business was growing so rapidly they had to expand the premises and Bertie told me he was taking on the hardest assignment of his life. "I'm going to move the Ballinamallard River," he said.

And he did. In a massive operation they diverted the river to create more space but the biggest headache was the wildlife which lived in and around it. Environmental experts had to be called in to ensure all the little creatures migrated safely to their new home. It caused months of delay but the job was done properly.

That, perhaps, was the Fisher hallmark - do it right. He hated second best. There was only ever one place to finish and that was first. He did it more than any other Irish driver in history as his 20 Tarmac rally victories testify.

And no one who was ever beaten by him could ever say he didn't do it fairly and squarely. A man of total integrity.

James Henderson, Secretary of Bertie's business Fisher Engineering (excerpt from Belfast Telegraph in 2001)

Bertie was a hard-working man. He knew everyone of his workforce by their Christian name and he treated everyone as an equal.

Vincent Kogan, Journalist (excerpt from Irish Independent in 2001)

There's something you probably should know about Bertie Fisher. It relates to the '98 Circuit of Ireland rally, an infamously contentious four-day battle that culminated with Fisher receiving the garlands beneath a finish arch in Bangor. Bertie was deemed to have won the rally by nineteen seconds from his greatest rival, Austin McHale.

But had he? Due to some quite bewildering heel-dragging on the part of the organisers, the rally ended with McHale's appeal against a twenty second penalty still pending.

That penalty had been wrongly imposed on the first day of the event, yet – three days later – Fisher and McHale went to the start of the final stage (an eighteen mile test just north of Castlewellan) neither man quite sure of the requirements for outright victory. Technically, Fisher led the rally by 45 second. But a suc-

cessful appeal by his Dublin rival would reduce the margin to 25. Confusion reigned.

Over Begny Hill, McHale – driving like a man possessed – out-paced Fisher by a startling 26 seconds. Yet, it was still Fisher's rally by nineteen seconds, right? Wrong.

One week later, after three layers of appeal had been activated, McHale was deemed to have won the 'Circuit' by the margin of a single second! For the previous fifteen or so years, Fisher and McHale had been involved in many riveting battles but this was, by far, the tightest. And, potentially, the most acrimonious. Yet, one of the first phone calls of congratulation McHale received on hearing that he was 'Circuit champion came from Fisher. It was the style of a man impervious to pettiness. Fisher simply confirmed that he would have done "exactly the same" had roles been reversed.

The chaos of 'Circuit '98 was not of the drivers' making. It would not break a friendship.

…

Bertie Fisher's gift as a driver was an uncanny precision. He had the gift of natural rhythm, he never wrestled with a car and stress never seemed to penetrate his world. He won more international rallies than any other Irish driver. Sometimes, the in-car camera pictures seemed implausible given his extraordinary speed. Bertie could look like he had an elbow on the sill and there was a Perry Como number humming down the intercom.

…

But he is gone now and, in his absence, we all feel a good deal older. We extend our deepest sympathy to the family.

Rory Kennedy, Co-driver to Bertie 1985 - 2000 and friend

As I sit here today in my office writing this eulogy, I am surrounded by photographs of treasured memories Bertie and I shared together and it almost feels surreal. – it's as if he's looking out at me to check what I write !

I was honoured and privileged to be Chosen to be Bertie's co-driver when Austin retired, little did I know then the incredible journey this would take me on over the next 14 years.

Being part of the team was like being part of the family, with everyone firmly focused on the same thing ... Success.

Bertie had an incredible will to win, something I picked up on very quickly and still carry with me to this very day, he was a man of steely determination with great leadership qualities.

I loved being part of the team, not only was it a sporting education but also an education on how to live your life.

I was lucky enough to work very closely with Bertie over a long period of time, I embraced his competitive spirit and learned first hand how to conduct yourself in life, business and sport. He was a born leader with a huge appetite for life in general.

Bertie epitomised the spirit of Irish rallying, raised the level and set the standards and most of all knew how to enjoy himself, we had many memorable celebrations which were never complete without Bertie giving us a few bars.

Everywhere I go I am constantly being reminded of Bertie and the golden years, people come up to me all the time and recount their story and memories of him which is always a pleasure . Apparently, Molls Gap still echoes with the sound of the Toughmac BMW, Sierra and Subarus ...

There's not an event I do now that at some point I think of Bertie, I feel in some small way I carry his memory , and am very proud to do so.

Michael Kirby, former head of Sales and Marketing in Subaru Ireland

Bertie was a consummate professional and a most unselfish man. His attention to detail was of the 'no stone left unturned' thinking, even down to pre-agreed food menus for the motor home and minute details of team gear as examples were just unheard of in Irish rallying at the time. He never forgot the marshals and helpers, and anywhere he went he was always highly respected, he wasn't just for the royalty, he was for everyone, he was a man of the people, available to everybody.

Adrian Kirkland, former Meeke mechanic

He was very straight and if he had to tell you something he would have told it to you, and you didn't hear it from somebody else.

Wesley N Knox
Finance Director · Fisher Engineering Limited 1989 · 2015

With a smile I recollect a morning when Bertie zoomed into the office, walking as always at top speed and, without so much as a hello, said, "Give me your tie!" Being handed the tie, he promptly put it on and went to meet the journalists for the photoshoot he had forgotten was occurring that day. And that speed was the way everything went. Bertie would give you three vital words out of a rush of thought, analysis and strategy; you had to read his mind and piece together the rest. The precision and demands of both business and sport were dealt with at high speed; Bertie would run up the stairs and in and out of building sites, racing every bit as swiftly as his motorcars. Everything was – metaphorically and literally – oiled to perfection and Bertie would fly seamlessly into the office and into his cars with everything organised along his guiding lines, the teams simply awaiting his arrival. He was, in every way, a leader. He surrounded himself with the best teams in business and in sport, inspired respect and admiration, making every individual feel valued, respected and heard.

Bertie gave his full self into anything he did. As on a number occasions he once summoned me to his office at midnight to look over some details of a tender; he hadn't yet made his way home. The office was a cloud of smoke and he was running at 100mph, his smartly ironed suit half covered in mud from the building site he had visited earlier in the day. We sat down and worked, his determination was steely and his focus absolute in everything he did. At first glance one might have thought his passion for motorsport was at odds with his success in business – and indeed once or twice, as Finance Director, I confess to having winced at the financial requirements of the sport Bertie so loved, but having seen his ruthless focus and enjoyment of both, I believe the opposite was true. Not only did the entire office and factory feel a certain excitement for working alongside a motorsport hero, but Bertie was able to lead innovation in both engineering and sport, the one fuelling the other, his enthusiasm for both ever unflagging.

Ultimately, he was a kind and generous man with a large heart who took all that life offered and gave back thousandfold to all who knew him.

In the 1980's the business jumped from performing fabrication projects at 200 tonnes to those at 3000 tonnes, the CastleCourt building Belfast - for which Bertie kept a particular fondness - was the springboard which catapulted the company into the premiership league and even greater success in the following decades. We all grew together and that excellence and excitement mirrored Bertie's rallying prowess. As one of the top Irish rally drivers and the head of one of Ireland's most successful businesses he could have been made arrogant by success, but the reverse was true: he was generous with his triumphs and every member – from the mechanic to the steel worker, the office junior to the engineer – felt part of a pioneering and winning whole.

There are stories about work and tales which show humanity, anecdotes full of laughter and lists of wild successes, memories of challenges overcome, yet none of these can fully explain my feelings with regard to Bertie Fisher. These are summarised in a word: Bertie was a Hero. A man I respect and revere, a man who set the highest standards and values which I attempt to follow, a man who gave opportunity to so many.

Kieran McAnallen, friend, sponsor (excerpt from Tarmac Titan DVD)

He was an ambassador for sport, business, and anything else that you can think of. There will never be anyone that will ever fill his shoes, or Mark's either, for Mark was his double, and Emma she was a bundle of joy too. They were just an exceptional family, the whole family, exceptional. And Bertie, Mark and Emma have been sorely missed since.

Sean McCaffrey, Radio Presenter and rally enthusiast

The Day the Big Boys came to Town…. Life is funny and in the way the things can be thrown up… Having always been a fan of rallying, in my early years it was not as easy to get to see the action on the stages but when the Circuit of Ireland in its proper format (I know, an argument for another day) had a stopover at the Hillgrove Hotel Monaghan in April of 1991, I was sure to be there armed with a camera, roll of film (none of your fancy digital equipment), paper and pen.

As the cars rolled up to the control it was a young motorsport fan's dream to see his heroes step out of their burbling beasts and chat among each other about the stages that morning and what was to come.

Obviously with pen and paper in hand (the paper being Brian & Liz Patterson's Rally News.. the only way of knowing what was going on at that time) it was shoved in the direction of every man wearing a rally suit… did we know exactly who they were, No but who cares these were rally drivers… Colin Mc Rae was leading the rally in his Subaru Legacy, we were just beginning to hear about him, Austin Mc Hale was holding 2nd in his BMW (Have to admit now I was an Austin man) and Bertie Fisher was 3rd in the Ford Sierra… (Knew him from the telly of course and he was the main competitor to Austin)…. Photos were taken and autographs were grabbed and then all was put away in a photo album to be forgotten until almost 20 years later that same photo album with the Rally news sheets folded neatly were found in a box and great memories

of the day the big boys came to town were recalled.

It was only 20 years later that I discovered the significance of the names on the back of the Rally news sheet. Names such as James Cullen, Bob Fowden, Robbie Philpott, Kenny McKinstry and even best wishes from George Hamilton (who was following the event for RTE I believe) jumped off the page, but it was 2 signatures in the top left hand corner that had me stunned.

Obviously being bombarded with pens and scraps of paper, an autograph/signature soon becomes a scrawl but not so Bertie's which was so easy to distinguish. Time and patience taken to ensure a motorsport fan got his moment and above it Colin McRae, this one took a little bit of time to confirm, well as long as it took me to grab the Playstation game and look to see were the signatures the same. They were, so here on the back of a page that had not seen the light of day for 2 decades was the autographs of two of rally's best known competitors, little did I know what I had for so long.

That page is now laminated for safe keeping and prosperity with the Rally news on front giving a snap shot of time… Even just reading that report and looking at the "poorly" taken photos brings back wonderful memories of the day the big boys came to town and it is the extra wee bit special to have the signatures on the back…

Robbie McGurk, former Meeke mechanic

Just home from the 2015 Donegal international Rally won by Gary Jennings & Rory Kennedy in a Subaru Impreza S12B. 20 years

ago Bertie Fisher & Rory Kennedy won this rally in a Subaru Impreza GpA, standing at the finish banner at Portsalon there was a lot of old memories from 20 years ago, the one that stays with me is mid-day on Saturday .The Impreza clutch started slipping and as luck would have it next service was only 20min so maximum attack in service and the clutch was changed in 16min. To the ordinary Joe blogs this might not sound very exciting but your local Subaru dealer could spend 4 hours at this job! Bertie Fisher always rose the bar in Irish rallying and was a pleasure to work for whatever the result and believe me it wasn't all champagne!! Great Memories.

Austin McHale, rally driver and friend

He was the best competitor that I ever had, the one I respected the most, right across the board. In motorsport he is an icon, and I think right across the island of Ireland and the UK he's probably better known and better recognised than a lot of the top people in the world. He is also well known in this country with his business and so on but I think that most people would be the same by saying he would be an icon and an awful lot of people would have a great height of respect for him over the years.

John McIlroy, Journalist (excerpt from Autosport)

The Tarmac Rally Championship is the biggest motorsports series in Ireland. And for 20 years, Bertie Fisher was its biggest player. He made his name in Ford Escorts and Opel Mantas, enjoying thrilling scraps with other local aces like Austin McHale and Kenny McKinstry, as partisan followers hung off every vantage point. It was pure theatre played out in front of thousands of people, and the cast became heroes.

But the bulk of the Fisher legend was created in Subarus. He used the Legacy and Impreza models to boost his tally of Ulster Rally wins to four and rack up three Circuit of Ireland victories. Of the Tarmac Championship rounds, only the Manx eluded him, although he came agonisingly close to rattling Armin Schwarz's works Toyota on the event in 1996. In total, he won 20 Irish internationals and lifted the Tarmac crown four times, although his impact on the country's rallying scene went further than mere figures. He played key roles at organisational level, and was a crucial voice to call for improved spectator control.

Outside the car, Bertie was a modest, quiet man, blessed with an impish sense of humour that regularly flourished in the presence of his long-time sponsor Kieran McAnallen, and the shrewd preparation wizard behind so many of his cars, Sydney Meeke. Together, they were a formidable team.

I must confess that as a boy from Banbridge, my allegiance growing up would have been firmly in the McKinstry camp. But when my professional life took me to time controls and service parks in search of Bertie's story, I always found him a gentleman to deal with - as determined as any factory driver, but always interested in the wider story. And that's all that any rally journalist could ask for.

Bob McKeown, auto electrician

I would like to think Bertie is remembered for a very, very, very long time for being known as not only a true character in sport but also in business, a multi-talented man as well and a very modest man to boot. He was a brilliant motorsport man, a good businessman, but also, he could sing, and one of the best moments I enjoyed was in 1985 during the Manx Rally prize giving when Bertie sung 'Where have all the Audis gone', it was a brilliant night, very memorable.

Kenny McKinstry, rally driver [excerpt from Carsport]

Bertie was one of life's gentlemen and a wonderful rally driver and competitor with a skill that could not be taught. In a strange way it might have been easier to accept if Bertie or Mark had been killed in a rally car, knowing the risks we all take.

[The late] Colin McRae, 1995 World Rally Champion [excerpt from Autosport]

Bertie was a driver I looked up to, he was a trier right to the end. As a private driver he could compete against the works drivers and mix it with them. That was something I respected so much about him. He was special.

Jimmy McRae, rally driver and former GMOS team-mate [excerpt from Carsport]

I've known Bertie since my first rally in Ireland in 1976 and we remained friends as well as competitors ever since. We had many great rally battles but he was always a gentleman, as was Mark.

[the late] Frank Meagher, rally driver [excerpt from Tarmac Titan DVD]

I think for the last 15 years we have tussled with Bertie on all sorts of rallies be it the Circuits, the Galways, the Donegal rallies. I mean, he's been there a long, long time, a fantastic competitor in every respect. He always had a good word to say about you, and really he was my hero in my early days starting off and if we could compete against Bertie Fisher it was a big thing

Sydney Meeke, car builder, Team manager and friend

I first met Bertie in the early 1970s, and though he was younger than me, I knew quickly that he was a very astute engineer, as was his father. A few years later he had not the time to work at his own rally car so he asked me to look after his car and from then I did all his work until the year 2000. In all that time we never had an argument, he would ring me every day from where ever he was (sometimes from USA). Many times he gave me advice and I always took it. He was one in a million!

Stephen Murphy, rally driver

I first got to know Bertie personally, when I started in business, manufacturing structural steel. I've always admired him as a rally driver and remember standing on a ditch on the famous Skeaghvasteen, Graiguenamanagh stage of the Circuit, in the early 80's, when he was driving CIL999. I greatly admired him as a competitor, and his preparation with his driving, car and team was second to none. Bertie was the ultimate rally driver, and I feel he could have been a successful professional driver had he taken that route in his early days.

I dealt with him on a business level also, and always found him to be very professional, a great man to deal with. We were both in a similar line of business, and had many business interactions. I always valued his comments. Also, we both shared similar interests in aviation.

I have a story from the Circuit one year when we had a long road section at night, very relaxed time wise, going through Enniskillen. MJ (Morrissey) suddenly saw Bertie going off rally route and said "Lets follow Bertie, he's taking a short cut". When Bertie realised we were following him he stopped and said for us to follow him home. He took us to his house, where we had a lovely cup of tea and a snack. I remember the chat we both had there with the late Tommy and Mrs Fisher.

In March 2000, I bought Bertie's Subaru, R555FEL the week before the West Cork Rally. I had already entered, and collected the car a few days before. I only did a few miles testing, but the car was so good that MJ and I went on to win the rally. I'll never forget when I met Bertie in St Angelo airport to check the car out before I bought it. Bertie arrived driving the car into the airport, accompanied by 2 mechanics. He handed me a helmet, and said "Let's go for a test drive". Bertie was trying hard to impress me, when he came to the first '6 Right' he pulled the handbrake and I was looking out the side window at the view! He continued to do the same on all four corners. When the test drive was completed, we stopped and got out. Bertie placed his helmet on the roof of the car and I likewise. "See here Young Murphy" he said, "What do you think of that car now?". To his laughter I replied, "I can't

understand why you didn't win more rallies in it".

A pure gentleman in business and in rallying.

Andrew Nesbitt, rally driver and friend

Bertie Fisher was a great friend of mine, and I often think of the lessons in life, sport and business that I learned from him, even 15 years after that tragic day that took Bertie, Mark and Emma from us all too soon. It was a great privilege for my family and I to get to know Bertie and his family personally, and although he is best remembered for his exploits in rallying, my fondest memories of him are away from the spotlight.

The first thing to say about Bertie is that he was a consummate professional, and he was one of the first Irish drivers to bring to bear his knowledge of high level business in his approach to rallying. His ability to compete against professional drivers on the British scene, including Jimmy McRae, Russell Brookes and Tony Pond to name a few, were an inspiration to all young drivers in Ireland. Along with Austin McHale and Billy Coleman, he was a great ambassador for Irish sport and they brought rallying to another level in this country, ultimately culminating in the World Rally Championship visiting Ireland in 2007 and 2009.

Having spent many years looking up to Bertie, it was a huge challenge for me to find myself racing against him in the early 1990's when he occasionally competed in National rounds. Monaghan 1992 was the first time that I felt I was close to matching his stage times, and finishing runner up to him in his state of the art Subaru Legacy was a great milestone in my career. A couple of weeks later in Cavan,

Brian Murphy and I had a real white knuckle ride in our Metro 6R4 to stay ahead of Bertie. We pulled into a pub after the 9th stage assuming we had won the rally but thankfully a spectator spotted us and reminded us that there were 10 stages in Cavan that year! Bertie was extremely gracious in defeat and this was the start of a long relationship, both in and out of competition.

Bertie and I had many great duels on the stages throughout the 1990s, but the one that really stands out for me above all others was the Circuit of Ireland 1999 when James O'Brien and I battled Bertie and Rory Kennedy in identical Group A Subaru Impreza 555s. This stands out for me ahead of any of my International wins as one of the best rallies I was ever involved in. We had a ding dong battle for 3 days, through day and night, practically inseparable on the clock. I suffered a broken differential on the last stage of the penultimate night, and it took a huge effort from my team to get the gearbox changed (with great help from Kenny McKinstry) and ready for the final day.

Unfortunately, I picked up a puncture on the final morning and Bertie was able to cruise to a thoroughly deserved victory. Little did any of us know that this would be his last victory, and the classic footage of his parents greeting him at the finish line is still very emotional for me. That night, I visited Bertie and his team in their hotel before the prizegiving to give him a bottle of champagne in congratulations, returning the favour that he had done for me when I won my first International rally in Donegal in 1996. Bertie was sitting at the end of the table, surrounded by family and friends, with his head on the table, sound asleep! We were both completely exhausted by the emotional and physical efforts of the previous 4 days of rallying and there was a huge amount of respect between us. Incidentally, the bottle of champagne he bought me in 1996 was never opened and still takes pride of place in my trophy cabinet.

After that 1999 season, Bertie took a step back from competition in order to support Mark in his rally career and Emma with her charity fundraising. He helped organise the Summit Rally in 2000, and saw this as a way of giving back to the Tarmac Championship he enjoyed so much. When he stood down from full time competition, Bertie approached me about the possibility of me picking up his lucrative sponsorship deals with Subaru Ireland and Pirelli. He put the deal in place for me with Neville Matthews in Subaru Ireland and Dick Cormack in Pirelli, an extremely honourable thing to do for a fellow sportsman and something that allowed me to go to the next level in terms of machinery and ultimately to win 2 Tarmac Championships.

We had agreed that I would do the same for Mark once I was moving on from the sport, and it is a thing of immense sadness that this never came to pass. Mark was an extremely talented competitor who was destined to go much further in the sport than rallying in Ireland. I have no doubt he would have succeeded on the world stage, and this was a source of great pride to Bertie. I remember Mark finishing runner up to me that year in a Group N car in the Isle of Man, and I look back fondly on that rally as an opportunity to get to know this ambitious young man better.

Sadly, we will never know how far Mark would have made it due to the tragic events of January 21st 2001. That awful day was a tragedy, not only for the rally fraternity in Ireland but for all the people of Fermanagh and the island of Ireland. The only small grace was that

Gladys and Roy overcame their injuries and survived.

The Fisher family are known far and wide for their generosity, charisma and success in life and business. Bertie epitomised all of these qualities and stands out as one of the most impressive people I have ever known. The world as a whole lost three great people that day but I lost a great friend. Through those sad times in 2001 come fantastic memories, and I am grateful for the times we shared together – R.I.P. Bertie, Mark and Emma.

Graeme Nesbitt

I spent my whole childhood running around rally service areas and watching rally videos, so it was no surprise that Bertie Fisher was my idol growing up, along with Austin McHale and Colin McRae. Bertie visited our house when I was about 3 years old to have a look at the Manta 400 that my father, Andrew, had recently bought from Eian Pritchard. Dumbfounded at seeing this man from the TV in my kitchen, all I could say was "Hi Bertie, why are you not rallying today?!"

I can vividly remember the time my Dad and I were invited to join Bertie, Stephen Finlay and Kieran McAnallen to go and spectate on a rally down in Portlaoise, where Austin McHale was testing his Toyota Corolla WRC. When we landed into a particular field the farmer there couldn't get over having Bertie Fisher in his field and we were ushered into his house for tea and sandwiches and to be introduced to the whole family. My Dad and Stephen were 2 of the top drivers in the country at that time but they were only secondary to Bertie that day, I honestly don't think Roy Keane or Brian O'Driscoll would have got a warmer welcome!

Seeing the adulation that man had for Bertie shows what a legend he was, and I am truly privileged for the time I got to spend with him.

Hugh O'Brien, team member and friend

I first got friendly with Bertie after our trip to Haspengouw in Belgium in 1981 as a 3 car team out of Sydney Meeke's stable with us, Bertie, and Willie John Dolan. We kept in touch and got friendlier over the years, going to social functions, going on holidays and the likes. For years we organised a golfing holiday each year. Ourselves and our wives and friends would have gone to Spain or Portugal. There was golf every day, serious money involved, £10 or £20. He was a good enough golfer but his putting wouldn't have been up to much. He used to dance from one foot to the other for a 4ft putt, and I recall him one time saying to Paddy Kelly "I could slide a car to within an inch of a wall at 100mph and it wouldn't phase me but now I'm standing shivering over a 4ft put, I don't need all this stress."

All the rallying times we had were a serious bit of craic, indeed we would often joke about his driving techniques, slagging and so on but he was meticulous in everything that he did, and when you sat with him in a car, his reactions were fast, his focus on the road superb. You would know that his adrenaline and everything had gone up two or three margins. He had to be first, second was no good to him.

Bertie was probably on the fringe of being capable of a full time professional rally driver but it's a very difficult game being a full time professional rally driver and a full time businessman, you can't be both, you finish up a better and all rounded person when you decide that this is going to be my pass time. So with his successful business he could justify spending money with the top fella to produce his rally cars and compete at the level that he wanted to in this car. Bertie probably did it the proper way, looking at everything the right way. He was just that bit away from the cutting edge. The Friday two days before the accident he phoned and since it was Gladys' birthday he invited us out to the Manor House for something to eat.

Amongst the things we chatted about were the possibility of altering the business, and a new World Rally car he was looking at ordering. He was also talking about going to John Haughland's Ice School in Norway and asked me if I'd come along with him for a few days. After I told him it was a bad time of the year he said "Sure what the hell, we may as well, we'll not be here forever" and we had sort of half thrashed it out that we would go but nothing was set in stone.

The last thing he said to me was "We're going down to Ashford tomorrow and if I get back in time on Sunday evening maybe you would come up with me to see my dad in hospital in Belfast but it'll depend on what way the thing works out" so that was the first thing that came into my head when, whilst I was out walking with Phyllis, I got the phone call from Stephen Kirpatrick to tell me there had been an accident.

Bertie was as decent and genuine a fella as I have ever known and straight down the middle, that's how he run his business, very straight forward and generous.

He was like a brother to me, no doubt about it. He certainly enriched my life for sure.

Michael O'Carroll, Broadcaster & Journalist [excerpt from Irish Motorsport Annual in 2002]

Bertie was an outstanding businessman, an outstanding sportsman, a great family man and a solid churchman. If he was dedicated to his childhood sweetheart Gladys, his family, the business, and the close-knit community in Ballinamallard, he was addicted to rally sport. Motor rallying gave him delight – an adrenaline rush – and in the space of twenty years, he grew to be a living legend.

His ability to make a powerful rally car dance and dart at high speed on a closed road stage was what made him popular with rally fans in all parts of Ireland and even further. Courage and control were his trademarks. He was greatly admired by his fellow competitors for his sense of fair play and sportsmanship. And, when he was involved with bodies within the sport such as the Enniskillen Motor Club, the Association of Northern Ireland Car Clubs or the Irish Rally Competitors Association.

Bertie Fisher was highly competitive in rally trim, but he would offer advice to even his closest opponent and there was always the strong handshake and the warm friendly and sincere smile. He was a cornerstone and an ambassador, while forever enjoying the challenge of controlling a rally car. And, when it came to digging out the sport he was never slow to step forward, whether that was acting as a Safety Officer, on an event he was not competing in, or sponsoring an event such as the Summit 2000.

Mark was destined to follow his father both in the business and rally sport. He had taken to both the business partnership and the sport with total dedication and he did benefit from the support given to him by his family. Emma was a vivacious and bubbling hockey player and chiropodist who played a special and private role in charity work, particularly in the area of leprosy.

In a sporting sense it was ironic he died on January 22 2001 – one hundred years to the exact date when the Irish Automobile Club was founded to further automobile sports in this country.

Dr Frank O'Donoghue, Co-driver to Bertie 1980-1982

A fantastic driver and a gentleman to his fingertips. He was one of the nicest fellas you could go to a rally with, there was never a cross word with him. He was just good fun to deal with, and absolutely straight as a die, dead on bloke. While other drivers would have been a lot more focussed and serious Bertie was more open and liked having a bit of craic.

Brian Patterson, Journalist [excerpt from Motoring News in 2001]

Tribute to the King Fisher – A sportsman with integrity, humour and an iron will

Three coffins side by side in Ballinamallard's Magheracross Church. Bertie Fisher, his son Mark and daughter Emma, all victims of a horrific helicopter crash. In the church and in various locations around the town were rally, business people and friends from all over Britain.

As Austin McHale spoke one of the tributes, just one of his comments being "Bertie was my motivator. Rallying for me will never be the same again", it allowed a few moments to reflect the significance and the influence

Bertie Fisher had on rallying North and South, in Ireland.

For Bertie there were no borders of course, politically, geographically or religiously. He had time for everybody and was a great man for the mobile phone. The calls were always to the point, whether he was on the phone to a government minister or a handicapped child. The very fact that top politicians were in the congregation spoke for itself. Bertie almost single-handedly, over a period of 20 years, raised the profile and standard of rallying in Ireland to a new plane, not just of awareness, but credibility. From when he won the Ulster Rally in 1982, right through to his four Tarmac Championship titles and 20 major wins, he saw that as a responsibility.

Over the past few years we have seen the introduction of a safety officer on WRC events. Put this into perspective: On the Galway International in 1986 Bertie had a frightening incident when he stood on the middle pedal of his Manta coming into an open square right. With a clearly audible crack, a front calliper bolt had sheared, and the brake pedal went straight to the floor.

Bertie grabbed for the handbrake and gears, all graphically caught on in-car camera. He was ahead of the pack in that department as well. He had no chance of making the corner. There was only one place to go, and faced with a barrage of Galway stone walls and spectators on and behind every one, Bertie aimed the Manta for a narrow escape road, even though there were spectators in there as well.

Somehow he missed everyone, deliberately ramming the side of the Opel off walls in the process to scrub off speed. It was a horrific accident.

In typical Fisher fashion, Bertie decided something had to be done about this. He took 15 months off from competing to offer his services to rally organisers, going over the stages with the various clerks of the courses to check junctions, escape roads and hazards were properly set up, taped and marshalled. Only when he felt that all reasonable precautions were being taken did Bertie return to competing. As ever he was ahead of the pack, almost 15 years in front of the WRC safety measures.

Similarly when Irish rallying faced the insurance crisis Bertie more than lent his weight to fund raising and campaigning in order to bring the sport back. He was a founder member of the I.R.C.A, pushing for increased awareness of the sport. He condemned illegal reconnaissance, which he abhorred and which was totally opposed to Bertie's code and creed, in life as well as rallying. He worked hard to increase the public perception of the Tarmac and National Championships.

It wasn't all sweetness and light with Bertie, as with all of us. He could get into a temper with the best of them. He often spoke strong words. But always, for Bertie that was the end of it. It was said and done, over. It was one of his hallmarks, up front and out with it. He never put anything off. He was the same with phone calls. He was one of the busiest men in the country. But he never, ever, failed to either take or return a phone call. It was the way he was.

In his early days of rallying, past the period of the Minis and the early Escorts, Bertie, along with then co-driver Austin Frazer and preparation expert Sydney Meeke, sat down and discussed the way forward in the sport. They approached Shell with a professional proposal. The oil giant decided to take him on board and he moved onto another new frontier.

Whereas the norm in rallying in Ireland was to pile a few spares into any old van available and set off for a rally, Bertie moved up a level with proper dedicated vehicles. Seems a simple thing now, but then he set new standards that others were to follow.

Similarly, with Pirelli he built up a relationship and worked with Andy Hallam developing tyres specifically for the peculiarities of Irish Tarmac. Andy freely admits that it was Bertie's skills as a driver and engineer that brought them so much success in Ireland, and to a certain degree, beyond.

Bertie developed a similar relationship with Prodrive, which became almost a partnership with regard to his Subarus. Dave Richards was at the funeral, and one of the things he talked about was Bertie's enormous efforts for the community, as well as his (at that time) 180-strong workforce and his involvement with charities. Along with his close friend and sponsor Kieran McAnallen, they raised £40,000 for charity at the Summit Rally in 2000 for example.

Nothing fazed Bertie. His ability to communicate was huge, his sense of duty endless. He carried that sense of duty right through his rallying. No matter how pushed for time, he always attended functions which he felt were beneficial to the sport.

Remember this was a man who received many awards for business excellence. Although personally not all that interested in computers, Bertie reckoned that he had developed the most cost effective, computerised structural steel plant in Europe, if not the world.

When he was putting the domed single-span roof on the Waterfront Hall in Belfast, he had 100mm tolerance to play with and intense interest in the project from politicians and the public.

He rented a building at Harland & Wolff's shipyard, which had been used to house the Titanic, to construct the roof and hired huge cranes to put it on. He hired helicopters to fly over the building on the critical day, giving politicians, dignitaries and press a bird's eye view.

On the day, it was a perfect fit. This was a man of terrific confidence and great influence. Bertie used all his qualities and reserves of strength to carry that through to his perceived responsibility as a rally champion to safeguard and promote the sport.

Bertie Fisher, Rally Champion, helped the sport and almost everyone he came in contact with. He will be sadly missed.

Freddie Patterson, rally driver and friend

My first memories of Bertie are of him as a young man rallying in the Minis and I got to know him in the next few years after that. Then on a national rally in the mid-1970s Bertie navigated for me in my non-lightweight 2.7 litre Porsche Carrera. While he was one of the bravest ones to even take on the job he wasn't the best co-driver in the world. I remember him lecturing at me the whole way through and on a particular mountain stage we went off the road. She went up a drain and the bog water was flying everywhere, and I never lifted her as I was always told you had a better chance if you kept the foot in so we went in at one end of the drain, came out the other and he said "Heck, Talk about luck!" that there was nothing in the drain but despite that we finished well up in the rally.

Then at the end of 1977 I bought the Group 1 RS2000 KIA 2220 from him and I suppose over

the years we had done other bits of business, but in any kind of business dealings I had with him they were all 100%. If all your customers were half as good you wouldn't be worried.

I also sat with him once, in 1986. I had asked him if he wanted to sit with me for the fun on the Lurgan Park rally but the car let us down just before the event, so since we weren't going to get that sorted, as a replacement he invited me to navigate for him on the Lakelands rally, which we won outright, and we certainly didn't run away from the finish with the prize giving and all the rest, a great night ensued.

I remember when Sydney's boys would be working hard to get something changed or fixed in a quick turnaround speed in service and they would finally get it in Bertie would come out with a saying "Our dog has it".

Over the years I got to be one of the ones invited by him if there was a party in their house or whatever, and we went on holidays when the kids were small to Jersey, and skiing holidays and so on too. I always found him so genuine and down to earth, no airs and graces about him, and he was one of the very good people as far as rallying and business and everything in general are concerned.

Brian Quinn, Co-driver to Bertie 1973-1977, Friend and Mud Notes Crew

Well I know in my time with Bertie and particularly when I went to Enniskillen, the Fisher family and particularly Bertie and Gladys treated me unbelievably well. I was up in Enniskillen, and I would have got the call, and he would have invited me out for tea and God knows what job he would have lined up for me to do and it was always a pleasure to do it. They treated me like one of the family, and that's

how he treated me the whole time I knew him. And when he built his new house which he really looked forward to, he said "There it is Brian, you do the M&E and get it sorted for me and keep us right" so I done the drawings and all for his house and kept him right.

Sean Quinn, business client and friend

I knew Bertie Fisher on several levels - 80% - 90% business but the rest socially and so on. I was first introduced to him around the time of the construction of the prestressed concrete factory in 1984, but I really got to know him during the two-year construction project of the first cement factory, opened in 1989, when we would have been chatting on a daily and weekly basis through to the time it was finished, and thereafter too. I would have considered Bertie outgoing, not afraid to let the hair down, have a few drinks and sing a few songs. He had a great personality, he got on well with people, he wasn't overly imposing on people, so if you got friendly with Bertie he wouldn't abuse that, he would always know when to stay close, when not to get too close, and so on.

I remember Bertie Fisher as a decent and generous man and if somebody invited him to an event or if there was something he felt he would like to support, he would always be there to support it even if it didn't suit him. When there was any money or sponsorship for community, sport, and so on needing to be collected, whatever or wherever it was Bertie would be first.

One day I was chatting to Bertie and he asked me was I going to Joe McGurk's the rally driver's funeral, Joe having done work for both our companies. We went to the funeral together and, now I suppose I would be as well a known man as anybody in Cavan, but for every one person who shook hands with me, three shook hands with Bertie. And I said to him, "What sort of hoor are you coming up here and taking my limelight and me thought I was well known in this area, and you far better known than me!" but it was a serious rallying crowd there.

Bertie Fisher wouldn't have had many enemies, nor any of the Fishers for that matter. And that's the respect I had for the Fishers. Bertie was a leader of the people.

Dave Richards, Prodrive Chairman [excerpts from Autosport & Tarmac Titan DVD]

Bertie was a driver of great talent and enthusiasm, and we felt Mark would follow him and perhaps surpass him. He was unlike all the other customers though, We had lots of customers come through our premises and they would take their cars away but he became part of the family.

Annette Sheridan

It was the Saturday morning of the Donegal Rally, I think around 1990. I was 19 years old and I was marshalling in the service area, which that year was around the Killybegs pier and half a mile on the main Donegal Town road. There was a small petrol station on this road and when I was coming into Killybegs that morning I noticed Bertie's service crew setting up there. By the time service was set up, the place was in chaos! There were boats and crates and forklifts; service vans, chip vans and ice cream vans. There were course cars, flashing lights and sirens, tyres, jerry cans and way too many seagulls. And the whole shebang was parcelled up with about 6 miles of fluttering stripy tape.

And then, God love them , into this gaudy labyrinth arrived the front runners. Already under pressure they now had to find their service crew in this maze. I was doing my best to shepherd spectators and dodge seagull droppings when I happened to notice that Bertie Fisher was doing frantic laps of the pier. It suddenly dawned on me that he didn't realise that the service area extended out the road a bit, so, knowing that in service every minute counts, I ran over and flagged him down. I knocked on the window and shouted to him that he needed to go out the road to the petrol station and gestured in that direction. Now, between engine noise and him still having his helmet on I don't think he really heard or understood me, so somewhat dismissively, he shook his head and drove off again. I was a bit disappointed that I hadn't managed to get the message across but I resumed my attempts to direct traffic (an exercise in futility) and was too busy to think about it after that. However, a while later I noticed that Bertie was touring about again and seemed to be looking for something. By now, I was starting to worry about Rory's navigating skills but then Bertie drove over to me, stopped, opened his window and said "sorry about earlier, thanks for your help", and off he went (in the right direction)! It surprised me how much it meant to me! I really appreciated that he took the time to come back and speak to me. People often use the phrase 'how a person treats a waitress says a lot about them', well, I think 'how a person treats a marshal also says a lot about them' and from that day on, I always admired Bertie Fisher. I didn't know him BUT I wish I had!

Phil Short, former Works Team manager [excerpt from Tarmac Titan DVD]

Bertie was the spirit of Irish rallying. A fierce competitor, but a very straight guy, very friendly, good sportsman. I had a lot of good memories competing against Bertie in the Irish Championship in the 80s, first when he was in the Escort, then, later when he was in the fabulous BMW M3. He was always a tough guy to beat

Derek Smyth, former navigator and friend

For me Bertie was just a great sportsman, he competed hard and drove hard on the stages but he would have helped anybody. That struck me in the 70s but Bertie led the way for me in terms of being selfless. If he had something another crew needed he would have given it to them, and that just summed Bertie up. Inside the car, when it went 5,4,3,2,1, he was unbelievably competitive but outside the car and in service or whatever he would help anybody and was a model.

Alan 'Plum' Tyndall, Broadcaster and friend

What is it that has been so special about the Fisher family? There is one word that seems to weave its way through all their activities – integrity. Integrity in their personal lives, in their business dealings, and in their sporting activities.

I was privileged to know Bertie almost throughout his long rallying career from reporting on his achievements with the BBC, UTV and RTÉ and later of course on our own RPM programmes. I even competed against him once at a St. Angelo Sprint when we were both driving Escort Mexicos and beat him!

"Boy you were going well Plum." Said a by-stander. "You beat Bertie Fisher!" "Bertie who?' I asked, as the young Fermanagh driver was only beginning to get a reputation in his own local. It is history of course that Bertie climbed from these lowly beginnings to the very top of the rallying tree often matching and beating the very best professionals in the game, where as I disappeared behind a microphone and a laptop.

In the no pacenote years of multi-cheating, Bertie was almost unique in refusing to bow to the temptations of having a wee look at the roads before the rallies. He would play the physiological tricks as all the top drivers did, that was all part of the game, but he never broke the rules a hallmark of the man's integrity.

I also had an insight into the way Bertie and Ernie handled their business as my public relations company was employed by them on many occasions. It was always a happy relationship as you were dealing with a company that was greatly admired in the building trade throughout Ireland and further afield.

Through the rallying and the business I really got to know Bertie and the family. The boy's lovely parents had instilled an extraordinary work ethic in all the family. Bertie was the front man and Ernie the strong and quiet partner in the background who deserves equal credit for Fisher Engineering's success. Ivan was the man on the shop floor and of course there was Kenny who wasn't in the business but was very much in the business of rallying as a long time worker in the press offices of so many of the Irish Tarmac Rally rounds.

Gladys Fisher went quietly about the considerable task of bringing up their children, Mark, Emma and Roy, probably, it has to be said, with little help from Bertie as the hours that he spent in the factory developing the business were legendry.

It was one of Bertie's thinly veiled ambitions to see Mark reach a height in rallying that he had never been quite able to achieve - The World Rally Championship. And few would deny that that lovably cheeky chappie was well on his way to reaching that summit when the helicopter tragedy dashed so many of the Fisher family's hopes.

I was there almost at the beginning of the Fisher story with Bertie, and also Ernie and Kenny as the two young brothers lugged their heavy Betacam equipment around after me on one of the first video experiments I ever got involved with on an Enniskillen rally.

And I was also sadly there at the end on that dark day in Ballinamallard's history when we buried Bertie, Emma and Mark. The rallying world were packed into the tight streets in the Fermanagh town that day that owed so much of its prosperity to the Fisher family, and we all felt richer that day for knowing and experiencing the integrity of these wonderful people.

Plum Tyndall, Broadcaster and friend [excerpt from Tarmac Titan DVD]

Bertie, Mark and Emma will be remembered wherever there is fair play and sportsmanship on this island.

Ari Vatanen, 1981 World Rally Champion [excerpt from Autosport]

I came to Ireland so much in the early part of my career and got to know Bertie. He was so modest and a very good driver. This shattering news hurt me and my family so much

Gary Wilson, former Meeke mechanic

In typical Gary fashion, he described Bertie as "A miserable, generous gentleman." I think we all know what Gary meant.

Malcolm Wilson, Ford World Rally boss [excerpt from Autosport]

Bertie was not only a personal friend but a tough competitor. He epitomised the sport of rallying, mixing humour, generosity and guile. Like many people I was shocked by his loss and that of Mark and Emma. They will all be sorely missed.

The following poem gives the flavour of a number of poems which were sent to the Fisher family in the aftermath of the tragedy which were much appreciated

The Fisher Family Tragedy

Another Ulster Hero has met a tragic end
But not on his beloved roads or tricky left-hand bend
Like Joey he was gifted in a crazy sort of way
By taking risks with danger they were heroes of our day.

Success and dedication had brought him rich rewards
A private helicopter crash just wasn't on the cards
A man with skill unequalled behind the steering wheel
This freak encounter in the air was a raw and bitter deal.

In a long planned outing for a celebration meal
Tragedy was lurking and on their lives set its seal
The children Mark and Emma were cut off in their prime
While Bertie, Roy and Gladys clung on for a time.

But sadly two days later in another twist of fate
Bertie too was taken from a prayerful bedside wait
Dear God for Roy and Gladys, a wife, a son, a mother
Bring them through this crisis as support for one another.

In days and weeks and years to come may they dare to look ahead
And live in pride and dignity in hour of their dead
And may the trophies and honours that Bertie once Received
Bring courage for a future in which they all believed.

And in Mark's potential in his chosen racing scene
May despair turn into hope again as they view what might have been
A talent so uncanny, a life lived to the full
So prematurely ended an exception to the rule.

In memory for Emma may they for her be brave
In twenty-five short useful years what love and joy she gave
In sport, in work, in leisure, she was everybody's friend.
To know her was to love her, a truth right to the end.

While terrorists may come and go, forgotten in a day,
Good people like the Fishers will in our memories say,
For Bertie and for Joey you've reached another shore,
And the country roads that knew you once
will know you now no more.

Anon.

Appendix Z:
Events and Results

Year	Event	Date	Result	Co-Driver	Comp No.	Car	Reg
1968							
1968	Erne Safari	25-26/10	Finish - Unknown	Neil Paget	79	Mini 848	7685 IL
1969							
1969	Omagh Pre Circuit Rally	14/03	1st in Cl 3	John Brown		Mini 848	7685 IL
1969	Circuit of Ireland	4-8/04	N/F - Accident	Driver - Ernie Campbell	120	Mini 848	6672 IB
1969	Tostal Trial	28/06	3rd in Cl	Neil Paget		Mini Cooper 998	3328 SZ
1969	Scallon Cup	13/09	3rd in Cl 2	Neil Paget	58	Mini Cooper 998	3328 SZ
1969	Erne Safari	25/10	N/F	Neil Paget	56	Mini 848	3737 IL
1970							
1970	Circuit of Ireland	27-31/03	N/F - OTL	Driver - Ernie Campbell	177	Mini 848	3161 AZ
1970	Enniskillen Autotest	29/05	Unknown	N/A		Mini Cooper 998	AIL 2840
1970	Enniskillen Autotest	22/08	1st in Novice Cl	N/A		Mini Cooper 998	AIL 2840
1970	Erne Safari	23-23/10	Finish - Unknown	John Magee	55	Mini Cooper 998	AIL 2840
1971							
1971	Omagh Pre Circuit Rally	19/03	Finish - Unknown	John Magee		Morris Cooper 998	6258 JZ
1971	Circuit of Ireland	9-13/04	N/F - Codriver ill & mechancial	John Magee	193	Morris Cooper 998	6258 JZ
1971	Enniskillen Rallysprint	6/08	2nd in Cl 2	N/A		Morris Cooper 998	6258 JZ
1971	Manx	9-10/09	N/F - Mechanical	John Magee	51	Morris Cooper 998	6258 JZ
1971	CAM Rally	18/09	Finish - Unknown			Morris Cooper 998	6258 JZ
1971	Erne Safari	22/10	Finish - Unknown	Driver - John Lunny	56	Ford Escort Mk1 1600	HEK 158G
1972							
1972	EMC Winter Rally	28/01	Unknown	John White	19	Mini Cooper	AIL 6222
1972	Galway	4-6/02	N/F - Accident	John Lunny	84	Mini Cooper	AIL 6222
1972	Erne Trophy Rallysprint	15/07	Unknown	N/A		BMW 2002	
1972	Gortin Glen HillClimb	22/07	Unknown	N/A		BMW 2002	
1972	Dun-Om-En Rally	21/10	16th O/A	Driver - John Lunny	49	Ford Escort	HEK 158G
1973							
1973	Omagh Pre Circuit Rally	16/03	2nd O/A	Brian Quinn		Ford Escort Mk 1 Mexico	DEA 736J
1973	Circuit of Ireland	19-22/04	2nd in Cl 4, 3rd in Gp1, 17th O/A	Tony Anderson	74	Ford Escort Mk 1 Mexico	DEA 736J
1973	Donegal	16-17/06	N/F - Accident	Neil Paget	47	Ford Escort Mk 1 Mexico	DEA 736J
1973	Erne Trophy Rallysprint	20-21/07	2nd in Cl 3	N/A		Ford Escort Mk 1 Mexico	DEA 736J
1973	Scallon Cup	26/10	3rd in Cl, 3rd O/A	Brian Quinn	8	Ford Escort Mk 1 Mexico	DEA 736J

Year	Event	Date	Result	Co-Driver	Comp No.	Car	Reg
1974							
1974	Omagh Pre Circuit Rally	15/03	12th O/A	Brian Quinn	2	Ford Escort Mk 1 RS 2000	TMM 17M
1974	Circuit of Ireland	12-16/04	1st in Cl 3, 2nd in Gp 1, 12th O/A	Tony Anderson	88	Ford Escort Mk 1 RS 2000	TMM 17M
1974	Donegal	21-23/06	N/F - Accident	Brian Quinn	36	Ford Escort Mk 1 RS 2000	TMM 17M
1974	Texaco	28-29/06	N/F - Influenza	Brian Quinn	20	Ford Escort Mk 1 RS 2000	TMM 17M
1974	Erne Trophy Rallysprint	19-20/07	1st in Cl 4A	N/A		Ford Escort Mk 1 RS 2000	TMM 17M
1974	CAM Rally	7/09	7th O/A	Frank Burns	10	Ford Escort Mk 1 RS 2000	TMM 17M
1974	Autumn	27/09	N/F - Accident	Roy Sloan	2	Ford Escort Mk 1 RS 2000	TMM 17M
1975							
1975	Welsh	9-11/05	2nd in Gp 1, 25th O/A	Tony Anderson	79	Ford Escort Mk 1 RS 2000	GVX 833N
1975	Donegal	20-22/06	1st in Gp 1, 10th O/A	Derek Smyth	36	Ford Escort Mk 1 RS 2000	GVX 833N
1975	Texaco	28/06	N/F - Mechanical	Derek Smyth	19	Ford Escort Mk 1 RS 2000	GVX 833N
1975	Erne Trophy Rallysprint	19-20/07	1st in Cl A	N/A	52	Ford Escort Mk 1 RS 2000	GVX 833N
1975	Bushwhacker	23/08	1st in Cl 2, 1st in Gp 1, 7th O/A	Derek Smyth	16	Ford Escort Mk 1 RS 2000	GVX 833N
1975	Manx	12-13/09	N/F - Accident	Derek Smyth	21	Ford Escort Mk 1 RS 2000	GVX 833N
1975	Foreward Trust Rallysprint	1/11	N/F - Accident	Wesley Abraham		Ford Escort Mk 1 RS 2000	GVX 833N
1976							
1976	Galway Rally	6-8/02	N/F - Mechanical	Driver - James Davison	77	Ford Escort MK1 RS 2000	GVX 833N
1977							
1977	Snowspinner	22/01	1st in Cl 1, 2nd O/A	Brian Quinn		Ford Escort Mk2 RS 2000	KIA 2220
1977	Hellfire	26/02	6th O/A	Wesley Abraham		Ford Escort Mk2 RS 2000	KIA 2220
1977	Circuit of Ireland	08-12/04	N/F - Mechanical	Wesley Abraham	39	Ford Escort Mk2 RS 2000	KIA 2220
1977	C'Derg Car Club Circuit Opening Day	23/04	3rd O/A	N/A	3	Ford Escort Mk2 RS 2000	KIA 2220
1977	Burmah 'Orchard' Rally	30/04	1st O/A	Desi Wilson		Ford Escort Mk2 RS 2000	KIA 2220
1977	Midland Moto Rally	7/05	9th O/A	Willie Hunter	7	Ford Escort Mk2 RS 2000	KIA 2220
1977	Permapost	14/05	2nd O/A	Ivan Fisher	3	Ford Escort Mk2 RS 2000	KIA 2220
1977	Donegal	17-19/06	1st in Gp 1, 5th O/A	Trevor Hughes	18	Ford Escort Mk2 RS 2000	KIA 2220
1977	Erne Trophy Rallysprint	16-17/07	1st in Cl 4, 3rd O/A	N/A		Ford Escort Mk2 RS 2000	KIA 2220
1977	Tour of the Sperrins	30/07	N/F - Unknown			Ford Escort Mk2 RS 2000	KIA 2220
1977	Burmah International	19-20/08	N/F - Accident	Trevor Hughes	37	Ford Escort Mk2 RS 2000	KIA 2220
1977	Ulster	2-3/09	2nd in Gp 1, 11th O/A	Robert Harkness	20	Ford Escort Mk2 RS 2000	KIA 2220
1977	Cork '20	1-2/10	2nd O/A	Austin Frazer	11	Ford Escort Mk2 RS 1800	BIL 5700
1977	Autumn	14/10	N/F - Mechanical	Brian Quinn		Ford Escort Mk2 RS 1800	BIL 5700
1977	Donegal Highlands Rally	22/10	1st O/A	Austin Frazer	1	Ford Escort Mk2 RS 1800	BIL 5700
1978							
1978	Galway	10-12/02	N/F - Mechanical	Austin Frazer	9	Ford Escort Mk2 RS 1800	BIL 5700
1978	Hellfire	25/02	1st O/A	Austin Frazer	6	Ford Escort Mk2 RS 1800	BIL 5700
1978	West Cork	18-19/03	N/F - Mechanical	Austin Frazer	4	Ford Escort Mk2 RS 1800	BIL 5700
1978	Circuit of Ireland	24-28/03	N/F - Mechanical	Austin Frazer	21	Ford Escort Mk2 RS 1800	BIL 5700
1978	Circuit of Munster	4-5/06	N/F - Mechanical	Austin Frazer	3	Ford Escort Mk2 RS 1800	BIL 5700
1978	Donegal	16-18/06	N/F - Accident	Austin Frazer	8	Ford Escort Mk2 RS 1800	BIL 5700
1978	Permapost	1/07	4th O/A	Sammy Hamill	6/13	Ford Escort Mk2 RS 1800	BIL 5700

Year	Event	Date	Result	Co-Driver	Comp No.	Car	Reg
1978	Erne Trophy Rallysprint	14/07	1st in Cl	N/A	41	Ford Escort Mk2 RS 1800	BIL 5700
1978	Monaghan Autocross	15/07	1st O/A	N/A	41	Ford Escort Mk2 RS 1800	BIL 5700
1979							
1979	Hellfire	24/02	10th O/A	Austin Frazer	1	Ford Escort MK2 RS 1800	CIL999
1979	West Cork	17-18/03	4th O/A	Austin Frazer	7	Ford Escort MK2 RS 1800	CIL999
1979	Hills of Donegal Rally	10/03	1st O/A	Austin Frazer	3	Ford Escort MK2 RS 1800	CIL999
1979	Circuit of Ireland	13-17/04	3rd O/A	Austin Frazer	19	Ford Escort MK2 RS 1800	CIL999
1979	Midland Moto Rally	28/04	2nd O/A	Austin Frazer	2	Ford Escort MK2 RS 1800	CIL999
1979	Erne Trophy Rallysprint	8/06	1st in Cl 10	N/A	39	Ford Escort MK2 RS 1800	CIL999
1979	Donegal	15-17/06	2nd O/A	Austin Frazer	4	Ford Escort MK2 RS 1800	CIL999
1979	Permapost	7/07	11th O/A	Robert Harkness	4	Ford Escort MK2 RS 1800	CIL999
1979	Andrews Heat for Hire' Rally	18/08	5th O/A	Austin Frazer	19	Ford Escort MK2 RS 1800	CIL999
1979	Tyneside Stages Rally	18/08	2nd O/A	Austin Frazer	6	Ford Escort MK2 RS 1800	CIL999
1979	Bushwhacker	1/09	2nd O/A	Austin Frazer	5	Ford Escort MK2 RS 1800	CIL999
1979	Cork '20	6-7/10	3rd O/A	Austin Frazer	11	Ford Escort 'MK2 RS 1800	CIL999
1979	Ulster	19-20/10	5th O/A	Austin Frazer	7	Ford Escort MK2 RS 1800	CIL999
1979	Hitachi RallySprint	25/11	9th O/A	Austin Frazer	5	Ford Escort MK2 RS 1800	CIL999
1980							
1980	Galway	8-10/02	3rd O/A	Austin Frazer	4	Ford Escort MK2 RS 1800	CIL999
1980	Circuit of Ireland	4-8/04	N/F - Mechanical	Austin Frazer	12	Ford Escort MK2 RS 1800	CIL999
1980	Lurgan Park	3/05	1st O/A	David Johnston	1	Ford Escort MK2 RS 1800	CIL999
1980	Erne Trophy Rallysprint	5/05	1st in Cl 3B	N/A	45	Ford Escort MK2 RS 1800	CIL999
1980	Sligo	17/05	1st O/A	Frank O'Donoghue	2	Ford Escort MK2 RS 1800	CIL999
1980	Donegal	13-15/06	N/F - Accident	Peter Scott	4	Ford Escort MK2 RS 1800	CIL999
1980	Galway Summer Rally	30/08	2nd O/A	Frank O'Donoghue	2	Ford Escort MK2 RS 1800	CIL999
1980	Wexford Rally	20-21/09	1st O/A	Frank O'Donoghue	2	Ford Escort MK2 RS 1800	CIL999
1980	Bushwhacker	27/09	3rd O/A	David Johnston	4	Ford Escort MK2 RS 1800	CIL999
1980	Cork '20	4-5/10	N/F - Accident	Frank O'Donoghue	3	Ford Escort MK2 RS 1800	CIL999
1981							
1981	Galway	6-8/02	3rd O/A	Frank O'Donoghue	13	Ford Escort MK2 RS 1800	GVX 489T
1981	Circuit of Ireland	17-21/04	N/F - Mechanical	Frank O'Donoghue	8	Ford Escort MK2 RS 1800	GVX 489T
1981	Lurgan Park	2/05	1st O/A	Roy Cathcart	3	Ford Escort MK2 RS 1800	GVX 489T
1981	Erne Trophy Rallysprint	4/05	1st in Cl 4	N/A		Ford Escort MK2 RS 1800	GVX 489T
1981	Haspagnow Rally, Belgium	29-31/05	7th O/A	Austin Frazer	14	Ford Escort MK2 RS 1800	GVX 489T
1981	Lakeland Stages	4/07	1st O/A	Trevor McGaughey	3	Ford Escort MK2 RS 1800	RRM 912R
1981	Carsons Quarry Rallysprint	18/07	1st in Cl 4	N/A		Ford Escort MK2 RS 1800	RRM 912R
1981	Ulster	7-8/08	2nd O/A	Frank O'Donoghue	3	Ford Escort MK2 RS 1800	RRM 912R
1981	Manx	11-12/09	N/F - Mechanical	Robert Harkness	16	Ford Escort MK2 RS 1800	RRM 912R
1981	Rally of the Lakes	5-6/12	N/F - Accident	Austin Frazer	3	Ford Escort G3	OOO 96M
1982							
1982	National Rally, Longleat	6/03	3rd O/A	Frank O'Donoghue	2	Ford Escort G3	CIL999
1982	Rothmans Rallysprint	7/03	5th O/A	Keith Oswin / N/A	6	Ford Escort G3	CIL999
1982	Lurgan Park	8/05	2nd O/A	Austin Frazer	1	Ford Escort MK2 RS 1800	8 ZIK

Year	Event	Date	Result	Co-Driver	Comp No.	Car	Reg
1982	Moffetts Quarry Rallysprint	29/05	6th in Cl, 13th O/A	N/A	74	Ford Escort MK2 RS 1800	CIL999
1982	Scottish	12-15/06	N/F - Mechanical	David Johnston	11	Ford Escort MK2 RS 1800	CIL999
1982	Sligo	24/07	1st O/A	David Johnston	2	Ford Escort MK2 RS 1800	CIL999
1982	Ulster	5-7/08	1st O/A	Austin Frazer	9	Ford Escort MK2 RS 1800	CIL999
1982	Manx	15-18/09	3rd O/A	Austin Frazer	18	Ford Escort MK2 RS 1800	CIL999
1982	Bushwhacker	25/09	N/F - Accident	David Johnston	2	Ford Escort MK2 RS 1800	CIL999
1983							
1983	Mintex	25-26/02	9th O/A	Austin Frazer	14	Opel Ascona 400	DIL 999
1983	Circuit of Ireland	1-5/04	2nd O/A	Austin Frazer	11	Opel Ascona 400	DIL 999
1983	Welsh	6-8/05	N/F - Accident	Austin Frazer	12	Opel Ascona 400	DIL 999
1983	Lurgan Park	21/05	7th O/A	George Deane	1	Opel Ascona 400	DIL 999
1983	Moffetts Quarry Rallysprint	4/06	5th in Cl, 15th O/A	N/A	71	Opel Ascona 400	DIL 999
1983	Scottish	10-12/06	N/F - Mechanical	Austin Frazer	17	Opel Ascona 400	DIL 999
1983	Donegal	17-19/06	N/F	Austin Frazer	1	Opel Manta 400	DIL 2307
1983	Ulster	29-30/07	2nd O/A	Austin Frazer	10	Opel Manta 400	DIL 2307
1983	Manx	14-17/09	N/F - Accident	Austin Frazer	14	Opel Manta 400	DIL 2307
1983	Cork '20	1-2/10	N/F - Accident	Austin Frazer	2	Opel Manta 400	DIL 2307
1983	Bushwhacker	15/10	6th O/A (Rally cancelled)	Ernie Campbell	2	Opel Ascona 400	DIL 999
1984							
1984	National Breakdown	17-18/02	N/F - OTL	Austin Frazer	11	Opel Manta 400	DIL 2307
1984	Hills of Donegal Rally	03/03	1st O/A	Austin Frazer	2	Opel Manta 400	DIL 2307
1984	Circuit of Ireland	19-24/04	N/F - Mechanical	Austin Frazer	8	Opel Manta 400	DIL 2307
1984	Welsh	5-6/05	6th O/A	Austin Frazer	14	Opel Manta 400	DIL 2307
1984	Davagh		1st O/A	Austin Frazer	1	Opel Manta 400	DIL 2307
1984	Scottish	9-12/06	N/F - Mechanical	Austin Frazer	10	Opel Manta 400	DIL 2307
1984	Donegal	22-24/06	3rd O/A	Austin Frazer	4	Opel Manta 400	DIL 2307
1984	Lurgan Park	30/06	3rd O/A	Brian Patterson	2	Opel Manta 400	DIL 2307
1984	Sligo	21-22/07	1st O/A	Austin Frazer	1	Opel Manta 400	DIL 2307
1984	Ulster	27-28/07	4th O/A	Austin Frazer	8	Opel Manta 400	DIL 2307
1984	Manx	12-15/09	2nd O/A	Austin Frazer	12	Opel Manta 400	DIL 2307
1984	Audi Sport	20/10	14th O/A	John Millington	6	Opel Manta 400	DIL 2307
1984	RAC Rally	25-29/11	9th O/A	Austin Frazer	37	Opel Manta 400	DIL 2307
1985							
1985	National Breakdown	22-24/02	5th O/A	Austin Frazer	12	Opel Manta 400	DIL 2307
1985	Cavan	24/03	1st O/A	Rory Kennedy	1	Opel Manta 400	DIL 2307
1985	Circuit of Ireland	5-9/04	3rd O/A	Austin Frazer	6	Opel Manta 400	DIL 2307
1985	Welsh	4-5/05	N/F - Mechanical	Austin Frazer	9	Opel Manta 400	DIL 2307
1985	Davagh	22/05	1st O/A	Austin Frazer	1	Opel Manta 400	DIL 2307
1985	Scottish	8-11/06	4th O/A	Austin Frazer	9	Opel Manta 400	DIL 2307
1985	Donegal	21-23/06	N/F - Mechanical	Austin Frazer	13 & 008	Opel Manta 400	DIL 2307
1985	Lurgan Park	29/06	2nd O/A	Austin Frazer	1	Opel Manta 400	DIL 2307
1985	Lakeland Stages	6/07	1st O/A	Crawford Harkness		Opel Manta 400	DIL 2307
1985	Ulster	26-27/07	5th O/A	Austin Frazer	6	Opel Manta 400	DIL 2307

Year	Event	Date	Result	Co-Driver	Comp No.	Car	Reg
1985	Manx	11-14/09	3rd O/A	Austin Frazer	10	Opel Manta 400	DIL 9482
1986							
1986	Galway	8-9/02	N/F - Accident	Austin Frazer	3	Opel Manta 400	DIL 9482
1986	Lurgan Park	26/07	N/F - Mechanical	Austin Frazer	3	Ford Orion	IIB 5931
1986	Lakeland Stages	6/09	1st O/A	Fred Patterson	5	Opel Manta 400	DIL 9482
1987							
1987	Manx National	16/05	1st O/A	Austin Frazer	2	Opel Manta 400	DIL 9482
1987	Donegal	19-21/06	1st O/A	Austin Frazer	3	Opel Manta 400	DIL 9482
1987	Lurgan Park	4/07	2nd O/A	John McManus	4	Opel Manta 400	DIL 9482
1987	Ulster	31/07-1/08	2nd O/A	Austin Frazer	11	Opel Manta 400	DIL 9482
1987	Manx	9-12/09	N/F - Mechanical	Austin Frazer	18	Ford Sierra Cosworth GpN	C234 HVW
1987	Cork '20	3-4/10	N/F - Accident	Austin Frazer	3	Opel Manta 400	DIL 9482
1987	Rally of the Lakes	5-6/12	N/F - Mechanical	Austin Frazer	4	Opel Manta 400	DIL 9482
1988							
1988	Cartel	20-21/02	N/F - Accident	Austin Frazer	9	Ford Sierra Cosworth	D773 SVW
1988	Circuit of Ireland	2-4/04	N/F - Accident	Austin Frazer	10	Ford Sierra Cosworth	D773 SVW
1988	Welsh	30/04-1/05	12th O/A	Austin Frazer	16	Ford Sierra Cosworth	D773 SVW
1988	Donegal	17-19/06	3rd O/A	Austin Frazer	1	Ford Sierra Cosworth	D773 SVW
1988	Lurgan Park	2/07	N/F - Accident	Austin Frazer	3	MG Metro 6R4	Q630 BFQ
1988	Ulster	29-30/07	N/F - Mechanical	Austin Frazer	9	Ford Sierra Cosworth	D773 SVW
1988	Manx	13-16/09	N/F - Mechanical	Austin Frazer	12	Ford Sierra Cosworth	D773 SVW
1989							
1989	Circuit of Ireland	24-27/03	6th O/A	Austin Frazer	12	BMW M3	GXI 9427
1989	Manx National	20/05	1st O/A	Rory Kennedy	3	BMW M3	GXI 9427
1989	Donegal	23-25/06	2nd O/A	Rory Kennedy	3	BMW M3	GXI 9427
1989	Lurgan Park	1/07	2nd O/A	Jacqueline Berkeley	3	BMW M3	GXI 9427
1989	Ulster	28-29/07	4th O/A	Austin Frazer	11	BMW M3	GXI 9427
1989	Manx	12-15/09	N/F - Mechanical	Austin Frazer	14	BMW M3	GXI 9427
1989	Rally of the Lakes	9-10/12	N/F - Mechanical	Austin Frazer	2	BMW M3	GXI 9427
1990							
1990	Galway	10-11/02	2nd O/A	Rory Kennedy	2	BMW M3	GXI 9427
1990	Circuit of Ireland	14-16/04	N/F - Accident	Rory Kennedy	11	BMW M3	GXI 9427
1990	Donegal	22-24/06	2nd O/A	Rory Kennedy	4	BMW M3	GXI 9427
1990	Ulster	27-28/07	2nd O/A	Rory Kennedy	9	BMW M3	GXI 9427
1990	Manx	11-14/09	2nd O/A	Rory Kennedy	19	BMW M3	GXI 9427
1990	Cork '20	6-7/10	N/F - Accident	Rory Kennedy	2	BMW M3	GXI 9427
1990	Rally of the Lakes	8-9/12	1st O/A	Rory Kennedy	4	BMW M3	GXI 9427
1991							
1991	Talkland International	22-24/02	N/F - Mechanical	Rory Kennedy	13	Subaru Legacy GpN	G330 TUE
1991	West Cork	16-17/03	N/F - Accident	Rory Kennedy	1	Ford Sierra Cosworth 4x4	E28 JWK
1991	Circuit of Ireland	30/03-1/04	2nd O/A	Rory Kennedy	2	Ford Sierra Cosworth 4x4	E28 JWK
1991	Donegal	21-23/06	N/F - Accident	Rory Kennedy	2	Ford Sierra Cosworth 4x4	E28 JWK
1991	Lurgan Park	29/06	2nd O/A	Rory Kennedy	1	Ford Sierra Cosworth 4x4	E28 JWK

Year	Event	Date	Result	Co-Driver	Comp No.	Car	Reg
1991	Ulster	26-27/07	1st O/A	Rory Kennedy	3	Ford Sierra Cosworth 4x4	E28 JWK
1991	Manx	11-13/09	N/F - Mechanical	Rory Kennedy	7	Ford Sierra Cosworth 4x4	E28 JWK
1991	Cork '20	5-6/10	N/F - Mechanical	Rory Kennedy	1	Ford Sierra Cosworth 4x4	E28 JWK
1991	Rally of the Lakes	7-8/12	1st O/A	Rory Kennedy	1	Ford Sierra Cosworth 4x4	E28 JWK
1992							
1992	Galway	7-9/02	2nd O/A	Rory Kennedy	3	Ford Sierra Cosworth 4x4	E28 JWK
1992	Circuit of Ireland	17-20/04	N/F - Mechanical	Rory Kennedy	3	Subaru Legacy RS	H187 GUD
1992	Carlow	3/05	1st O/A	Rory Kennedy	1	Subaru Legacy RS	H187 GUD
1992	Monaghan	10/05	1st O/A	Rory Kennedy	105	Subaru Legacy RS	H187 GUD
1992	Manx National	16/05	1st O/A	Rory Kennedy	2	Subaru Legacy RS	H187 GUD
1992	Cavan	24/05	2nd O/A	Austin Frazer	3	Subaru Legacy RS	H187 GUD
1992	Donegal	19-21/06	1st O/A	Rory Kennedy	2	Subaru Legacy RS	H187 GUD
1992	Lurgan Park	27/06	2nd O/A	Rory Kennedy	2	Subaru Legacy RS	H187 GUD
1992	Ulster	31/07-1/08	N/F - Mechanical	Rory Kennedy	5	Subaru Legacy RS	H187 GUD
1992	Manx	8-11/09	2nd O/A	Rory Kennedy	7	Subaru Legacy RS	H187 GUD
1992	Cork '20	3-4/10	1st O/A	Rory Kennedy	2	Subaru Legacy RS	H187 GUD
1992	Rally of the Lakes	5-6/12	1st O/A	Rory Kennedy	2	Subaru Legacy RS	H187 GUD
1993							
1993	Galway	5-7/02	3rd O/A	Rory Kennedy	2	Subaru Legacy RS	H187 GUD
1993	Circuit of Ireland	9-12/04	2nd O/A	Rory Kennedy	1	Subaru Legacy RS	H187 GUD
1993	Rally of the Lakes	7-9/05	1st O/A	Rory Kennedy	1	Subaru Legacy RS	H187 GUD
1993	Donegal	18-20/06	1st O/A	Rory Kennedy	1	Subaru Legacy RS	H187 GUD
1993	Ulster	30-31/07	2nd O/A	Rory Kennedy	2	Subaru Legacy RS	H187 GUD
1993	Manx	14-17/09	N/F - Accident	Rory Kennedy	2	Subaru Legacy RS	H187 GUD
1994							
1994	Galway	5-6/02	N/F - Accident	Rory Kennedy	4	Subaru Legacy	H187 GUD
1994	Welsh	19-20/03	5th O/A	Rory Kennedy	7	Subaru Impreza 555	L444 MCA
1994	Rally of the Lakes	30/04-1/05	1st O/A	Rory Kennedy	3	Subaru Impreza 555	L444 MCA
1994	Donegal	17-19/06	5th O/A	Rory Kennedy	3	Subaru Impreza 555	L444 MCA
1994	Ulster	29-30/07	N/F - Mechanical	Rory Kennedy	6	Subaru Impreza 555	L444 MCA
1994	Manx	14-16/09	N/F - Mechanical	Rory Kennedy	8	Subaru Impreza 555	L444 MCA
1994	Cork '20	1-2/10	2nd O/A	Rory Kennedy	4	Subaru Impreza 555	L444 MCA
1995							
1995	Circuit of Ireland	14-17/04	1st O/A	Rory Kennedy	3	Subaru Impreza 555	L408 FUD
1995	Donegal	16-18/06	1st O/A	Rory Kennedy	6	Subaru Impreza 555	L555 FEL
1995	Lurgan Park	1/07	3rd O/A	Rory Kennedy	4	Subaru Impreza 555	L555 FEL
1995	Ulster	28-29/07	1st O/A	Rory Kennedy	10	Subaru Impreza 555	L555 FEL
1995	Manx	13-15/09	N/F - Mechanical	Rory Kennedy	10	Subaru Impreza 555	L555 FEL
1996							
1996	Galway	16-18/02	1st O/A	Rory Kennedy	3	Subaru Impreza 555	L555 FEL
1996	Circuit of Ireland	5-8/04	4th O/A	Rory Kennedy	1	Subaru Impreza 555	L555 FEL
1996	Rally of the Lakes	3-5/05	1st O/A	Rory Kennedy	1	Subaru Impreza 555	L555 FEL
1996	Donegal	21-23/06	3rd O/A	Rory Kennedy	1	Subaru Impreza 555	L555 FEL

Year	Event	Date	Result	Co-Driver	Comp No.	Car	Reg
1996	Ulster	2-3/08	1st O/A	Rory Kennedy	4	Subaru Impreza 555	L555 FEL
1996	Manx	11-13/09	N/F - Mechanical	Rory Kennedy	7	Subaru Impreza 555	L555 FEL
1997							
1997	Circuit of Ireland	28-31/03	1st O/A	Rory Kennedy	1	Subaru Impreza 555	L555 FEL
1997	ALMC National Rally	24/08	2nd O/A	Rory Kennedy	1	Subaru Impreza 555	P161 EUD
1998							
1998	Galway	20-22/02	2nd O/A	Rory Kennedy	2	Subaru Impreza 555	R555 FEL
1998	Circuit of Ireland	10-13/04	2nd O/A	Rory Kennedy	1	Subaru Impreza 555	R555 FEL
1998	Rally of the Lakes	1-3/05	N/F - Accident	Rory Kennedy	2	Subaru Impreza 555	R555 FEL
1998	Donegal	19-21/06	N/F - Accident	Rory Kennedy	3	Subaru Impreza 555	R555 FEL
1998	Cork '20	3-4/10	2nd O/A	Rory Kennedy	2	Subaru Impreza 555	R555 FEL
1998	Galloway Hills Rally	6/12	1st O/A	Rory Kennedy	2	Subaru Impreza 555	R555 FEL
1999							
1999	Galway	5-7/02	1st O/A	Rory Kennedy	2	Subaru Impreza 555	R555 FEL
1999	Circuit of Ireland	2-5/04	1st O/A	Rory Kennedy	2	Subaru Impreza 555	R555 FEL
1999	Rally of the Lakes	30/04-2/05	5th O/A	Rory Kennedy	2	Subaru Impreza 555	R555 FEL
1999	Donegal	18-20/06	5th O/A	Rory Kennedy	2	Subaru Impreza 555	R555 FEL
1999	Lurgan Park	14/08	5th O/A	Rory Kennedy	3	Subaru Impreza 555	R555 FEL
1999	Cork '20	2-3/10	N/F - Accident	Rory Kennedy	2	Subaru Impreza 555	R555 FEL
1999	RAC Rally	21-23/11	21st O/A	Rory Kennedy	53	Subar Impreza WRC	R16 WRC
2000							
2000	Monaghan	16/04	2nd O/A	Rory Kennedy	2	Subaru Impreza 555	P136 XBW

DEMO / NON COMPETITIVE RUNS – Note: this list is not fully comprehensive						
1980	Ulster Rally	22-23/08	00 Car	Driving COC Robert Harkness	Ford Escort Mk2	CIL 999
1983	Sligo		00 Car for Day 2	00 Car duties on day2 w/ Austin Frazer	Opel Manta 400	DIL 2307
1984	UAC Rally School		N/A - Demo only	Demonstration runs	Nissan 240 RS	WIA 3104
1985	North West 200 Motorcycle Race	16/05	N/A - Demo only	Demo run	Opel Manta 400	DIL 2307
1987	Forum, Enniskillen	16/06	N/A - Demo only	Filming of 'Get Fresh' ITV programme	Opel Manta 400	DIL 9482
1996	Instonians Rugby Club, Belfast	01/06	N/A - Demo only	Charity demo runs	Subaru Impreza 555 GpN	M435 XFC
1999	Motor and Accessories show, Fintona	15-17/06	N/A - Demo only	Charity demo runs	Subaru Impreza 555	R555 FEL
1999	RallySchool Ireland ,Monaghan		N/A - Demo only	Demo run	Subaru Impreza 555	R555 FEL
2000	Summit Rally setup	May	Stage setups	Stage setups	Mitsubishi Evo GpN	XJI 1464
2000	Millenium Motorsport Festival, Stormont	29/08	N/A - Demo only	N/A	Peugeot 205 T16	B555 SRW

Appendix 3: Competition Cars

YEARS DRIVEN	CAR TYPE	CAR REG NO.	PREVIOUS DRIVERS	FIRST FEW FOLLOWING DRIVERS
1968-1969	848 CC Mk1 Mini	7685 IL	N/A	N/A
1969	998 CC Mk1 Morris Mini Cooper	3328 SZ	Harry Cathcart	Ron Neely as autocross car, Ernie Fisher
1969	848 CC Mk1 Morris Mini	3737 IL	Jackie Thompson, Raymond Carroll	Unknown
1970	998 CC Mk2 Morris Mini Cooper	AIL 2840	Wesley Johnston	Unknown
1971	998 CC Mk1 Morris Mini Cooper	6258 JZ	Ralph Armstrong	Dessie Orr
1972	998 CC Mk2 Morris Mini Cooper S	AIL 6222	Mervyn Johnston	
1973	Ford Escort MK1	DEA 736J	Lepley 'Derby Road Motors'	
1974	Ford Escort MK1 Mexico	TMM 17M	Lepley 'Derby Road Motors'	as BIL 787 - Roy Cathcart
1975	Ford Escort MK1, RS 2000	GVX 833N	Russell Brookes	James Davison
1977	Ford Escort MK2, RS 2000	KIA 2220	Wesley Abraham	Fred Patterson
1977-1978	Ford Escort MK2, RS1800	BIL 5700	Roy Cathcart	Roy Cathcart
1979 - 1980	Ford Escort MK2, 1800	CIL 999	N/A, NEW SHELL	
1981	Ford Escort MK2, RS1800 'Monte Carlo Special'	GVX 489T	Russell Brookes, Billy Coleman	Vincent Bonner
1981	Ford Escort MK2 RS1800	RRM 912R	Malcolm Wilson	Alan Fraser, Hugh O'Brien
1981	Ford Escort G3 Gartrac	OOO 96M & CIL 999	Billy Coleman	As FJI 2- Ken McMillen
1982	Ford Escort MK2 RS1800	8 ZIK	John Burns	
1982	Ford escort MK2 RS1800, BDA engine	CIL 999	N/A, NEW SHELL	Martin Freestone, Chris Mellors
1983	Opel Ascona 400	DIL 999	Jimmy McRae	Billy Coleman, as SOI 4694 - Mark Reynolds, as 606 ZP - Vincent Bonner
1983 - 1985	Opel Manta 400	DIL 2307	N/A, NEW SHELL	as 809 RZK - AJ Keating, Donie Keating, Luke McCarthy, Donal O'Donovan
1985 - 1987	Opel Manta 400	DIL 9482	N/A, NEW SHELL	as 606 ZP - Vincent Bonner, James McDaid
1986	Ford Orion RWD development car	IIB 5931	N/A NEW SHELL	as XIJ 548 - Stephen Finlay, Barry McGuigan, Kenny McKinstry
1987	Ford Sierra Cosworth GpN	C234 HVW	Chris Mellors hirecar	Gwyndaf Evans, Don Bailey
1988	Metro 6R4	Q630 BFQ	John Price	
1988	Ford Sierra Cosworth	D773 SVW	Ex Boreham car	Gwyndaf Evans
1989 - 1990	BMW M3	GXI 9427	Marc Duez, Bernard Beguin, Billy Coleman	Billy Connolly, Andrew Nesbitt, Gene Meegan, Denis Cronin
1991	Subaru Legacy Group N	G330 TUE	David Gillanders	Richard Burns
1991	Ford Sierra 4 x 4 Cosworth	E28 JWK	Russell Brookes	Stephen Finlay
1992 - 1994	Subaru Legacy RS	H187 GUD	Markku Alen, Colin McRae	James Leckey, Doherty Brothers, Peter Green
1994	Subaru Impreza 555	L444 MCA	As L555 STE-Markku Alen (First ever 555 Chassis, 001)	
1995 - 1997	Subaru Impreza 555	L408 FUD & L555 FEL	Ex Prodrive Test car including Pre Monte Carlo 1994 test	Tom Spence, Frank O'Mahony, Barry Coleman
1997	Subaru Impreza 555	P161 EUD	ALLSTARS	Hugh O'Brien, Ryan Champion, Kris Meeke
1998 - 1999	Subaru Impreza 555	R555 FEL	N/A NEW SHELL (Last ever 555 Chassis, 061)	Stephen Murphy, Tim McNulty
1999	Subaru Impreza WRC	R16 WRC	Andreucci (Procar)	Alan Dickson, James Belton
2000	Subaru Impreza 555	P136 XBW	Kenny McKinstry, James Cullen	

Note: To avoid confusion or error in relation to potentially reshelled cars and multiple identities I have in some instances only listed the first drivers to have driven the identities of cars after Bertie had driven the cars

Appendix 4: Co-drivers

BERTIE'S CO-DRIVERS		
NAME	FROM (County)	PERIOD
Neil Paget	Fermanagh	1968 - 1969 & 1973
John Brown	Fermanagh	1969
John Magee	Fermanagh	1970 - 1971
John White	Tyrone	1972
John Lunny	Fermanagh	1972
Brian Quinn	Tyrone	1973 - 1974 & 1977
Tony Anderson	Down	1973 - 1974
Frank Burns	Fermanagh	1974
Roy Sloan	Down	1974
Derek Smyth	Tyrone	1975
Trevor Hughes	Limerick	1977
Sammy Hamill	Antrim	1977
Desi Wilson	Fermanagh	1977
Robert Harkness	Tyrone	1977 & 1980
Ivan Fisher	Fermanagh	1977
Wesley Abraham	Fermanagh	1975, 1977
Willie Hunter	Armagh	1977

NAME	FROM (County)	PERIOD
Austin Frazer	Fermanagh	1977 - 1989 & 1992
Peter Scott	Tyrone	1980
Dr. Frank O'Donoghue	Dublin	1981
Roy Cathcart	Fermanagh	1981
Trevor McGaughey		1981
David Johnston	Fermanagh	1980-82
Keith Oswin	England	1982
George Deane	Fermanagh	1983
Ernie Campbell	Fermanagh	1983
John Millington	England	1984
Brian Patterson	Antrim	1984
Crawford Harkness	Antrim	1985
Fred Patterson	Tyrone	1986
John McManus		1987
Jacqueline Berkeley		1989
Rory Kennedy	Donegal	1985 & 1989 - 2000
Rory Kennedy	Donegal	1985 & 1989 - 2000

DRIVERS FOR WHOM BERTIE SAT AS CO-DRIVER		
NAME	FROM (County)	PERIOD
Ernie Campbell	Co. Fermanagh	1969 & 1970 Circuit of Irelands
John Lunny	Co.Fermanagh	1971 Erne Safari, 1972 Dunomen
James Davison	Co. Antrim	1976 Galway

Appendix 5:
Memorial Awards and Trophies etc

Bertie Fisher Memorial Perpetual Cup

North Armagh Motorcycle & Car Club – Lurgan Park Rally
To the highest placed Subaru car in the overall finishers list

Bertie Fisher Perpetual Memorial Award

In 2001 at the Greenmount Sprint in Limerick RT Communications (main sponsor) commissioned a painting of Bertie that was presented to Austin McHale who said that he was "deeply honoured to receive this award in memory of a great rival and a great friend."

Bertie Fisher Cup

Killarney & District motor Club – Killarney Rally of the Lakes, Awarded to the driver setting fastest time on Molls Gap each year. Open to all sections of the Rally. Time may be recorded on any run on the stage unless the start and finish locations are altered between runs, in which case the first run will count.

Fisher Perpetual Cup

Trophy awarded to the winners of the Irish Tarmac Rally Championship, a series organised by TROA (Tarmac Rally Organisers Association). The cup, sponsored by Kieran McAnallen and family, has three handles on it, one each to represent Bertie, Mark and Emma

Entry Lists left blank

There were not many rallies held on the island of Ireland in 2001 due mainly to the Foot & Mouth Crisis of the farming world which ultimately due to rallying's agricultural nature, affected the sport massively. But of the few that there were, such was the respect the Fishers had in the rally world in Ireland that a number of events left their Number 1 spot blank in memory of the tragedy. These included:
Birr Single Stage Rally, 12th Feb,
Punchestown Rally Masters, 27th May
Lark in the Park, 14th July
Stonethrowers Rally, 12th August
Monaghan Single Stage, 2nd September

Music

Dance to Tipperary – Great moments with you

Bertie was also awarded Fermanagh Herald's first Hall of Fame award in 2008

Note of Interest

The Fisher Complex at Armagh City Hotel, including bars, lobbies and four Fisher function suites which can seat up to a total of 1,200 delegates (the location of the launch of this book), is one of the largest hotel function rooms in Northern Ireland. This suite was named in memory of Bertie Fisher, who was a director at the time the hotel was being planned and built.

.... thanks for the memories my friend.

Kevan